Palgrave Studies in Comparative East-West Philosophy

The purpose of Palgrave Studies in Comparative East-West Philosophy is to generate mutual understanding between Western and Chinese philosophers in a world of increased communication. It has now been clear for some time that the philosophers of East and West need to learn from each other and this series seeks to expand on that collaboration, publishing books by philosophers from different parts of the globe, independently and in partnership, on themes of mutual interest and currency.

The series also publishs monographs of the Soochow University Lectures and the Nankai Lectures. Both lectures series host world-renowned philosophers offering new and innovative research and thought.

Sitansu S. Chakravarti
Amita Chatterjee • Ananda Chakravarti
Lisa Widdison
Editor

Traditional Indian Virtue Ethics for Today

An East-West Dialogue

palgrave
macmillan

Editors:
Sitansu S. Chakravarti
New College
University of Toronto
Toronto, ON, Canada

Ananda Chakravarti
International Society for World Philosophy
Toronto, ON, Canada

Amita Chatterjee
Jadavpur University
Kolkata, India

Lisa Widdison
St. Mary's University
San Antonio, TX, USA

ISSN 2662-2378 ISSN 2662-2386 (electronic)
Palgrave Studies in Comparative East-West Philosophy
ISBN 978-3-031-47971-7 ISBN 978-3-031-47972-4 (eBook)
https://doi.org/10.1007/978-3-031-47972-4

Cover illustration: Dialogue between Krishna and Arjuna in the Bhagavad Gita' The Picture Art Collection / Alamy Stock Photo

This Palgrave Macmillan imprint is published by the registered company Springer Nature Switzerland AG.
The registered company address is: Gewerbestrasse 11, 6330 Cham, Switzerland

Paper in this product is recyclable.

To Rosalind Hursthouse, who enthusiastically encouraged the Editor-in-Chief of this volume to keep on bringing Indian philosophical thoughts in the fold of virtue ethics. But for her academic support over the years, this book might not have been ventured into.

To the sacred memory of Buddhadev Bhattacharya (1933–2015), affectionately called "Dada"—the older brother—in the publishing world in India. He upheld the cause of Indic studies with his brilliance in the art of book making, as he lovingly dedicated himself to publication of philosophy books in India.

Foreword

I am very pleased to have been asked to write the foreword for this volume that mainly contains essays focusing on virtue ethics in relation to Indian thought. I am somewhat new to Indian philosophy, but as you will see briefly in what follows, I am more than willing to recognize that India has a pivotal place in what I take to be the best way forward for contemporary work in philosophy. This needs some explaining.

Let's begin at the beginning. There are three places on this planet where philosophy originated in endogenous fashion: India, China, and Greece. Ancient Israel, despite the high rate of male literacy, produced nothing we can properly call philosophy. The same holds for ancient Egypt and Babylonia; and Japan has venerable philosophical traditions but they originally stem from the influence of Chinese and then later German philosophy. Further, philosophy flowered in India before it developed in either Greece or China, but we need to go beyond these origins.

The conference in Shimla from which the present volume emerged also gave rise to an International Society for World Philosophy. The idea or project of world philosophy is an important new development for the field of philosophy, and I shall say briefly what that idea/project involves. World philosophy is not comparative philosophy in the manner of Archie Bahm. The latter compares and contrasts philosophical traditions without seeking to advance any new philosophical ideas of its own. By contrast, world philosophy makes use of two or more of the autochthonous traditions mentioned above to argue for ideas and perspectives that cannot be found within any single one of those traditions. Arguably, Schopenhauer was doing world philosophy in this sense more than a hundred and fifty years ago, but he never proposed the idea of world philosophy, and such a suggestion came only at the end of the twentieth century from the Chinese philosopher Feng Qi. His student and successor at East China Normal University, Yang Guorong, has defended the appropriateness of doing world philosophy, but perhaps more significantly another Chinese philosopher, Mou Zongsan, actually engaged in world philosophy toward the end of the twentieth century. He sought to integrate all three of the main philosophical traditions—invoking Buddhism, the Kantian idea of the thing in itself, and Mencius' striking example of our reactions to a child about to fall into a well, in order to advance a total philosophical worldview. This effort in world philosophy came from the Chinese end, so to speak, but when I started trying to integrate Chinese and Western ideas into one overall philosophy, the world philosophy originated from the Western end—though in the early stages of my work I was unaware of the concept of world philosophy that had been suggested by Feng Qi.

We have reason to regard world philosophy as an important philosophical approach if we become convinced that it has insightful things to say that aren't discussed in any one tradition, and I have argued that Chinese thought can serve as a corrective to the longstanding Western idea that thinking can occur in the absence of any emotion. The Chinese themselves never thought to correct Western thinking in this way, but if the arguments I give at all work, then one has shown that Western thinking stands in need of a major course correction. I have also argued that Western thinking can be enhanced by bringing in updated versions of the traditional Chinese categories of yin and yang. Again, if this is on the right track, then the importance of world philosophy as an idea and project is vindicated in philosophical terms.

Some of the essays in the present volume bring Indian ideas together with Western ones in an effort to clarify certain issues and argue for certain conclusions and thus count as examples of world philosophy. But perhaps the most significant fruit of the Shimla conference was the International Society for World Philosophy (ISWP) that was founded in 2021 and will be housed at Massey College in the University of Toronto. My lecture at the conference called for the founding of such a society, and the mainly Indian philosophers attending the conference were quick to respond positively to that suggestion. More particularly in practical terms, Sitansu Chakravarti and others worked to establish the ISWP and were successful in their efforts. In a way, then, what happened in Shimla has come full circle in this book. My call at the conference for an International Society led to the founding of such a society, and the society, the ISWP, has created the present volume of essays originally given in Shimla. Needless to say, I think we should all be very happy with this virtuous circle.

More broadly, I don't think we should be surprised that so much of the effort to put world philosophy on a proper footing comes from ethnically Indian philosophers. The British Raj brought Western ideas to the attention of Indian thinkers, and Indian thinkers have become comfortable making use in combination of the Western ideas together with ideas from their own longstanding philosophical traditions. (We see some of this in this volume.) By contrast, Western philosophers pay no attention to ideas coming from India, and at least recently Chinese philosophers have paid little or no attention to India and have had a kind of schizoid reaction to Western philosophy. Many today think that all philosophical truth comes from the West and to that extent give up on the world philosophy whose concept and practice originated within China itself. Other Chinese thinkers withdraw from present-day philosophical thinking and regard all philosophical truth as completely contained within traditional Chinese thought. The Indians are more comfortable with world philosophy and continue to practice it very naturally and without any self-consciousness (as per the present volume). But as a Western philosopher I have hopes that the West will eventually pay attention to what has gone on in Indian and Chinese philosophy—will eventually, in this increasingly internationalized world, pay attention to the promise and prospects of world philosophy.

University of Miami
Coral Gables, FL, USA

Michael Slote

Preface

In November 2018, Professor Sitansu Sekhar Chakravarti, after a panel on Hinduism at Parliament of the World's Religions (PWR), Toronto, said to me, "You know, Makarand-ji, we should have a conference on Virtue Ethics in Hinduism. There is very little work on this topic." I immediately said, "Why not? Provided you organize the conference and publish the proceedings."

That this casual-seeming, albeit hopeful, conversation on the side-lines of PWR-Toronto is actually coming to a remarkable fruition today is a matter of great satisfaction and pride for all those associated with the project. We are especially grateful to Sitansu-da, the moving spirit behind it, for all the persistent and unflagging hard work that he has put into this enterprise to bring it to this successful juncture.

Looking back, one reason I gave that instant affirmation to his suggestions was that I was then Director, Indian Institute of Advanced Study (IIAS), Shimla. IIAS, founded by India's second president, Dr. S. Radhakrishnan, himself a philosopher, was the perfect place to host such a conference. In fact, Radhakrishnan had a life-long interest in ethics, his very first book being on *The Ethics of the Vedānta and its Metaphysical Presuppositions* (Madras: Guardian Press, 1908). It was based on his B.A. thesis. Later, Radhakrishnan was the Spalding Professor of Ethics and Religion at Oxford from 1936 to 1952, the first Indian to hold a chair at Oxford. IIAS has had an abiding interest in the area, with numerous fellows pursuing this interest and producing well-regarded publications and monographs.

When we hosted the International Symposium on "Traditional Hindu/Indian Virtue Ethics in Today's Perspective: Sharing Ideas between East and West" from 17 to 19 October 2019, it was a relatively happier time for all of us. The COVID-19 world pandemic had not yet broken out. International travel was possible, as attested to by the many participants from abroad, some from distant places even as far away as Hawaii. Thanks to the untiring efforts of Sitansu-da and his son, Ananda, who was also present, the conference, superbly organized and well executed, was a great success.

A number of learned, well-researched, and engaging papers were presented, some from North America in virtual mode. It was resolved not only to publish the proceedings but also to start the International Society for World Philosophy (ISWP). This first of its kind initiative would incorporate "perspectives of the ancient traditions of philosophizing to the benefit of the academic pursuit of philosophy itself. An important by-product of this venture is finding solutions to persistent problems afflicting today's world, relating to the natural environment as well as a global human society situated amid an accelerating technology disruption that is re-defining human existence." The not-for-profit organization is incorporated in Canada, with its headquarters located at Massey College, University of Toronto. Professor Kumar Murty of the University of Toronto, who was present at our conference, is currently Chair of the Board of Directors.

I am glad that this volume, with a vitality of its own emanating from the seed sown in the conference, enriched with a Foreword and major intervention by Professor Michael Slote, is being published. As can be seen from such promising and exciting developments, world philosophy is no longer a tantalizing but impossible dream. It is an urgent imperative and demand of the times. For years, it was believed, especially in the West, that Indian philosophy was only religion and mythology. Hardly taught in Philosophy departments the world over, even in India only a few universities studied it seriously. The rich tradition of systematic thinking and philosophizing was, thus, often relegated to religious and area studies departments abroad and more traditional, Sanskritic institutions in India.

The change came recently, with the pioneering efforts of philosophers such as Ben-Ami Scharfstein, whose path-breaking volume, *A Comparative History of World Philosophy, From the Upanishads to Kant* (Albany, SUNY Press, 1998), for the first time tried to study Indian, Chinese, and Western philosophy in an integrated fashion. Scharfstein defined a philosophical tradition as "A chain of persons who relate their thought to that of their predecessors and in this way form a continuous transmission from one generation to the next, from teacher to disciple to disciple's disciple." He placed the world's earliest systematic philosophising in India, as far back as 900 CE: "This first encounter with Indian philosophers has five protagonists: Uddālaka Āruṇi (son of Aruṇa), his son Śvetaketu, his student Yājñavalkya, Maitreyī the more philosophical of Yājñavalkya's two wives."

When it comes to Virtue Ethics, I hope this volume will show quite conclusively that it pervades all the spheres of the human life world in Indian thought, covering each of the cardinal aims of life, Dharma (virtual and righteousness), Artha (wealth and power), Kāma (pleasure and desire), not excluding Moksha (liberation and perfection). In the Ashtānga Rāja Yoga of Patañjali, Virtue Ethics as Yama and Niyama become the groundwork for higher states of realization and superconsciousness, Dhyāna, Dhāraṇā, and Samādhi. From Kauṭilya to Mahatma Gandhi, Virtue Ethics has informed Indian ideas of good governance and political economy. In arts and crafts, ranging from the culinary to the erotic, the relish or flavour is invariably predicated to purification of senses and refinement of taste, both of which are linked to sacralization and consecration. In this very day and time, commerce, industry, consumerism, climate change, digitization, and artificial intelligence—all must have a Virtue Ethics component if human civilization itself is to have a future and survive its present crises.

The Indian way of life emphasizes *abhyudaya* or the socio-economic welfare and *niḥśrēyasa*, ultimate liberation, of all beings from the very ancient of times. As Saṅkara says in his commentary on the Bhagavad Gītā:

> *Dharma (the preferable way of life), as mentioned in the Vedas, accommodates both the human inclinations, and abstention, …thus leading to peoples' prosperity, as well as attainment of the ultimate becoming.*

Virtue Ethics, for the Indian tradition, thus had both *pravṛtti* or the normal, natural course of life, as well as *nivṛtti*, the higher, turning away towards transcendence and the peace that surpasses understanding, as its twin aims and imperatives. Earlier, Kaṇada (c. 400 CE), the root rishi of the Vaiśeṣika, sometimes called the naturalist, physicist, or atomist philosopher of India, famously said: *that is the greatest good and highest success which combines worldly welfare and spiritual liberation or cessation of suffering.*

Given this age-old and ever-relevant orientation of the Indian way of life, the present volume on Traditional Indian Virtue Ethics, combined with the establishment of the International Society for World Philosophy (ISWP), could not be more welcome or timely.

Jawaharlal Nehru University
New Delhi, India

Makarand R. Paranjape

Acknowledgments

First, my sincere thanks to the contributors for having acceded to my request to participate in this challenging, ground-breaking venture on traditional Indian virtue ethics in the mode of World Philosophy. I appreciate the overwhelming cooperation received from them all through as they revised their drafts several times in response to thoughts from my end for the benefit of the reader with clarification of the subject matter.

Thanks to Michael Slote for writing the Foreword for the book, in the wake of his ongoing support favouring a venture in World Philosophy with a significant inclusion of Indian Philosophy. Thanks also to Makarand Paranjape for writing the Preface; but for his participation the work would not have originated.

Continuing cooperation from New College, University of Toronto, has certainly helped. Fang Zhang, Executive Assistant in the Principal's office has always looked after my academic facilities resulting in benefits for the book.

Outside of the other three editors—Ananda Chakravarti, Amita Chatterjee and Lisa Widdison—Amitabha Bagchi, Amitabha Das Gupta, and Chandreyee Niyogi have offered substantial editing assistance.

I must thankfully mention the detailed report from the anonymous referee to Palgrave, who expressed full-blown support toward publication of the book, highlighting the spirituality aspect the anthology emphasizes as the philosophical grounding for virtue ethics, with no suggestions for revisions.

I am thankful to Sage Publications for permission to reproduce two articles from the *Journal of Human Values*, published on behalf of

Management Centre for Human Values, Indian Institute of Management, Calcutta. These are: (1) "Ethical Message of the Mahabharata in the Wake of the Global Financial Crisis" by Sitansu S. Chakravarti [15:2 (2009); 97–105 DOI: 10.1177/097168581001 500202] and (2) Review of the book *Ethics in the Mahabharata: A Philosophical Inquiry for Today* in the 'Book Reviews' section, by Amita Chatterjee, [13:2 (2007); 179–184 DOI:10.1177/097168580701300208]. Both the authors are editors to the present anthology where the articles are being reproduced.

Words of inspiration from Swami Bhajanananda of the Ramakrishna Math and Mission (RKMM), Kolkata, India went a long way in the preparation of the book. Indeed, he found and emphatically took exception to the fact that the area of ethics was not receiving as much attention as it deserves in the Indian philosophical system being dealt with today. Swami Bodhasarananda not only provided a sustained inspiration but indicated some bibliographical references, even in the midst of his heavy responsibilities at the RKMM, which were of great help to me in writing the Introduction.

Without constant help and cooperation from my wife Rina, this work could not have been done. My whole family supported me: our son Ananda as an editor with whom I would be in touch whenever needs would arise so often; my daughter Vidula would occasionally help in the editing process from Middleton, MA.

This book owes its life to the tradition many of the contributors imbibed from the department of philosophy, Jadavpur University, in the capacity of students or teachers—a tradition instilled by the philosophy stalwarts Gopinath Bhattacharya and his student Pranab Kumar Sen. This tradition is thankfully acknowledged as incorporated in the making of the anthology.

Book Description

This book, as the title indicates, brings into focus some prominent, fundamental virtue ethical concepts present in the traditional systems of Indian thought in and through the transformations they underwent in modern times. The concepts are presented in the mode of the ongoing discussions on virtue ethics in the West. In essence, this book is an exercise in World Philosophy, a concept highlighted by Michael Slote in the two opening articles by him (Chaps. 2 and 3), as ethical issues have been dynamically dealt with here combining Eastern and Western perspectives toward solution of philosophical queries.

A unique feature of this anthology lies in its attempt at de-alienating the philosophical exercise by (1) making philosophy accessible to non-philosophers following the style of Socratic visits to the marketplace, and (2) having incorporated important contributions made by non-philosophers, even from outside of academia. Chapter 7 originally appeared in a journal from a reputable Institute of Management; it contains philosophical thoughts from the Mahabharata for the benefit of non-philosophers in their world of operation. Chapter 15 deals with concepts in the Mahabharata combining ideas of Saul Kripke relating to Wittgenstein. Chapter 12 puts to philosophical use ideas from the Gita in helping Hursthouse's endeavour to construct an environmental virtue ethics.

All the chapters convey some hitherto unexpressed novel thoughts pertaining to the flourishing of the humankind in a harmonious fold.

Contents

Notes on Contributors

Abhishek Bandyopadhyay did his Ph.D. in Biochemistry at Cambridge University in 2004, supported by the Nehru-Cambridge Fellowship. He is an Assistant Research Scientist at Purdue University at the Purdue Institute for Inflammation, Immunology and Infectious Disease. His research area is macromolecular structure and dynamics, with a particular focus on structural and molecular virology and immunology. Bandyopadhyay is well versed in the Ramakrishna-Vivekananda literature in Bengali as well as English.

Nirmalya Narayan Chakraborty did his Ph.D. in Philosophy from the University of Waterloo, Canada. He is presently Professor of Philosophy Rabindra Bharati University Kolkata, where he was formerly Vice-Chancellor. Chakraborty's research areas include Philosophy of Language (Classical Indian and Western Analytical), Epistemology, Philosophy of Religion, Environmental Ethics. He is a Former Member-Secretary, Indian Council of Philosophical Research, New Delhi. Some of his recent publications include: "Self-knowledge: The Moral Dimension" (2023), "Realism, Anti-realism and Quietism: Has Philosophy Become Dispensable?" (2022), "On the Very Idea of the Authority of the Vedas" (2020), "Tagore and the Idea of Emancipation" (2020).

Sitansu S. Chakravarti did his Ph.D. in Philosophy from Syracuse University, concentrating on the Philosophy of Language. He was formerly a Visiting Professor in Logic and modern western Analytical Philosophy at the Department of Philosophy, University of Rajasthan,

Jaipur; in Comparative Religion at the Department of Philosophy and Religion, Visva-Bharati, Santiniketan. He is currently Affiliated Scholar, University of Toronto, New College.

Chakravarti has published in *The Journal of Indian Philosophy* and the *Notre Dame Journal of Formal Logic.* He has authored the books: *Hinduism—A Way of Life* (1991), *Modality, Reference and Sense—An Essay in the Philosophy of Language* (2001) and *Ethics in the Mahabharata—A Philosophical Inquiry for Today* (2006).

Being well versed in the Western as well as the Indian philosophical traditions, he has combined them in his various writings.

Ananda Chakravarti did his undergraduate studies in political science, specializing in political theory, and mass communication at York University, Toronto. He has held several international management positions within the Big Four accounting firms, specializing in audit and ESG assurance markets and business development.

Chakravarti contributed an invited paper on virtue ethics in the contemporary business world at an international conference on Indian virtue ethics held at Indian Institute of Advanced Studies, Shimla, India in 2019. He is currently Secretary, International Society of World Philosophy (ISWP), headquartered in Toronto.

Amita Chatterjee did her Ph.D. in Philosophy from Calcutta University in 1981. She is Emeritus Professor at the Department of Philosophy and School of Cognitive Science, Jadavpur University. She was the Editor-in-Chief of the *Journal of Indian Council of Philosophical Literature* (2014–2017). Widely published, her books include *Bharatiya Dharmaniti* (Indian Ethics in Bengali, co-edited, 1998, 2015), *Indian Philosophy and Meditation, The Study of Internal States in Theory and Practice: A Perspective from Indian Psychology* (2021).

Shefali Moitra did her Ph.D. in Philosophy from Visva-Bharati University, India. She retired as Professor of Philosophy, Jadavpur University, Kolkata. She has played a leading role in familiarizing Tagore's philosophy to the English-reading scholars in India and abroad. Her works on Tagore in English include: "Thoughts of Tagore on Man, Freedom and Value," *Ethics and Culture*, 2010. "Tagore's Perception of the West," *Philosophy in Colonial India*, 2015. Her areas of specialization are Tagore, Feminist Theory, Ethics and Philosophy of Language.

V. Kumar Murty received his Ph.D. in Mathematics from Harvard University in 1982. He is Director of the prestigious Fields Institute for Research in Mathematical Sciences. His mathematical accomplishments cover diverse areas including analytic number theory, algebraic number theory, information security, and arithmetic algebraic geometry. Murty has served on the Canadian Mathematical Society Board of Directors and held vice-presidency at the Canadian Mathematical Society. He was elected a Fellow of the Royal Society of Canada in 1995, Fields Institute Fellow in 2003, and Senior Fellow of Massey College in 2020.

Murty has offered courses on Indian philosophy, in the world-philosophical format, which have been enthusiastically received by students at the department of Philosophy, University of Toronto.

Indrani Sanyal did her Ph.D. in Philosophy from Jadavpur University, Kolkata, in 1981. She retired as Professor of Philosophy, Jadavpur University. Sanyal is a founder and former coordinator of the Center for Sri Aurobindo Studies, and the Director, Center for Comparative Religion and Culture, National Council of Education, Bengal, Kolkata. Her areas of specialization are Ethics, especially Indian Ethics, Philosophy of Language (Western), Metaphysics, Philosophy of Sri Aurobindo. Sanyal's publications include: 2016, Through the Lens of Dharma Ethics, 2015, and Modality, Essence and Possible Worlds, 2002.

Balbir Singh Sihag received his Ph.D. in Economics from Massachusetts Institute of Technology (M.I.T.). Serving as Professor of Economics at the University of Massachusetts for twenty-two years, he is now Professor Emeritus of Economics. Sihag has published research papers in journals of international repute such as the *Journal of History of Economic Thought, Journal of Public Economics and Quarterly Journal of Economics*, and two Books, *Kautilya: The True Founder of Economics*, 2014, and *Kautilya on Moral Hazard, Poverty and Systemic Risk*, 2019.

Michael Slote received his Ph.D. in Philosophy from Harvard University. He is currently UST Professor of Ethics at the University of Miami. He taught at Columbia University, at Trinity College Dublin (where he was a Fellow), and at the University of Maryland, College Park, before coming to Miami in 2002.

He is the author of several books and many articles: most of these publications are in ethics, but in recent years his work has extended into epistemology, metaphysics, philosophy of language, and philosophy of mind. Slote is a pioneering force in doing World Philosophy, as demonstrated in his book, *The Philosophy of Yin and Yang*, published in 2018.

Lisa Widdison did her Ph.D. in Philosophy at the University of Hawaii in 2021. She is a researcher in the history of philosophy and philosophy of art, nature, metaphysics, emotions and theories of knowledge, East and West. Currently, she is Visiting Assistant Professor at St. Mary's University, San Antonio, Texas. Widdison has studied philosophy and literature in far reaching locales, from Los Angeles to Bangalore. Her dissertation incorporated cross-cultural research on theories of *taste* and the *sublime*.

Dennis Wittmer is a professor in the Management Department of the Daniels College of Business at the University of Denver, where he has taught for 32 years. He currently teaches courses related to ethical leadership, business ethics, organizational ethics, business and the public good, as well as AI and leading in the digital age. Dennis received his Ph.D. in public administration from the Maxwell School of Citizenship and Public Affairs at Syracuse University. He has an MA in Philosophy from Syracuse University. Wittmer has published numerous articles in professional journals, and he has taught a variety of international audiences in Kuwait, Taiwan, and Mexico.

List of Figures

List of Tables

CHAPTER 1

Introduction

Preliminaries

Sitansu S. Chakravarti

'Yatra Vishvam Bhavatyeka-Nidam' (Mahanarayana Upanishat 2.3)
(Where the World Becomes One Single Nest)

I start with a quote from Bernard Williams:

> The resources of most moral philosophy are not adjusted to the modern world. I have tried to show this is partly because it is too much and too unknowingly caught up in it, unreflectively appealing to administrative ideas of rationality. … It is not a paradox that under these very new circumstances very old philosophies may have more to offer than moderately new ones. (Bernard Williams, *Ethics and the Limits of Philosophy*, pp. 197–8)

The words above have inspired us to go back to the 'very old philosophies' of India today in our anthology keeping in view possible benefits for modern times.

S. S. Chakravarti (✉)
New College, University of Toronto, Toronto, ON, Canada

S. S. Chakravarti et al. (ed.), *Traditional Indian Virtue Ethics for Today*, Palgrave Studies in Comparative East-West Philosophy,
https://doi.org/10.1007/978-3-031-47972-4_1

This book is a product of intense hard work extending over a three-year period. To do world philosophy effectively, combining Indian philosophical thoughts relating to virtue ethics with those in the West for the benefit of philosophy itself, has been the goal that has taken the full attention of the people carrying the mission of this book for quite a while. Getting contributors to open up and relate their areas of expertise, in philosophy and beyond (even outside of academia) to the field of virtue ethics was the first hurdle we started with. The authors of articles, however, have been consistently receptive to ideas from the editor, and unbelievably cooperative all through. It has been a humbling experience for me as academic stalwarts in their fields ended up revising their papers many times while accommodating cues I happened to advance.

We have aimed at de-alienating philosophy in taking the wisdom associated with Indian philosophical systems to all, following the Socratic way of taking philosophy to the marketplace. The de-alienation process works both at the receiving end of the readers of this anthology and at the contributing end of writers who are not necessarily accomplished philosophers. Kumar Murty, Balbir Sihag and Dennis Wittmer are academics established in their own fields outside of philosophy—Mathematics, Economics and Business Administration to be specific—and have contributed to this philosophical anthology on virtue ethics where their areas of expertise have been of relevance. Abhishek Bandyopadhyay, an academic in Chemistry, deeply acquainted with the Ramakrishna-Vivekananda field of literature, has done us a great service in seeing things from a novel perspective that portrayal in a paper on Swami Vivekananda deserves. Ananda Chakravarti has incorporated his perspective from the corporate world he is situated in, in the philosophical language of virtue ethics befitting the mood of World Philosophizing the book adopts. The wisdom associated with Indian Philosophy has been drawn upon as belonging to the dimension of secular spirituality, to be strictly segregated from the religious, that aims at bringing about an existential becoming at the receiving end in the pursuer, thus paving the way for the proper functioning of society from the virtue ethical point of view.

We intend the book to reach readers outside of the field of philosophy in order for them to benefit from it. The articles 'Business Leadership and Virtue Ethics for the 21st Century: Barton through the Lens of Tagore' by Ananda Chakravarti, 'Ethical Message of the Mahabharata in the Wake of the Global Financial crisis' by Sitansu S Chakravarti, 'Reflections on Teaching Virtue Ethics in a Business Curriculum' by Dennis Wittmer and

'Kautilya's Ethics-based Economics vs Modern Economics' by Balbir S Sihag are examples of entries in the book that are expected to be of relevance to everyone, hopefully, including philosophers. I would expect people from outside of the rank of philosophers to start with the article just referred to above, by Sitansu S Chakravarti, which was written explicitly with non-philosophers in mind, in order to introduce them to the world of Indian Philosophy, within the frame of reference of philosophy as such, for solutions to serious problems in the world today.

We keep in mind that many of the ills that are conspicuously present around us in the area of administration in general, including at the political level of statecraft, in addition to the ones relating to severe environmental issues along with those connected with the functioning of the business world—and not the least of all, in the sphere of the pandemic of drug addiction—are all intimately associated with social and individual ethical lapses. These ills demand their proper addressal at the ethical level by virtue of their ethical mooring. Here indeed the ancient wisdom of India as contained in its philosophy, relating, for example, to the philosophical area of existentialism, assumes a deserved relevance. In this anthology the articles by Ananda Chakravarti, Dennis Wittmer, Sitansu S Chakravarti and Balbir S Sihag relate to the ethical dimension connecting to the areas of business, environment and macroeconomics. Here is our response to UNESCO's call to philosophers in finding solutions to world's problems, as the world body celebrates annually the World Philosophy Day every third Thursday in November. We, on our part, approach philosophy in a comprehensive way, combining the East with the West, while we do away with the East-West dichotomy altogether.

My close friend Robert Heard, along with his wife Leslie McGrath, formerly in the faculty of Library and Information Sciences, University of Toronto, has been associated with the planning process of the book as well as editing some parts. Another close friend of mine, Richard Ficek, with his background as a Librarian, has been helping me in a concurrently continuous way. My very dear Brother-In-Law, Amitabha Bagchi, has provided valuable editing assistance. Ananda Chakravarti, Amita Chatterjee and Lisa Widdison, all members of the editorial team, have helped at different levels whenever the need arose. Amitabha Das Gupta, the famed philosopher of India, has provided immense editorial help. I certainly have had the chance to practise the virtue of *interracial amity*, and partake of the joy in it, in the process of preparing this book on virtue ethics as I received invaluable support from varied sources. This book aims toward the integration of cultures in the nested web that World Philosophy seeks to provide, sharing the plus points of any one culture with all. In the process of doing World Philosophy, it does not mean to establish the superiority of one culture over another.

Dealing with Indian Philosophy, I had to make an unavoidable compromise in not including perspectives from the rich traditions of Buddhism and Jainism. I personally feel content, though, in what little worthwhile we are able to produce in our limited capacity heeding the challenge of breaking new grounds in World Philosophy. Our motto is to do well what we attempt to do, accommodating exclusions necessitated by limited capability. Apart from the Buddhist and Jain perspectives, I would have liked to include a unique syncretism India has shown the world. This relates to the forging of Islam with Hinduism in India as Sufism. Sufi Islam assumed a special form in contact with the ancient tradition of mysticism present in India, amalgamating Indian philosophical wisdom with Islam during the process of assimilation and integration.

The two outstanding philosophers of the day I am most indebted to for the book are Michael Slote and Rosalind Hursthouse. Slote has been associated with the book from the very inception of the thought of it. It is far from a sheer accident that the present anthology is appearing in the series PALGRAVE STUDIES IN COMPARATIVE EAST-WEST PHILOSOPHY where he is a joint editor. In email correspondences I had initiated, Hursthouse has continually encouraged me, for over a decade, to indulge in doing World Philosophy while bringing in more material from the area of Indian Philosophy in my writings.

The fairly long Introduction consists of several sections. We start with PART I, leading on to PART II, PART III and PART IV, in successive sections. In the second section of Introduction dealing with Part II of the book entitled 'Traditional views reformulated' I have taken an opportunity to acquaint the general reader in broad outlines with Swami Vivekananda, Rabindranath Tagore and Sri Aurobindo, the three stalwarts of our times, on each of whom an article has been included in Part II. In the course of providing brief introductions on them, I have indicated some relevant areas where further work in philosophy relating to them may benefit the cause of philosophical pursuit.

Before we get started with the articles individually in the book, I would like to mention a salient point of departure obtaining in the Indian tradition from the spirit of the Western way of doing Ethics. Indian Ethics is basically nested in virtue ethics, while dispensing with the spirit of exclusiveness among virtue ethics, deontology and consequentialism that took shape in the West. Accommodating the positive points of all three is characteristic of an overall inclusiveness pursued in the Indian way of doing things.

'I ever look for an abode
That locates me at all places' (Tagore)

Part I: World Philosophy

PART I deals with the concept of World Philosophy, which stands for a style of philosophizing where philosophical approaches of more than one tradition in the world combine toward the benefit of clarity and wisdom relating to discussion on philosophical issues. In this anthology we have included Indian Philosophical perspectives, as combining with the Western, for philosophical deliberations on virtue ethical issues. While Michael Slote is well known for having involved himself in the practice of World Philosophy by connecting Chinese Philosophy with his own background in Western Philosophy, the inclusion of Indian Philosophy in the World Philosophy fold has been a long-cherished desire that he has entertained to ensure that proper justice is done to the cause of philosophy itself. In the mode of pursuing his academic interest in World Philosophy, which he hopes to be the future shape of philosophy one day soon, Slote has contributed two papers to this volume, the second one of them being an unsolicited gift from him. Rather than summarizing the papers myself in the Editor's Introduction, I prefer to reproduce below the two long Abstracts he sent me some time back on his papers.

In this connection I feel tempted to make a comment or two pertaining to the thoughts contained in the papers by Slote relating to World Philosophy, while I incorporate the Indian perspective. First comes the history of World Philosophy. We accord all respect to Feng Qi (1915–1995) doing pioneering, and meaningful, work in the field in China during the mid-fifties, as he broadened the area of philosophy accommodating the wisdom accumulated in a cultural tradition. This led him in its wake to redefine the concept of philosophy itself. Without an intention to minimize the thrust and novelty of Qi's contribution, it seems but fair on our part to take note of the historical event of World Philosophy pursued in an academic setting by Swami Vivekananda as he presented an address entitled 'The Vedanta Philosophy' before the Graduate Philosophical Society of Harvard University in March, 1896, following which he was offered the Chair of Oriental Philosophy at Harvard's department of Philosophy. We must not be oblivious of the first-rate World Philosophical work that started being produced by Indian philosophers after this event. Sarvapalli Radhakrishnan (1888–1975) did extensive work in the area, and eventually became the Spalding Professor of Eastern Religion and Ethics at Oxford. K C Bhattacharya (1875–1949) is globally famous for his innovative thoughts accommodating Indian and Western perspectives harmoniously. His younger son, Kalidas Bhattacharya (1911–1984), famously followed the tradition his father had built. His older son Gopinath Bhattacharya (1903–1990) became famous in India teaching World Philosophy, and eventually devising for the department of Philosophy, Jadavpur University, a World Philosophy curriculum geared to teaching the diverse areas of Philosophy at the university level—the first of its kind anywhere. T R V Murti (1902–1986), Sivajivan Bhattacharya (1926–2005) and J N Mohanty (1928–2023) are three other luminaries. The most recent is Bimal Krishna Matilal (1935–1991), another Spalding Processor at Oxford, perhaps the latest in line who did pioneering work interpreting the intricate niceties of Indian Epistemology in the language of Western philosophy.

We must keep in mind that deep study in Indian philosophy with the help of Western analytic tools has not been confined to philosophers of Indian origin only. We might mention Frits Staal, UC Berkeley; and Stephen Phillips, UT Austin, for having done substantial work in the area.

While doing World Philosophy with the incorporation of Indian Philosophy, the minimum attitude of respect to the ancient Indian culture has not unfortunately been maintained always. Admitted that cultural practices need to be subjected to an analytic probe, we certainly have to ensure that the norms of philosophical rigour are strictly maintained in the course of the analysis, and do not get tilted by one's political stand. Amartya Sen, in his 'Consequential Evaluation and Practical Reason' objects to the 'high deontology' he finds present in the Gita, without citing textual and philosophical reasons in some academic detail for his position. Also, he ignores the counsel of Sri Krishna to Arjuna, his friend, at the end of the long process of deliberations that is the Gita, 'to act as [the latter] think[s] proper, after having gone minutely over [in his mind what has been discussed so far]', (Gita, 18,63) a language indeed not approximating a deontological dictate by any stretch of the imagination. No doubt, the ancient Indian (Hindu) philosophy is at fault from the author's ideological standpoint.

Let us come back to our reflections on Slote's papers. I believe that ideas can be gathered relating to making life positively and sustainably enjoyable from the traditional Indian perspective based on the articles contained in this anthology. They will hopefully mitigate Slote's concern to the contrary as expressed in his essay 'Questioning Buddhism on Way to World Philosophy'. Certainly, the philosophical question he raises is welcome in the spirit of World Philosophy. Slote bases his misgivings centring on the first of the four noble truths of Buddhism, viz., that life is evil, as the great historian of Indian Philosophy, Hiriyanna translates it. He sees the shadow of the first noble truth of Buddhism, especially as relating to the place ordinary desires occupy in a positive shaping of life, cover the entire canvas depicting Indian Philosophy. We leave the task of handling the philosophical point pertaining to Buddhism that Slote raises to future endeavours in the area of World Philosophy. However, as I take a look at the paper on Kautilya in this anthology, I can see the importance Indian macroeconomics would place about two millennia before Adam Smith on the flourishing, including in the material world, of people in daily life, grounded on the cultivation of ethical virtues, leading the way to a spiritual awakening onto an existential becoming on their part. This emphasizes the reflection of the philosophy of the day on the material wellbeing in life, while life is not looked upon as evil in itself. It is of relevance to bring to mind the stir the discovery of the rare, handwritten manuscript of the *Arthashastra* in a library in India in 1905 created in the world outside for the message of the book not fitting into the existing model of otherworldliness that the traditional Indian mind was believed to promote. Challenging the consequences entailed by the supposed Indian philosophical stand, the inclusive look of the philosophy is brought to the fore in the paper by Sihag, highlighting the value of the charm of life in course of its daily living, with desires properly attuned, and certainly not thwarted or forsaken.

Hopefully, academic work will be pursued on the history of World Philosophizing, including Indian Philosophy dealt with in terms of Western philosophical concepts, taken together with Western Philosophy, and covering the philosophical areas of Epistemology, Metaphysics, Philosophy of Mind, Ethics, Phenomenology and Existentialism.

Here are the abstracts on the two articles by Michael Slote that comprise PART I, in the author's own words:

'World Philosophy: The Importance of India':

World philosophy involves bringing together two or more of the world's three main endogenous philosophical traditions (the Indian, Chinese and Western) in order to make philosophical progress. My own take on this possibility involves combating Western skepticism about Chinese thought and demonstrating that ideas from China can serve as a course correction for largely mistaken Western views about the mind in particular. The West sees cognition and emotion as separable, but Chinese thought subscribes to the idea of a heart-mind where these elements are vitally interconnected. And we nowadays are in a position to support the Chinese view against the Western. All thinking and reasoning involves belief, but given that confidence that p is strong belief that p, belief and confidence lie on a single scale of increasingly positive epistemic feeling. If confidence involves feeling, so do belief and mental activity in general. Further, yin and yang understood in modern generalized terms as receptivity and directed purpose respectively can be used to understand all the cases where cognition and emotion come together. In compassion receptive yin empathy coincides with purposeful yang motivation to help. Yin and yang are (necessarily) complementary in this and a host of other cases involving the mind or, better, heart-mind. So Chinese categories can take us philosophically further with the idea that cognition and emotion cannot be separated.

This is an instance of world philosophy, but the West isn't interested in such a thing, and the domination of Marxism in China would make it difficult for it to establish roots there. But Indian philosophy has a tradition of philosophical interest in more than one world tradition, and Indian philosophers have now set about establishing an International Society for World Philosophy at the University of Toronto.

'Questioning Buddhism on the Way to World Philosophy':

The idea of world philosophy originated with Feng Qi in China, and its most committed recent practitioner was Mou Zongsan. It must bring together at least two of the world's endogenous philosophical traditions: those of China, India and the West. (Ancient Israel had no real philosophy, and Japanese and Korean philosophical ideas are rooted in Chinese and/ or German thought.)

Although I have generally worked only with Chinese and Western philosophy, the present essay addresses itself to some ideas out of India. Indian and, especially, Buddhist thought is skeptical about the possibility that ordinary life can be satisfactory or good, and despite the influence of India on Chinese metaphysics, the Chinese never bought into such skepticism. To complicate matters, the West is of two minds on this issue: Plato clearly thinks ordinary life is unsatisfactory, but the French philosophes and many Western philosophers and psychologists today hold that ordinary lives can, on the whole, be good ones.

Here I want to call into question two main arguments that Indian or India-influenced philosophers have mounted against the possibility of good ordinary human lives. The familiar first one points out that human lives are full of desire(s) and asserts that desire is a lack that cannot be anything but unpleasant. But some gestalt psychologists take issue with this pessimistic assessment of desire. Someone who hasn't recently eaten can very easily anticipate a fine meal with great pleasure. However, one can take a larger view, as Eckhart Tolle recently has, and claim that everyone eventually becomes unsatisfied with their life. This would certainly lead us toward questioning the possibility of good ordinary lives, but is it true?

Let's assume we have someone who doesn't want to 'rest on their laurels'. They have accomplished great things, let us say, but eventually want to do more. Does this mean they were ever unsatisfied or discontented with their life? With food, we can be satisfied after a meal but eventually want to eat again. Does this mean we were ever dissatisfied? I think not, and the same holds for accomplishing things in life. Indian and partial Western pessimism about life aren't at all obviously correct. This is world philosophy, but nothing prevents such philosophy from favouring one of the traditions it considers over others.

'O my mind,
You don't know the art of tilling the soil –
Alas, the land of human existence
Lies barren. –
It would've yielded a golden harvest
Well cultivated.'
(Ram-Prasad)

Part II: Traditional Views Reformulated

Part II comprises three articles, one each on the three Indian geniuses of our times who happen to be three outstanding personalities of the world. They are Rabindranath Tagore, Sri Aurobindo and Swami Vivekananda.

All three have brought the Indian philosophical wisdom to a new height in their distinct, and yet, complementary ways.

Swami Vivekananda (1863–1902), the first of the three to shine on the world scene, came all the way to Chicago from Calcutta, India to represent Hinduism at the World's Parliament of Religions, 1893. While representing Hinduism at the Parliament, Vivekananda touched a deep universal chord for the whole of humankind, ushering in a turn to creative unity at the secular spiritual level that transcends the narrow confines of religious bigotry and exclusiveness that give rise to intolerance leading, in its wake, to human suffering, both intra- as well as inter-religious. This contribution of Vivekananda took an abiding shape in the West as he crisscrossed America, and later Europe, delivering series after series of talks at every place he visited. If we see the spirit of Enlightenment in operation at the holding of the Parliament in America at the end of the nineteenth century, Swami Vivekananda certainly added an innovative base for the onward flow of Enlightenment on which human flourishing can be structured in and though an elevation of the world religions toward opening themselves up to positive phenomenological heights in mutually beneficial coexistence with each other. All this the Swami did while exposing the world to the spirit of the universal messages inherent in Hinduism. He was by far the first in human history to have indulged in the task of doing World Philosophy. His address on the Vedanta Philosophy delivered before the Graduate Philosophical Society of Harvard University on March 25, 1896,[1] along with two afternoon discussions with Harvard students preceding the address, demonstrate his involvement in the task of doing World Philosophy. On the heels of his presentation at Harvard, Vivekananda got an offer of appointment from the university for its chair in Oriental Philosophy, while almost a concurrent offer for a chair in Sanskrit came

1

Janmashtami
September 6, 2023

International Society for World Philosophy (ISWP)
www.iswphil.org
C/O
Massey College
University of Toronto
4 Devonshire Place
Toronto, ON, Canada
M5S 2E1

from Columbia University. As acceptance of an academic position would interfere with his commitments to the cause of a Hindu monk; he had to decline both offers.

No wonder, Romain Rolland, the great French creative writer, a contemporary of the Swami, was literally overwhelmed by the thoughts he generated, so much so that he wrote a biography of him highlighting the thoughts, the first of its kind to appear on the world stage. As a matter of fact, Vivekananda's ideas and influence were so pronounced on him, that he wrote to Freud in response to the latter's book *The Future of an Illusion*, highlighting the thoughts he had gathered from Vivekananda and mentioned the Swami in his personal correspondence to Freud. Rolland specifically emphasized attaining the phenomenological state of immersion in the 'oceanic feeling' associated with an existential becoming within oneself at the spiritual domain, transcending the narrow confines of the religions that Freud targeted for criticism in his book. Situated in the state of the oceanic feeling one indeed is fortified with a unifying sense that helps resolve tensions arising out of conflicts relating to diversities as harmony manifests itself in unity. In his letter to Freud dated December 5, 1927[2] Rolland writes the following to Freud that corroborate the observations I made above:

> … I would have liked to see you doing an analysis of *spontaneous religious sentiment* or, more exactly, of religious *feeling*, which is wholly different from *religions*, in the strict sense of the word, and much more durable.

He continues with his thought in the letter relating to the feeling grounding all religions, from a psycho-philosophical perspective, and adds:

> I am going to study, in a future book, two personalities who were almost our contemporaries (the first one belonged to the late nineteenth century, the second died in the early years of the twentieth) and who revealed an aptitude for thought and action which proved strongly regenerating for their country and for the world. I myself am familiar with this sensation. All through my life, it has never failed me; and I have always found in it a source of vital renewal… I may add that this 'oceanic' sentiment has nothing to do with my personal yearnings.

[2] Parsons, pp. 173–4.

The second of the personalities Rolland draws Freud's attention to in the extract above is none other than Swami Vivekananda, the first being the latter's revered guru, Sri Ramakrishna. Freud himself refers to this conversation originating from Romain Rolland as he starts his book *Civilization and its Discontents* with the concept of the 'oceanic feeling' in us that Rolland had highlighted in his letter as 'the true subterranean source of the religious energy'[3] laudable in itself, even as it is channelled through 'the various Churches and religious systems' following questionable ways as pointed out in Freud's book *The Future of An Illusion*. Making a distinction between 'the source of the religious energy' (to borrow the language Freud uses) and the various religions originating from the source, Rolland seems to make a deep/surface level distinction in the realm of spirituality famously made later by Noam Chomsky in the linguistic field. The 'oceanic feeling' belongs to the innate deep level, and is untouched by the faults of the religions at the surface level that Freud finds in them. Rolland's claim seems to amount to this: While Freud's criticisms against religions in *The Future of an Illusion* Rolland finds broadly justifiable, he does not see them applicable against the deep level.

Freud mentions in the footnote to *Civilization and Its Discontents*[4] the two books on the lives of Sri Ramakrishna and Swami Vivekananda by Rolland, already published, while the latter had hinted at authoring 'a future book' on them in his letter. Rolland seems to have got inspiration from both the spiritual leaders for the 'oceanic feeling' at the deep level, as he takes a special care to mention their names in his letter.

Here are two excerpts I consider relevant to quote from the writings of Rolland on Swami Vivekananda:

> Rolland concludes the Prelude to his book on the Swami with a reference to the untimely passing of the great master:
>
> He was less than forty years of age when … [he] lay stretched on the pyre … But the flame of that pyre is still alight today. From his ashes, like those of the Phoenix of old, has sprung anew the conscience of India—the magic bird—faith in her unity and in the Great Message, brooded over from Vedic times by the dreaming spirit of his ancient race—the message for which it must render account to the rest of mankind.

[3] Parsons, p. 174, Also, Freud, p. 11.

[4] Freud, p. 11, Footnote #2.

Elsewhere the author says:

> His words are great music, phrases in the style of Beethoven, stirring rhythms like the march of Handel choruses. I cannot touch these sayings of his, scattered as they are through the pages at thirty years' distance, without receiving a thrill through my body like an electric shock. And what shocks, what transports must have been produced when in burning words they issued from the lips of the hero.[5]

Abhishek Bandyopadhyay starts his article 'Virtue Ethics in Swami Vivekananda: a Novel Perspective on Vedanta' with the Swami's presentations at the Parliament, pointing out that he was the only speaker present at the august gathering who did not confine his speeches exclusively to the excellence of the faith he represented, but urged on paying our attention to the greatness of all faiths. Bandyopadhyay highlights the emphasis Vivekananda lays on the acceptance of the state of phenomenological awareness of the non-dual (Advaita) on which ethics is grounded. The author is quick to point out that the Swami's acceptance of the foundational non-dual is not in keeping with the traditional, nihilistic interpretation following from the great philosopher Shankaracharya according to which the world is cancelled (vadhita) the moment the realization dawns. The author continues his thesis focussing his attention on the non-dualism in place in the Tantra, as Vivekananda's revered guru Sri Ramakrishna would emphatically assert the abiding, dynamic identity between the Primordial Energy of the universe, Shakti, or Prakriti, with Siva, the Primordial Passivity, or Purusha, comprising the other end, if we translate the concepts in the Tantra using the terminology in the Sankhya system. This identity is certainly contrary to the static non-dualism of the Shankarite kind. Having attained the coveted non-dualistic experience following the Shankarite tradition, as his guru did, Vivekananda took Advaita Vedanta to a dynamic direction, where the world remained, and would not disappear following the realization of non-dualism, waiting for service from the realized soul as needs arise. This certainly is a major contribution to the ancient thoughts in Indian Philosophy by Swami Vivekananda that seems to have escaped the attention of the philosophers of today. Bandyopadhyay mentions the relevance the Swami finds of the awareness

[5] Rolland, LV (1984, 146).

of the non-dual to the ethical overtures of an agent. The following quote from the author relates to a major contribution of the Swami to the Ethico-spiritual area in the Hindu tradition in continuation of his contributions to the Non-dual Vedanta:

> Vivekananda added an important strand of yoga to the group of existing yogas in the Indian system, viz., that of service to God in and through service to humans, considering them as manifestations of divinity in our very presence, while the suffering souls wait for the proper attention and treatment from us. This turns out to be inclusion of Care Ethics in the fold of virtue ethics on the Swami's part in the Hindu system, in the frame of reference of the philosophy of Vedanta before the birth of Care Ethics as a distinct system in the West at the end of the twentieth century.

In this short paper Bandyopadhyay, an academic scientist, with a strong grounding in the Ramakrishna-Vivekananda literature, has brought a number of innovative thoughts relating to Swami Vivekananda in the context of the theme of this book which hopefully a philosopher will be able to develop further in a potent philosophical shape at some future date. It is indeed interesting to note that the Swami developed the ancient spiritual thoughts of Hinduism in the West centring around Advaita Vedanta around a time when the Neo Hegelian thoughts of the great Oxford philosopher F H Bradley, e.g., *Appearance and Reality*, had a pronounced impact on the metaphysics of the day. It would be great to philosophically relate the concepts of Purusha and Prakriti prevalent in the Indian system with Yang and Yin in the Chinese, keeping in mind that Prakriti, which is manifestly geared to activity, contains two constituents—sattva and tamas, that combine an element of passivity in their own distinctive ways. We would look forward to philosophers doing work relating Romain Rolland's thoughts pertaining to the 'oceanic feeling' to those of Swami Vivekananda, grounding the entire conversation in the deep/surface level model touched upon earlier in the Introduction.

Rabindranath Tagore (1861–1941) was an outstanding thinker, on top of his super acumen in composing poems and other forms of creative writing, while he concurrently pursued with remarkable distinction many other ways of aesthetic pursuit like music, dance, dramatic performance and painting. He was the first Asian to be honoured as a recipient of the Nobel Prize. He received the prize in Literature in 1913 with a special mention of his book of poems, *Gitanjali (Song Offerings)*, that contained

English translations of some of the poems by the poet from the original Bengali. Certainly, the Nobel Committee honoured itself awarding the Prize to this very special litterateur who occupies a high place among literary figures in all languages for all times. I feel tempted to quote from the Introduction to the original edition of the book written by W. B. Yeats, a British Nobel Laureate in Literature who helped Tagore in copy editing the final translated version of the manuscript. 'I have carried the manuscript of these translations about with me for days,' he says, 'reading it in railway trains, or on the top of omnibuses and in restaurants, and I have often had to close it lest some stranger would see how much it moved me. These lyrics—which are in the original, my Indians tell me, full of subtlety of rhythm, of untranslatable delicacies of colour, of metrical invention—display in their thought a world I have dreamed of all my life long. The work of a supreme culture, they yet appear as much the growth of the common soil as the grass and the rushes... These verses will not ...be carried about by students at the university to be laid aside when the work of life begins, but as the generations pass, travellers will hum them on the highway or men rowing upon rivers. Lovers, while they await one another, shall find, in murmuring them, this love of God a magic gulf wherein their own more bitter passion may bathe and renew its youth.' 'A whole people, a whole civilization, immeasurably strange to us', Yeats continues on, 'seems to be taken up into this imagination, and yet we are not moved because of its strangeness, but because we have met our own image, as though we had walked in Rossetti's willow wood, or heard, first time in literature our voice as in a dream.'

In the above extract we find Yeats touch upon a universal, cross-cultural philosophic moment he finds present in the poems of Tagore, a philosophy the poet devoted his entire life to develop in his characteristically poetic way of philosophizing where the worlds of philosophy and poetry coalesce in an intimately creative thrust of unity.

Tagore was involved in activist efforts geared to peace in the world, in company with his friend Romain Rolland. He was in intimate touch with Albert Einstein whom he visited several times.

In her paper on Tagore entitled 'Tagore's Philosophy of Man: Reconciling Opposing Forces' Shefali Moitra brings out Tagore's concept of human freedom in secular spiritual terms which stands remarkably different from the standard views in the West. Although Tagore rejects the reputation of being a philosopher, the author disagrees, for she takes him to be a philosopher in a broad sense where his poetic mood is incorporated in his vision of life as an ever-continuing onward journey, in the evolutionary process starting from matter and life, toward achieving an inner freedom, as we move deep within, beyond our surface level lying in the jurisdiction of science. This account may sound very poetic and romantic, says Moitra, to anyone with a scientific orientation, as Tagore emphasized the welcome incorporation of imagination of poetic as well as artistic creation in the spiritual pursuit of humans stretching beyond the surface level leading onto the pursuit of the infinite via the finite. Moitra posits that in Tagore's creative thinking the finite and the infinite are united in one seamless whole, an idea to cause a stir in the realm of science. Moitra starts her paper with the apology for an effort to put the rich thoughts of Tagore within the short compass of one single paper. As she shows the area of ethics emerge in course of her discussion on Tagore's thoughts relating to one's journey within, she indicates the possibility of a virtue ethical connection the inward journey might suggest.

Hopefully, this paper by Moitra, in combination with the thoughts presented in Ananda Chakravarti's presentation in Part III, along with the comments made in the Introduction here, will inspire future philosophical work on Tagore and his virtue ethics.

Sri Aurobindo (1872–1950) is one of the brightest luminaries in the galaxy of Indian spirituality and philosophy for all times. Born Aurobindo Ghosh, he was a junior contemporary of Swami Vivekananda as well as Rabindranath Tagore, the place of birth for all three being Calcutta, India. He was educated from early boyhood in England, as his father wished, and passed the Tripos in Cambridge in the first class, the university education being supported by a senior classical scholarship. He displayed his brilliance in Greek and Latin during the school days. Since his father was intent on the son growing up saturated in British thoughts and culture, segregated from the Indian environment, Aurobindo did not have a chance of learning Sanskrit, Bengali—his mother tongue—or any other Indian languages toward attaining a sound grasp of the Indian culture till he finished his Cambridge days to come back to India at the age of twenty-one. He started learning Sanskrit, Bengali and some other Indian languages after getting settled in India, and made tremendous progress within a short time in mastering the roots of the Indian culture. Later, he started analytic writing on areas relating to Indian culture, along with philosophico-spiritual prose writings, and composing poems in English. A deep spiritual turn in his life became the basis of all his work, including his writings. His razor-sharp intellect, mounted on the exalted spiritual state he eventually attained, did certainly put to an effective use the intensive training in the classics he had received in England.

Sri Aurobindo's prose writings encompass various levels. In *The Foundations of the Indian Culture*, in polemical mood, he lays bare the true foundations of the Indian culture for his readers against wrong, distorted portrayal of them originating and circulating in the West. Even at the comparatively preliminary level of exposition the book is apt to pose a challenge to the reader in having a thorough grasp of the subtlety and depth relating to the thoughts presented. In the booklet *The Mother* he unveils the philosophical subtleties connected to the concept of the *Mother* prevalent in the Tantra. *The Secret of the Veda* with its own polemical stride brings out the unity of the intent, purpose and content of the Rig Veda, the oldest of the Vedas, on the one hand, and Vedanta, or the Upanishads, on the other. Here Sri Aurobindo meticulously goes into the story of the journey of the Angirasas found in the Rig Veda and lays bare the deep philosophico-spiritual significance of the story standing at par with the messages imbedded in Vedanta. Our physical distance from the sacrificial language used in the Veda creates an inaccessibility on us—later users of the language—which amounts to an inability on our part to see the same message present in the Veda and Vedanta, he observes. The *Essays on the Gita* is another very important interpretive work on his part where he follows the tradition of the Indian way of philosophizing while creating new ideas by way of writing a commentary on an existing text. Perhaps it is time now for an able scholar to demonstrate that Sri Aurobindo's interpretation of the Gita stands out in lifting the understanding of the text to a new height in comparison with the other standard commentaries made through the centuries. Certainly, it is imperative to consult his interpretation of the Gita, in conjunction of the other standard ones, to arrive at a proper understanding of the philosophy of the Gita today.

It is important to keep in mind that Sri Aurobindo, though respectful of Shankaracharya as a philosopher and a super individual, was critical of the latter's interpretation of Vedanta, an interpretation he found nihilistic with the world considered illusory. In his magnum opus, *The Life Divine* Sri Aurobindo develops his own philosophy of attainment of a next step for humans in the ongoing evolutionary process, with practice of the *Integral Yoga* where there is a co-presence of knowledge and action, as transcendence and immanence coalesce. The epic *Savitri: A Legend and a Symbol* he composed is considered a super poetic expression of his philosophy.

Since Sri Aurobindo's philosophy imparts all the importance on the world we live in, accommodated in the spiritual perspective he lays his emphasis on in his philosophy, a question naturally comes to mind relating to the relevance he might find of the ethical dimension in his philosophy. Indrani Sanyal, in her paper 'Sri Aurobindo's Metaphysics of Morals *vis-à-vis* Western Models of Virtue Ethics' deals with the specific area of the presence of the ethical perspective in Sri Aurobindo. 'Sri Aurobindo's not authoring any … text dealing exclusively with morality or ethics', she assures us, 'is not to be read as a reflection of Sri Aurobindo's backing for an insignificant role for morality or ethics in his whole narrative of spiritual growth, progress and unfolding.' 'Ethics prepares for "our growing into the nature of the Godhead"', she quotes from him. In her paper she explores the part ethics plays in the scheme of Sri Aurobindo's philosophy of human growth into fullness in the process of an existential becoming where ethics is found to play a very important, though transitory role. She does us the great service of collecting from the vast corpus of Sri Aurobindo's writings many passages relating to his thoughts on ethics, which, hopefully, will facilitate future philosophical work relating to his ethics. Although it is difficult to confine the comprehensive holism of Sri Aurobindo to a single brand of ethical theory, as she observes, she ends her paper with the suggestion that virtue ethics comes closest to the categorization of his ethical thinking.

Work needs to be done connecting the Shankarite interpretation of Maya, the primordial cause of the universe, as Falsity in the construction of his system of Non-dualism, with the opposing Tantric model, leading finally on to the unfolding of thoughts that Sri Aurobindo weaves in his comprehensive philosophy of *Integral Yoga*.

'Uttisthata, Jagrata, Prapya Varan Nivodhata' (Kathopanishat 1.3.14)
(Arise, Awake and Stop Not Till the Goal is Reached; [Translated by Swami Vivekananda])

Part III: Virtue Ethics For Current Application

This book has many unique features about it. To start with, this is the first book on the area of virtue ethics, spelling out its mooring in the Indic tradition. Also, this book on philosophy opens itself up to contributions from people outside of academic philosophy, to include their relevant perspectives into a broader philosophical fold. Ananda Chakravarti, from the corporate world, meaningfully treads into the world of philosophy for guidance in his professional existence. Here he follows the general advice of Dominic Barton, the great consultancy guru in the world of business/ administration, articulated in talks at business schools, and elsewhere, to access philosophy for the sake of doing business. Ananda is ensuring that doing philosophy, at least to an extent, is the sure way to access it while he attempts to make a contribution to the existing thoughts in philosophy. In his essay 'Business Leadership and Virtue Ethics for the 21st Century: Barton through the Lens of Tagore,' he highlights the views of Wim Vandekerckhove and others relating to business grounded on virtue ethics, and eventually brings all the relevant conversations into the fold of the thoughts of Tagore where the ancient wisdom of India has found a creative expression for the modern world.

Dennis Wittmer, in his article 'Reflections on Teaching Virtue Ethics in a Business Curriculum' gives us a glimpse of how he introduces virtue ethics to his students in a prestigious business school in America in the credit courses he offers. Wittmer mentions four strategies he combines in his business ethics courses, starting with discussion on the purpose of business in the broad spectrum of life, leading to an exposure to Aristotelian virtue ethics as he proceeds on the way. He ends the paper with expression of encouragement he feels regarding a positive receptivity on the part of the students in their venture into ethics courses at the business school.

In his paper 'Kautilya's Ethics Based Economics vs Modern Economics' we find Balbir Sihag, an accomplished economist, providing an excellent, innovative introduction of a philosophical backdrop to the science of economics of today, incorporating ancient philosophico-economic ideas from India he finds manifest in the work of the economist Kautilya, 300 BCE. Sihag highlights the strong emphasis Kautilya laid on building an effectively productive, prosperous and happy society grounded on virtues situated in the all-inclusive structure of the virtue ethics in place in ancient India, to be found in scriptures such as the Srimad-Bhagavad-Gita, one may feel tempted to point out. However, Kautilya does not leave administration to the task of development of virtues only in society. The legal system is there in place backed by the might of the administration to ensure that justice prevails with the needed deontological support, while social prosperity ensues as a consequence of economic measures meticulously spelt out toward the purpose, accommodating consequentialism within the frame built on virtue ethics. Thus, an all-out, harmonious blend of all three theories: virtue ethics, deontology and consequentialism makes

Kautilya's system so attractive, effective and innovative in the history of humankind. The paper claims superiority for Kautilya's system in comparison with Adam Smith's formulated two millennia later. We may conclude that the blend of the three ways mentioned above, to be found in Kautilya in ancient India, is missing in Adam Smith. This paper paves the way to prospective serious World Philosophical work by academic philosophers on virtue ethics/virtue theory geared to the task of building prosperity and happiness in society.

The topics of the three papers are by themselves quite novel in an anthology on virtue ethics. The two papers relating to the world of business are after all complementary to each other if we consider the emphasis mentioned in Chakravarti's article that Dominic Barton lays in his talks at business schools on the need he feels for people in the business world to access philosophy. Chakravarti involves himself in doing philosophy while arranging the ideas of Barton with application of recently developed concepts in business ethics, stretching eventually into the rich area of Indian Philosophy where the expanse of life has come to be delineated with a novel mode of purpose and meaning in joy. Wittmer concentrates on the task of teaching business ethics in a business school, focusing on virtue ethics, thus laying the foundation for the upcoming business administrators to benefit from Philosophy, a favourite idea of Barton's. We might expect that the horizon of World Philosophy will one day be meaningfully included in the laudable attempt he makes at introducing philosophy to the students at business school. This would fall in line with the importance Barton places on the Eastern emphasis of a long-term goal in administration, while he finds character as the most important element in the leader.

PART III, where the above three papers by Ananda Chakravarti, Dennis Wittmer and Balbir Sihag belong, begins with a paper by Sitansu S Chakravarti, 'Ethical Message of the Mahabharata in the Wake of the Global Financial Crisis'. The paper, originally written for people associated with business administration not conversant with the world of philosophy, makes observations relating to virtue ethical issues in the Mahabharata in a language accessible to educated non-philosophers. It shows the relevance today of the ancient Indian scripture of the Hindus dating way back from Kautilya's era of 300 BCE, in so far as it contains secular thoughts for today's world, in the language of virtue ethics, as they relate to mitigating systemic greed toward the smooth running of the financial system, thus averting a catastrophe of the kind the world witnessed to originate in 2008. In the paper the author relates the thoughts in the Mahabharata to those present in the stalwarts of the modern day—Tagore and Gandhi.

The author relates the appropriateness of an act involved in a moral situation combining the perspectives of the Act Dharma and the Attitude Dharma, in so far as the virtue constituting an attitude is vital to the performance of an act. The content of the article provides readers without prior in-depth knowledge of virtue ethics, and Indian philosophy, a stepping-stone for entry into the subject virtue ethics for everyday benefit in life. Those eager for further elaboration of ideas involved here may like to go into the article 'Environmental Virtue Ethics: A Traditional Indian Perspective on Hursthouse's Quest' by the same author in Part IV of this anthology.

'Vasudhaiva Kutumvakam' (Maha Upanishat 6.72)
(The World is But One Family)

Part IV: Indian Virtue Ethics For Theory Building Today

Part IV starts with Amita Chatterjee's 'Why Virtue Ethics Comes Closest to Indian Moral Praxis' where the author intends to establish that a prominent trend of Indian Ethics is virtue ethics. She briefly covers the route of the emergence of virtue ethics in modern times in the West from its source in the Greek beginnings in ancient times. While indicating the presence of a virtue ethical trend in traditional Indian philosophy, she moves on to modern writings on Indian virtue ethics. In her discussion she has freely negotiated her journey in the area of Indian virtue ethics with sources in the Ramayana, the Mahabharata, which contains the Gita, intertwining her movement with thoughts in the diverse schools of Indian philosophy, viz., the Nyaya, Mimamsa and Vedanta. She has touched upon Islam and Sikhism in her survey. Here is an abstract of the paper:

> Right from its inception, Indian Ethics has been *dharma*-centric, which can justifiably be translated as virtue-centric. Yet, in most of the global ethical literature, ethicists have been found to engage in Greek ethics and Chinese ethics in discussions of virtue ethics where Indian ethics is conspicuously absent. The author intends to highlight in the paper the nature of Indian ethics as a virtue ethics. Drawing on the resources of the *Dharma-Shastra-s*, the Vedanta literature and the *Bhagavadgita*, the starting point of the author is to establish that though Indian theorists have laid down definite sets of rules of conduct, moral prescriptions and prohibitions, yet these have always

been subservient to the goal of attaining a kind of excellence, i.e., being a certain kind of person by realizing the divinity already existing in man. Finally, the author attempts to show that Indian ethics is a genuine brand of virtue ethics and not merely a virtue theory though many interpreters of the Gita have often placed its ethics within a consequentialist or deontological frame.

The next paper 'Environmental Virtue Ethics—A Traditional Indian Perspective on Hursthouse's Quest' by Sitansu S Chakravarti mentions the possible routes indicated by Hursthouse to building a viable environmental virtue ethics in her landmark 2007 paper. He follows the basic comprehensive structure for such an ethics as delineated by the foremost virtue ethicist of today, and incorporates Indian philosophical concepts from ancient times as he builds a model for environmental virtue ethics grounded on the virtue Indian philosophy has especially emphasized in character building, viz., *harmony within*. He maintains that harmony has a threefold aspect: (a) the *harmony within*, which is the virtue leading to the wellbeing of the agent herself; (b) the harmony amongst human beings—in one's own society and the whole social world—that the virtue is meant to, and helps promote; and (c) the harmony of the individual and every society with the natural world, which we delight in and promote on the basis of the virtue.

Chakravarti claims this anchor virtue implies the presence of other needed virtues, thus pointing to the unity of virtues, as Hursthouse comments in personal communication on previous versions of this paper, where she encourages the author to bring ideas from the East in the paper enriching its philosophical moment. Here Chakravarti has followed the spirit of World Philosophy in his attempt at finding a solution to the philosophical problem of building environmental virtue ethics with the help of philosophical insights and wisdom from the Indian tradition as the East and the West join hands together in a common philosophical venture. He attempts to elaborate on Ronald Sandler's concepts of the meaning of life, knowledge and autonomy suggested as distinctive emergent features in the process of evolution reaching its final state of rationality where we humans are situated. In fact, finding the meaning of life in knowledge and autonomy is a move toward a state of existential becoming where the virtue *harmony within* seems to be of quite a relevance. This existential becoming is what the author understands as spirituality involved in the process of our relation to nature while character is considered important in Sandler's book with the significant title 'Character and Environment'. 'The meaning of life based on ***harmony within***,' says Chakravarti, 'which is 'intentional' in character, prompts one to look for harmony all the way, and help maintain, and build it if found missing by any chance…' All in all, this a philosophical paper, done in the spirit of World Philosophy, where the wisdom of India has not been left out in the process of doing philosophy.

In 'Emotion Concepts for Virtue Theory: From Aesthetic to Epistemic and Moral', Lisa Widdison addresses a meta-philosophical issue in virtue theory, the historically problematic role of emotions in moral judgement, and in motivating virtue. Contemporary virtue epistemologists look to character traits that are relevant to inquiry, such as intellectual courage, carefulness and open-mindedness as marks of intellectual virtue. Both virtue ethicists and virtue epistemologists may also construe emotions as embodied judgements which express moral and epistemic value. However, the cognitive language of emotions as 'self-interested judgments of value' leaves a gap aesthetic judgment may fill. In contrast with egotistical or deterministic emotions, a path to empathy, harmony and compassion is affectively regulated by judgments of taste. By following Bharata (*Nāṭyaśāstra*, 200 CE) and Abhinavagupta (950 CE) on a paradigmatic model of fully graded aesthetic emotion-type distinctions, the discourse around bhavas and rasas (ordinary and universalized emotion, respectively) provides a basis to link the aesthetic stance to free will, agentive responsibility and an infusion of pathos required to motivate a character trait of harmony. Widdison maintains that in processing aesthetic judgments, emotions become reflective, or operate without a settled objective, and so can harmonize actions with moral interests. It is possible to make a fine-tuned analysis of cognitive, occurrent states of personal emotion, and open-ended, universalized emotions, which constitute aesthetic experiences. The finely graded distinctions of affect in Śaiva non-dualism reveal an emotional spectrum which presupposes the unity of cognition with affect.

This paper is a smooth transition from the Vedantic perspective highlighted in the preceding paper by Chakravarti to the perspectives of Indian aesthetics as well as the philosophy of the Tantras, while the author engages herself with doing World Philosophy using relevant thoughts from the West in course of her philosophical deliberations. Widdison's paper provides ample evidence of Indian philosophy accommodating the emotive dimension in an analytic way of philosophizing since ancient times, maintaining a heart-mind continuity Michael Slote keenly seeks in philosophy.

In his paper 'Science, Spirituality and Virtue Ethics', Kumar Murty, a mathematician of international repute, has ventured into an area which hardly ever receives academic attention of philosophers. He deals with spirituality in his paper from the perspective of the Indian philosophical system of Vedanta where there is no prerequisite for a commitment to a personal God. Vedanta emphasizes the growth and transformation of the individual, and this is well aligned with virtue ethics. While discussing the relationship of spirituality and virtue ethics to science, he quotes extensively from Swami Vivekananda. It would not be an exaggeration to say that in modern times, Vivekananda's lectures, especially his widely acclaimed Harvard address of 1896, have thrown new light on the way we understand Vedanta and its ramifications on all aspects of life. Drawing on his decades-long experience as a practising scientist, and combining it with the insights of Vivekananda, Murty gives a nuanced and holistic description of what science is, how it is practised and how it is expressed. He pays particular attention to the human being who is doing the science. In this way, Murty sees science and spirituality, along with virtue ethics, of mutual relevance, keeping their identities intact. Making the paper in the spirit of World Philosophy, the author does not adopt a parochial attitude outside of the field of philosophical reasoning. We expect this article to be a precursor to future investigations. It builds on his course of lectures to philosophy students at the University of Toronto on "Knowledge, Identity and Behaviour: An introduction to Indian philosophy".

In 'The Challenge to being Virtuous: A Lesson from the Mahābhārata,' Nirmalya Narayan Chakraborty situates the search for liberation on a tumultuous path of rule following, versus moral particularism in an epic tale of war and peace, tolerance and ignominy, truth and lies, vengeance and forgiveness. In the realm of moral dilemmas, he focuses on the morality of deception. Nirmalya explains how the quintessential moral player, Yudhiṣṭhira, who is an embodiment of truth, is justified, *or not*, to lie to his teacher, Droṇa. Is such an act universalizable? Even more strange and questionable, Yudhiṣṭhira attempts to make his false statement appear like the truth and arguably deceives himself about his own fall from virtue, after Bhīma kills an elephant belonging to the Pāṇḍava side whose name happens to be Aśvatthāman, like Drona's son. Unaware of the intentional equivocation, Droṇa goes on rampage and falters. Is all fair in war, *or is morality impossible*? We shall learn from his analysis the context in which dharma ripens as the fruit of properly motivated action. The moral fruit comes in the form of a direct perception of 'the real' across different appearances. This is clear in lessons from Mahābhārata's authority, Bhīṣma, whose allegiance to non-monotonic reasoning reveals scepticism about universal rule-following. Bhīṣma implies a philosophical account of moral reasoning cannot be given from some external standpoint, outside the *worldly conventions* of life. Nirmalya Chakraborty pleads for waiver of universalism in favour of moral particularism developing a point from Kripke's treatment of Wittgenstein in *Wittgenstein on Rules and Private Language.* This is Chakraborty's stance relating to the criticisms levelled by Jonardon Ganeri in his paper 'A Cloak of Clever Words: The Deconstruction of Deceit in the *Mahabharata*' in *Conceptions of Virtue: East and West*, Ed. Chong, Kim-Chong, Marshall Cavendish, Singapore, 2006.

Epilogue

Incorporating Ideas From the Mahabharata

This long review article by Amita Chatterjee on *Ethics in the Mahabharata: A Philosophical Inquiry for Today* by the author Sitansu S Chakravarti brings into focus the ethical insights found present in the Mahabharata. She brings in relevant ethical insights from the stalwart Indian philosopher Bimal K Matilal relating to the discussion in the book on ethical issues covered in the epic. 'The Mahabharata,' Chatterjee says, 'is the richest document available on society, polity and value system of ancient India.' In this anthology we had intended to include more than just two articles on the epic. However, since we did not succeed in fulfilling our desire, we inserted the meticulously crafted review as a compromise, as it contains a thorough overview of ethics in the epic.

References

Burke, Marie Louise. *Swami Vivekananda in the West: New Discoveries*, Part Two, Advaita Ashrama, Calcutta, 1986.

Freud, Sigmund. *Civilization and its Discontents*, Translated and edited by James Strachey, W.W. Norton, New York, 1961.

Parsons, William B. *The Enigma of Oceanic Feeling: Revisioning the Psychoanalytic Theory of Mysticism*, With an *Appendix* 'The Letters of Sigmund Freud and Romain Rolland,' Oxford University Press, New York, 1999.

Rolland, Romain. *The Life of Ramakrishna*, Translated from the original French by E.F. Malcolm-Smith, Advaita Ashrama, Calcutta, 1984.

______. *The Life of Vivekananda: And the Universal Gospel*, Translated from the original French by E.F. Malcolm-Smith, Advaita Ashrama, Calcutta, 1984.

Sen, Amartya. 'Consequential Evaluation and Practical Reason, *The Journal of Philosophy*, vol. XCVII. No. 9, September 2000.

Williams, Bernard. *Ethics and the Limits of Philosophy,* Fontana Press/Collins, London, 1985.

PART I

World Philosophy

CHAPTER 2

World Philosophy: The Importance of India

Michael Slote

1

The idea of world philosophy originated toward the end of the last century in the work of the Chinese philosopher Feng Qi. His student and successor at East China Normal University in Shanghai, Yang Guorong, has kept the idea alive till this day, but the chief practitioner of world philosophy has been Mou Zongsan, another Chinese philosopher. World philosophy deliberately and self-consciously draws on more than one of the world's main historical philosophical traditions, and there are only three places where philosophy as a discipline has developed sua sponte on this planet: China, India, and Greece. There was no real philosophy in ancient Israel, Egypt, or Babylonia, and the same is true of the three societies in the Western hemisphere that possessed a written culture: the Maya, the Aztecs, and the Incas. World philosophy at its most basic, then, draws on India, China, and the Western thinking that developed out of Greek thought (with help from the Arabs during the Western "dark ages"). Mou Zongsan made use of Chinese ideas derived from Mencius/Mengzi, of

M. Slote (✉)
University of Miami, Coral Gables, FL, USA
e-mail: mslote@miami.edu

S. S. Chakravarti et al. (ed.), *Traditional Indian Virtue Ethics for Today*, Palgrave Studies in Comparative East-West Philosophy,
https://doi.org/10.1007/978-3-031-47972-4_2

Kant and Hegel's philosophies, and of Buddhism to achieve an overall philosophical vision that indeed deserves the title of world philosophy.[1] But subsequent to Mou and up till very recently no one has been seriously or systematically pursuing the idea of world philosophy. No one was doing philosophy in a way that takes India, China, and the West seriously into account. But in this increasingly internationalized world we *should* be thinking and writing in world-philosophical terms, and that has increasingly been my own aim and practice.

But there is one objection that must be overcome if we are all, everywhere, to be or become devoted to the pursuit of world philosophy, and that objection comes from the West. When Western philosophers look, e.g., at Chinese thought, they think they see lots of confusion and lots of philosophically primitive ideas; and when they are willing or able to see merit in things the Chinese have said about philosophy (e.g., their obvious interest in virtue ethics), Western philosophers have believed that those same ideas are already prevalent in the West. What need, then, to pay serious philosophical (as opposed to historical) attention to Chinese ideas?

If world philosophy is to get off the ground, it is imperative that it be able to answer such skeptical doubts (which the West would raise against India as well), and it has been one of my main purposes in recent years to show the West that it has a lot to learn from the Chinese. In my 2018 book *The Philosophy of Yin and Yang* (PYY) and in an earlier article in the journal Dao, I have sought to show that the West misconceives the mind and our cognitive life in a way Chinese thought never has.[2] Western philosophy stands in need of a major course correction, and PYY goes on to argue that updated or purified versions of the Chinese concepts of yin and yang, and of yin/yang, can help the West and all the rest of us to a better understanding of issues in ethics, epistemology, and philosophy of mind. Now I obviously don't have the space to fully give all those arguments here, but I would like to summarize what I have said in order to give you readers some understanding of why I think Western thought needs the help of other philosophical traditions. I shall thereafter introduce India into the picture—all in the service of the idea and the hoped-for reality of world philosophy

[1] See Mou's *Nineteen Lectures on Chinese Philosophy* available online at www.nineteen-lects.com.

[2] See my *The Philosophy of Yin and Yang: A Contemporary Approach*, Beijing: Commercial Press, 2018 (with side-by-side Chinese language and English language texts); or my article "Yin-Yang and the Heart-Mind, *Dao* 2017.

2

Western philosophy has by and large seen the mind and our cognitive functioning as independent of emotion (even the moral sentimentalist Hume saw things this way). But the Chinese and other peoples of the Far East don't think in terms of mind thus understood and prefer to speak/write of a heart-mind instead. The Chinese term *xin*, the Korean term *maum*, and the Japanese term *kokoro* are all typically translated heart-mind, and that is because these cultures don't view cognition and emotion as separable as the West standardly views them (the only exceptions I know of are the German Romantics Herder and Scheler). Sanskrit and other Indian languages have no equivalent to heart-mind, and we shall delve further into that when Indian philosophy becomes the center of our attention here, but one has to ask, given that this idea of inseparability has no currency in the West or (as far as I have been able to determine) in India, whether the assumption of inseparability built into the Far Eastern languages is true to the reality of our cognitive lives. Maybe thought/cognition really can be separated from emotion, and in that case the Western assumption to that effect is acceptable and far from problematic. Let us see.

First, let's look at the cognitive operations/processes philosophers of mind in the West typically talk about. They include reasoning, making inferences, seeing things as, intuiting (truth), planning, intending, and criticizing. All these operations/processes clearly involving believing something or other. Even in a reductio ad absurdum argument, one believes the premises entail one's untenable conclusion. When one plans or intends, one has beliefs about what the future may bring and about what one will do or is likely to do in one or another future situation. If one thinks about it, the same holds true for the other main cognitive operations listed above. The real question, then, is whether belief can occur in the total absence of emotion.

All the Western philosophers I know of (except the German Romantics) assume that it can. For example, Hume thought that beliefs about the world are inert and, unlike moral judgments, purely cognitive, a form of what he called reason. Today's philosophers think of belief and desire as having opposite "directions of fit," with the world (ideally) fitting desire, but (true) belief simply reflecting and cognitively fitting the world. And in his classical explanation of means-end rationality in the 1963 article "Actions, Reasons, and Causes" (available in many anthologies), Donald Davidson puts desires, attitudes, and values in a category entirely separate from beliefs. The implicit assumption, then, is that unlike these other psychological states, beliefs are purely cognitive.

But I believe this is a huge mistake. Belief is or involves an emotion or affect, but the emotion or affect has an epistemic character. Consider what it is to be confident that something is the case. Everyone in the West would agree that confidence is a positive epistemic feeling or emotion and that certitude represents an even more positive epistemic emotion toward some propositional content p. Well, several dictionaries define confidence (that p) as strong belief (that p); and if that is accurate, then belief is on the same scale as confidence and certitude. It represents or entails a positive epistemic attitude toward some proposition, though one that is less positive than confidence just as confidence is less positive than certitude. These are all epistemic emotions, forms of epistemic affect, and in that case all the cognitive operations mentioned above—and they surely represent the main examples we have of our cognitive life—involve affect or emotion. The cognitive cannot, therefore, be separated from the emotional, and the West is mistaken to assume it can be—just as the Far Eastern idea of heart-mind expresses an implicit assumption that cognition and emotion *cannot* be separated. I have speculated in the *Dao* article about why the Chinese or Japanese have never explicitly made this point, but the point, in any event, *can* be effectively made. Since much of Western ethics, epistemology, and philosophy of mind involves the separability assumption, Western philosophy stands in need of a major course correction, and as I think it is fair to put it, that correction has to come from the direction of China and other East Asian nations. (Korean philosophy comes mainly from China, as did Japanese philosophy till the influence of German philosophy began to be felt strongly in Japan.)

So the West has been philosophically mistaken about some elemental truths about cognition, but I have also argued that once that fact is acknowledged, the West (not to mention India) can learn a lot from the use of application of Chinese categories. Once we see that cognition and emotion or feeling cannot be separated, the Chinese categories yin and yang can offer us positive illumination about the way they are related. Now those categories have traditionally been conceived in two rather different ways. The main historical tradition concerning yin and yang sees them as contraries or opposites, with yin being viewed, respectively, as dark, wet, cold, and acidic and yang as bright, dry, warm, and alkaline. Such contrasts were originally used for purposes of natural explanation, explanation, for example, of why the sun sets and brings on darkness after shining brightly. Such explanation was cyclical and conformed to our common experience of natural cycles: not just between dark night and bright day, but between cold winter and warm summer and between wet weather and dry weather operating in some sort of cycle. Such explanations in terms of a temporal cycle of opposites or contraries may have made sense in earlier times, but modern science has given us reason to reject them in favor of more quantitative non-cyclical explanations. So the explanatory use of a yin and yang cycle is no longer viewed by Chinese academic thinkers as relevant to how we should view things today, and cultural practices that make use of yin and yang—e.g., macrobiotic diets, feng shui, and Chinese medicine—are also viewed as outmoded or even superstitious by present-day forward-looking Chinese academics. The fact is that no significant Chinese philosopher of the past 800 or so years has relied on yin and yang as part of their basic view of human life or the natural universe.

However, there is another tradition of thinking about yin and yang that sees them not as mutually opposed, but, rather, as complementary. This way of conceiving them has roots as far back as the *I Ching* and can be seen, for example, in the idea that Heaven (Tian) is yang and Earth (Di) is yin. In Chinese thought Heaven and Earth are not seen as contraries or opposed, but rather as in some sense needing each other and complementing each other: without the order of Heaven, Earth and what happens on Earth is left blind or rudderless, and without Earth, Heaven is empty of all purpose. (Shades of Kant on percepts and concepts.) The idea of yin and yang as mutually friendly and necessary complements is also visible in the traditional depiction of yin and yang as curvy half-circles within a larger circle, with the yin half-circle containing an element of yang and the yang half-circle containing an element of yin—all very peaceably. (By contrast, dark doesn't contain an element of brightness, and coldness doesn't contain an element of warmth. The curvy half-circles *don't* illustrate the conception of yin and yang as total opposites.) It is the complementarity tradition of yin and yang and yin/yang that I have made central use of in attempting to show how these concepts can help Western (and other) philosophy to an improved picture of the realms of ethics, epistemology, and philosophy of mind.

My understanding of yin and yang has deep roots in Chinese thought and culture, but it also involves a kind of philosophical updating or purification of ancient ideas. Yin has been variously equated with passivity, receptivity, and pliancy/pliability (Chinese: rou), and I think receptivity is probably our best candidate for philosophically updating yin and yang. If yang contains the idea of directed activity of some sort, then yin passivity is the polar opposite of yang activity rather than its necessary complement, and obviously such an understanding doesn't conform to the traditional depiction of yin and yang (you can find it on the Internet) because passivity contains no element of activity and vice versa. However, receptivity *does* involve at least a minimal element of activity: when one is receptive, one is motivated to *take things in*. So conceiving yin as receptivity rather than as passivity will allow us to view yin as necessarily (and simultaneously) involving and "friendly" toward yang as activity. Similarly, when we are active we are necessarily responsive or receptive to something that stirs our activity, so if we conceive yin and yang, respectively, as receptivity and (directed) activity, we can understand how they can be mutually necessitating (with respect to any given time) and also mutually friendly or non-hostile complements. The idea of yin as pliancy can then be dismissed or discarded because it is so narrow. Pliancy contains elements of yin receptivity and yang activeness but it is a fairly narrow concept. We can find many instances of yin and yang that have little or nothing to with pliancy, and the equation of yin with receptivity and yang with activity allows us to deploy the yin/yang complementarity in a very broad and philosophically desirable way. Let me now mention one (I believe) illuminating way in which yin and yang as I am suggesting we conceive them can help us better understand philosophical issues.

Compassion is today widely viewed as involving empathy with the distress or suffering of others together with motivation to relieve that distress or suffering. Most psychologists view these elements of compassion as only contingently related: empathy leads to altruistic motivation but that is thought to be a merely contingent causal fact. I think this is a mistake. Empathy with suffering and altruistic motivation are on conceptual grounds necessarily connected. Consider a father who is infected with his daughter's enthusiasm for stamp collecting. This is an empathic process that can occur without the empathic father's being consciously aware that it is happening, but the empathy clearly involves him in more than sheer enthusiasm; it involves his acquiring enthusiasm *for stamp collecting*. Empathy standardly involves sharing both a feeling/attitude and its intentional object, and the same holds for the empathy that is integral to compassion.

Imagine someone who is distressed by the intense throbbing pain in their arm. Distress at something by its very definition involves a desire to eliminate or lessen what one is distressed about, so the person in question desires or is motivated to alleviate the pain in their arm. But then someone who empathizes with that person will not only feel distress but feel distress at what distresses the other person. So the empathizer feels distress at the pain *in the other person's arm*, and we have already seen and said that distress at something involves a desire to eliminate or lessen it. So by its very concept empathy with another person's distress necessitates a desire to eliminate or lessen the object of that distress: in this case the intense pain the *other person* feels in their arm. It follows that in such a case empathy necessarily involves (altruistic) motivation to help the other person, the person who is the focus of one's empathic compassion.

In compassion, then, empathy necessitates altruistic motivation, but it is obvious, too, that there cannot be such a thing as altruistic compassionate motivation without empathy with the person or persons one is motivated to help. To help someone because it is one's duty to do so or because the world will be a better place if one does is not to help them out of *compassion*. Compassion needs to be based in empathy, so in the phenomenon of compassion empathy entails altruistic helping motivation and vice versa.

Does this remind you of anything? Well, it eventually came to remind me of yin and yang. Empathy (when we take in the feelings or attitude of another) is a form of receptivity to the reality of another person (or animal) and can readily be seen as yin; and altruistic motivation to help is clearly a matter of directed purpose and so can be viewed as yang. Moreover, these two sides of compassion necessitate one another in just the way yin and yang viewed as (simultaneously) compatible and friendly complementaries are supposed to. The same points apply to other moral sentiments like benevolence and gratitude.

Further, all of this is related to the idea that cognition and emotion/feeling cannot be separated, to the idea that we have heart-minds, not minds as they are understood in the West. When we emotionally empathize with another person's pain distress, we know or are directly acquainted with that distress through our capacity for empathy. We don't infer or theorize that the person is in distress but rather empathically feel or register that distress. Of necessity, though, as we have seen, the empathy involves compassionate feeling and motivation toward the person in distress. So in such a case cognition and emotion/feeling are inextricably connected, and the concepts of yin, yang, and yin/yang (as their inextricable complementarity) allow us to conceptualize the indissoluble relationship between cognition and feeling/emotion in such a situation.

But this is not just one isolated example. Consider thirst. We can desire to drink for reasons other than thirst (e.g., for reasons of conviviality or to please a host), but when thirst motivates us to drink, we have both knowledge and emotion-clad motivation in inextricable relationship. If one is really thirsty, one will feel unhappy or even angry if one is not able to drink, and so thirst is internally connected to certain emotional dispositions. But by the same token a state doesn't count as thirst if it doesn't register and involve acquaintance with a parched state of one's body. So as with compassion, the phenomenon of thirst embodies a necessary connection between cognition and emotion, and, once again, talk of yin/yang can enable us to conceptualize the structure of thirst as a phenomenon. Thirst involves the yin of receptivity to a certain state of one's body and the yang of motivation to alleviate or do away with that state.

Now I have already argued that all cognitive processes involve the epistemic emotion of belief, but if I had the time and space I think I could show you that wherever any such process or operation occurs (in a functional way), there are inseparable yin and yang sides to it. All mental or, as we might now better say, all heart-mental functioning can be conceptualized in yin/yang terms, so yin and yang give us invaluable insights into our functioning psychology, once we recognize the inseparability of cognition and emotionality. The West needs to make a major course correction and come to see the inseparability of cognition and emotion in a way that Chinese thought always implicitly has. But then the Chinese categories of yin and yang help us conceptualize what cognition involves in a way that would not be necessary if the West had been right in holding that cognition/belief and emotion/motivation can be separated.[3] Yin and

[3] In his *Instructions for Practical Life*, the neo-Confucian philosopher Wang Yangming argued for the inseparability of cognition and emotion. He was the first philosopher East or West to ever do so, but he never recognized the conceptual role yin and yang can play in helping us understand what is involved in the inseparable connection between cognition/knowledge and emotion/motivation. Similarly, Mencius in the *Mencius* puts great emphasis on compassion, but, once again, fails to see how the ancient Chinese categories of yin and yang can help us better understand the nature, the metaphysical constitution, as it were, of compassion. Overall, Chinese philosophers have, in my opinion, underused and underappreciated the idea of yin/yang.

yang offer us a better understanding of moral virtues like compassion and benevolence, but also help us frame a general picture of what is conceptually required in order for functional heart-mental processes to occur.

Now the reader may wonder why I introduce the notion of functionality here, but I do so because not all things that occur in the mind or heart-mind involve yin and yang. In thirst we are cognitively receptive to a state of our body and motivated to act in a more or less specific way to change that state. But consider panic. A panicked person (as opposed to someone who merely feels fear) is no longer receptive or sensitive to what their environment has to teach them and is incapable of concerted action. That constitutes the dysfunctionality of panic, but the important point is that what we have just said about panic shows that it involves a lack or absence of both yin and yang. In general, I want to say that yin/yang marks the distinction between psychological/cognitive functionality and psychological/cognitive dysfunctionality, so once again yin and yang help us to a better overall understanding of our heart-mental life.

Note, however, that this understanding is conceptual, not causal or empirical. Yin and yang doesn't explain why fear sometimes turns into panic and doesn't tell us when that is likely to happen; what it tells us is that whenever there is a dysfunctional state or process like panic, yin and yang are not present in the way they so often are when someone merely fears some person or event. This is the philosophical attribution of conceptual structure, not the offering of a scientific/causal explanation. It is time now to bring in Indian philosophy.

3

As I mentioned in passing earlier, neither Sanskrit nor any modern Indian language contains a word that specifically connotes heart-mind rather than mind. And the same is true, I am told, of every other Indo-European language. This means that not only Western philosophers but also Indian ones can learn an interesting philosophical lesson from the way the Chinese think about our psychology and, more explicitly, from the arguments briefly given above to show how and why cognition cannot be separated from emotion/motivation. Then too, once the assumption that cognition and emotion are separable has been cleared away, it is possible that both Indian and Western philosophers can be brought to see how Chinese yin and yang conceptually/philosophically structure or constitute various moral virtues and our functioning psychology more generally.[4] (If there were space, I would show you how I think yin and yang can work in and for epistemology.) So both the West and India have a lot to learn from China, but as regards what I hope will be the run-up toward vital world philosophizing, I think India is for a number of reasons in a better position than the West.

Above, I offered a critique of a basic and pervasive Western assumption (to some extent shared by Indian philosophy) to the effect that cognition and reasoning don't require emotion/feeling. But Western philosophers almost everywhere are sure they have nothing to learn from other philosophical traditions, and this cannot be said either about the Chinese or about the Indians. All too often Chinese philosophers today tend to dismiss their own country's intellectual traditions and to regard the West as the source of all philosophical wisdom and potential future progress, so they may be more open to the idea of world philosophy because they already look beyond their own traditions and because national pride might persuade them to acknowledge the newly revealed value in such notions as yin and yang. Yin and yang are totally alien to the West, so it doesn't make the West look philosophically better if they turn out to be philosophically important; but China will look better if they do, and that is surely some sort of motive or push toward recognizing the value of Chinese thought alongside the frequent Chinese fondness for philosophical things Western. China and Chinese philosophers thus have a motive for acknowledging the value of more than one philosophical tradition that the West lacks, and one might therefore find that our earlier arguments about heart-mind and yin and yang meet greater resistance among Western philosophers than among most Chinese philosophers. In effect, China is more geared toward an inter-traditional world philosophy than the West is.

But then consider India. Up till now India has not taken Chinese thought into account, and I have attempted to show you why they should start doing so. (For example, Indian virtue ethicists are interested in compassion, and yin/yang helps us to a better understanding of what compassion involves or is.) But Indian philosophy as I understand it doesn't think it has all the answers the way the West does. Indian philosophy, and

[4] Traditional Indian philosophy has and makes use of the distinction between active and passive, but, as I pointed out earlier, neither of the latter categories involves the other. It is the fact that yin and yang involve each other that allows us to make the useful philosophical explanations we have been arguing for here.

especially recent Indian virtue ethics, reaches out toward Western thinking in a welcoming way, and some of this was apparent at the conference on virtue ethics held in Shimla in October of 2019. This means, once again, that Indian philosophy is more capable of acknowledging and more willing to acknowledge the value of non-Indian philosophy in marked contrast with the tendency of Western philosophy to reject outside philosophical traditions. So both India and China are in a better or more likely position to move the philosophical world toward world philosophy than Western philosophy is.

However, it was the Chinese, not the Indians, who came up with the idea of world philosophy, so isn't it more plausible to think they can or should play the leading role in moving philosophy toward world philosophy? Does India have any kind of essential or important role here? I think it does.

After the recent conference at Shimla, I suggested that Indian philosophers might be in the best position to found an International Society for World Philosophy that might play a useful future role in making the possibilities of world philosophy more real and more attractive to philosophers all over the world. India was the first place where philosophy was done on this planet, but it was the Chinese who introduced the notion of world philosophy, and it is a Western philosopher, myself, who is now urging that we philosophers start thinking in a world-philosophical manner. But this still leaves India with an opportunity to *take the lead in moving philosophy and philosophers toward the doing of world philosophy.* The founding of an International Society for World Philosophy would be one way to take the lead, and, as I indicated, I urged Indian philosophers, after the Shimla conference, to do just that. And the response has been quite enthusiastic. I think many Indian philosophers can see that by founding such a society and developing its activities in various ways, India can play a crucial and unique role in philosophy's future.

Moreover (and these are some new points), Indian philosophy is in a better position to accomplish this than either Chinese or Western philosophy is. The West, as is obvious, is too closed-minded about the value of other philosophical traditions to be a fertile place, at this point, for advocacy of world philosophy. And China has a couple of disadvantages in regard to such a potential project. India is a democracy, and there is little chance that its government would seek or be able to interfere with any Indian project of developing an international society devoted to the promulgation and development of world philosophy. By contrast China is ruled by its communist party, a party which, given its official Marxist ideology, wouldn't be all that likely to welcome a society devoted to a world philosophy that didn't (and it wouldn't) give automatic pride of place to Marxism. No, India is a better place than either China or the West for the project I have proposed, the project of founding an international society capable of promulgating world philosophy. I have made this point to my colleagues in India, and they seem to agree with me about it, in which case India may indeed have a uniquely important role to play in philosophy's future.

4

What I have been saying has been intended to show that future philosophy should operate as world philosophy. But what I have been saying has downplayed or minimized the role Western thought can and should play in world philosophy, and in this final section I would like to say more about the Western role in world philosophy and about how the three main traditions encompassed in world philosophy relate to each other.

Western philosophy demarcates different areas or subfields of philosophy in a very articulate way. The demarcated subfields of philosophy include ethics, epistemology, metaphysics, philosophy of science, philosophy of mind, aesthetics, philosophy of language, philosophy of logic—and I could go on. These subfields raise questions that are individual to themselves, as when aesthetics asks about the criteria of beauty and about how or whether one can know that something is beautiful; or as when philosophy of science asks about the criteria for rationally accepting a given scientific explanation of some natural phenomenon or phenomena. Those in China who have advocated for world philosophy—most notably Feng Qi and Yang Guorong—haven't thought in terms of particular subfields of philosophy, but the questions raised in the West in or about those subfields are important ones, and there is no reason why world philosophy shouldn't be relevant to answering them. For example, Western thought asks about the nature and role of beliefs within what it calls the mind, and a world philosophy can answer such questions differently from the way the West does. The West sees beliefs as emotionally inert and purely cognitive, but a world philosophy that learns from what China thinks about heart-mind will answer the question about the nature and role of beliefs very differently from the way the West typically has. The question arises within a field, philosophy of mind, demarcated in the West, but the answer world philosophy gives to it is a basically Chinese, not a Western or Indian, answer.

Then there is Western analytic method. There has not been a lot of that in China; there has been more, traditionally, in India, but analytic thinking is useful and arguably indispensable toward the answering of the questions that arise within the subfields of philosophy. Or so, at least, this Western philosopher thinks. So I am saying that world philosophy needs to acknowledge Western subfields of philosophy and Western questions asked within those subfields; that Western analytic techniques are indispensable to any plausible attempt to answer those questions; but that the answers arrived at may not be at all in line with the ways Western philosophy has sought to answer those questions. The motto of world philosophy could in a nutshell be: *Western fields, Western questions, Western methods, but non-Western world-philosophical answers.*

I shall now say a bit about how the three main original philosophical traditions—India, China, and the West—might interact with one another in the context of the project of developing a genuinely world philosophy. Let's first consider epistemology. India was doing epistemology hundreds of years before anyone in the West was thinking about epistemology, and in fact, as is well known, Chinese thought never went into issues of epistemology. However, since the concept of (justified) belief is basic to almost all epistemology, it should be clear at this point that Chinese ideas about belief—e.g., that like the other operations of the heart-mind it cannot be separated from feeling—will play a significant role in what world philosophy has to say about epistemology. The Chinese may not have been interested in epistemology, but their ideas can serve to illuminate the world epistemology of the future.

Then there is the issue of individuality. By individuality I don't mean individualism of the sort that tells us we needn't care about the welfare of other people (as with the American philosophy of libertarianism or Ayn Rand's virtue of selfishness). I mean rather the placing of importance on the individual and his/her interests even while one leaves room for or morally insists on concern for the welfare of others. Traditional Indian philosophy placed less emphasis on morality or moral virtue than Chinese thought did. There was a preoccupation with the difficulty and painfulness of ordinary living that catered to the individual's desire to do what was best for himself and to the idea of finding a way for the individual to suffer less in this life. This meant, I believe, less concern for what is good for the group, hence the lesser emphasis on moral virtue that one finds in Indian philosophy as compared with Chinese philosophy. The Chinese, by contrast, were less interested in defining or saying what is good for individuals and more interested in focusing on virtues that concern themselves with group (or family) welfare.

One finds both tendencies in different places in Western philosophy. There is sometimes, often, an emphasis on describing what is necessary or sufficient for an individual to have a good life: as with the Epicureans and Aristotle. Such preoccupation with the individual has more in common with traditional Indian philosophy than with traditional Chinese philosophy. On the other hand, Plato in the *Republic* emphasizes the need for the philosopher to take care of the state rather than focus on his or her own satisfactions or well-being; and Kant thinks we have a basic duty to promote the happiness of others but no such duty toward ourselves. These tendencies in the West are more reminiscent of Chinese philosophy than of the Indian. To that extent the West mixes elements that come out more separately or more purely, though in different directions, in Indian and Chinese thought. Dare this Western philosopher suggest that world philosophy try to compromise between Indian and Chinese thought by advocating an individuality that places emphasis on what is good for the individual while at the same time insisting that such individuality is compatible with and may even entail moral concern for others?

Finally, let's consider what China, India, and the West have to say about the value of life itself. Traditional Indian philosophy (like Buddhism) thinks ordinary human life is inherently unsatisfactory or worse, but the Chinese have never bought into such a pessimistic picture of human life. Even at the height of Buddhist influence on Chinese metaphysical thought (in the centuries before the emergence of a neo-Confucianism that deliberately sought to resist Buddhist influences), the Chinese never accepted the idea that ordinary life is inevitably painful and unsatisfactory—in fact the Chinese have mainly been very optimistic about what ordinary life can bring us.

Chinese thinkers have recognized the difference between Chinese and Buddhist thinking about the value of ordinary life. For example, in work that has yet to be translated, Feng Qi notes this difference in attitude and quite firmly sides with Chinese tradition. But Indian and Buddhist philosophers have presented *arguments* purporting to show why ordinary human life is so unacceptable, and as far as I know, Feng Qi doesn't take on or criticize those specific arguments. However, a world philosophy that takes seriously the three main historical traditions of philosophy on this planet will need to pay attention to the arguments Indian philosophers have given for doubting the value of ordinary human living. India will need to be given a chance to defend its view(s) on human life against contrary Chinese opinions, and this is all the more obviously so in the light of the fact that Western philosophy has also offered arguments for considering ordinary human life unsatisfactory. In the *Republic* Plato says we should try to escape bodily existence and make ourselves as much as possible like the timeless pure Forms of Beauty, Truth, and Goodness (etc.) as we can. And in the *Groundwork of the Metaphysic of Morals*, Kant says that everyone would prefer to lose their ordinary desires/appetites if they could.

But in the West there is a division of opinion on this issue that one doesn't find in either China or India. India is pessimistic about human life, China is optimistic about it, and the West has a diversity of opinions on this question. Hume didn't question the possibility of good human living and modern-day psychologists like Erik Erikson hold that it is a mark of mental health that one be able to acknowledge that one's life has overall been good (if in fact it has been).[5] So there is a division of opinion *within* the West and *between* China and India as to the possibility of good ordinary lives, and it makes sense for a developing world philosophy to focus on this question and see whether it can find resources within its different traditions and sub-traditions that can enable it to answer this question or else perhaps tell us why it cannot be answered.

Note that in regard to the last two issues I have considered for their relevance to world philosophy—the issue of individuality and the issue of the potential satisfactoriness of ordinary life—the Chinese and Indians hold totally opposed views whereas Western thought seems to accommodate, within different approaches, both possible takes on the issue at hand. This indicates a certain flexibility within Western thought that one doesn't find in India or China, but flexibility is not the same thing as insightfulness or philosophical wisdom. For example, India might turn out to be right about the unsatisfactoriness of human life and its inflexibility regarding the matter a sign of its superior understanding, relative to univocal Chinese and bifurcated Western thought, of what human life is like. But my point is that we can only get a better understanding of this whole issue if Indian, Chinese, and Western views are allowed to confront each other in a way that up till now has not happened. It will take the development of world philosophy to make it happen.

[5] See, e.g., his *Childhood and Society*, NY: Norton, 1950.

CHAPTER 3

Questioning Buddhism on the Way to "World Philosophy"

Michael Slote

1

In this essay I want to focus on one prominent, even central, aspect of Buddhism, its negativity about ordinary human life. But I have a larger purpose in mind. In the last century the Chinese philosopher Feng Qi proposed the idea of (a) world philosophy, and I think that questioning or challenging Buddhist views about human life can play a role in such philosophy. China, India, and Greece are the three loci on this planet where philosophy developed endogenously. Japan developed philosophy under the influence of Chinese thought and then, much later, under the influence of German philosophy—which like all philosophy in the West had its ultimate origins in Greek thought. Korea too developed philosophically under a largely Chinese influence, and other places on this planet pretty much entirely ignored philosophy. Despite its highly literate traditions, Judaism never promoted or participated in philosophy on its own. A Greek

M. Slote (✉)
University of Miami, Coral Gables, FL, USA
e-mail: mslote@miami.edu

S. S. Chakravarti et al. (ed.), *Traditional Indian Virtue Ethics for Today*, Palgrave Studies in Comparative East-West Philosophy,
https://doi.org/10.1007/978-3-031-47972-4_3

influence on Jewish thought came later than the Hebrew Scriptures, and Egypt and Mesopotamia never gave rise to anything explicitly philosophical. The same holds for the three literate cultures of the New World: the Incan, the Mayan, and the Aztec. So if there is to be something properly called world philosophy, it needs to take in India, Chinese, and Greece/the West in a central way, even if ideas, say, from Japan can play a role too.

Later in this essay I shall say more about what world philosophy essentially is, but for now I would like to concentrate on one major issue that any world philosophy worthy of the name needs to focus on. Indian thought and most particularly Buddhism tend to believe that ordinary human life is painful and unsatisfactory, and on this issue Chinese thought has an entirely different opinion. During the early years of the common era, Buddhism had a great influence on Chinese metaphysical thought, but that influence never extended to making the Chinese doubt the value of ordinary human life. So there is a great divergence of opinion between the two on this very important philosophical question. World philosophy needs to address, to sort out, this issue, and I am going to do some of that here.

It is also worth noting that Western thought is somewhat divided on this question. Plato was skeptical and more than skeptical about the value of ordinary life—telling us in the *Republic* that we should try to escape our bodily existence and commune as much as possible with the eternal verities, the Forms. Kant, in the *Groundwork of the Metaphysics of Morals*, says that every person would want, if possible, to be rid of all appetitive and other worldly inclinations. But I dare say the French philosophes of the eighteenth century expressed no doubts about the value of earthly satisfactions (they were Frenchmen, after all). And very few Western philosophers today show any inclination to doubt the value of ordinary human living. All the more reason, then, for a world philosophy to address this issue and take its conclusions into an overall philosophical picture of things. So let us address the question directly. The Chinese, despite their skepticism about the Buddhist negativity (regarding human life) never, as far as I know, proposed any arguments to controvert the Buddhist view of human life, so if we really want to do world philosophy and if we believe, as I do, that the Chinese were right to value ordinary human life, we must supply arguments in favor of what they seem to have largely taken for granted. Buddhism proposes arguments for doubting and denying the value of human life, and we must now consider just how cogent they are.

2

There are two ways in which or levels at which Buddhism rejects ordinary life, views it as unsatisfactory or worse. At the most general or universal level, the Buddha and Buddhists regard desire as inherently painful, and since all of ordinary human life involves desiring things (or people), they believe ordinary life is full of misery and on the whole miserable, unhappy. This assumes, of course, that desire is unpleasant, and it is worth noting that the ancient Greeks, most notably Plato, came to a similar conclusion. The reasons or arguments that have been given for this conclusion are well known. Desire is thought to represent the lack of something that is desired, and this is analogized, for example, with a state of thirst in which water is lacking and desired. Thirst is not pleasant so it can be argued that for similar reasons having to do with lack or absence, desire in general must be unpleasant. Then there is the related argument that desires are like itches, and no one would want to have an itch in order to be able to scratch it, so if itches are undesirable, desires are too.

As I said, both Greek philosophy and Buddhism bought in to such arguments.[1] However, even when Buddhism was at its most influential in China, the Chinese were never pessimistic about ordinary human life and never deployed arguments about the painfulness of desire in order to show that ordinary life can't be good. In my opinion, they were right to hold back on such assumptions and simply accept what most non-philosophers believe, namely, that some lives—not perhaps most lives, but certainly some lives—can be overall pleasant and good. But to show this we have to look more deeply or sensitively at human desire.

The gestalt psychology movement (along with Edmund Husserl) sought to show, sometimes very successfully, that previous descriptions of human experience have failed to capture what is actual and palpable in some of those experiences. Before gestalt psychology, for example, many philosophers and psychologists held that the world presents itself to us in two-dimensional visual terms, but of course we now know, and know it through the efforts of the gestaltists, that our vision is experientially,

[1] Buddhism places some of the weight for its view that human desire and human life are miserable on the assumption that all apparent differences between things are illusory. The Greeks didn't buy into such metaphysics, and the Buddhist defense of the idea that all differences are illusory is—how shall I say this?—pretty weak in relation to present-day Western standards of philosophical argument. I shall keep assuming that there is more than one thing and more than one person in the universe.

phenomenologically, three-dimensional. At least one gestalt theorist, Karl Duncker, paid similar close attention to the phenomenology of desire or wanting, and his conclusion was that not all desire is unpleasant.[2] To choose an obvious example, when one is looking forward to a great French meal at a Michelin-starred restaurant, the anticipation can be exceedingly pleasant even if this occurs in a context where one wishes to eat. Literal hunger and thirst may be unpleasant, but not all desire for food and drink is based on literal hunger and thirst, so the general idea that all desire is unpleasant and the conclusion drawn on that basis that human life is overall unpleasant are simply not compelling. They oversimplify our experience and our lives. (When one is the last stages of writing a book, does there have to be something unpleasant about wanting to finish one's book project? If one can be satisfied with what one *has* accomplished, one can also be satisfied with what one knows one is *about* to accomplish.)

3

So I think the Buddhists and Greek philosophers were wrong so quickly to reject ordinary human life, and the Chinese showed good sense in firmly rejecting that rejection. But, as I indicated above, there is another level at which one can reject ordinary human life. That other way doesn't focus on desire in general and as such, but rather on certain structural or larger desires that occur within human life: e.g., the desire to find love and the desire for a successful career in some area. Buddhists as such would treat such larger desires in the manner of other desires, but it is worth noting that questions can be raised about such larger desires or medleys of desire that don't depend on the immediate assumption that desire in itself is painful or unpleasant. The present-day neo-Buddhist writer/lecturer Eckhart Tolle doesn't assume or argue that desire is in itself undesirable, but he does question whether, say, the desire for career achievement or success can lead toward a happy life. (See his many video internet lectures at Google.) He thinks that human beings are inevitably disappointed with anything they achieve, that they eventually want more and are dissatisfied until they get that more. And then, of course, the cycle of dissatisfaction is supposed to begin again.

[2] Karl Duncker, "On Pleasure, Emotion, and Striving," *Philosophy and Phenomenological Research* 1, 1941, esp. pp. 420–25.

On that basis Tolle, with his different arguments, joins Buddhism in concluding that human life as we ordinarily live it is invariably unsatisfactory or even miserable. But this conclusion in common with the Buddhists doesn't lead him to the Buddhist solution of seeking the nothingness of nirvana. Rather, he thinks the solution to these difficulties lies in the seeking and possession of fuller, more spacious experiences of current moments. Buddhist negativity in that case is replaced with a positive view of human happiness, one that demands or recommends dwelling richly in the moment. Still, this recommendation is substantially based in the idea that ordinary achievements/accomplishments and ordinary relationships are inevitably unsatisfying, and we have to ask whether Tolle is right about this.

I very much doubt that he is, and I think modern psychology offers some support for resisting Tolle's conclusion(s) here. Tolle tells us that someone with great power will always want and feel the need for more power, and he generalizes this to people's careers. But that seems a mistake. To put things as the psychologist Erik Erikson does in various of his works, if things go well or well enough in one's life, one can at the end of that life look back and see the whole of one's life as good, as satisfactory.[3] There may have been many sad or painful moments in that past life, but one will accept one's previous long life as a whole, rather than finding fault with it or wishing it to have been otherwise.

But surely we cannot or should not avoid considering the implications of Tolle's view, a view I believe he shares with other Buddhists, that we are invariably dissatisfied with our careers, whether they be in philosophy, in science, in literary criticism, in business, or in industry, etc. Such dissatisfaction can loom large in the mind of anyone who looks at human life objectively, and maybe Erikson's final stage of accepting and valuing one's life as a whole and despite its setbacks and unpleasantnesses really shies away from what a life, a whole life, is really like.

To consider this issue, I think we should compare careers with ordinary appetitive satisfactions and also home in on what careers are actually like. Consider someone who has done good work, say, in philosophy and who is satisfied with and even proud of what they have achieved. May their creativity not give out or slacken at a given point later in their life, and will they not regret that loss or diminution? They may at that point console themselves with the thought of all they have previously accomplished, but this implies there is something they have to be consoled for, their lack of

[3] See, for example, Erikson's *Childhood and Society*, NY: Norton, 1950.

continuing creativity, and this more than suggests that the loss of creative power is felt as a regrettable and even a bad thing about their later years. Consider too how they will feel if somehow that creativity revives unexpectedly late in their lives. Won't they feel relieved at the new surge or burst of creativity, and doesn't that then likewise imply that their period of fallow creativity made them to some extent unhappy?

But this sword cuts two ways. If a permanent loss of creativity occurs, they will perhaps have much to regret about their life, but if it doesn't, that source of dissatisfaction and unhappiness will not exist, and so in present terms there will be nothing for them to regret about their careers. And even if they regret certain earlier setbacks, if they have been spared war, pestilence, hunger, and the premature deaths of family members and friends, why shouldn't we say that their life on the whole has been a good one?

Still, there is the fact that they need to keep up their creativity in order to have a happy life. Each time they create something that they and others think well of, they will eventually want more than that. Doesn't that show that all along, whatever they accomplish, they are not fully satisfied with what they have done, and doesn't that indicate a pervasive kind of dissatisfaction nestling very prominently in all their accomplishments?

4

Here it will be useful to bring in a parallel with appetitive pleasures and satisfaction. If someone wants to eat a good (or gourmet) meal and ends up doing so, they may well be satisfied after the meal with that whole experience. But that doesn't mean that at some later (not so distant) time, they won't want to eat well again. Will it follow that they are at the later time dissatisfied with what they earlier enjoyed? I think not. Appetite rises again and makes them seek a new pleasure and new appetitive satisfaction, but there doesn't, realistically, have to be any sense of dissatisfaction with what they enjoyed previously. Rather, there is a certain periodicity to (some) human desire, and if each new desire is satisfied, there doesn't have to be any feeling of dissatisfaction on the part of the person with the desires. And looking at them from the outside I think we can find no reason to hold that such thinking and such attitudes involve some sort of self-deception or some sort of absence of realistic perspective. Sure, at the later time, the person isn't satisfied just to have had what they enjoyed in the past, they now want something beyond what they had earlier. They want, for example, a new meal or a new kind of food. But none of this entails any feeling of dissatisfaction or unhappiness. So there need be nothing disappointing or dissatisfying about their appetitive life, and to that extent their life, their pretty ordinary life, can be viewed as satisfactory and more than merely satisfactory in this area.

This analysis can then be transferred or transposed to the career of a philosopher or scientist, etc. If they at a certain point cease to be active or creative in their field, they will have something to regret, even intensely regret. But if they continue creatively throughout their lives (like Kant, John Dewey, and many others), there need by nothing unsatisfactory or dissatisfying about that career. At a certain later point they may continue to want to be creative and will not, therefore, be entirely satisfied to rest on their laurels. But if they continue creatively, there will be no source of dissatisfaction in their careers, no feeling of inadequacy about them. There can be a kind of periodicity about creativity just as there is about certain appetites, but in both fortunate cases the overall picture will be a pleasant and happy one.

To be sure, everyone suffers setbacks. One may not be able to go to the restaurant one wants to eat at, and one's article or book may not meet with as much praise as one would hope for. But these are contingent facts. If they compromise career or appetitive satisfaction over a lifetime, it is only a contingent fact that they do, and there is thus nothing in the structure of career creativity or the resurgence of appetitive desires over time that entails anything less than satisfactory (or more) about these. Buddhists like Tolle think that the very structure of (having) a creative career is inherently less than satisfactory, but our previous arguments show, to the contrary, that this needn't be so. And those arguments point to the possibility that such lifetime projects or motives can often be more than merely satisfactory, that these can be part of and contribute to a good life overall. Life can contain an ongoing systole and diastole of desires and projects, but there is nothing inherent in the psychology of such developing lives that should make us doubt, what most of us and certainly the Chinese think, that ordinary life can be good.

5

India's most distinctive or well-known philosophy, Buddhism, is in need of major course corrections, and a world philosophy that seeks to integrate the best of different traditions of philosophical thought has reason to reject Buddhism's rejection of ordinary life and its arguments on that basis in favor of our seeking a nirvana of nothingness. There is no reason to believe what Buddhism tells us about the value of ordinary human life, but I have elsewhere and at great length argued that Western philosophy also stands in need of major course corrections. They are not the same corrections that Buddhism needs to make, but, once again, they come from the direction of Chinese thought and philosophy.

Chinese thought assumes, without any obvious argument, that ordinary life can be good, but Chinese philosophy also doesn't make the kind of rigid distinction between reason(ing)/cognition and emotion that is standard in the West (German romantics like Herder and Scheler are an exception). I have argued elsewhere that that distinction is illusory, that we have heart-minds, not minds; but I don't intend to repeat those arguments here.[4] The relevant point, rather, is that contemporary philosophy ought to consider the merits of the different main traditions of philosophy and accept or reject different aspects of them within an eventual to-be-hoped for world philosophy that takes them all into account.

Thus far I have been recommending that world philosophy ought to develop in a way that is more consonant with Chinese thought than with Indian or Western philosophy, but of course, historical Chinese thought is itself far from perfect, and most notably so, perhaps, in its failure to reckon with plausible notions of individuality and human rights and in its never having fully developed the analytic philosophical techniques that the West has learned to use. And now let me make a couple of further points about world philosophy.

As I have implicitly indicated, world philosophy isn't just a new form of what has been called comparative philosophy, which seeks to compare and contrast different philosophical traditions without offering any judgment or judgments about which are, and in what ways, more plausible in current-day philosophical terms. (This is the sort of thing Archie Bahm famously went in for.) This assumes that in this increasingly internationalized world philosophers from different traditions can learn to see what is valuable and also what is weak or criticizable in traditions outside their own, and it also assumes or proposes that attempts to integrate what is

[4] See my book *The Philosophy of Yin and Yang: A Contemporary Approach* published with side-by-side English language and Chinese language texts by the Commercial Press, Beijing, 2018.

best from different traditions into a philosophical whole, a world philosophy, make sense and are worth pursuing.

We already have a historical example of such an attempted world philosophy. In the twentieth century and as I have already mentioned, the Chinese thinker Feng Qi called for world philosophy in the sense I am speaking of, but another Chinese philosopher, Mou Zongsan, actually provided us an example of such a thing. In his "Nineteen Lectures on Chinese Philosophy" and in other works, this "New Confucian" philosopher brought elements from Chinese, Western, and Indian/Buddhist thought into connection within one overall system of philosophical thought. But his emphasis or direction was mainly historical: his emphasis in Western philosophy was mostly on Kant. A contemporaneous world philosophy needs, by contrast, to bring in the best of recent Western philosophical thought and show how it can be integrated with the best that can be derived from the Indian and Chinese (and other) traditions.[5]

Mou's world philosophy was in a certain degree *syncretistic*. It brings in ideas from different philosophical traditions without spending a lot of time criticizing some of the other ideas of those traditions. What I think we need, rather, is a more *synoptic* kind of world philosophy, one that takes a good hard look at assumptions from or within the different traditions and is willing to criticize them in forceful terms where it finds reason to do so. But also to employ and deploy other ideas from the main traditions (or elsewhere) where this is thought to contribute to an overall more plausible philosophical picture than any one or two traditions provide us with.

[5] I realize that I have mainly written of one kind of philosophy coming from India, Buddhism. But world philosophy will need to consider other kinds of Indian philosophy. To be sure and as a rule, Indian philosophy is skeptical of the value of ordinary life, and we have been arguing here against such skepticism. But world philosophy needs to consider the possibility of Indian (or, for that matter, Western) ways of questioning the value of ordinary life that could possibly differ from anything I have discussed in this essay. And more generally Indian philosophical thought needs to be examined carefully if one is really committed to doing world philosophy.

PART II

Traditional Views Reformulated

CHAPTER 4

Tagore's Philosophy of Man: Reconciling Opposing Forces

Shefali Moitra

Preamble

Rabindranath Tagore (1861–1941) says, '…the world in its essence is a reconciliation of pairs of opposing forces'.[1] In Sanskrit, the word for opposition is *dvandva*. The oppositions when reconciled are unified in a harmonious relation. Tagore uses the metaphor of the left hand and the right hand working in unison. He holds that no force can break away from harmony indefinitely it has to come back to its equilibrium. Creation could not be a chaos for then there would be no rhythm—creation has a rhythm, a cadence that is marvellously beautiful. This account may sound very poetic and romantic to anyone with a scientific orientation. Tagore was aware of such a possible reaction. He knew that if a scientist were told

[1] 'Sadhana' (1913), *English Writings of Tagore (EWRT)*, vol. 2, New Delhi: Sahitya Akademi, 1996, p. 316.

S. Moitra (✉)
Jadavpur University, Kolkata, India

S. S. Chakravarti et al. (ed.), *Traditional Indian Virtue Ethics for Today*, Palgrave Studies in Comparative East-West Philosophy,
https://doi.org/10.1007/978-3-031-47972-4_4

that two opposing forces like the finite and the infinite were united in one seamless whole then he would think this to be an insane thesis. Tagore says, 'I have nothing to say in my defence except that this paradox is much older than I am'.[2] He also refers to this as the '…sublime paradox that lies at the root of existence'.[3] Sublime in the sense, the paradox can only be appreciated when man's finite identity is sublimated by his infinite identity; when the deterministic laws of causality are surpassed by Man's surplus manifested as creative freedom. The co-presence of freedom and determinism has its roots in the above mentioned paradox. Science is not willing to accept the paradox of the infinite assuming finitude—for science, the finite and the infinite denote two separate worlds. According to Tagore, in the final stages of evolution the hostile dualism of the finite and the infinite is transformed to a relational dualism—the disjunction between the two no longer remain exclusive.[4] This is not only a paradox this is a mystery; he laments, '…there are men who lose that feeling of mystery…'[5]; as a result they fail to savour the delight of witnessing a unity between opposites.

In his 'The Religion of Man', Tagore categorically rejects the reputation of his being a philosopher.[6] There is no substantial ground on which such a rejection can be justified, his refusal merely betrays his modesty. Of course, much depends on how one defines philosophy, in its narrow sense philosophy stands for analysis. Tagore is a philosopher in a very broad sense of the term. His way of doing, philosophy does not employ the methodological tools commonly used by philosophical systems. He has taken the liberty to reinterpret scriptures. While making an implicit reference to classical scholarship he says, '…they lose their significance when exhibited in labelled cases—mummied specimens of human thought and aspiration…'.[7] Tagore always introduced himself as a poet and referred to his religion as 'the poet's religion' which does not adhere to any doctrine or to any injunction. Doctrines and injunctions compromise man's freedom and creativity—the two aspects of man's humanity.

[2] 'The World of Personality' (1917), *EWRT*, vol. 2, p. 368.

[3] 'Sadhana', p. 316.

[4] See Shefali Moitra, 'Science and the World of Personality', *Tagore Einstein and the Nature of Reality*, ed. Partha Ghosh, New York: Routledge, 2019, pp. 92–106.

[5] 'Sadhana', p. 317.

[6] 'The Religion of Man' (1931), *EWRT*, vol. 3, 1996, p. 138.

[7] Preface, 'Sadhana', p. 278.

A convenient entry point into Tagore's philosophy of man could be through his writings on the religion of man—clearly outlined in his Hibbert lectures on, 'The Religion of Man' (1931) as well as in his 'Sadhana' lectures (1913) and 'The World of Personality' (1917). His religion is fluid and devoid of firm conclusions.[8] Religion does not promise a fixed final destination. He frequently refers to himself as a traveller without a road map. His journey is an 'onward journey' and his god is none other than a fellow traveller, '*panthajaner sakha*', which could be translated as 'travel-companion'. Tagore observes that religious preachers are in the habit of talking with a finality as if they have already arrived at their destination of Truth and therefore can speak with unquestioned authority. He refrained from all forms of proselytizing, be it moral or religious.[9] He speaks from the perspective of a seeker who is proceeding on an eternal journey. However, in the context of reconciliation of opposing forces one may expect that there must be some culmination of a journey where the final reconciliation takes place, but in Tagore there is no such final end-point, there are only a series of reconciliations, opening up into new possibilities. In a 'Gitanjali' poem he writes, '...But I find that thy will knows no end in me ... where the old tracks are lost, new country is revealed with its wonders'.[10] Freedom and creativity the two markers of humanity resist any final culmination or closure.

In the scope of a single essay, it is not possible to map the umpteen oppositions and locations needing reconciliation in man's life-world, discussed by Tagore, therefore, one has to be selective. Keeping in mind the present context of deliberation on ethics, we shall focus on the following oppositions: detachment / attachment, negative freedom / positive freedom, scientific knowledge / imagination and finite / infinite. Segmenting his thoughts into neat compartments is not in keeping with Tagore's oeuvre since he is not a systematic philosopher—some overlap here and there in our discussion is therefore unavoidable.

[8] '...the poet's religion is fluid ... It never undertakes to lead anybody anywhere to any solid conclusion...' 'The Poet's Religion', 'Creative Unity' (1922), *EWRT*, vol. 2, p. 500.

[9] 'I do not believe in lecturing, or in compelling fellow-workers by coercion; for all true ideas must work themselves out through freedom. Only a moral tyrant can think that he has the dreadful power to make his thoughts prevail by means of subjection.' 'Letters to a Friend', *EWRT*, vol. 3, p. 245.

[10] 'Gitanjali', *EWRT*, vol. 1, New Delhi: Sahitya Akademi, poem 37, 1994, p. 54.

Stages of the Onward Journey

There is a genesis to the foregrounding of oppositions in man's onward journey; it all began with the first moment of creation. Tagore speaks of man's universe as a product of evolution. In his 'The Religion of Man', he speaks of light as the radiant energy of creation. He says, in the beginning 'the planets came out of their bath of fire ... then came a time when life was brought into the arena. ... Before the chapter ended Man appeared and turned the course of this evolution...'.[11] With the advent of man, a shift took place, 'from an indefinite march of physical aggrandizement to a freedom of a more subtle perfection'.[12] Man is in search of the meaning of the universe, the meaning of reality, and he seeks to develop his personality in tandem with truth and reality. Truth and reality are not static substantive endpoints of evolution. Some scholars find a similarity between Henry Bergson's emergent evolution giving expression to the elan vital and Tagore's vital moving force in evolution.[13] Similarly, some philosophers draw a comparison with Alfred North Whitehead's process philosophy and Tagore.[14] Needless to say, these comparisons have their limitations. For Tagore, in the early phases, evolution was the result of natural selection. With the appearance of man and his mind, evolution was transformed to, '...the purposeful selection of opportunities with the help of his [man's] reasoning mind'.[15] The first two stages of the evolution drama are marked by matter and life respectively. In the third stage, Man's consciousness of his own creative personality ushers in a new regime. Now Man directly attempts to fully capture the government of the world and make his own laws prevail.[16] In this stage of evolution, the regime of life recedes to the background and the regime of the Spirit of Man occupies the foreground. Since man embodies both the biological realm of life and the Spiritual realm of Mind, he has a dual identity of being both man the

[11] 'The Religion of Man', p. 87.

[12] Ibid.

[13] Sashi Bhusan Dasgupta, *Upanishader Patabhumikay Rabindra Manash* (in Bengali), Calcutta: Supreme Publishers, 1992, p. 186.

[14] Sachindranath Gangopadhyay, 'Sattadarshan', *Rabindradarshan*, Santiniketan: Visva-Bharati, 1968, pp. 17–18.

[15] 'The Religion of Man', p. 98.

[16] 'It is the consciousness in Man of his own creative personality which has ushered in this new regime in Life's kingdom. And from now onwards Man's attempts are directed fully to capture the government and make his own Code of Legislation prevail without a break.' Ibid., p. 99.

mortal and Man the eternal. Tagore refers to man, mind and personality in the realm of life by using initial lower-case letters; the same nomenclatures are referred to in the third realm, which is the spiritual, by using initial capital letters—Man, Mind, Personality and Spirit.

Man misses himself when he is isolated and unrelated; he finds himself in his wide human relationship to other individuals as well as to nature. Tagore disapproved of the tendency to view things in disassociation.[17] Just as there is a relationship in our body, there is an uninterrupted relatedness throughout the world. Relationships keep expanding and get more and more inclusive with the growth of personality. Interpersonal relationships keep widening as man's relation with the universe grows. In the early stages of evolution, progress took place in a linear direction; with the advent of man, the direction of progress changed to the ever-expanding relation of concentric circles with man at its centre reaching out to wider and wider horizons. Tagore writes, 'From individual body to community, from community to universe, from universe to Infinity,—this is the soul's normal progress'.[18] He refers to this unity as an 'energizing truth'.[19] For him the consciousness of this unity is spiritual and to be true to it is our religion.[20] In this ideal unity, Man realizes the eternal and the boundless in his love.[21] All living things are finite and infinite; both descriptions are simultaneously valid. Even though the forces come from opposite directions, they act in absolute harmony. He uses the metaphor of our two eyes working in unison.[22] How the opposite forces are reconciled in creation is incomprehensible—we tend to forget that this is the mystery of all mysteries.[23] Science is partly responsible for this forgetting. Science seeks to unite oppositions by formulating laws to explain unity in diversity. These laws are no doubt useful, but the problem is that we tend to stop at these laws and fail to probe deeper. By speaking of 'unity in diversity', unity is foregrounded and diversity is back grounded thus man proceeds on his onward

[17] 'For the world is not atoms and molecules or radio-activity or other forces ... You can never come to the reality of creation by contemplating it from the point of view of destruction.' 'The World of Personality', p. 366.

[18] 'The Religion of Man', p. 169.

[19] 'The unity becomes not a mere subjective idea, but an energizing truth.' Ibid., p. 88.

[20] 'Whatever name may be given to it, and whatever form it symbolizes, the consciousness of this unity is spiritual, and our effort to be true to it is our religion.' Ibid.

[21] Ibid.

[22] 'Sadhana', p. 316.

[23] Ibid.

journey in the unidirectional unifying path of science. By limiting the universe to the world of science the problem of reconciliation is dissolved rather than resolved. Tagore reminds us that law in itself is a limit—therefore the realm of the infinite cannot be comprehended through scientific laws.[24] He speaks of the two modes of man's relation with nature: one is the external relation where laws suffice to satiate one's curiosity, that is the domain of strict causation, the other is the internal relationship that presents an entirely different picture, here one experiences the limit and the beyond, the law as well as the liberty as being co-present.[25] Through this experience, a true reconciliation takes place between unity and diversity without minimizing either dimension. The experience, however does not come as a sudden flash, it comes through a tedious process of growth involving a series of trials and tribulations.

Negative Freedom Followed by Positive Freedom

Just as relatedness and unity are pivotal concepts in Tagore's scheme of things so is the concept of freedom. As a manifestation of the infinite, all living things must possess freedom in some form or the other. Multiple forms of freedom are mentioned in his scheme; each form has a significant role in the ongoing evolution of the world. Before the arrival of man freedom in the realm of living things was like the circumscribed freedom of the cage. In the initial stages, man was also confined to this cage-like existence till he realized his additional potential for agency. Man's unique agency or freedom progresses through two discernible stages. In the first stage, man asserts his agency by freeing himself from the oppression of the cage; he tries to transform hostile nature into a conducive habitat. Through his scientific endeavours man has constantly been gaining the capacity to unlock the mysteries of nature and to overcome its debilitating control. In this way, he has succeeded in freeing himself from the vagaries of nature and gained increasing power and control over his natural surroundings. This newly earned freedom is gained primarily through a better understanding of man's surroundings. Science and technology play a major role in freeing man from the oppressive clutches of nature. This, however, does not imply a detachment or alienation from nature. Nature has always been acknowledged as a healer and an energizing force by Tagore. Nature has

[24] Ibid., p. 317.
[25] Ibid.

another dimension as well where it constrains man's growth. Tagore speaks of various regressive forces from which man constantly strives to gain freedom. In his 'The Religion of Man', several natural obstacles to growth and flourishing are listed, such as physical injuries and disease, then there are factors that retard our intelligence such as stupidity, ignorance and insanity. There are also the uncontrolled exaggerations of passion that cause an imbalance in our personality.[26] All these factors cause disorientation of our personality and stand in the way of further flourishing. A deeper knowledge of the physical world as well as our mental world enables us to identify the impediments to growth. By controlling nature, man is able to gain freedom from these negative forces such as physical or mental injuries or injuries to personality.

Knowledge is the key to such emancipation. Through the pursuit of knowledge, man gains his first taste of freedom as a human being. Such freedom is acquired by the means of detachment from the sources of pain and disharmony. In this context freedom refers to something in the world from which emancipation is gained, therefore, this freedom could be characterized as 'freedom from…' which is also a form of negative freedom. Here the ellipses could refer to any of the obstacles that stand in the way of man's onward journey towards greater and greater unity with fellow men and with the universe at large. According to Tagore, scientific knowledge is one of the principal forms of knowledge that facilitate the growth and development of the first phase of freedom. Knowledge intrinsically involves a distancing between the knowing subject and the content of knowledge. As Tagore says, 'Objects of knowledge maintain an infinite distance from us who are the knowers'.[27] The epistemic virtue upheld by knowledge in general, and scientific knowledge in particular, is the virtue of objectivity. Objectivity could be understood as a distancing between the knowing subject and the known object; alternatively, 'objective' could mean that which is not subjective. Initially such a detached stance in our understanding of our surroundings is necessary in order to distance ourselves from the obstacles that constrain man's growth and development. Distancing is also necessary for the sake of self-preservation. Through detachment, man is able to establish a self-hood, which is distinct from the rest of creation. Negative freedom through detachment is a necessary condition for the onward journey towards unity. One cannot proceed by skip-

[26] 'The Religion of Man', p. 161.
[27] Ibid., p. 157.

ping the initial steps and passing on directly to the second mode of freedom. Tagore reminds us, 'we do not attain our goal by destroying our path'.[28] He observes, the verb *gamaya*, to move, to travel, is of great significance in the prayer *tamaso ma jyotirgamaya* (lead me from darkness to light); the journey is as important as the goal. However, it must be remembered, though 'freedom from…' gives man his first experience of freedom, it is not to be treated as an end in itself—detachment cannot be a goal. The goal of evolution is union, 'therefore the further world of freedom awaits us…'[29]—the world of positive freedom. The union in this instance is a unifying game played between the finite and the infinite it is unending and continues till the next detachment leads to '…a new ceremony of life'.[30]

Man's singularity is established by the means of this second freedom, namely, 'freedom to…'; that leads to creativity and new forms of union. If this singularity is lost, the creative joy of the individual is gone. Creative joy is the only thing that man can call his own; once it is missing the individual is bankrupt.[31] Man's freedom and creativity may proceed in varied directions. There is no prescribed pre-determined highway. In one of his poems Tagore writes, 'Where roads are made I lose my way. … I ask my heart if its blood carries the wisdom of the unseen way'.[32] 'Freedom to…' enables man to pave new roads, strike new relationships and to broaden the unity with his surroundings. Such rejuvenation would not be possible by treading a beaten path. The purpose of this second form of freedom, positive freedom, is 'to reveal the endless in unending surprises.'[33]

Here the perplexing question is how does the path of evolution shift gears from a journey of detachment and avoidance of injuries towards a path of union strewn with obstacles and associated pangs of growth? One cannot escape the pain and sorrow associated with positive freedom. The journey towards rejuvenation is tedious and troublesome. Man, gains strength to proceed through his dual identity, as he is both finite and infinite.

[28] Ibid., p. 168.
[29] Ibid., p. 157.
[30] Ibid., p. 123.
[31] 'Sadhana', p. 306.
[32] 'Fruit-Gathering', poem 6, *EWRT*, vol. 1, p. 158.
[33] 'The Religion of Man', p. 105.

The Finite and the Infinite

Man has a stand-alone independent identity as well as an identity of being a part of one cosmic whole, the infinite. The splitting of the infinite into the finite and the infinite is the primary purpose of creation. This has been clearly expressed in Tagore's poem, 'The world is yours at once and for ever. / And because you have no want, my king, you have no pleasure in your wealth. / It is as though it were naught. Therefore through slow time you give me what is yours, and / ceaselessly win your kingdom in me…'.[34]

The infinite will intentionally limits itself by making room for the finite will. The infinite needs the finite in order to experience the emotion of love. The infinite will 'creates' the finite will through love, the purpose of creation is to fully cherish the experience of love. The unitary lover can neither fully cherish the joy of unification (*milan*) nor the pangs of separation (*biraha*)—the lover needs a beloved. Therefore, it is very much in the interest of the infinite to give form to the finite so as to fully imbibe the emotion of love and thereby the fullness of Being. This is well expressed in a 'Gitanjali' poem, '…Thus it is that thou hast come down to me … where would be thy love if I were not?'[35] Without the finite, without 'the other', the infinite is incomplete. Both the infinite and the finite are mutually locked in a relation of love, in a relation of independence and dependence. In love, there is the warmth of proximity as well as the independence of self-expression.

With Man's ability to break away from the circumscribed freedom of the cage what comes into prominence is his Spirit. Spirit manifests the infinite dimension of the individual, which is the dimension of self-expression and creativity. Consciousness of the self begins with the sense of detachment and gradually widens towards unity with the infinite. Having accomplished the breakaway from the oppression of the finite the infinite, which is attuned to unity, becomes the primary consideration and separateness now becomes the secondary consideration of the onward journey of evolution.[36] Tagore makes a distinction between the surface level of our being and the deep level. At the surface level we have the ever-changing phases of the individual self.[37] In the deeper level of existence

[34] 'Fruit-Gathering', poem 77, p. 187.

[35] 'Gitanjali', poem 56, p. 62.

[36] 'The World of Personality', p. 385.

[37] 'The Religion of Man', p. 88.

dwells the Eternal Spirit of human unity.[38] The Spiritual and mental are co-present and both play a prominent role in an individual's personality-formation. Acquaintance with the Spiritual level provides a new perspective on the world. The Spiritual experience underscores the importance of emotions like love as well as the pivotal role of imagination. According to Tagore, 'Love is the perfection of consciousness'.[39] A relationship of love leads to greater and greater unity.[40] Reason is important but imagination broadens our horizon of understanding; imagination must not, however, be confused with fantasy. We gain a vision of the infinite through imagination, the infinite is not a creation of our mind.[41] Imagination signifies a form of mental freedom that transcends man's instinct of self-preservation; it works at the surplus.[42] Man has a special relationship with the infinite by virtue of his unique human characteristics. What differentiates man from other creatures is his faculty of imagination.[43] Imagination in its higher stage is special to man, Man the Eternal, and has been referred to as luminous imagination. It offers man a vision of wholeness; it also urges man to realize this vision. It inspires creations that reveal man's humanity as well as his freedom of activity, which is not meant for utilitarian purposes but for man's ultimate expression. Traditionally, reason not imagination is cited as the differentiating characteristic of humans. Tagore's notion of luminous imagination does not rule out the co-presence of reason. He says, 'We must realize not only the reasoning mind, but also the creative imagination…'.[44] Creative imagination brings about a qualitative change in our understanding of the world. In evolution we pass from the negative freedom of detachment to the positive freedom of creative imagination with which is associated the freedom of view. Thus man gains the sense of wholeness which has no role in the biological necessity of survival. We can now comprehend our relationship of unity with the infinite—we realize the vastness of the infinite along with our located connection with it. The accumulation of more and more objective knowledge does not lead to the

[38] Ibid.

[39] 'Sadhana', p. 321.

[40] Shefali Moitra, 'Tagore's Thoughts on Religion', *The Cambridge Companion to Rabindranath Tagore*, ed. Sukanta Chaudhuri, Cambridge: Cambridge University Press, 2020, p. 406.

[41] 'The Religion of Man', p. 144.

[42] Ibid., p. 104.

[43] Ibid.

[44] Ibid., p. 91.

same goal. Unity with the universe cannot be comprehended through a discursive practice. The qualitative distinction between the two modes of comprehending the world—the scientific mode and the spiritual mode—could be differentiated by the expressions, 'knowledge' and 'wisdom' respectively. Man has a vision of a Being who exceeds him in truth and with whom he has an intimate relation of kinship.[45] In this context attachment honours difference. Tagore says, 'the mistake that we make is in thinking that man's channel of greatness is only one…'.[46] The relationship between the finite individual and the infinite Being is one of love and mutual respect. This leads us to a new kind of emancipation, a new kind of freedom. He says, 'For love is freedom; it gives us that fullness of existence which saves us from paying with our soul for objects that are immensely cheap'.[47] The acquaintance with this freedom enables an individual to create, to relate and to unite. Since Spiritual freedom is integrally related to surplus, to imagination and to love it leads to the inner perfection of personality, which is an endless asset for humanity.[48] The notion of surplus has a central role in Tagore's conceptual scheme. Spirit has a surplus far in excess of man's biological needs. Surplus allows man the space and leisure to fulfil his dreams and to create.

Leisure, Relationality and the Infinite

Leisure has a special significance in Tagore's writings; it is related to a broad perspective and to a space through which an individual can contemplate on the meaning and value of existence. Tagore says, 'man has his two phases'.[49] In one phase, 'he mastered his resources and utilizes them for his own indomitable purpose … through the manipulation of Nature's law…'[50] The other phase of man's life pertains to wisdom where quantification has no role, where according to Tagore, '…the value of truth is realized by matured mind through patient devotion, self-control and concentration of faculties. It has its atmosphere of infinity in a width of leisure…'[51] Speed is related to the domain of the finite and slow time to the

[45] Ibid., p. 108.
[46] 'Nationalism', *EWRT*, vol. 2, p. 457.
[47] 'The Religion of Man', p. 160.
[48] Ibid., p. 167.
[49] 'The Philosophy of Leisure', *EWRT*, vol. 3, p. 615.
[50] Ibid., p. 616.
[51] Ibid., p. 617.

realm of the infinite. Man's awareness of Spirit and its surplus sensitizes him to this atmosphere of infinity produced through leisure. He is now able to free himself from the 'compelling claim of physical need'.[52] The journey towards the union with the infinite Being is facilitated by leisure. It carries with it an atmosphere of infinity by providing hospitality to the silent voices of creation. Quiet time is essential for individual maturity. Leisure is commonly contrasted with speed. Tagore believes, leisure and speed are two attitudes that may be jointly cultivated. We cannot and should not try to stop the increasing quickness of speed, which is a necessary corollary of our modern lifestyle, side by side we must also value slow time so as to give balance to the reckless rush of ambition and to give rhythm to life that misses its happiness in the absence of a proper balance between speed and solitude. Speed has usurped the major part of our life in the name of progress, which relates to our external existence, at the cost of neglecting our deeper life process, 'which requires depth of leisure for its sustenance'.[53] Tagore concludes his essay on 'The Philosophy of Leisure' by saying, 'compressed and crowded time has its use when dealing with material things but living truths must have for their full significance a perspective of wide leisure'.[54]

Man gains a new kind of freedom with his awareness of surplus which is different from the prior negative freedom which provides independence without content, he now has positive freedom. With the foregrounding of the Spirit, evolution now follows a new direction. Tagore says, 'we must have the possibility of the negative form of freedom, which is licence, before we can attain the positive freedom, which is love'.[55] For him, love is to realize ourselves in others; he says, 'this is the definition of love'.[56] Perfect freedom lies in a perfect harmony of relationship.[57] Only a perfect arrangement of interdependence engenders positive freedom. This state is not one of passive equilibrium. Action has not been neglected by Tagore. We must strive to attune activity closer and closer to eternal harmony. In order to be united with the infinite Being we have to become *viśvakarmā*, 'the world-worker'[58]—one who works for all, for the good of all, through

[52] 'The Religion of Man', p. 99.
[53] 'The Philosophy of Leisure', p. 618.
[54] Ibid., p. 619.
[55] 'Sadhana', p. 312.
[56] 'The Religion of Man', p. 102.
[57] Ibid., p. 157.
[58] Ibid., p. 110.

love and sympathy. The infinite Being needs man's love and cooperation. In this respect, man's relation to the infinite Being is a personal relationship. The world also has its impersonal aspect, which is the subject matter of science. The relation between the finite and the infinite is beyond the comprehension of science. In the absence of surplus and imagination, it would not be possible to widen our scope of understanding to the infinite.

With the coming of positive freedom, Man is called upon 'to give' and no longer incessantly appeal 'to get'.[59] He takes on the role of a sovereign creator who builds his world as well as governs it.[60] Man, however, does not build his world on a clean slate; as Tagore says, 'But man ... is born also to his home, his society and his country. These afford him the background, the perspective needed for the expression of his complete being'.[61] Each society provides its own context and perspective for expression. Every society is an organ of universal man (*viśvamānab*). The stability of a society is dependent on what it contributes to the growth and development of universal man. The stability of traditional Indian society was sustained by relationality. Tagore refers to the traditional Hindu custom of daily remembering our blessed-relation (*mangalsambandha*) with God, with the rishis, with our forefathers, with all human beings and all birds and animals. If this is remembered and followed it will be propitious for the individual and for the world at large.[62] We need to know things in their relationship to the universe. A unity exists through the harmonious mutuality of elements. There is a rhythm of cosmic motion that produces the creative emotion. The best opportunity for the blossoming of this emotion is in man's society,[63] unless the society degenerates. Man feels the mystery of unity in the life of social communion; he cannot gain unity with the Supreme Being in isolation. Tagore says, '...man's ideal of human perfection has been based upon a bond of unity running through individuals culminating in a supreme Being who represents the eternal in human personality'.[64] Through the cooperation of minds, through hospitality, and love's sacrifice creative ideals slowly develop over the centuries. Many years of hard labour have led to the development of human civiliza-

[59] Ibid., p. 99.

[60] Ibid., 100.

[61] 'The Philosophy of Leisure', p. 615.

[62] 'Atmashakti' (in Bengali), (translation mine) *Rabindra-Rachanabali*, vol. 3 (1916), Calcutta: Visva-Bharati, 1969, p. 538.

[63] 'The Poet's Religion', *EWRT*, vol. 2, p. 503.

[64] 'The Religion of Man', p. 146.

tion. No creature has to work so hard as man, making and reformulating laws, constantly thinking, searching and suffering so as to become that which he is yet not.[65]

With the growth of civilization, man learns to cherish the value of civility, which according to Tagore, 'is beauty of behaviour'.[66] Civility can be perfected only through patience, self-control and an ambiance of leisure. Genuine courtesy is like an artistic production in which there is a harmonious blending of voice, gesture, movement, word and action. Courtesy is an expression of expansiveness of conduct through which man is revealed without any further motive. Civilization is created with the objective of realizing our vision of the spiritually perfect.[67] To be spiritually perfect one need not shun one's finite physical identity and remain confined to the domain of the infinite. A split between man's finite and infinite identity is unwarranted. Tagore makes his point abundantly clear through his free translation of the ninth verse of the Ishopanishad, 'They enter the region of the dark who are solely occupied with the knowledge of the finite, and they into a still greater darkness who are solely occupied with the knowledge of the infinite'[68] The two identities serve two equally important complimentary purposes. For perfection man has to be vitally savage, which means he has to be natural, uncultivated (savage does not mean cruel or fierce) with nature; at the same time, with human society he has to be human which means he has to be mentally civilized.

The humanity of man is revealed through love and goodness. A distinction needs to be drawn between pleasure and goodness. Pleasure is for oneself, it is contingent; whereas, goodness is concerned with the happiness of all humanity, it is timeless. When we realize ourselves in 'love' we gain the greatest delight. The spirit of love is the spirit of civilization. To be happy we must establish harmonious relationships with all things with which we have dealings. In the absence of harmony, we are aliens in this world. Lack of harmony with one another leads to pain and suffering. Harmony can only be achieved through creatively modifying relationships; it cannot be achieved through compulsion. We must learn to keep step together for this we need to nurture 'man-love' for all creatures. According to Tagore from the time Man became truly conscious of his

[65] 'Sadhana', pp. 327–8.
[66] 'The Poet's Religion', p. 495.
[67] 'The Religion of Man', p. 137.
[68] 'The World of Personality', p. 368.

own self he also became conscious of a spirit of unity manifested through him in his society. Relationality, harmony and love do not, however, act as a scaffolding of a new model of well-being, nor do they function as regulative forces. The more evolved form of life being envisaged here has been compared to the life of a music-maker or poet. The resistance to expressions like 'scaffolding' or 'regulative forces' must not be interpreted as an invitation to epistemic anarchy. Tools like 'reason' or 'form' are essential for the onward journey; they, however, need to be remodelled according to the changed mode of passage. Beyond science the path is radically different, therefore the existing epistemic tools also need modification. The importance of 'reason' and 'form' cannot be denied. Tagore writes, 'The guidance of reason constantly varies its course, in its perpetual process of adjustment with unforeseen circumstances; its scope is ever being widened by contact with new data'.[69] Like reason form also shifts its course; Tagore says, 'For revealment of idea, form is absolutely necessary. But the idea which is infinite cannot be expressed in forms which are absolutely finite. Therefore forms must always move and change…'[70] Stagnation is a sign of finitude. Unifying relationships are constantly transcended to form new unities that is the insignia of the infinite. 'Therefore when the world takes its shape it always transcends its shape; it carelessly runs out of itself to say that its meaning is more than what it can contain'.[71] Creative imagination facilitates the passage beyond existing boundaries.

Moving Beyond the Norm of Utility

In contemporary times we are made to understand that our 'compelling claims of physical needs can be well looked after by market forces. Tagore laments that in former times intellectual and spiritual powers had their independence and dignity whereas today money-power has taken full charge of our existence. This implies that profit and production are now in full command—both morality and Spirituality are subsumed under market control. As a result, our social equilibrium is destroyed and moral callousness has gained ground.[72] Tagore says, '…they [profit and production] play havoc with our love of beauty, of truth, of justice and with our love

[69] 'Thoughts from Tagore', *EWRT*, vol. 3, p. 80.
[70] 'The World of Personality', *EWRT*, vol. 2, p. 370.
[71] Ibid.
[72] 'Construction versus Creation', *EWRT*, vol. 3, p. 405.

for our fellow-beings'.[73] At times utilitarian demands forge a kind of mechanical unity; as for example market-forces create a unity through the creation of a uniformity in demand. Tagore was vehemently opposed to the ideal of uniformity. For him human dignity and freedom have always been of utmost importance. He was against both consequentialism and essentialism as human ideals. By forwarding a kind of process philosophy he always endorsed an open-endedness in every sphere of life including ethics and religion. Unfortunately, we have allowed utility to occupy the leading position in our daily life. Through excessive greed, we degrade ourselves, we degrade others and we degrade our surroundings. If we get into this habit and constantly deride human sentiments in favour of material gains then we shall never be able to free ourselves from serfdom. When confined to negative freedom man concentrates on gaining more and more power leading to an arena of fierce competition, which Tagore does not approve of, he asks whether we were borne to make the world a 'marketable commodity'.[74] Tagore feels the only way to stem the rot is to realize, '…the ultimate truth in man is not in his intellect or in his material wealth; it is in his imagination of sympathy, in his illumination of heart, in his activities of self-sacrifice, in his capacity for extending love far and wide across all barriers of caste and colour…'.[75]

If the people of a society fail to follow a design that will transform them from being utility maximizers to forming an organic whole, then the interminable expansion of greed will continue. Self-assertion plays a major role in a utilitarian set up. When we concentrate on our immediate self-interest, we ignore our unity with the All. Same is the case with success. Tagore does not consider success to be a human ideal even though success has emerged as a value in modern times. He points out that in earlier times, even in the context of war success was not looked upon as the objective—it was honour that was at stake. He categorically rejects the proposition that, man merely has use-value and the man who is above usefulness is not recognized.[76] Man belongs to a greater reality; he aspires for the dignity of being.[77] Man constantly refuses to accept the permanent status of being objectified, which means he is searching for ways of expressing his person-

[73] Ibid., p. 406.

[74] 'Sadhana', pp. 321–2.

[75] 'Construction versus Creation', p. 409.

[76] Ibid., p. 406.

[77] 'The Religion of Man', p. 131.

ality. Tagore says, 'our course is not so much through ... the battle of the good and evil, as through the inner concentration of mind ... to reach that serenity of the infinite in our being which leads to the harmony in the all'.[78] One may find a close affinity between Tagore's goal and the goal of virtue ethics. Tagore, however, has never made an explicit reference to virtue. He says, '...we know when we have touched Truth by the music it gives, by the joy of greeting it sends forth to the truth in us ... not through the explanations of theologians, not through the erudite discussion of ethical doctrines'.[79]

This does not mean that Tagore did not engage with the problems of good and evil. An entire chapter has been devoted to 'The Problem of Evil' in his book 'Sadhana'. There he says, evil and imperfection are one and the same in an evolutionary process. The direction of human evolution is from evil to good. When man gains an extended vision of himself, he begins to get conscious of his moral nature. Moral and immoral belong to the same gradient; what is immoral is imperfectly moral.[80]

The important lesson that man can learn from life is that '...pain, disease and poverty of power are not absolute, but that it is only the want of adjustment of our individual self to our universal self which gives rise to them'.[81] It depends on man to turn pain into a good and that it is possible for him to further transform it into joy.[82] Good comes from our moral endeavour, and joy is related to our spiritual side. The enrichment of the spiritual side is related to the nurturing of surplus, creativity and unity. Creativity and unity cannot flourish in isolation from the whole that integrates the finite with the infinite. In his 'The World of Personality' essay, Tagore warns us against separating the finite, which is associated with the moral side from the infinite, which is associated with the spiritual side of our lives, and subsequently focusing exclusively on one or the other. According to him, the moral side needs to work in tandem with the spiritual side of our existence. He writes, 'the cultivation of the merely moral side of our nature leads us to the dark region of narrowness and hardness of heart, to the intolerant arrogance of goodness; and the cultivation of the merely spiritual side of nature leads us to a still darker region of revelry

[78] Ibid., p. 118.
[79] Ibid., p. 127.
[80] 'Sadhana', p. 301.
[81] Ibid., p. 304.
[82] Ibid., p. 305.

in intemperance of imagination'.[83] The same notion resonates in his 'The Religion of Man' where he speaks of two aspects of perfection in man: the perfection of being and the perfection of doing. It is possible though not desirable to separate these two aspects. Doing in isolation may be requisitioned for the purpose of achieving the normative goals of truth beauty and goodness. Such segregation marks a confinement to the realm of the finite. In this detached isolated finite domain, it is possible to do outer—not related to the inner being—good work leading to good results. These works maybe valued and praised beyond an individual's lifetime. These actions have a utility, though Tagore is not willing to attribute moral perfection to these deeds. In order to gain moral perfection an action must be rooted in man's being. It must manifest man's spiritual perfection, the perfection of unity and love. Neither a rule-guided perfection nor a utility-guided perfection is real perfection. At most, a cost-benefit-harmony leads to a type of mechanical perfection. Nevertheless, utilitarian considerations are necessary for the growth and sustenance of human society, but they must not be treated as ends in themselves. Tagore holds man's inner personality has immense value for the individual as well as for humanity even though it may not be acknowledged. The inner perfection of personality is nothing but spiritual freedom.[84] What is needed is the moral side of our nature, which represents unselfishness and control of desire, should never be separated from the spiritual side.[85]

Tagore's occasional pronouncements on ethics do not neatly fit into a rubric of any standard western ethical position like, consequentialism, deontology or care ethics. He does not engage with a systematic study of mainstream western ethical concerns, such as, rights, duties, motives and intensions, moral choice or a theory of justice. His views on each one of these moral issues could, however, be extrapolated from his varied writings relating to the human situation. The conventional categorization of moral issues is well suited to a compartmentalized approach to existential predicaments where a stand-alone moral choice is to be made. Tagore does not subscribe to a purely local perspective. Man is situated in the paradoxical context of the finite and the infinite simultaneously, ideally represented by the ethical and the spiritual, working in unison. In 'The Religion of Man' Tagore writes, 'Man in his detachment has realized himself in a

[83] 'The World of Personality', pp. 373–4.
[84] 'The Religion of Man', p. 167.
[85] 'The World of Personality', p. 373.

wider and deeper relationship with the universe. In his moral life, he has the sense of his obligation and his freedom at the same time, and this is goodness. In his spiritual life his sense of the union and the will which is free has its culmination in love'.[86] Man has to struggle to unite this dualism of the finite and the infinite in a harmonious way. The relation between the finite and the infinite is neither sequential nor aggregative, it is hyphenated leading to a co-constitutionality. The struggle leads to an unending journey of deeper and wider unification. At times Tagore seems to be inclined towards an existentialist becoming where the journey is unending because both the finite and the infinite are involved. Though the infinite participates in a self-limiting process, the infinite always moves beyond limits. Since the onward journey is a human effort to achieve deeper and wider unity and harmony through love the passage could be termed a journey involving virtue ethics, keeping in mind: at the final stage ethics merges with spirituality.

[86] 'The Religion of Man', p. 100.

CHAPTER 5

Virtue Ethics in Swami Vivekananda: A Novel Perspective on Vedanta

Abhishek Bandyopadhyay

Presentations at the Parliament of World Religions

A key turning point in East-West comparative philosophy was an event we might call the first opportunity for a true confluence of ideas. The 1893 World's Parliament of Religions held in Chicago was unique in the sense that it provided a global platform for open dialogue between different religions for the first time in modern history. The event was held for 17 days in September 1893. Though the general aim of the parliament was in the spirit of what we have come to know as interfaith dialogue, this spirit was not shared by all. For example, the Archbishop of Canterbury was quite clear that his disapproval of the Parliament rested on "the fact that the Christian religion is the one religion". He claimed: "I do not understand how that religion can be regarded as a member of a Parliament of

The author benefitted from the many discussions he had with Sitansu S. Chakravarti.

A. Bandyopadhyay (✉)
Purdue University, West Lafayette, IN, USA

S. S. Chakravarti et al. (ed.), *Traditional Indian Virtue Ethics for Today*, Palgrave Studies in Comparative East-West Philosophy,
https://doi.org/10.1007/978-3-031-47972-4_5

Religions without assuming the equality of the other intended members and the parity of their position and claims." Another example is that of John Henry Barrows, the chairman of the General Committee of the Parliament, who stated, "The Parliament has shown that Christianity is still the great quickener of humanity, that it is now educating those who do not accept its doctrines, that there is no teacher to be compared with Christ, and no saviour excepting Christ … The non-Christian world may give us valuable criticism and confirm spiritual truths and make excellent suggestion as to Christian improvement, but it has nothing to add to the Christian creed" (Cornish and Clement 2011).

Such views stand in stark contrast to the message Swami Vivekananda wished to communicate at the Parliament. It is a well-known fact the Swami's addresses and assertions resonated deeply with the attendees of the Parliament as well as a wider audience of American and later British society, continuing in many other parts of the world.

Swami Vivekananda presented a vision of spirituality that transcends ordinary boundaries without sacrificing individualistic approaches towards it. His vision of spirituality is drawn heavily from the Hindu tradition, which he proudly represented, yet it transcended the tradition itself, while accommodating other traditions. This particular vision is remarkable in its originality and its scope, which was absent from any other presentation at the Parliament.

The Unique Perspective of Swami Vivekananda's Non-Dualism

Among the many talks that Vivekananda delivered in the West, one was at the Graduate Philosophical Society of Harvard University. His spiritual vision was largely based on the Vedantic school of philosophy. In the Indian traditions, which are Dharmic in nature, philosophy and spirituality are intimately related. In fact, great spiritual teachers of India were also great philosophers. Thus, Vivekananda's vision of spirituality also represented his unique thoughts in the light of modern philosophy. Charles Carroll Everett, Dean of the Faculty of Divinity at Harvard University (1878–1900), notes in his introduction to 'The Vedanta Philosophy', a talk that the Swami delivered before the Graduate Philosophical Society, Harvard University, that "Hegel said that Spinozism is the necessary beginning of all philosophizing. This can be said even more emphatically of the Vedanta system. We occidentals busy ourselves with the manifold. We can, however, have no understanding of the manifold, if we have no sense of the One in which the manifold exists. The reality of the One is the truth which the East may well teach us; and we owe a debt of gratitude to Vivekananda that he has taught this lesson so effectively" (Vivekananda 1901). In a way, Swami Vivekananda was also truly the first philosopher who utilized both western and eastern ideas to synthesize a contemporary philosophical vision rooted in the Vedantic tradition.

In his very first address to the Parliament, Vivekananda proclaims, "I will quote to you, brethren, a few lines from a hymn which I remember to have repeated from my earliest boyhood, which is every day repeated by millions of human beings: 'As the different streams having their sources in different places all mingle their water in the sea, so, O Lord, the different paths which men take through different tendencies, various though they appear, crooked or straight, all lead to Thee.'" (Vivekananda 2014, Vol 1, 'Response to Welcome'). This verse is from an ancient Book of Prayers called *Śiva-Mahimnah Stotram*, and the Swami reiterates it in the context of the unity in plurality of faiths. This introduces the idea of viewing different religions as different streams travelling towards the same destination. What that 'destination' actually is and most importantly, how we are indeed related to it, forms the basis of the series of lectures that Vivekananda presented over the next few years in the west and also in India. The central pillar of Vivekananda's philosophy rests on Advaita or the non-dualistic view of existence, where we are not really 'separate' from one another, but it is the 'One' which appears as many. This conclusion, as propounded in several Upaniṣads as well as the Srimad Bhagavad Gītā, is the inevitable conclusion of critical analysis of our phenomenological experience. Most importantly, this analysis is neither tied to any particular deity or prophet or specific rituals, nor does it belie our broader spirit of accommodation; thus, it never demands the abandonment of an individual's tradition or religious identity. The Swami in his very last address at the Parliament envisions a remarkable trajectory for this journey of the different streams of religion in this way: "The Christian is not to become a Hindu or a Buddhist, nor a Hindu or a Buddhist to become a Christian. But each must assimilate the spirit of the others and yet preserve his individuality and grow according to his own law of growth." (Vivekananda 2014, Vol. 1, 'Address at the Final Session'). There is an enormous thrust on the individualistic nature of human growth in his message. It is important to note that there is a direction in this growth, and that direction is towards the realization of 'oneness of existence'. Swami Vivekananda in his talk titled 'The Atman' as part of his lectures on Jnana-Yoga, says "The Self—the Atman—is by Its own nature pure. It is the same, the one Existence of the universe that is reflecting Itself from the lowest worm to the highest and most perfect being. The whole of this universe is one Unity, one Existence, physically, mentally, morally and spiritually". Vivekananda goes further and states in the same talk: "No books, no scriptures, no science can ever imagine the glory of the Self that appears as man, the most glorious God that ever was, the only God that ever existed, exists, or ever will exist" (Vivekananda 2014, Vol. 2, /Jnana-Yoga, 'The Atman'). This is a remarkable statement in itself. Indeed, Vivekananda notices how hard it actually is for anyone to even think about it, let alone comprehend and live by it, as exemplified by his following statement, "Very few men ask for the truth, fewer still dare to learn the truth, and fewest of all dare to follow it in all its practical bearings" (Vivekananda 2014, Vol. 2). The most important aspect of emphasis here is the phenomenological, as distinct from a metaphysical underpinning. Thus, he presents our goal as the realization of 'oneness of existence', the conclusion of Advaita Vedanta, and challenges us to live our lives accordingly. He further states, "We know how very few in this world can come to the last, or even dare believe in it, and fewer still dare act according to it. Yet we know that therein lies the explanation of all ethics, of all morality and all spirituality in the universe" (Vivekananda 2014, Vol. 2, /Jnana-Yoga, 'The Atman'). With this assertion he connects all ethics, morality and spirituality to the non-dual.

Non-Dual Is the Mooring of Morality

Whether for a serious spiritual aspirant or ordinary beings going about their daily lives, ethics and morality are integral and critical components of every individual's existence. Clearly, ethical frameworks and moral dimensions vary significantly between different cultures and traditions. Moreover, our understanding of morality is often confronted with the changing circumstances that we find ourselves in. Swami Vivekananda's representation of the non-dual as the repository of all ethics and morality provides us with an ethical and moral framework capable of evolving with the changing circumstances yet never deviating from the fundamental truth of existence. This is again exemplified in his address titled the 'The Vedanta Philosophy' at the Graduate Philosophical Society of Harvard University in 1896, where he states, "Behind everything the same divinity is existing, and out of this comes the basis of morality" (Vivekananda 2014, Vol. 1/ Lectures and Discourses, 'The Vedanta Philosophy'). Thus, the basis of morality lies in the non-dual, not a personal god, yet all personal gods, denominations and traditions emanate from this. It is a concept that goes beyond all individuality, accommodating all of them nonetheless. In such a view, the world is not abandoned either. Because if it were so, morality and ethics would have no place at all, yet Vivekananda categorically connects morality and ethics with the non-dual. Herein lies the import of his message in its phenomenological emphasis as distinct from the metaphysical or ontological. The Swami's vision, centered around non-dual *Brahman* and *maya*, does not desist from action. The very fact that he connects ethics and morality with the non-dual clearly shows us the importance of action. Interestingly, a classical interpretation of Advaita Vedanta (as systematized by the great non-dual philosopher of India, Adi Shankaracharya) could lead to inaction, because there is no explicit impetus to work or moral action given that the world (*jagat*) is *mithya* (neither existent nor non-existent and, consequently, an illusion). Yet Vivekananda, just like his Guru Sri Ramakrishna, does not suggest inaction. He emphatically states that the non-dual *Brahman* (*Puruṣa* or *Śiva*) is no different from *Śakti*, the primal force manifesting as the world at large. According to him, they are one and the same (Nikhilananda 1984, p. 321). This remarkably places non-duality in a dynamic perspective relating to moral agency.

Thus, the phenomenological world is certainly not cancelled as in being considered '*mithya*' but is completely transformed into a lived reality of *Śakti* manifesting as the multitudinous diversity of phenomenal existence. There is boundless *Ananda*, bliss that is not dependent on causality, in such an experience of the transformative reality. This vision of Sri Ramakrishna is much closer to a *Tantradvaitic* position rather than a purely classical idea of Advaita as proposed by Shankaracharya (Nikhilananda 1984, p. 298) "... One can also turn this world into a mansion of mirth"; also, "... after the attainment of knowledge, the vision of God, this very world becomes ... a mansion of mirth" (Nikhilananda 1984, p. 310). He inspired young Narendranath Dutta (later Swami Vivekananda) to serve humanity as service to the divine and teach this message to the world at large after attaining the grand spiritual experience of *nirvikalpa samadhi*. In fact, he did chide Narendranath for aspiring to stay immersed in the rich non-dual realm of *nirvikalpa samadhi* following his guru's guidance where the world (*jagat*) stands cancelled according to the traditional interpretation. Going beyond this to serve humanity, according to Sri Ramakrishna, would be a much higher calling than any other spiritual pursuit for Narendranath.

We find in *The Gospel of Sri Ramakrishna* that he is urging all of us to live this transformative reality as he advises both the householders and his sannyasi (monk) disciples. In such a view of existence, 'action' is an inevitability, since 'experiencing' is after all an 'action'. We can all aspire towards this great goal which is rooted in the non-dual, yet it takes a monumental effort to begin this journey for most of us. The major obstacle to this journey is the pull of our inherent tendencies, otherwise known as character flaws. Swami Vivekananda describes character as follows: "If you take the character of any man, it really is but the aggregate of tendencies, the sum total of the bent of his mind" (Vivekananda 2014, Vol. 1, /Karma-Yoga, 'Karma in its effect on character'). These tendencies compel us in certain directions and it is a constant struggle to overcome some of these tendencies that take us away from the goal. Therefore, the key to overcoming the obstacle is transforming the mind. The struggle is also in the mind.

Character can be defined by the virtues and vices ingrained in us. Character states, therefore, are reflections of the virtues and vices that define it. Since character is basically the 'bent of the mind', character states are essentially states of the mind. Therefore, virtues and vices are also features of the states of the mind. In the realm of virtue ethics, morality is not simply a product of rationality alone. It encompasses a range of wider impact on human experience as a whole. In this regard, the concept of 'harmony within' (Chakravarti 2024) as derived from the concept of '*samatva*' enunciated by Sri Krishna to Arjuna in the Srimad Bhagavad Gītā, is a central virtue and thereby a character state/mental state. This '*samatva*' is after all '*yoga*' as propounded by Sri Krishna in the Srimad Bhagavad Gītā (Tapasyananda 1984, chap. 2, verse 48). Since 'action/karma' lapses only in the non-dual, the state of mind is the key to performing any 'action'. Having the appropriate state of mind is after all the greatest challenge that we all face. We find in the Srimad Bhagavad Gītā, that the key to performing the correct 'action' lies in establishing the mind in '*yoga*' (Tapasyananda 1984, chap. 2, verse 50). Thus, having the mind establish itself in the 'harmony within' prepares it to take the correct 'action'. The question then becomes, what exactly is the basis of this 'harmony within'? The answer lies in Swami Vivekananda's message based on Advaita Vedanta. The oneness of existence becomes the bedrock of 'harmony within', thereby providing the necessary framework for an ethical and moral landscape capable of continuously adapting to the changing circumstances without ever deviating or dissociating from the fundamental reality.

An Exalted Non-dualistic Vedanta Emerges

We would like to touch upon the novelty of Sri Ramakrishna's philosophical thinking with regard to Advaita Vedanta as he inspired Swami Vivekananda towards serving the world for the well-being of others. In the Dharmic Hindu traditions, the effect is metaphysically contained in the cause, a position known as *satkaryavada*. There are two forms *satkaryavada* has assumed in the philosophical history of Hinduism: *parinamavada* and *vivartavada*. The former means that the effect, contained as it is in the material cause, is a real manifestation of transformation. This is the position of Sankhya-Yoga, Vedanta in general, excluding the Advaita variety, and the Tantras. According to *vivartavada*, upheld by Advaita Vedanta, the effect, manifestation though it be, is a falsity and apparent transformation, as the material cause is the only reality in the ultimate analysis. Attaining *nirvikalpa samadhi* in the Advaita lineage, yogis would denounce the world as false. This has been the tradition in India.

Sri Ramakrishna questioned this traditional position having himself reached the non-dualistic (Advaita) state following the Advaita way, and yet he did not abandon non-duality which he would enrich in terms of the Tantric non-dualism, or Advaita. This is Sri Ramakrishna's unique contribution passed on to his disciple Vivekananda towards the well-being of the world.

After descending on to the planes of Calcutta, having constructed a temple in the non-dualist Vedantic tradition at Mayavati on the Himalayas, where no provision was made for placing images, including that of his guru Sri Ramakrishna, in absolute reverence to the spirit of Advaita Vedanta, Swami Vivekananda started the annual ritualistic worship of Mother Durga at the headquarters of Ramakrishna Mission. Vivekananda's attachment to the non-dualistic Vedanta did not find it hard to yield place to the non-dualism of the Tantras.

Thus, Non-dualistic (Advaita) Vedanta assumes a new dimension in the Swami's ethical involvement, with the theoretical as well as the practical inspiration that the disciple received from the guru. Vivekananda added an important strand of yoga to the group of existing yogas in the Indian system, viz., that of service to God in and through service to humans, considering them as manifestations of divinity in our very presence, while the suffering souls wait for the proper attention and treatment from us. This turns out to be inclusion of Care Ethics in the fold of virtue ethics on the Swami's part in the Hindu system, in the frame of reference of the philosophy of Vedanta before the birth of Care Ethics as a distinct system in the West at the end of the twentieth century.

References

Chakravarti, Sitansu Sekhar. (2024). 'Environmental Virtue Ethics – A Traditional Indian Perspective on Hursthouse's Quest,' *Traditional Indian Virtue Ethics for Today: An East-West Dialogue*, eds. Sitansu S. Chakravarti et al. Palgrave Macmillan. New York.

Cornish, A., Clement, J. (2011). Excerpt from Faith like a River: Themes from Unitarian Universalist History. Unitarian Universalist Association. https://www.uua.org/re/tapestry/adults/river/workshop14/178841.shtml.

Nikhilananda, S. (Translator). (1902). The Gospel of Sri Ramakrishna. (1984). Foreword by A. Huxley (Aldous). Ramakrishna-Vivekananda Center. New York.

Tapasyananda, S. (Swami). (1984). Srimad Bhagavad Gita – The Scripture of Mankind. Sri Ramakrishna Math. Mylapore, Madras.

Vivekananda, S. (2014). The Complete Works of Swami Vivekananda (8-vol. set). Advaita Ashrama. Kolkata.

Vivekananda, S. (1901). The Vedanta Philosophy: An Address Before the Graduate Philosophical Society of Harvard University, March 25, 1896. Introduction by C. C. Everett. Fourth Edition. Vedanta Society. https://www.vedanta.gr/wp-content/uploads/2012/03/SwVivek_The-Vedanta-Philosophy-Harvard_ENA5.pdf.

CHAPTER 6

Sri Aurobindo's Metaphysics of Morals vis-à-vis Western Models of Virtue Ethics

Indrani Sanyal

Introduction

To begin a discussion of Sri Aurobindo's metaphysics of morals is a challenging task. Sri Aurobindo did not offer any specific text dealing exclusively with his viewpoints on ethics, morality, or more specifically a metaphysics of morals. Sri Aurobindo's writings do, however, provide ample evidence of a view on the metaphysics of morals, particularly in *The Life Divine*, *The Synthesis of Yoga*, *Essays on the Gita*, and *Isha Upanishad*. Sri Aurobindo disagreed with the opinion that there is a want of ethical content in Indian philosophical discourse. He suggested instead that: "Hindu thought and literature might almost be accused of tyrannously pervading ethical obsession; everywhere the ethical note recurs. The idea of Dharma is next to the idea of the Infinite, its major chord; Dharma, next to Spirit, is its foundation of life... Buddhism with its high and noble ethics, Jainism with its austere ideal of self-conquest, and Hinduism with

I. Sanyal (✉)
Jadavpur University, Kolkata, India

S. S. Chakravarti et al. (ed.), *Traditional Indian Virtue Ethics for Today*, Palgrave Studies in Comparative East-West Philosophy,
https://doi.org/10.1007/978-3-031-47972-4_6

its magnificent examples of all sides of the Dharma are not inferior in ethical teachings and practice of any religion or system, but rather take the highest rank and have had the strongest effective force."[1] To comprehend Sri Aurobindo's position, we ought to recapitulate his primary sources of inspiration. Sri Aurobindo writes: "the highest morality of which humanity is capable finds its one perfect basis and justification in the teachings of the Upanishads and the *Gita*."[2]

In common practice, morality and ethics are interchangeably used quite frequently, but in Sri Aurobindo's writings, a subtle distinction between ethics and morality is noticeable. To commence broadly, morality may consist of a well-regulated individual and social conduct. The remark, viz., 'morality safeguards society,' seeks to explain morality as the protective shield for society against social turmoil. Thus understood, Sri Aurobindo echoes the dictum, '*dharmo dhārayati*,' i.e., he conveys the core of dharma-ethics by saying that morality protects society, and he further elucidates how far morality provides a drive towards more rational, considerate, sympathetic and self-disciplined behavior toward one's fellow-beings.[3] Sri Aurobindo carefully draws a line of demarcation between morality and ethics, for he assigns ethics a corrective role in disciplining the human mind. Ethics provides guidelines for moral conduct by formulating rules and laws from the egoistic principle of life and proceeds further to the altruistic principle of life. Ethics has been described as corrective. Ethics tries to discipline further to the principle of altruism.[4] Sri Aurobindo, in one place, writes, "Ethics deals only with the desire-soul and the active outward dynamical part of our being; its field is confined to character and action. It prohibits and inhibits certain actions, certain desires, impulses, and propensities—it inculcates certain qualities in the act, such as truthfulness, love, charity, compassion, and chastity. When it has got this done and assured a base of virtue, the possession of a purified will and blameless habit of action, its work is finished."[5] This statement is also about ethics from the ordinary point of view.

Ordinarily, ethics is regarded as epistemically indispensable to right action. But for the Yogi, the action is important not for its own sake but

[1] CWSA, Vol. 20, p. 148.
[2] CWSA, Essays in Philosophy and Yoga, vol. 13, p. 9.
[3] CWSA, vol. 25, p. 632.
[4] CWSA., vol. 25, pp. 627–628.
[5] Ibid., vol. 24, p. 644.

rather as a means of the growth of the soul. In its refined sense—from the spiritual point of view, ethics is the path for developing our actions and, still more, essentially for creating the character of our being the diviner self. Ethics prepares for "our growing into the nature of the Godhead."[6] He writes: "Ethics must eventually perceive that the law of good which it seeks is the law of God... and depends on the being and nature of the Master of the law." Sri Aurobindo points out that "ethics in its essence is not a calculation of good and evil in the action or a labored effort to be blameless," for those are only crude appearances, it is instead an attempt to grow into the divine nature.[7]

The ethical aim of Yoga, from Sri Aurobindo's perspective, is different from that of the external idea of virtue. Since the Yogi's actions are means for the growth of the soul, and Indian spiritual writings lay stress not so much on the quality of the action to be done but the quality of the soul from which the action flows, upon its truth, fearlessness, purity, love, compassion, benevolence, absence of the will to hurt, and upon right actions. Some philosophers with a typically Hobbesian attitude may believe that humans are innately selfish and that human nature is intrinsically evil; hence, it may be maintained that despite man's sinful nature, a trait that is antithetical to nature needs to be taught. This belief about human nature does not find support in the writings of Sri Aurobindo, inspired by the ideas of the Yogin from ancient times and his commitment to the ideology of *Srimadbhagavadgītā*. According to the *Gita*, it has been upheld that human nature contains passionate rajasic elements and its down-tending tamasic quality; but that is not the whole picture about human nature. There is a purer sattvic element, and the encouragement of this, the highest part of it is the concern of ethics. This enables the heightening of the divine nature, *daivi prakṛti*, which is present in human nature, and the ability to get rid of the demoniac elements, *asūri prakṛti*.

Sri Aurobindo identifies a sharp contrast between the Hebraic righteousness of a God-fearing man and a God-loving man; however, the concept of the Hebraic righteousness of a God-fearing man is a loaded concept, and without entering detail, it would be better to keep in hold any such comparative account. In the Indian view, what is very important is its requirement for growing in the divine nature; in this view, this is the consummation of the ethical being. This can be done best by realizing

[6] CWSA, vol. 24, pp. 564–565.

[7] CWSA, vol. 20, p. 35.

God as the higher S elf, the guiding or uplifting Will or the Master whom we love or serve. This much may be added if fear is understood from the commonsense perspective; in the growing of the Self, fear has no role to offer.[8] Sri Aurobindo emphasized in the Indian tradition that the love of God and aspiration for the freedom and eternal purity of his being must be the motive.[9] This begins an answer to the question, from where do moral impulses, instincts, and activities originate?

Sources of Morality

For Sri Aurobindo, ethics is a stage in evolution. That which is common to all phases of evolution is the urge of *sachchidānanda*,[10]—the One, Ultimate, and the Absolute in Sri Aurobindo's metaphysics, toward self-expression. Sri Aurobindo provides the explanation of how this urge toward self-expression was to be characterized differently stage-wise. This urge is first non-ethical, then infra-ethical in animals, and even in intelligent animals anti-ethical, for it permits us to approve harm done to others. Just as all below man's level is infra-ethical, there is above man, which is supra-ethical and does not need ethics. This is unequivocally what Sri Aurobindo did maintain. He writes: "The ethical impulse and attitude so crucial to humanity is a means by which it struggles out of the lower harmony and universality based upon Inconscience and broken up by Life into individual discords towards a higher harmony, and universality based upon conscient oneness with all existences."

From the above discussion, it is clear that Sri Aurobindo's presentation of a three-tier existential level of: *suprarational*, *rational*, and *infrarational*, does admit the ethical to be the feature of the rational level. Some questions may arise regarding the justification for Sri Aurobindo's exclusion of the suprarational and infrarational levels from being ethical. However, before discussing how far Sri Aurobindo could have responded to these objections, it would be better to draw attention to some texts from which Sri Aurobindo quoted lines at the very beginning of his chapter entitled, "The Origin and Remedy of Falsehood, Error, Wrong and

[8] CWSA, vol. 24, pp. 564–565. According to some interpretations, the concept of 'Hebraic fear of God' signifies awe or reverence. These details have not been worked out in the present article.

[9] *The Synthesis of Yoga*, CWSA, vol. 24 for details.

[10] *sachchidānanda*, composed by *sat-cit-ānanda*, broadly speaking is the Absolute Conscious Energy, behind all creation. For details *The Life Divine*, Sri Aurobindo.

Evil."[11] In this source, we may attend to the following two relevant quotations:

> One whose intelligence has attained to Unity casts away from him both sin and virtue. (*Gita*, II.50)[12]

> He who was found the bliss of the Eternal is affected no more by the thought, 'Why have I not done the good? Why have I done evil?' One who knows the Self extricates himself from both these things. (*Taittiriya Upanishad*, II.9)

Sri Aurobindo's Metaphysics of Morals: Some Central Issues

In this section, I consider it imperative to touch upon some focal points from Sri Aurobindo's metaphysics of morals to elucidate further why being ethical has been projected as a feature only at the mental level—the level of human existence. He sought to answer the mystery of our own individual existence, cosmic existence, and problems of evil by positing ignorance, which in his view has been considered as a "power of manifoldly self-absorbed and self-limiting concentration" of the Absolute *sachchidānanda*. In his metaphysics, one of the capacities of the Conscious being is to become ignorant of the Self by the power of self-absorption. Thus, it gets itself engaged in working on individual existence, cosmic existence, and problems of evil, among others. The first emergence from the Inconscient is Matter, but in Matter, he explained that falsehood and evil could not exist. To an extent, falsehood and evil, in his model, share the same beginning process since these two expressions are used simultaneously. This is because falsehood and evil are created by a divided and ignorant surface consciousness and its reactions. The indwelling secret consciousness, which is none other than the bona fide Ultimate Absolute, is one, undifferentiated, mute; it is inertly inherent and intrinsic in the Energy that constitutes the object. Fire warms a man or burns him, a medicinal herb cures a person, or a poison kills another. But the value of good or evil is brought into action by the user; The world of pure Matter

[11] 'The Origin and Remedy of Falsehood, Error, Wrong, and Evil,' CWSA, vol. 21, *The Life Divine*, p. 618

[12] Ibid.

is neutral and irresponsible; the values insisted on by human beings do not exist in material Nature: as the superior Nature transcends the duality of good and evil, so this inferior Nature falls below it. 'The duality of good and evil is not native to the material principle, it is absent from the world of matter.'[13]

The duality begins with conscious life and emerges fully with the development of the mind in life; the vital mind, the mind of desire and sensation, is the creator of the sense of evil and the fact of evil. Sri Aurobindo comments that in animal life, evil is present, in the form of suffering and the sense of suffering, the evil of violence, cruelty, strife, and deception, but the sense of moral evil is absent[14] may sound odd to some. But Sri Aurobindo had explained his position sufficiently. In animal life, what he intended to account for is that there is no duality of sin or virtue; in his view, all action is neutral or permissible to preserve life and its maintenance and the satisfaction of life instincts or what Sri Aurobindo calls, "the vitals," i.e., the vital aspects of being that all of us are endowed with. Good and evil are inherent in the form of pain and pleasure, vital satisfaction, and vital frustration. The distinguishing mark of evil is at the animal level. Still, mental ideas, and the moral reaction of the mind to corresponding ideas of value, are human creations.[15]

Are Moral Values Subjective?

One may well be inclined to ask: did Sri Aurobindo assume that moral values are creations of the mind, or that moral values are unreal? This, however, is not Sri Aurobindo's view on the matter. Sri Aurobindo did not agree that ethics is a mental construct. In his opinion, this sort of statement that the moral responses of the mind to some values are mental constructions only is based on hastily drawn inferences. Furthermore, he did not prescribe one true way to accept the activities of Nature, but rather did so in the following, three broad ways:

[13] CWSA, vol. 21, 'The Origin and Remedy of Falsehood, Error, Wrong, and Evil,' *The Life Divine*, pp. 631–632.

[14] In recent literature on ethics, the issue of animal ethics has often been discussed and debated. In these discussions, however, the question of how the possibility of animal ethics is to be addressed, whether from the perspective of animals or humans, is still indecisive.

[15] CWSA, Vol., The Origin and Remedy of Falsehood and Evil, p. 632.

1. neutral indifference
2. equal acceptance, or
3. intellectually, as a divine or a natural law, in which everything is impartially admissible.

This kind of approach was never considered sufficient for capturing the truth in its totality. In this context, his remark: "That is indeed one side of the truth"[16] is worthy of notice. Sri Aurobindo's endeavor consisted of spanning the characteristics of truth from different levels. From the infrarational level—from the level of Matter and Life—such infrarational truth, as spoken of by Sri Aurobindo, is, what he would say, impartial and neutral. He did not find any reason for denying that whatever happens at this infrarational level are facts of Nature. He also believed these happenings at the infrarational level are serviceable for carrying on three modes of Nature, creation, preservation, and destruction. In his view, the truths disclosed at the infrarational level are never to be belittled, for the infrarational truth through the modalities of creation, preservation, and destruction of life is, what he described as "the three necessary and inseparable movements of the universal Energy." Thus understood, "these movements are necessary and connectedly indispensable."[17]

According to Sri Aurobindo, there is a suprarational truth that forms in spiritual experience. In it, one can observe the play of universal possibility and accept all impartiality as the true and natural features and consequences of a world of inconscience and ignorance. This is the level where mysteries and puzzles of Falsehood and Evil may be remedied. Of course, the belief in a level of suprarational truth is controversial and many strong arguments may come forth to refute the possibility of any such claim. However, what is of considerable importance in the present discussion is to keep in view that Sri Aurobindo does not fail to ascertain the importance and dire necessity of the medium level of consciousness, which makes us sensitive to the values of good and evil.[18] This intermediate step is indispensable in the evolutionary process. We ask, from where does this evoking or rousing of moral values come into being, in the intermediate step of the evolutionary process? If so, there is a further conceptual question.

[16] Ibid., p. 630.
[17] CWSA, vol. 21, p. 630.
[18] CWSA, *The Life Divine*, vol. 21, p. 633.

Morality and the Ongoing Evolutionary Process

How do human beings conceptualize moral values? What gives a concept power and a place for the senses of good and evil? Sri Aurobindo points out that it may seem that the vital mind makes the distinction. He entrusts the vital mind with the initial role for distinguishing between good and evil. The valuation that comes from the vital mind is sensational as an individual's egotistical life; it goes by all that is beneficial, and useful to the life-ego as good, and whatever is malefic, destructive, and unpleasant to the life-ego is evil. The second type of valuation assumes different contours, thus being utilitarian and social; all that promotes sustenance, development, etc., of associated life and its unity is considered good. This is so in cases overriding selfish interests; hence, whatever is contrary to the betterment of a society is considered evil.

With the arising of a reflective or thoughtful mind, the "thinking-mind" tries to find some law or principle, rational or cosmic, or something like the law of karma, or to develop an ethical system founded on reason, emotion, or aesthetics. In many instances, religion has come to the fore as the law-giver. Religion teaches the role of God in determining what is good or evil. Again, though some seek a more profound hidden truth, something within us has the intuition of that truth. Thus, by this approach, total weightage has been laid upon the inward spiritual psyche. In traditional literature, this is known as inner conscience. But much more than the mind or life, the soul-personality is of a higher order. Questions may be raised about the nature of this spiritual or psychic witness and what is the value of a sense of good and evil to it, though. The following are some possible answers:

1. Some may suppose that the embodied being becomes aware of this world of ignorance, suffering, and evil, and then a sense of evil and good inclines one to turn away from the relative nature of this world of good and suffering towards the absolute. This is the standpoint of the Māyāvādin Advaitins.
2. According to the Buddhists, a sense of good and evil may prepare one for the dissolution of the ignorant ego-complex and transition into an escape from personality and suffering.
3. According to Sri Aurobindo, the awareness of an embodied being about good and evil is a spiritual necessity of evolution itself; it is a step towards the growth out of Ignorance into the truth of divine unity.

In this connection, it needs to be reiterated that Sri Aurobindo upholds the reality of one Brahman, which necessarily constitutes all-knowledge.

Here, we must touch upon some observations of Sri Aurobindo. It has already been discussed pace Sri Aurobindo, that duality begins with life and the mind. But a psychic being is more concerned with the distinction between good and evil in a larger sense than mere moral difference. Our soul, as has been conceived by Sri Aurobindo, is always inclined toward the Truth, Good, and Beauty. The soul's progression is a growth out of the darkness into light, out of falsehood into Truth, and out of suffering into its supreme and universal *ānanda*. This is his final contention. The soul's perception of good and evil may not coincide with the mind's artificial standards. The superior spiritual light is beyond all good and evil. According to Sri Aurobindo, the sum and substance of metaphysics that the evolutionary Nature, the terrestrial cosmic Force, seems then at first to have no preference for either of these opposites, that of good and evil; it uses both alike for its purpose. The exact Nature, the same Force, has burdened man with the sense of good and evil and insists on its importance; Sri Aurobindo discovers an evolutionary purpose in this working of Nature: he emphatically asserts that it must be necessary, "it must be there so that man may leave certain things behind him, move towards others, until out of good and evil, he can emerge into some Good that is eternal and infinite." However, not all of these details fall within the scope of the present discussion.

The Evolutionary Process

Sri Aurobindo, unequivocally, asserts his belief in the evolutionary intention of Nature to fulfill itself. But Evolutionary Nature must require some 'power, means, impulsion' and some 'principle and process of selection and harmonization' to execute the intended goal. We ask, how is this evolutionary intention in Nature to fulfill itself? Sri Aurobindo points out that a mind perennially pursues the principle of selection and rejection; this principle presented itself differently either in a garb of religious sanction, social and moral rules of life, or as an ethical ideal. These means adopted by one's mind are empirical and lack any comprehension of the root. Sri Aurobindo was never willing to allocate primacy to the mind, and had strong grounds for his stand. He alleged the mind is unfit for tracing the cause and origin of 'the malady of the problem it attempts to cure.' Mind deals with the problem of good and evil with the 'symptoms' and 'perfunctorily,' thus implying minds dealing with objects are with their superficial appearances but not in-depth and from a casual perspective. Mind does not know about the significance of the opposites like good and evil concerning the intention of Nature and why mind and life support them and sustain their being. Sri Aurobindo affirms relative characteristics of human good and evil; the proclaimed standards are also to a certain extent uncertain and lead to relative evaluation. It has been often found that religions differ regarding what is permitted and forbidden; the standard or criterion prescribed by ethics varies specifically from one culture to another, from period to period, and from country to country. Similarly, we find social norms are also subjected to diversification. What is considered useful for a society, what is considered good by social opinion, or what is considered beneficial for society are not absolutely settled forever. Hence Sri Aurobindo includes all these factors along with moral and ethical to the domain of relatives. The amalgamation of all these factors constitutes the complex subject matter of morality. Mind plays the role of a controller over our vital and physical desires and instincts. Mind also regulates our dealing with other members of society and our individual and personal checks with ourselves. However, the control exercised by the human mind on humans can never claim to be perfect. Sri Aurobindo would say that this managerial check done by the mind is an expedient one, never a solution: "man remains always what he is and has ever been, a mixture of good and evil, sin and virtue, a mental ego with an imperfect command over his mental, vital and physical nature."[19]

However, Sri Aurobindo expresses a high opinion about the human endeavor to sustain the good, casting out evils and remolding themselves in the ideal model. This he characterizes as a 'more profound ethical motive' for it comes closer to the real issue. In Sri Aurobindo's view, this human endeavor to purge all evils from our consciousness and action relies on the belief that human life is a becoming and there is something which we must evolve and be. There are undoubtedly human limitations, so the ideal opted by the human mind has limits. "But the ideals selected by the human mind are selective and relative."[20] This ascription of limitation and restriction to shape our ideal nature is not favorable for the growth of human consciousness. The statement, viz., "The true call upon us is the

[19] 'The Origin and Remedy of Falsehood and Evil,' CWSA, vol. 21, p. 651.
[20] Ibid., p. 651.

call of the Infinite, and the Supreme"[21] is what expresses the viewpoint of Sri Aurobindo. Self-abnegation and self-affirmation are both the ways of Nature, or so to say, movements of Nature to discover the Absolute. The conflict between yes and no that we find in Nature is not the final, but through that, we need to discover the Infinite.

Sri Aurobindo maintains that true ethic is Dharma, the right fulfillment and working of the higher nature. Right action should be the product of right motive. He maintains further that a right done for its own sake is truly ethical and ennobles the growing spirit. Right action merely done for material reward or fear may be eminently practical and useful for the moment. Still, it is not in the slightest degree ethical but is instead a lowering of the soul of man, or at least the principle is a concession to his baser animal and unspiritual nature. Sri Aurobindo distinguishes between a natural man and a dharmic man or a genuinely ethical man: in his opinion, in an honest man, before *dharma* has arisen, *kāma*, attraction, and *artha*, wealth or material goods or, non-material possession like *vidya* (knowledge) are motives for his actions. In an average natural man, thus desire and pleasure of enjoyment accompanied by the fear of loss and frustration govern the man.

Sri Aurobindo maintained that God is beyond good and evil; man moving Godward must become of one nature with God. He must transcend good and evil. From Sri Aurobindo's analysis of the phrase, 'God is beyond good and evil' the following implications may be drawn:

1. God is not below good and evil.
2. God is not existing and is limited by good and evil.
3. God is not above good and evil.
4. God is, in an absolute sense, exceeds and transcends the ideas of good and evil.

Perhaps the most significant part of the totality is either supramoral, inframoral, or simply amoral. Good and evil come in with the development of mental consciousness; they exist in their rudimentary elements in the animal and the primitive human mind, and they develop with human development. Good and evil arise during the process of evolution. If this is so, on the same logic, it can be claimed that they will disappear in the

[21] Ibid., p. 651.

process of evolution. They will remain if they are essential to their highest point of culmination.

Sri Aurobindo's other writings also provide evidence for the exploration of three models:

1. The humanitarian-secular model
2. The religious-ethical model
3. The spiritual model

Sri Aurobindo admits that some more comprehensive ideals are provided by the secular mind of man based on some ethical standards. The distinctions are sharply drawn between emotions sanctioned by ethical sense and those prompted by selfish and egoistic instincts and emotions. The ideals of altruism, philanthropy, compassion, benevolence, humanitarianism, and labor for the well-being of all men and creatures are such ideals. Sri Aurobindo was convinced that these ideals would appeal to the secular mind of man. Broadly speaking, the humanitarian-secular model is indeed one of the routes that could enable getting out of the fold of narcissism and self-obsession; positively, this model as promoting and encouraging the growth of the soul in the ideal of self-sacrifice for the well-being of others is indicative of a man's inner evolution. Sri Aurobindo's views on humanitarianism were the product of a consistent thought. He commented on the failure of this 'too secular and mental view' and considered the deeper religious-spiritual aspect of being. The gap in this model, however, consisted in its failure to cover the whole of a human being within its span. The law of universal goodwill, or universal compassion and love to one's neighbors, had its religious-ethical basis in Vedanta, Buddhism, and Christianity. Sri Aurobindo rejected xenophobia and called for a humanitarian approach in society. The religious-ethical and secular ethical systems differ very much in their perspective regarding the law of works; in the religious systems, this law of works is a means for seeking the Divine or passage to Nirvana. In the secular system, the greatest good is an end. It promotes happier life in the world, a better society, and more unified life for people.

Sri Aurobindo could not deny the need for liberating human beings from the ego-sense through the secular and the humanitarian model. In his view, this secular model accepted most of the valuable ideas from the tradition of religious-ethical ideals; but, Sri Aurobindo found in these models the very lack of the spiritual flame of Divine love. The egoistic trends often remain attached to the secular model of philanthropy or humanitarianism. Of course, in such instances, it has to be conceded that truly speaking, often egoistic models may survive under the camouflage of humanitarian models. Undoubtedly, via these secular models, however, a possible way of diminishing the egoistic trends does persist. Sri Aurobindo also does not without any reservation support the religious-ethical ideal. In his view, the spiritual consciousness belongs to a higher plane where dualities of the mind cease to exist.[22]

Sri Aurobindo maintains that through the principle and law of our religious being, through the principle and law of our aesthetic being, the universal principle or a law that is suitable to all beings and which is steadily applicable with regard to all human activities may be discernible. These principles may as well be citable as resting on truth on which sages have always agreed. However, intellectual thinkers, especially, those who are more empirically inclined, would raise objections questioning the ground that "It is the truth that all activities of being is a seeking for God, a seeking for some highest self and deepest Reality secret within, behind and above ourselves and things, a seeking for the hidden Divinity; the truth which we glimpse through religion lies concealed behind all life; it is the great secret of life, that which it is in labour to discover and to make real to its self-knowledge."[23] "The seeking for God is also subjectively seeking our highest self. It is the seeking for a Reality that the appearances of life conceal because they only partially express it or because they express it from behind veils and figures, by oppositions and contraries, often by what seem to be perversions and opposites of the Real."[24] Sri Aurobindo mentions that this truth is expressed in Religion and Art. "There lies the immense value of Religion, the immense value of Art and Poetry to the human spirit, it lies in their immediate power for inner truth, for self-enlargement, for liberation."[25]

In other spheres of life, particularly in practical life, men are not ready to acknowledge this sort of universal truth. Sri Aurobindo was aware that it might take a long time to admit it, even partially in theory; he could also guess that there may exist a sporadic preparedness to follow it in practice. In all practical life, as maintained by him, human beings, in general, are all

[22] *The Synthesis of Yoga*, vol. 1, CWSA, vol. 23.
[23] CWSA, vol. 25, 'The Suprarational Good', p. 146.
[24] CWSA, vol.25, The Human Cycle, 'The Suprarational Good', p. 146.
[25] CWSA, vol. 25, The Human Cycle, pp. 147–148.

content to be the slaves of an outward Necessity and admit as the law of their thought, will, and action the yoke of immediate and temporary utilities.

He was not, however, blinded by negative trends. Sri Aurobindo quite optimistically remarked, "Yet even there, we must arrive eventually at the highest truth. We shall find out in the end that our daily life and social existence are not things apart, are not another field of existence with another law than the inner and ideal."[26] He had the understanding that harsh and agonizing problems of practical life and their resolution and meaning can be understood only when men learn to see in them a means towards the discovery for the individual and collective of their highest, therefore their truest and fullest self, their largest most imperative principle and power of existence. He writes, "All life is only a lavish and manifold opportunity given us to discover, realize, express the Divine."[27]

The truth of practical life and all practical aspects of it, become apparent in our ethical being. The rational man has tried to examine ethical life as a matter of reason. Hence, they have resorted to some principle or law of reason for determining nature, its law, and practical action. Sri Aurobindo straightforwardly pointed out the failure of reason to tackle ethical life and action problems. "He has never succeeded, and he never can succeed: his appearance of success are mere pretenses of the intellect building elegant and empty constructions with words and ideas, mere conventions of logic and vamped-up syntheses, in sum pretentious failures which break down at the first strenuous touch of reality."[28] Sri Aurobindo could decipher the gap remaining between the practical life and ethical life and rational principle or law of reason and the failure of it in grasping and discovering the nature and law of ethical life.

He criticized utilitarianism as being one such pretension of intellect and logic. Utilitarianism had its beginning in the nineteenth century, and Sri Aurobindo characterizes that century as "the great century of science and reason and utility," but he is happy that utilitarianism has been "now deservedly discredited." He considers utilitarianism as consisting of "shallow pretentious errors."[29] Utilitarian ethicists tried to substitute a practical,

[26] Ibid., p. 148.

[27] Ibid., p. 148. In this connection, this needs to be kept in view that Sri Aurobindo's concept of the 'Divine' is not to be interpreted in a narrower religious sense.

[28] Ibid., p. 148.

[29] CWSA, vol. 1, The Harmony of Virtue.

outward, and occasional test for the inner, subjective, and "absolute motive of ethics."[30] He called it the "impracticable jugglery of moral mathematics," which the utilitarian theorists tried to establish. The logical and so-called rational mind may find it entirely satisfactory. According to Sri Aurobindo, it is foreign to the whole instinct and intuition of the ethical being. He does not find any justification in the attempt to explain ethical being in terms of reason. Reason cannot provide or formulate principles or laws for ethical beings. The hedonistic account of virtue in terms of pleasure or satisfaction of the mind is not acceptable. Neither sociological theory advocates ethics as a system of conduct generated by social sense and impulses. He maintains that "ethical being escapes from all these formulas."[31] This is a point of contention. He is committed to the view that ethical being "is a law to itself and finds its principle in its own eternal nature which is not in its essential character a growth of evolving mind, even though it may seem to be that in its earthly history, but a light from the ideal, a reflection in man of the Divine."[32]

Sri Aurobindo, however, does not deny the worth of these contributions of reason and logic. He believes each of these errors has some truth behind their false constructions. He does not discard the concept of utility. For he finds in utility a fundamental principle of existence. He further believes that the basic principle of existence is aimed at the direction of the end. Hence, he argues that the highest good is also the highest utility. He does not advocate the utilitarian principle urging the balance of the highest good of the highest number. But the utilitarian ethicists' emphasis on going beyond oneself to others seemed more or less appropriate to Sri Aurobindo. Sri Aurobindo emphasizes that the good of others when taken most widely is the good of all. This is the ideal aim of our external ethical practice. But this does not help to regulate ethical practice. He also points out that from this, we do not get any clue about the inner principle of ethical being or action. But ethical beings do not get any insight into how to reach that goal and what is the real good of all. He finally proposes substituting the concept of utility with the idea of good. He fears "otherwise we fall into the hands of that dangerous pretender expediency, whose whole method is alien to the ethical."[33] He is also apprehensive of variation

[30] CWSA, vol. 25, The Human Cycle, p. 149.
[31] Vol. 25, p. 149.
[32] Ibid., p. 149.
[33] Ibid., CWSA, vol. 25.

of the standard of utility, the judgment of utility, its spirit, form, and application with the individual nature, the habit of mind, and the outlook on the world. His prescription for the ethical man is to stick to his principle of good, his instinct of good, his vision of good, his intuition of good, and to govern himself by his conduct. It would be erroneous to suggest that Sri Aurobindo was framing a set of practical rules for one to follow. Instead he is very much committed to the notion of *svabhāva* and *svadharma* as preached in the Gita. "The saying of the Gita is always true; better is the law of one's nature though ill-performed; dangerous is an alien statute however speciously superior it may seem to our reason."[34] He insists that the law of nature of ethical being in the pursuit of good cannot be utility.

Conclusion: The Virtue Ethics Connection

In this essay, an attempt has been made to collect and collate innovative ideas on morality, ethics, and metaphysics of morals from Sri Aurobindo's writings. In presenting his views in the way that has been done in this essay, naturally, a question may arise about how to assess his standpoint on ethics in the light of the prevalent form of characterizations of ethical theory. Primarily it should be kept in mind that Sri Aurobindo is subscribing to what has been called in this paper as the metaphysics of morals which is a prototype of Dharma ethics. In this essay, an endeavor has been made to show that there is a close connection between ethics and metaphysics in Sri Aurobindo's writings, though that connection may not always remain explicit. Sri Aurobindo provided a reasoned statement accounting for the cessation of the need for ethics at one stage of human existence. In ethics, especially western ethics, varied sorts of deliberations related to morals and their different kinds of ethical systematization are available. It has already been clarified that Sri Aurobindo would not support any version of egotistical hedonism for a person to cater to his self-interest and promote only his choices to satisfy his pleasure. Sri Aurobindo had no ground for laying claim to the Hobbesian belief that men are innately selfish. The model of ethics supported by him rules out this possibility. Of course, this needs to be borne in mind that utilitarianism encompasses various versions. This has already been discussed what were Sri Aurobindo's grounds to find some merits in the utilitarian perspectives. The urge of the utilitarians to go beyond one's narrow self-interest

[34] CWSA, vol. 25, p. 149.

did appeal to Sri Aurobindo. We have also discussed his viewpoint in detail regarding the failure of utilitarianism as a final answer. In Sri Aurobindo's writing, like Dharma ethical tradition in general, we find enormous importance has been attributed to the growth and development of character, which is also recognized as a significant aspect of the Western virtue ethics, whether in the Aristotelian model or its various recent models. Hence psychology of the individual mind in the context of character development is very significant. Sri Aurobindo's reference to the concept of desire-soul, as has already been discussed, accommodates desire, and emotions as well in projecting a moral agent in a concrete shape. It cannot be overlooked that versions of virtue ethics in the west are not confined to one particular model, so when we compare Dharma ethics in general and Sri Aurobindo's ethics as a prototype of that model, this is indeed a challenging task. This approach to ethics as developed by Sri Aurobindo if understood comparatively with any western model of ethics, is closer to what is known as virtue ethics, though its details may be worked out on some other occasion. Deontology and consequentialism as ethical theories are more concerned with right actions since these are more preoccupied with promulgating rules for the right actions. On the contrary virtue ethics concentrates on the concept of character. As a pioneer of virtue ethics, Aristotle emphasized the development of moral character. Sri Aurobindo's commitment to the view that an ethical being is "a law to itself."[35] He finds its principle in eternal nature makes it rather difficult to accept either a deontologist or a consequentialist ethical viewpoint. Sri Aurobindo preferably characterizes ethics as seeking the law of good, and so far, he sounds quite closer to Aristotle. But Sri Aurobindo's explanation of the nature of seeking the law of good which in his view, essentially is the seeking Law of God, wedges a demarcation between Sri Aurobindo's approach and Aristotle's approach to virtue ethics. In Sri Aurobindo's model, like Dharma ethical model, virtue ethics remains a preparatory tool for "our growing into the nature of the Godhead."[36] However I may add that Sri Aurobindo's comment is never to be read in a popular, narrow religious sense, which has been explained and argued through the elaboration of his metaphysics of morals.

[35] CWSA, vol. 25, p. 149.
[36] Ibid.

References

Sri Aurobindo, 'The Harmony of Virtue,' *Early Cultural Writings*, *CWSA*, Vol. 1, 2003a, Sri Aurobindo Ashram Pondicherry.

———, 'The Stone Goddess', *Collected Poems*, *CWSA*, Vol. 2, 2009, Sri Aurobindo Ashram, Pondicherry.

———, *Essays Divine and Human*, *CWSA*, Vol. 12, 1997a, Sri Aurobindo Ashram, Pondicherry.

———, *Essays in Philosophy and Yoga*, *CWSA*, Vol. 13, 1998, Sri Aurobindo Ashram, Pondicherry.

———, *Isha Upanishad*, *CWSA*, Vol. 17, 2003b, Sri Aurobindo Ashram, Pondicherry.

———, *Renaissance in India*, *CWSA*, Vol. 20, 1997b, Sri Aurobindo Ashram, Pondicherry.

———, *The Life Divine*, *CWSA*, Vols. 21 and 22, 2005, Sri Aurobindo Ashram, Pondicherry.

———, *The Synthesis of Yoga*, *CWSA*, Vols. 23 & 24, 1999, Sri Aurobindo Ashram, Pondicherry.

———, *The Human Cycle: The Ideal of Human Unity War and Self-Determination*, *CWSA*, Vol. 25, 1997c, Sri Aurobindo Ashram, Pondicherry.

PART III

Virtue Ethics for Current Application

CHAPTER 7

Ethical Message of the Mahabharata in the Wake of the Global Financial Crisis

Sitansu S. Chakravarti

The Epic and Today's Ethical Theories

The recent happenings in the financial world in the USA, whose repercussions have been felt all over, have turned our attention to Business Ethics again, this time with the deeper question of its relation to ethics as such.

Paper originally appeared:
Sitansu S. Chakravarti, Ethical Message of the Mahabharata in the Wake of the Global Financial Crisis. *Journal of Human Values*, 15:2 (2009), pp. 97–105. DOI: https://doi.org/10.1177/097168581001500202. Sage Publications. Copyright Holder: Management Centre for Human Values, Indian Institute of Management, Calcutta.

This chapter is a follow-up of the ideas in my book *Ethics in the Mahabharata: A Philosophical Inquiry for Today*, Munshiram, New Delhi, 2006. An earlier version was presented at an international conference held at Jamia Millia University, New Delhi, in 2009, organized by the Centre for the Study of Comparative Religions and Civilizations. I appreciate my son Ananda Roop's help towards its editing.

S. S. Chakravarti (✉)
New College, University of Toronto, Toronto, ON, Canada

S. S. Chakravarti et al. (ed.), *Traditional Indian Virtue Ethics for Today*, Palgrave Studies in Comparative East-West Philosophy,
https://doi.org/10.1007/978-3-031-47972-4_7

Excess greed harms in every sphere of life. When it is propagated as the only sure road to happiness, almost the whole society gives in and such an economic catastrophe follows. Here no special features pertaining to the world of business may be seen as coming under scrutiny, in as much as taking to task a few individuals at the top for breaking the rule of law fails to mend the situation. This is for two reasons. One, if the society does not find anything wrong with greed in so far as it is contained within the limits of law, and extols it as the value in life, greed tends to cross its limits prompted by its very nature. The Enron situation, in spite of the publicity of the legal wrongs involved in it and the punishments as a result of judicial handling of the case, is followed by the recent series of events culminating in the state of the late 2008, which led to catastrophic suffering to humanity across the globe in no time. Two, the economic structure of today's world furthers the greed of the few at the top so long as it is supported and fed by the greed of the masses that the people at the helm of affairs attempt to generate. Although breaking the law in the wake of fostering greed is a crime, flourishing by generating greed around is not discouraged in the liberal society and is not necessarily looked upon as criminal involvement. For us, the total greed in society is at play in the events under consideration which resulted in the economic chaos of 2008. Consequently, greed as such demands the attention of our ethical scrutiny.

In what follows I propose to uncover what the ancient epic the Mahabharata has to say in the situation under consideration, keeping in view the three main theories of ethics of today and see the relevance of the views expressed in the epic in the context. We intend to focus on the secular sense of spirituality in this connection adhered to in the epic compatible with atheism subscribed to in some schools of Hinduism.

The vast corpus of the Mahabharata incorporates a substantial amount of discussion on morality. The moral issues, it is interesting to note, are not decided on the basis of imperatives promulgated in the scriptures, with a resulting follow-up of punishment assigned by a legal standard as resting on such imperatives. Morality, in the ultimate analysis, is rather discussed here in the spiritual setting that holds an invitation to life's transformation into a state of harmony within and without, *sāmya* or *samatva*, in other words,[1] that spills over into doing good to all, while leading the individual to a state of existential freedom away from the sway of the senses. Such a setting offers both the concepts of morality and spirituality

[1] Bhagavadgita, 1977, 2/48; 5/19.

a welcome secular backdrop in that morality is not a result of authoritative dictates, while spirituality does not ground itself in an ever-demanding transcendental source to which the individual might find hard to relate in abiding friendship ushering in growth and the quality of life. The laws of morality indeed are laws of love leading one to the unfolding of one's real nature in harmony with oneself, the society, and the ecology we all are situated in. The goals of morality as well as spirituality coalesce in the epic at the level of harmony considered as the highest end of life, where the moral *ought* ceases into the *is* of the balance of truth and joy.[2] It is this state of harmony that is described in some detail in the second chapter of the Gita as the mark of a person who has attained the height of spiritual goal, without any ostensive reference to God.

The above, we may say, gives us a glimpse of a secular system of morality as well as spirituality in the Mahabharata, in so far as both morality and spirituality are accepted as philosophical concepts instead of theological. The realm of morality, as we indicated above, ends with the dawn of the highest spiritual value where one keeps on doing good to all, including the sub-humans, not from a sense of duty but as a matter of course. The scripture leaves a lot of room for rational discussion, although in the ultimate analysis both areas are found grounded on mindsets (*virtues*, to use the common parlance of modern Western Ethics) we choose to adopt aided by deliberations, with recourse to extra rational means. Attempts at imbibing in the needed virtues are spiritual, which in their turn ground the individual on her moral stand with increasing success on the journey to the goal of life. The different kinds of yoga and meditation are spiritual ways to facilitate the individual, and the society at large, to be established on the desired virtues.

With these preliminaries, we may go to the three main contending theories in today's Western Ethics, known as Deontology or Duty Ethics, Consequentialism, and Virtue Ethics, and see the Mahabharata's ethical position in their light. First we have to have some idea regarding what these theories mean.

According to the Deontological position duty is law-bound and is supposed to be unsparing in the mood of the legal system. In the Kantian system of Duty Ethics it is the rationality of the human being that dominates the moral situation without any room for sentimentality or concern for the consequences of an act. The motive of the act is the only concern

[2] Ibid., 6/20, 21, 27, 28, 32.

for Kant, and *duty for the sake of duty* is his slogan. The Consequentialist, in his turn, puts all his emphasis on the consequences generated by an act while extolling the altruistic virtue. Rationality in the ethical situation reduces to him to the calculation of the greatest benefit for all. According to the Virtue Ethicist, however, morality is not primarily an area of rationality, in so far as what counts here is virtue, not pertaining only to doing good to others, but to overall shining forth of the human existence, in balance and conformity with the animate as well as inanimate environment. It is at this point that the Mahabharata joins hands with the Virtue Ethicist, proposing harmony within and without, which prepares the individual, as well as the society, to do good to all.

In the academic world of the West it is generally believed that the Indian system subscribes to Duty Ethics, especially with reference to the Gita which is considered as containing the quintessence of the epic. The reason is that here we see Sri Krishna repeatedly urging on his devotee Arjuna, the chief General of the Pandava forces, who gives in to feelings of affection for the near and dear ones on the opposite side at the onset of the fight, to start fighting as a matter of duty, when the latter approaches him for counsel. The language of the imperatives used, however, indicates a friend's urgings as a counsellor to the one who has lost the balance of mind in order to restore him back to his own self, and should not be confused with commandments. Also, the fighting is insisted upon to restore justice, which is consequential consideration when all the other avenues for negotiation have failed. To my mind, it is primarily Consequentialism, as nested in Virtue Ethics, that reflects the stand of the epic on ethics, although there are strains of the other theory, viz., Deontology, to be found in the Mahabharata. The imperative of speaking literal truth certainly holds ground up to a point. It, however, yields finally to the ethics of being entrenched in the virtue of sympathy and care for others in conformity with the *truth of life* where actions are good or otherwise in consideration of the results that follow. The Mahabharata gives an example of a mendicant, Kaushika, who discloses the whereabouts of a fugitive to the approaching robbers when asked, for he has taken the vow of speaking the truth. The book takes this as an example of wrong behaviour on the part of the mendicant. While speaking the truth, he goes against the truth of life, viz., harmony and benevolence, which has a sway over the literal truth, i.e., the factual truth. Here consequential consideration is indeed important.

Duty Ethics certainly does not hold ultimate ground in the Mahabharata. After the long discourse with Arjuna through the seventeen chapters of the Gita, Sri Krishna requests the former to deliberate minutely over all he has said and act according to his own decision.[3] He does not dictate or command him to take to a certain course of action.

The distinctive feature of the Virtue Ethics in the Mahabharata is that the virtue harmony[4] seems to have an edge over the virtues benevolence and care, commonly taken as the support for human behaviour in today's Virtue Ethics, in that harmony implies these two other virtues in so far as real harmony is incompatible with neglect of others' needs. However, benevolence and care as virtues may not suffice for harmony, even with the support of empathy, to take Slote's suggestion,[5] for wrong understanding regarding what is good, as well as lack of needed expertise, may lead to disharmony through acts performed with a spirit of genuine benevolence and care, even when supported by the right empathy needed in the situation. The Virtue Ethicist tends to put less emphasis on the consequences of acts, and shy away from the *duty* aspect of ethics. The concept harmony, in contrast, does not make sense in isolation from the state of things

[3] Ibid., 18/63.

[4] The expression 'harmony' has two senses: (1) The first refers to a harmonious state that obtains on its own out there or is brought about on the basis of actions undertaken. The harmony one finds present in nature is of the former kind. Human intervention towards mass exploitation of nature eats into it and ecological imbalance results. Those who believe in Gandhian socialism think that the societal harmony it aims at is to be brought about by human involvement the right way. (2) The other sense pertains to an attitude, to wit, a disposition (courage is a mental disposition), typically a character state, which again one can work on towards its furtherance, as one can on courage. The Gandhian socialism is dependent on building this harmonious state within, on the basis of which one would be motivated towards proper actions leading to the goal of building a harmonious society. Harmony within is a disposition that inspires to build harmony around, resulting in doing good to others as well as contributing to ecological harmony. Here harmony is not just balance or equilibrium; like harmony in music, it is creative in its aesthetic mode present in the ethical dimension, and is pleasing overall—certainly not binding or depriving, either to oneself or to the other. (This position is very near to Tagore's.) Thus, harmony is not simply self-control that Aristotle talks about as a measure against self-indulgence or intemperance, but adds a meaning to the onward flow of life. Harmony in this second sense is a virtue. The virtue harmony is a character state, as indicated above, that equips, and prompts, the possessor of the virtue to furtherance of harmony within and without, a process accompanied by a sustaining, unconditional joy manifest even in the midst of failures and many challenges on the way, an intrinsic value which the person intends to share with others.

[5] Michael Slote, 2007.

holding a balance. It has the harmonious consequence ingrained in it that the agent takes upon herself to contribute. The virtue harmony is a disposition to attain inner and outer harmony, to be, in other words, in tune with the inner harmony of the universe. It is incomplete without the right state of mind having a glimpse of the harmony all around under the surface of conflict and discord to which the agent contributes. This I call a spiritual state. Benevolence and care coupled with empathy do not have to be associated with this spiritual dimension. That is why these virtues by themselves may land the agent into planning actions destined to have untoward consequences for the recipients, in spite of her good intensions. There is here nothing to protect her from a wrong notion of the good. Benevolent overtures mounted on nourishment of societal greed taken as the good in life to further would be a case in point. Harmony seems to have an advantage in comparison. The description of the harmonious state in the Gita does not leave any room for wrong actions based on greed or other egotist leanings, which it is possible to promote in a psychological theory in the name of science.[6] The Mahabharata not only talks about the importance of virtue in ethics in company with the other Virtue Ethicists; it also includes the aspect of duty in its discussion on morality, as we will see in the following chapter, to cover the shortcomings of the other Virtue Ethicists, towards contributing to a harmonious existence for all, ensuring peace, satisfaction, and well-being and not just happiness.

The Act and the Attitude

There is talk about propriety of acts according to the demands of situations. However, the acts are not considered proper if not carried out in the right spirit. The Mahabharata speaks about two kinds of ethical constraints or considerations: the *act dharmas* (or, the act constraints) and the *attitude dharmas* (or, the attitude constraints). The acts, in so far as they fit situational needs, are proper in view of the consequences expected to follow from them, determining their fit. From this angle, their value is consequential in respect to achieving the end for which they are performed. However, if the aim of an act is saving some unknown person from an impending danger where there is no personal benefit involved for the

[6] My discussion in *Ethics in the Mahabharata: A Philosophical Inquiry for Today* (Munshiram, New Delhi, 2006, pp. 112–120) on the scientific claim of Freud to denounce the age-old human values may have relevance in this connection.

agent, one must be committed, to an extent, to the altruistic goal of mitigating others' sufferings in order to be motivated for the action. Subscribing to the altruistic virtue is a necessary condition for performance of an altruistic act. The more the virtue takes root in the agent, the more she is committed to performing relevant acts. Also, laudable as the actions are, they are not strictly ethical if not done in the proper spirit. Thus, all actions may turn defective when associated with a motive of 'showing off' in order, for instance, to earn people's attention and respect. The ritual of sharing one's wealth with others may, under certain circumstances, become a meaningless practice, if not a harmful one of nepotism. All the actions of *dharma* must be guided by the principle of it that constitutes the other sense of the word, if they are to pass the test of morality.[7] Four virtues have been mentioned in the epic as the principles of *dharma*. They are truth, forgiveness, sympathy to others, and control on greed. Each of the four principles is a necessary and sufficient condition for the rest. Truth, for instance, manifests itself in forgiveness, and forgiveness itself is truth. Similar conditions can be shown to hold for the other three. Unlike the acts, however, the four virtues are without defects,[8] in so far as they are attitudes and not actions. These may be termed *attitude dharmas.*

Thus, an act is important in its own right, fitting the situational need which is consequential. Actions, however, may be performed rudely, with audacity, or with an ulterior, self-seeking motive in mind. From an ethical perspective, these associated attitudes would constitute the defects of the actions concerned. The attitudes of forgiveness, sympathy, and non-violence, however, may not be contaminated with any of the defective attitudes mentioned above. As attitudes, they have a serenity constitutive of them that eludes the defects. We have to keep in mind that it is not forgiveness as an act performed, say, in the court of law that we are talking about here. An act, of course, may be associated with the blemishes mentioned. We are concerned here with the mental *attitude* of forgiveness, which is closely connected with *ahimsa* or non-violence. Forgiveness as an act, performed with a declaration 'You are pardoned,' may take effect even when mixed with a show of pride or a gesture of rudeness. Forgiveness as an attitude, however, shuns such association. There may be gradations of achievement of forgiveness as an attitude through practice—a dimension absent in the case of the act. One may make a gift of one's property,

[7] Mahabharatam, 2060, 13/111/18–19.

[8] Ibid., 5/35/37; 3/2/76–77.

unfortunately with an unhappy show of rudeness, though it does not make much sense to say that the person concerned is in the process of making a gift, in exactly the same sense as a person may be said to be trying to inculcate the virtue of forgiveness.[9] Making a gift is an act that may be performed irrespective of its moral quality or tone. There is little room for improvement in the act itself. It is either performed or not. The moral quality of the act, however, can be improved upon. It is based upon the principles involved, as reflected in the associated attitudes.

Thus, performance of an appropriate action itself, in keeping with the nature of things, is demanded by the morality of the situation, even though this is not enough. Making a gift is a moral act that is to be based on the four principles of morality. An act and the attitude involved in performing it have to be basically differentiated in order to understand the logic of the moral situation. Attitudes manifest themselves in actions. In them lies the moral tone of an action, as we have already seen. The appropriateness, or otherwise, of an action, however, constitutes the other dimension of morality. It is an answer to the question: 'Is this action proper? If not, which one is?' For the moral tone, the question that would be in order is of the type: 'Is the action (which is appropriate for the occasion) performed in the moral way?' The appropriateness of an action is determined by the prosperity it generates for all creatures through sympathy and justice.[10] 'Wrong intention is the defect of dharma, hoarding of wealth, enjoyment for its own sake is the defect of desire; they [i.e., dharma, wealth and desire], however, lead to prosperity when shorn of the faults.'[11] Here moral tone is evidently suggested as generating prosperity out of actions, which, though proper for the occasions, do not lead to their utilitarian goal on their own. The moral tone is empty without the actions, and the actions are imperfect without it. It is in actions that the moral tone finds its expression; one on the way to perfecting the moral tone in life definitely suffers from the fault of non-performance[12] if the relevant actions are skipped by any chance. Virtues motivate the performance of an act,

[9] True, the procedure of making a gift may be complicated in a land, and one may get entangled in the process. This endeavour at making a gift does not correspond to the attitudinal sense, as in the case of trying to forgive the son's murderer. Neither does it correspond to the pathological case where making a gift means quite an endeavour on the part of the agent, because the person lacks in the requisite attitude normally expected of people.

[10] Ibid., 12/329/12–13.

[11] Ibid., 12/123/10.

[12] *Manusaṃhitā*, 11/44.

and promote the performance of it in a decent way, adding the touch of the moral tone; the performance of the perfect act for the situation under consideration is guided by consequential considerations.

Ethics and Spirituality: Tagore-Gandhi

The virtues not only set the moral tone of an act but also set the basis for performance of the right acts. The Wall Street crises have been triggered by acts based on intense greed and lack of respect for others. The relevant virtues were flouted. The acts certainly were morally wrong, not because the relevant laws of the land were disregarded, but more importantly because they led to undesirable consequences with disregard of the virtues that bring in harmony, even though the moral tone might not have been overtly affected. To come to an example of religious fundamentalism, raping and killing of women of a faith other than one's own with barbaric display of humiliation and cruelty, triggered by fundamentalist beliefs, is wrong not only because the act of rape has been performed disregarding the relevant virtues but also because the moral tone has severely suffered, as manifest in the brutal way it is performed. Atrocities perpetrated on innocent civilians as a part of religious war are on the rise in today's world.

The Mahabharata depicts how the civilians are untouched in the devastating war at Kurukshetra. This dates several millennia before the inception of the Geneva Convention. The Mahabharata war is not a religious war at all. During the long discourse through the eighteen chapters of the Gita Sri Krishna does not ever counsel Arjuna to fight inciting hatred towards his enemies. The relevance of the Mahabharata today lies also in its teaching regarding the place of the virtues in a faith. The people of the various faiths need to take a hard look today at their own faiths from this angle. In the secular area of the business world, too, there is need for a hard look at the relevance of the virtues in day-to-day living. A time may have come when Business Ethics may need to rise above the overarching mechanism of greed and exploitation where the world of business is imbedded. What has triggered the financial collapse today cannot be comprehended simply in terms of disregard of the legal system, but in terms of mismanagement of greed. Spirituality certainly has relevance here. Spirituality, however, needs to be comprehended here in terms of harmony, as the Gita says, so that a person striving for it does good to the cause of all beings, not only the humans.[13] People indeed take their spiritual inspiration from the religions so long as the religions in their turn uphold spirituality.

In the play *Red Oleanders*, where Tagore depicts the suffering of the human soul in the modern industrialist society, mounted as it is on greed, the King rises in revolt against the system of profit and production he leads, with its inbuilt conspiracy to distance the King from the inner values that he pines for in his deepest aspirations. However, there is no hatred involved, nor bloodshed other than perhaps in self-sacrifice. Gandhi revolted against the system in place in his country, certainly not in hatred and enmity precipitating killings. Sri Krishna did not incite hatred in his friend Arjuna to lead him to fight the battle of Kurukshetra in order to settle the score of justice. The virtue of human dignity and respect was maintained in the actions of all three figures.

All the relevant virtues above can be clustered around the virtue of harmony, as we indicated above. The virtues strengthen in the individual with spiritual practice. Morality, or its opposite, is the manifestation of the spiritual dimension in everyday life. One whose spiritual dimension has been thwarted to a pathological level may not mind indiscriminate killings or other kinds of harms to humanity as manifest in the incidents leading to Wall Street collapse.

Gandhi was uncompromising with holding on to the virtues in life. He stopped the freedom movement with the Chauri Chaura massacre, at a very opportune moment when the movement had turned into a strong, irresistible current, because the virtue of ahimsa had fallen prey during the progress of the movement. He wanted India to become Ram Rajya (the kingdom of God) where acts would always be nested in the virtues of ahimsa, care for others and restraint of one's greed.

For Tagore, 'the umbilical cord connecting the India depicted in the Mahabharata and of this century has not snapped, however much the two may differ in very many important matters.'[14] Tagore believed that the harmonious life is a life of artistic and poetic living. The deep meaning of life is not to be learnt from science, important as it is in its own frame of

[13] Bhagavadgita, 1977, 5/25, 12/4. Both couplets have the expression 'sarva-bhuta-hite-ratāh,' meaning the spiritual aspirant would be engaged in doing good to all creatures.

[14] '"Dhammapadam," Prachin Sahitya,' *Rabindra Rachanavali* (Collected Works of Tagore), Birth Centenary Edition, Government of W. Bengal, vol. 13, p. 162 (45), Calcutta, 1961–1966.

reference, but from poetry, art, and music where life's meanings are imbedded. Science starts with initial doubt and questioning, which is an excellent method so far as it goes, and lands us in hopes as a result of its questioning method, but never does it hold an unconditional hope in the human values, and a faith in reaching the goal in conformity with them. If a scientist happens to have the hope and faith, this fact needs to be explained in terms of parameters falling outside of his scientific pursuit even as they act as inspiration behind his scientific venture. Life is a totality, and the scientist's world does not hold in isolation, nor does that of the administrator and the business person. When indeed our acts get severed from the meaning of life, putting a block to harmonious living, the matter certainly deserves minutest attention.

It is interesting to look at the universal human psychology in the light of the Chomskyan linguistic model of the deep level of language we all are born with translating itself into the surface languages. The universal moral principles may be viewed via the virtues at the deep level we all are born with. The diverse practices are but the various ways the principles translate themselves in societies with invitation to individuals to be firmly imbedded in the virtues at the surface level of consciousness, in the existential mode, through practice of the societal ways. Severing ourselves off the virtues, taking to parochial means, keeps us away from the journey of life, which after all is a spiritual journey, whether one believes in God or not.

To Tagore the spiritual world was phenomenological rather than ontological. This means that the God of harmony realized in every breath of life, tying a knot of fraternity with oneself and with others around, where life is the aesthetic joy that the harmony manifests, is our true God, rather than the God far away in the heaven with whom we might have problem to relate. Gandhi did not intend a severance between spirituality and politics. Neither did Tagore. In the Gita the virtue of harmony is very much emphasized even when the war is going to be fought. Today we need to look for the virtues in our own secular world of business to make the world a place for living together in harmony, thereby making our business endeavour a success in the real sense, while real satisfaction follows as a result. This, I believe, is the message of the Mahabharata for us.

How To Go About It

It should be clear now that involvement in business aiming at success should not be taken in isolation within the narrow parameters of Business Ethics away from ethics as such in order to protect society from wrongs arising in the field. It rather needs to be taken as imbedded in the total lifestyle where ethics, spirituality, music, and the arts, as crystallizing the core human values, are the nesting ground for all human activities. Ethics is taken here not in the negative sense of shielding the human cause from harms generated by wrongs done, but in the sense of furthering the cause. Business Ethics needs to be viewed as entrenched in this overall ethical consideration. Wrongdoers certainly may need to be punished, but morality does not need to be reduced to judgemental overtures. It must be viewed instead as providing the very sap of life's sustenance. Discussions and trainings must take place in the business world and places of learning geared to this end. Certainly yoga and meditation would be a favourable aid. However, the whole process must need to be an existential involvement, both on the part of the individual and on the part of the society, so that there is no mechanical rule to ensure the holding ground of the positive ethics, although the rule of law would continue to protect and safeguard. The new President of the United States, Barack Obama, might be seen as offering a fresh perspective to this end for the whole of humanity. He emphasizes the element of pervasive greed that went to generate the financial catastrophe and gives out a call for sacrifice to all. He has also expressed profound concern over the continuing greed with which the administrators are handling the bail out money allocated for revamping of the fallen economy.

This chapter is an attempt at an analysis of the concept of greed in the backdrop of human values aimed at everyone's satisfaction and real prosperity. The above remark indicates that the virtue harmony has its consequential implication, even though it has an intrinsic value of its own, connecting ethics and aesthetics with the broader sense of truth, i.e., the truth of life, and not just the literal truth of facts. The alternative to today's failing liberalism, grounded as it is on the wrong human psychology, is not opting for the rule of law, or commandment, either of the rightist or of the leftist kind, but an existential involvement in the values. Today's Business Ethics certainly needs an emphasis on greed management geared to prosperity in its terms towards building of overall harmony. The Mahabharata may be a real help here. It does not dispense with spirituality, but depicts it in secular terms and bases ethics on it in terms of the virtue harmony which inspires one to acts generating desirable consequences to all, safeguarding ecological balance. Such is the position of the ethics in the Mahabharata in a nutshell. The rising interest of the world today in yoga and meditation need not stand in isolation from the theory and practice of morality in the Mahabharata, Business Ethics being one important area to benefit from it.

References

Mahabharatam, 6 vols., original with Hindi translation, Gita Press, Gorakhpur, 2060 (Vikrama Calendar).

Bhagavadgita, Translated by S Radhakrishnan, Blackie & Son (India), Bombay, 1977.

Slote, Michael, *The Ethics of Care and Empathy*, Routledge, New York, 2007.

CHAPTER 8

Virtue Ethics and Leadership in the 21st Century: Barton through the Lens of Tagore

Ananda Chakravarti

"It's not what you do as a leader so much as who you are." Hearing these words spoken in 2016 by Dominic Barton, renowned business leader and diplomat, to a group of MBA students at one of the world's top business schools, helped me realize that philosophical ideas I had explored in my undergraduate days were relevant—essential even—to the world of business in which I operated.

Background

I remember my introduction to formal philosophy through Plato's *Apology of Socrates* during my undergraduate studies in political theory. It was a revelation. Socrates' commitment to his values, even as he faced death, showed me that philosophy isn't just for the classroom but can shape

I have profited significantly from the many discussions I've had concerning the ideas in this paper with my father, Sitansu S. Chakravarti.

A. Chakravarti (✉)
International Society for World Philosophy, Toronto, ON, Canada

S. S. Chakravarti et al. (ed.), *Traditional Indian Virtue Ethics for Today*, Palgrave Studies in Comparative East-West Philosophy,
https://doi.org/10.1007/978-3-031-47972-4_8

real-world discussions. It challenges norms and encourages critical thinking—what we might today call "engaging stakeholders"—and it need not be confined to the ivory towers of academia but can thrive in the bustling marketplace of ideas.

Dominic Barton follows in the Socratic tradition, reminding us starkly of the need for philosophy to enter the arena of business leadership discourse as business leaders are compelled to think differently about their role in a thriving society that becomes more global by the day.

I will address the above in this paper, expanding our scope to world philosophy, the heart of which is to use established philosophical tools from various cultures and civilizations, offering a fresh and innovative way to approach established problems as well as new ones. I look specifically to the rich philosophical heritage of India, to which I have been exposed for decades, to move beyond abstract theorizing and into the realm of leveraging practical wisdom for today's world. By combining core concepts from Western virtue ethics with insights from Indian philosophy, this paper focuses on real-world concepts like Environmental Social and Governance (ESG) considerations in business and the role philosophy must play in its evolution.

Dominic Barton: Who You Are Versus What You Do

First, a few words to introduce Dominic Barton, who frames the problem I attempt to shed light on in this paper. Global managing partner emeritus of McKinsey & Company and an Oxford Rhodes Scholar, Barton is a noted business leader and strategist whose remarkable career path also led him to international diplomacy and academic administration.

In his thought-provoking address at the Darden School of Business, University of Virginia in 2016 [Beach 2016], Barton passionately emphasizes that amidst the sweeping changes in the world, the foremost expectation for a twenty-first-century leader lies in "who you are versus what you do," focusing on character as the primary driver of effective leadership. He contends that a leader's actions are shaped by the traits in their character, and in today's dynamic landscape of technological advancements, economic shifts, demographic changes, and political unrest, selflessness and judgment are vital qualities that leaders must cultivate through life experience and practice. Through Barton's thinking I found a clue as to how to bridge the worlds of academic philosophy and practical business realities, recognizing that the pursuit of ethical conduct and the cultivation of moral character were essential for a positively impactful business environment toward a flourishing society by various markers.

The idea that who you are transcends what you do is simple enough to grasp. Yet on closer examination, Barton's pronouncement stirs in his audience the timeless and foundational questions that philosophy sets out to explore, such as, "what constitutes my inherent nature?" and "what actions should I be undertaking?" These questions have deep-seated origins in the language of Ancient Greek philosophy, notably within Aristotelian ethics, and have in recent decades found resonance in the domain of virtue ethics. Barton's contribution lies in introducing these very questions to the realm of twenty-first-century business leadership. This significance endures, years after his discourse at Darden in 2016. As of the writing of this paper in 2023, a worldwide discussion is taking shape involving investors, corporate leaders, regulators, and stakeholders about reimagining the purpose of business, extending beyond financial performance. Specifically, the debate is about the extent to which environmental and social impact should be the strategic focus of a business over what many consider its primary or even exclusive duty of generating profits for shareholders. Much of this debate has become politicized at present. My focus in this chapter will be more on the philosophical underpinnings of the issues, leaving politics aside.

Barton's Novel Contributions: Philosophy and Business; East and West

Barton's remarkable influence in the business world distinguishes him from those who engage in philosophy related to business, as he anchors his approach in the pragmatic necessity of philosophy within business, rather than theoretical musings. His contribution combines insights from years of advising global business leaders, underpinned by a steadfast commitment to the practical application of philosophy for the betterment of both capital markets and society at large. In fact, his devotion to philosophy stems from dialogues with business leaders regarding the philosophical challenges they confront, exemplified in the case I elaborate on below, and their desire to learn more about philosophy—a pursuit often curtailed by the demands inherent to a corporate CEO's responsibilities. [Beach 2016]

In this chapter I will focus on two aspects of Barton's 2016 talk that I think are noteworthy, particularly as they relate to world philosophy. I should also point out that the talk at the University of Virginia's business school was part of a series of talks Barton gave between 2015 and 2017 at the world's top business schools—including Oxford and Stanford—an indication of his commitment to fostering a dialogue between the academic setting and the marketplace, in keeping with the Socratic philosophical tradition. This paper provides an introductory sketch of how we can give philosophical shape to Barton's ideas, which I would invite future scholars to build on, particularly using the tools of world philosophy. The two aspects are as follows:

(i) The need for more philosophy in business
(ii) The need to look Eastward for sustainable business practices

I will end by providing some specific commentary on the ESG phenomenon, which has swept across the world of business in recent years, building on the above two points, considering the interplay between stakeholder capitalism, ESG and virtue ethics.

The Importance of Philosophy in Business

I would like first to write a note on the importance of business, particularly in today's world. In his talk, Barton identifies four gravitational forces shaping our world in the twenty-first century [Beach 2016]:

- A shift in economic power eastward to Asia
- Sweeping technological change (exponential rise in computing power, data and connected devices)
- An aging population
- Geopolitics and the transformation to a new "social deal"

Any of these forces on their own, Barton suggests, is monumental. The prospect of their convergence at a single point in time will be transformational to human civilization. The role of business and government organizations in this context is manifestly important to this transformation. One has only to think at any given moment in today's world, as I do even as I type these words, how much of a role companies, regulatory agencies and public-private partnerships play in mediating all aspects of our lives. These are key areas for leadership to play out in the twenty-first century, where the very question of what it means to be human will be challenged and redefined.

In the context of *judgment* as an essential character trait—or virtue—in morally ambiguous situations, Barton refers to "Right versus right" decision making. He cites an actual case study where the CEO of a dairy company finds out from his Research & Development department that aborting a calf fetus will yield 30% more milk production [Beach 2016]. One decision, he suggests, could be going ahead with the efficiency gain without hesitation: a seemingly straightforward choice for a profit-driven dairy company. A second consideration could be understanding what the public perception would be of this practice, with a view to mitigating any damage to the company's brand reputation. What if we did it and the activists found out? A third view is simply considering whether this treatment of a sentient being is defensible. In philosophical language, the ethical choices represented here are informed by both consequentialist and deontological considerations. Though Barton does not delve deeper into the ethical underpinnings of the scenarios in his dairy company example, he makes two important points, both implicitly and explicitly: first, that the judgment orientation around this decision is fundamentally character rather than action-based; and second, that a deeper understanding of philosophy is essential to navigating the complexities of morally ambiguous decision making circumstances, which will be in abundant supply as Barton's gravitational forces mentioned above continue to converge and transform the human world.

It is important to note that philosophical reasoning, which is essential to determining our approach to an ethical problem—no matter how abstract or practical—is a different kind of process to scientific reasoning. An ethical problem does not entail playing around with or applying ready-made conclusions. Instead, it requires an agent to go through the process of argumentation based on first principles, herself becoming the philosopher in the process. This contrasts from the scientific reasoning process, commonly used in business decision making, which relies more on empirical understanding and experimentation to lead to conclusions which are definitive, or probabilistic. Barton's emphasis on business leaders requiring a deeper understanding of philosophy should, I believe, transcend an enumeration of conclusions arrived at by other philosophers, focusing instead on cultivating a foundational grasp of concepts required to reason out solutions to philosophical problems.

On the UNESCO World Philosophy Day in 2022, a message from UNESCO's Director-General emphasizes not only the need for more philosophy in various aspects of human life, but the need to seek perspective from various traditions of philosophizing:

> *Philosophy is not only a thousand-year-old science, nourished by traditions from all over the world; it is a living exercise in questioning and conceiving the world, not only as it is, but also as it could or should be. In order to build a better world, to move towards an ideal of peace, we know that we must adopt a philosophical approach—namely, we must question the flaws of our world, beyond the tumult of crises. Philosophy is therefore essential when it comes to defining the ethical principles that should guide humanity….* [UNESCO 2022]

Virtue Ethics as the Philosophical Framework for Barton's Proposition

It is relatively simple for anyone versed in the basics of ethics to identify the philosophical foundation for Barton's concept of who you are being more important than what you do as virtue ethics. The notion that virtue ethics is the most appropriate and consequently should be established as the dominant model for business ethics has garnered increasing interest in recent decades, pioneered by thinkers such as Robert Solomon in the early 1990s. In line with this perspective, Miguel Alzola, a prominent philosopher renowned for his contributions to the field of business ethics, contends:

> *A virtue ethical theory of business must be not only a normative theory about abstract principles and side constraints, but also a theory of practice that is accessible to the people for whom business ethics is not just a subject of study but a way of life. Accordingly, the appropriate ethical theory for business is then teleological and character based. It is a theory of the practice of business that is concerned with the character of those who engage in business. It must emphasize the role of virtue in contributing to the achievement of the purpose of that practice (business).* [Alzola 2017, 592]

Here Alzola advocates a departure from armchair philosophizing when it comes to business ethics in favor of a more practical approach. His teleological stance regarding business ethics underscores a focus on the ultimate purpose or end goal of ethical practices—moving away from the more deontological focus of "the ways in which theories of justice and democracy evaluate markets and firms to the study of the decision-making processes at the individual and organizational levels that promote and impair human flourishing" [Alzola 2017, 609]—within the business realm, which I will build on in the next section.

Virtue Ethics, Deontology, Consequentialism and the Long View in Business

In his 2014 article, "Virtue Ethics and Management" Wim Vandekerckhove challenges compliance-based business ethics, the normative business ethics of our time, advocating for what he refers to as an integrity-based approach that focuses on cultivating individuals of virtuous character. He goes further in emphasizing the need for organizational leaders to judge others based not just on compliance with policies but also on their virtues, as a basis for promoting the betterment of society through business practices [Vandekerckhove 2014, 342]. The character-driven or virtue approach diverges from compliance-based ethics rooted in deontological principles, which is reactive and as such not the best suited to long-term flourishing, particularly in the face of uncertainty.

If we envision compliance-based deontological ethics as a reactive and potentially counterproductive approach to organizational culture, as proposed by Vandekerckhove, it becomes apparent that solely adopting a consequentialist stance could give rise to what he calls "profit myopia" [Vandekerckhove 2014, 346]. This phenomenon blurs the distinction between a business's means (profit) and its ends (social values), particularly relevant to sectors like financial institutions, as he highlights. Contemplating the interplay of ethics and a business's long-term sustainability prompts a profound exploration of the business's fundamental purpose.

Virtue ethicists in the business world, including pioneering thinkers like Solomon and Ed Freeman, offer a distinct perspective on the interplay between ethics and purpose, which has given rise to the stakeholder capitalism movement, placing emphasis on the interests of all stakeholders, encompassing employees, customers, communities, and the environment, to foster responsible and sustainable business approaches.

A foundational theorist of stakeholder capitalism, Freeman illustrates the connection between profit and purpose through the metaphor of red blood cells. He emphasizes that, while red blood cells are vital for sustaining life, existence isn't solely about their production [Freeman 2010]. Similarly, the essence of business involves nurturing stakeholder well-being beyond mere profit pursuit. This underscores the importance of collective welfare in both business and philosophy.

Eudaimonia—Connecting the Purpose of Business to the Purpose of Life

What I perceive as absent in Freeman's red blood cell metaphor and much of the stakeholder capitalism discourse, especially in the business realm where I operate, is a clear delineation of the ultimate purpose served by business. Terms like "delivering value" and "community investment" hold a degree of directional utility, yet their clarity remains elusive. It is incumbent upon philosophers to step into this discourse and offer a precise articulation of the purpose that businesses can and should embody in the twenty-first century. After all, the purpose of business is intricately linked with the purpose of life.

Concerning the purpose of business, the Aristotelian term "eudaimonia" seems appropriate to use and build upon in the business world, where it is not yet widely recognized either at a practical or a theoretical level. While I appreciate not all virtue ethicists favor a eúdemonistic approach, it is clear that eudaimonia and virtue ethics can form an intriguing intersection in the realm of business ethics. Eudaimonia, often translated as "human flourishing" or "well-being," aligns with the ultimate aspiration of virtue ethics: the cultivation of virtuous character. In the context of business, this convergence leads beyond mere regulatory compliance but the development of ethical decision-makers guided by their virtuous principles toward the end of human flourishing. The alignment between eudaimonia and virtue ethics opens avenues for nurturing businesses that not only pursue financial success but also strive for the genuine well-being and moral growth of individuals and society as a whole.

I believe the nature of eudaimonia—or *what it means to flourish* whether at the level of society at large, the individual, or the business entity—needs to be explored from the perspective of world philosophy, expanding and enriching the philosophical toolkit to incorporate ancient traditions of philosophizing Western philosophy. That the nature of eudaimonia requires deeper investigation is in fact a concept Aristotle himself acknowledged:

Verbally there is very general agreement; for both the general run of men and people of superior refinement say that it is happiness, and identify living well and faring well with being happy; but with regard to what happiness is they differ, and the many do not give the same account as the wise. For the former think it is some plain and obvious thing, like pleasure, wealth, or honor; [Nicomachean Ethics, Book 1, Chapter 4]

I am tempted to mention at this point an idea from the philosopher Bernard Williams about the need for old philosophical perspectives to solve new philosophical problems. In the words of Williams:

The resources of most modern philosophy are not adjusted to the modern world. I have tried to show that this is partly because it is too much and too unknowingly caught up in it, unreflectively appealing to the administrative ideas of rationality. … It is not a paradox that in these very new circumstances very old philosophies may have more to offer than moderately new ones. [Williams 2011, 219–220]

Taking a cue from Williams, I find no reason to confine ourselves to the ancient West in delving into the past, excluding the wisdom of the East. Before doing so, however, I would like to reflect briefly from Barton's perspective on the underlying thinking behind short-termism, which is now broadly considered to be an undesirable mode of doing business.

Consequentialism and Short-termism

A "winner take all" mindset, entrenched in of a type of capitalism that grew into and out of the modern European colonialism era, is rooted in what Barton refers to as 'Anglo-Saxon capitalism'. [Beach 2016]. This form of capitalism prioritizes short-term gains by seemingly any means, disregarding the well-being of stakeholders. This is fundamentally characterized in ethical terms by a mix of hardcore consequentialism, with an abiding deontological mooring—potentially fostering blind adherence to the service of an organization whose goals (ends) are reduced to profit at any cost. There could be virtues at play here such as fortitude, empathy or even courage, but if improperly oriented, these virtues may not amount to any good, and could end up doing harm. This is reminiscent of a "my country, right or wrong" (or perhaps "my company" could be an appropriate substitute in this context) mentality, seeking domination without considering the broader consequences, offers no real benefits for any stakeholder involved.

From an investor's perspective, short-termism can pose a significant problem in that it prioritizes immediate returns, often at the expense of long-term sustainability and broader stakeholder welfare.

To address these shortfalls and risks, a long-term view is essential among investors and companies. This is where stakeholder capitalism has emerged as a counter force, promoting long-termism by advocating for businesses to consider the interests of all stakeholders, including employees, customers, communities, and the environment. This fosters a more inclusive and responsible approach to corporate decision-making, focusing on long-term value creation and sustainable development. Embracing a more comprehensive perspective that considers stakeholder interests can only be meaningful if it is driven by a genuine, forward-looking, inward-looking and sustainable vision.

In recent times, ESG considerations are seen as essential to addressing stakeholder capitalism and long-termism, as they integrate sustainability, ethical practices, and responsible decision-making into business strategies, aligning corporate interests with the well-being of all stakeholders and fostering a more inclusive and enduring approach to long-term value creation. However, some critics argue that these efforts may still be constrained by short-term thinking. It is essential to recognize that genuine stakeholder consideration, driven by a long-term view that values sustainability and the well-being of all involved parties, is inherently linked to the concept of flourishing at both individual and macro levels. Here, philosophers can play a crucial role by promoting a holistic understanding of flourishing that encompasses not only financial gains but also the overall fulfillment and prosperity of individuals, communities, and the environment. By integrating the principles of flourishing into corporate strategies, businesses can raise an ethical and sustainable environment, paving the way for the collective flourishing of stakeholders and contributing to a more thriving and harmonious society in the long run. The growing focus on ESG considerations in businesses has been influenced by a mix of factors, including government regulations, management decisions, board engagement, and shareholder activism. In this rapidly evolving landscape, there is ample space for philosophers and ethicists to step in and play a pivotal role in guiding the trajectory of the ESG phenomenon, helping companies navigate complex moral dilemmas and promoting a more sustainable and fruitful approach to business practices.

Virtue Ethics for Business: Looking Eastward

This leads us to Barton's second significant point from his Darden talk I want to focus on, which revolves around the importance of looking Eastward and embracing long-term thinking and the purpose of business. It is worth emphasizing again that that this is not theoretical rumination—Barton is speaking from his practical experience in Asia, having led McKinsey & Company's Korea office and then serving as the firm's Asia chairman based in Shanghai. Though Barton does not explicitly reference Eastern philosophy, he highlights how Western business leaders often struggle to plan for the distant future, while their Asian counterparts seem more naturally inclined to do so. Barton provides examples of Korean and Chinese business leaders who plan for over a century ahead, openly challenging the ability and willingness of Western leaders to adopt such long-term perspectives. Interestingly, Barton does not see the pivot from Western short-termism to long-termism as a departure from the roots of western capitalism but a reversion to it. He points out that in Adam Smith's *The Theory of Moral Sentiments*, Smith argues that it is the entrepreneur's duty to care for the society in which they operate. Smith himself frames the idea in the terms of the virtuous agent embodying the qualities of prudence, justice and beneficence [Smith 2002]. The resonance between Adam Smith's idea of social responsibility—balancing deontological, consequentialist and virtue-based considerations—and what Barton posits as an innately Eastern style of long-term thinking in business showcases the potential for a more sustainable and socially conscious approach to capitalism that transcends short-term profit motives.

We find an apparently consequentialist focus to Barton's concern regarding long-termism when tracing it back to his first "gravitational force" for the twenty-first century, as indicated above, which is a fast-moving global economic re-balancing back to Asia. Western business leaders must get into the long game argues Barton, because that will be the new game on the world stage. And how to get there? In another talk from 2018 at the University of Toronto, he invokes wisdom from the Buddhist tradition, in a decidedly secular spirit:

> *The more you do for others without expecting to get anything back, the more you will personally gain... although that cannot be tied to the thinking.* [Sorensen 2018]

It is incumbent on western leaders, argues Barton, to learn from Eastern wisdom, theory and practice to compete and lead in the new world.

In the context of virtue ethics related to short-term vs. long-term thinking, it will be critical for future scholars to build out an ethical theory that synthesizes ideas from the East with the West. The theory needs to problematize short-termism in the sense of not having the right perspective in life, lacking a concept of becoming, which can stifle one's inclination to build their virtue and character. Looking at the state of things now—economic disruption and volatility, wealth disparity, nationalism, declining trust in institutions, media, and so on, which is largely a western construction, we have a way to go for people to actually become happier and more at peace in their lives. Overlooking Eastern philosophical thinking in this context could have two undesirable implications, viewed through a consequentialist lens. Firstly, it could perpetuate the grip of short-term thinking, a phenomenon that gives rise to a multitude of challenges. Secondly, it could result in West falling out of step with the East as the latter rises and progressively asserts its distinctive perspective on the global stage.

There has been growing interest in Eastern thinking in virtue ethics for business in recent years, though the perspective of the East remains ripe and necessary to explore for a variety of reasons.

Alzola, Hennig and Romar have done some work in this area, highlighting how Eastern philosophy, particularly Confucianism, plays a vital role in shaping world business by emphasizing practical character cultivation and self-improvement through key concepts such as *li*, *yi*, and *ren*. They show how virtue ethics, drawing from both Western and Eastern traditions, offers valuable insights for business success, stressing the importance of social relationships, responsible behavior, and environmental consciousness in fostering organizational development and human flourishing [Alzola et al. 2020].

I will not delve deeper into Confucian or other Chinese philosophical systems within this paper. Instead, I would like to emphasize that when we discuss the philosophical realms of "East and West," we should recognize that the category of "East" can and should encompass the long and firmly established Indian tradition of philosophical inquiry, which is explored extensively in this volume.

Broadening the Eastern Gaze to Include Indian Philosophy

Let us head away now from the home of Confucius in Qufu, Eastern China—where Alzola and others fix their focus—and shift our gaze towards India, to gather a rounded view of Eastern thinking.

Rabindranath Tagore, the world-renowned poet who drew profound philosophical insights from his Hindu heritage and Western education, emerged as the first non-European Nobel laureate in Literature in 1913. His remarkable contributions reverberated across the world's philosophical landscape, offering a fresh and creative reinterpretation of Indian philosophy that resonated with the demands of modernity. Although Tagore's ideas had gained international attention, it was in the 1920s that Romain Rolland, an eminent French literary figure, played a crucial role in amplifying their reach and depth in the Western world.

Rolland's emphasis on Tagore's philosophy encouraged a more profound understanding of his work within the Western intellectual community, enriching the cross-cultural philosophical dialogue. This enhanced recognition led to the incorporation of Tagore's ideas into the curricula of esteemed institutions such as Oxford and Harvard, underlining their global relevance. Tagore's philosophy, thus, stands as a critical bridge between Eastern and Western thought. This East-West philosophical exchange has been significantly illuminated through the efforts of figures like Rolland, who championed Tagore's philosophy and its capacity to foster global philosophical discourse. In a letter to Tagore in 1919, Rolland wrote:

> *I wish that henceforth the intellect of Asia will take a more active part in the expression of European thought. It is my dream to see the union of these two hemispheres of the mind. I admire you for contributing to it more than anyone else. Allow me to say in conclusion how dear to us are your wisdom and your art.* [Guha 2018]

Philosophy, Spirituality and Long-termism in Tagore

In *Sadhana: The Realization of Life*, Tagore presents an engaging and profound exposition of Indian spirituality to the Western world. He elucidates Indian spiritual concepts with a unique blend of poetic grace and philosophical depth, making these ideas accessible and relatable to a

Western audience. Tagore's objective in *Sadhana* is to manifest philosophically the inherent unity of all life and illustrate the relevance of ancient Indian spiritual teachings to contemporary life. He presents the "realization of life," or "Sadhana," as a holistic quest, linking every individual's spiritual journey to a broader cosmic drama. By doing so, he offers a gateway to the philosophical treasures of the East, emphasizing the universality of spiritual wisdom and its application in everyday life.

Tagore expresses poetically the human nature of short-termism in exquisite language:

> When man's consciousness is restricted only to the immediate vicinity of his human self, the deeper roots of his nature do not find their permanent soil, his spirit is ever on the brink of starvation, and in the place of healthful strength he substitutes rounds of stimulation. Then it is that man misses his inner perspective and measures his greatness by its bulk and not by its vital link with the infinite, judges his activity by its movement and not by the repose of perfection—the repose which is in the starry heavens, in the ever-flowing rhythmic dance of creation. [Tagore 1932, 10]

In the above example, Tagore lays bare *that* spirit of capitalism which causes a man to lose his perspective in life, which leads him into short-term thinking.

Tagore's words emphasize the limitations of confining one's consciousness solely to immediate concerns. When individuals, including business leaders, focus only on short-term gains and immediate profits, they are akin to those whose consciousness is restricted to their "immediate vicinity." In the context of business ethics, this kind of short-term thinking often leads to decisions that prioritize immediate financial gains without considering the long-term consequences for all stakeholders involved.

Long-term thinking, on the other hand, aligns more closely with Tagore's idea of seeking the "deeper roots" of human nature and finding a "permanent soil" for our endeavors. Just as Tagore suggests that a person's spirit requires a connection with the infinite, businesses too can thrive by establishing a deeper connection with the broader community, environment, and society. Long-term thinking encourages business leaders to consider the sustainability of their actions, the well-being of their employees, the impact on the environment, and the relationships with various stakeholders beyond just shareholders.

This idea ties in with the concept of stakeholder capitalism, which emphasizes that a business's responsibilities extend beyond maximizing shareholder value. Stakeholder capitalism suggests that businesses should consider the interests and well-being of various stakeholders, including employees, customers, suppliers, local communities, and the environment. Tagore's notion of measuring greatness not by mere "bulk" but by its "vital link with the infinite" resonates with the idea that businesses should be evaluated not solely based on short-term financial metrics but on their ability to contribute positively to the larger human and ecological contexts.

Tagore's philosophy encourages us to move beyond short-sighted, immediate gratification and embrace a more holistic and long-term perspective. By integrating these principles into the realm of business ethics, we can better understand the merits of long-term thinking and the philosophical underpinnings of stakeholder capitalism. Just as Tagore's words invite us to find our "repose of perfection," businesses too can find their optimal state by seeking harmony and sustainability through a broader consideration of stakeholders and their interconnected interests.

Amidst the disruptions posed by Barton's gravitational forces outlined at the beginning of this article, integrating virtue ethics ought to serve as a moral anchor, guiding business leaders to act with moral conviction and embrace a naturally apparent interconnectedness with stakeholders. By aligning their endeavors with the harmony relating to the animate and inanimate world around, businesses can actively contribute to the well-being of humanity and the environment, embodying Tagore's timeless wisdom in their actions.

Returning to Aristotle's concern over the subjectivity of Eudaimonia, we have an opportunity to revisit this in the context of the demands of our changing world, receiving help and stewardship from Tagore's uniquely Indian perspective along the way.

This fusion of Tagore's philosophy with virtue ethics assumes a crucial role in shaping the future of business, especially when we consider the philosophical underpinnings of movements such as ESG and stakeholder capitalism. By embracing these ethical principles, businesses can foster a more sustainable and compassionate landscape, where character-driven leadership places a high value on the well-being of stakeholders. As the challenges and opportunities of the future unfold, the integration of Tagore's wisdom with virtue ethics offers a promising direction, motivating businesses to take responsibility and cultivate harmonious coexistence with society and the planet.

By concretely adhering to virtue ethics and infusing Tagore's timeless insights into practical strategies, businesses can transcend mere compliance with ESG standards. This approach encourages a deeper understanding of interconnectedness, leading businesses to adopt responsible practices that extend beyond mere profitability. In doing so, businesses not only benefit from sustainable practices but also appeal to conscious investors and consumers seeking genuine ethical leadership and socially responsible enterprises.

Ultimately, this integration of Tagore's philosophy with virtue ethics inspires a transformative shift in business leadership. It propels corporations towards a profound commitment to social and environmental responsibility, reflecting a future where ethical considerations, compassion, and interconnectedness form the bedrock of a thriving global community. Through this concrete and purpose-driven journey, businesses can truly become the catalysts of positive change, driving progress towards a more sustainable and harmonious world.

Reframing the Stakeholder through Tagore's Lens

> *We can look upon a road from two different points of view. One regards it as dividing us from the object of our desire; in that case we count every step of our journey over it as something attained by force in the face of obstruction. The other sees it as the road which leads us to our destination; and as such it is part of our goal. It is already the beginning of our attainment, and by journeying over it we can only gain that which in itself it offers to us.*
>
> *This last point of view is that of India with regard to nature. For her, the great fact is that we are in harmony with nature; that man can think because his thoughts are in harmony with things; that he can use the forces of nature for his own purpose only because his power is in harmony with the power which is universal, and that in the long run his purpose never can knock against the purpose which works through nature.* [Tagore 1932, 7]

This quote from Tagore emphasizes a profound perspective, one that carries significant relevance in shaping a business leadership mindset through virtue ethics for stakeholder capitalism in the twenty-first century amidst disruptions and uncertainties. The analogy of viewing a road as either an obstacle to overcome or a path leading to a destination resonates with the ethos of virtue ethics. This philosophy encourages business leaders to see challenges as integral parts of the journey toward creating meaningful, sustainable enterprises. By adopting the latter viewpoint, where the road symbolizes the synergy between human intention and the harmonious order of the universe, businesses can align their pursuits with the holistic well-being of stakeholders and the environment. In the contemporary context, marked by rapid changes and unpredictability, Tagore's perspective invites leaders to cultivate virtues, ethical principles, and long-term thinking. By recognizing their interconnectedness with both nature and the larger ecosystem of society, businesses can navigate complexities with integrity and contribute to a stakeholder-focused capitalism that embodies enduring values and shared prosperity.

Renowned management consultant and educator Peter Drucker's famous quote, "culture eats strategy for breakfast," underscores the pivotal role of character-driven leadership in fostering individual and macro-level flourishing, particularly in the complex and uncertain landscape of the twenty-first century. Philosophers, recognizing the interconnectedness of human, social, and environmental well-being, hold a crucial responsibility in shaping leadership mindsets that prioritize virtues like integrity, empathy, and adaptability. By infusing these ethical values into corporate culture, philosophers contribute to cultivating an environment where flourishing thrives at both individual and societal levels, leading to a sustainable and harmonious future."

A well-implemented virtue ethical paradigm fosters a corporate 'nice neighborhood' where integrity, empathy, and responsible decision-making thrive. In such an environment, trust flourishes among stakeholders, reducing the need for strict regulatory oversight, just as good character minimizes the need for policing. This virtuous approach not only enhances individual and collective well-being but also cultivates a positive social and environmental impact, creating a harmonious ecosystem of flourishing akin to the tranquility of a well-kept neighborhood.

Anchoring Virtue in an Eastern Conception of Eudaimonia?

I believe more work needs to be done to shape an innovative new direction for virtue-based business ethics that not only accommodates but also draws inspiration from Eastern Eudaimonia. A framework for twenty-first-century business ethics can be greatly enriched by the timeless insights of Tagore, particularly his philosophy as encapsulated in *Sadhana: The Realization of Life*. Tagore's emphasis on interconnectedness and spiritual growth can serve as a guiding beacon, illuminating the unique approach to anchoring virtue ethics within the context of Eastern philosophical ideals.

Tagore's deep contemplation on interconnectedness underscores the intrinsic value of considering the interconnected interests of all stakeholders, encompassing employees, customers, suppliers, and the environment. This broader perspective transcends short-term profits, contributing to the harmonious development of society and the planet.

Additionally, Tagore's philosophy underscores the importance of self-realization and holistic growth. This perspective is akin to our approach of infusing mindfulness and ethical decision-making into corporate culture, fostering environments conducive to the comprehensive well-being of employees. By nurturing a sense of purpose and fulfillment, companies can align their endeavors with the profound ideals of *Sadhana*.

Two other perspectives I would like to highlight briefly in relation to an important leadership quality emphasized by Barton, namely, "selflessness" as it relates to character, are Swami Vivekananda's concept of "man making" and Robert Greenleaf's "servant leadership." These converge on the principle of selflessness in service and character development, albeit grounded in distinct philosophical and cultural frameworks. Vivekananda draws from Hindu philosophy, advocating for personal growth through altruistic deeds, aligning with the idea of dharma and karma. In contrast, Greenleaf's modern leadership theory fosters a nurturing approach wherein leaders prioritize followers' well-being and growth. This resonates with Western ethical thought and echoes Plato and Aristotle's concept of eudaimonia, where flourishing arises through virtuous actions and the betterment of others. Research avenues encompass cross-cultural analysis, examining well-being effects, organizational performance implications, philosophical synthesis, and long-term character evolution. Both concepts harmonize with the notion of eudaimonia, aspiring to profound personal flourishing by embracing selflessness, character enrichment, and the elevation of individuals within the complexities of life and leadership.

Ultimately, the core principle we derive from Tagore's and other exponents of Indian philosophy including Vivekananda which seems lacking in established paradigms of business ethics is that of a well-defined eudaimonia—the pursuit of human flourishing and the realization of a life imbued with meaning. As businesses integrate these Eastern philosophical underpinnings into their ethical frameworks, they can realign their purposes, fostering not only financial success but also the collective well-being of society. This transformative ethos can pave the way for sustainable practices and a heightened sense of responsibility, allowing businesses to manifest positive change in our world.

In short, our vision for a twenty-first century business ethics embraces Eastern eudaimonia, guided by Tagore's timeless wisdom. The interconnectedness of all life, the pursuit of self-realization, and the harmony between humanity and nature—these principles hold the potential to reshape corporate ethics, cultivating a more holistic and purpose-driven approach to business that contributes positively to our global community.

The Way Forward: ESG and World Philosophy

In the final strides of this exploration into the intricate interplay between virtue ethics, world philosophy, and the unfolding realm of ESG principles, I revisit Freeman's red blood cell analogy: a vivid depiction of our interconnectedness with the broader world. What emerges is a profound illustration of business's role in society: just as red blood cells circulate through our bodies to sustain life, the tangible and intangible benefits generated by a thriving economic system circulate through business to invigorate the broader spectrum of human flourishing.

As we approach this crucial juncture, the current landscape of ESG comes into focus in a new light, where the echoes of compliance-based practices reverberate. Here the red blood cell analogy stands as a reminder of the purpose-driven future we aspire to cultivate, anchored in eudaimonia-based virtue rather than deontological compliance. ESG's metrics and disclosures, though crucial, must not transform into a mere checkbox exercise. Instead, they should be the vessels through which the ethical essence of business is channeled, in harmony with the larger pursuit of human and environmental well-being.

I would like to point out here a rather obvious point: world philosophy means a collaboration between West and East. In other words, the West is not excluded in this endeavor. By now I have hopefully established that ESG is a Western construct, largely solving for a Western framing of the need to reorient capitalism to serve a broader community of stakeholders than to deliver profits to shareholders. I have pointed out the growing interest generated in the West in recent decades to establish virtue ethics as the normative ethics for business, moving away from the compliance-based deontological ethics we see in most business today. Let us now conclude with some possible direction drawing from both Western and

Eastern thinking on the way forward with ESG, ethics and business leadership for the twenty-first century.

"E" for (Environmental) Ethics?

Today, in practice, ESG-related theory and practice in business is largely focused on the "E"—which stands for Environmental. It is almost exclusively focused on compliance with greenhouse gas emissions directives, and the like, which as stated above Vandekerckhove describes as essentially reactive and not conducive to long-term flourishing. In his book *Character and Environment*, Ronald Sandler eloquently underscores the significance of virtue in decision-making, particularly in environmental contexts. He astutely notes,

> *So while we might condemn removing mountaintops, filling wetlands, and poisoning wolves, and make our case against these practices before lawmakers, courts, and the public, we must also consider the character of people responsible for them.* [Sandler 2007, 1–2]

This observation poignantly underscores the necessity for an intrinsic shift in attitudes. Regulatory measures undoubtedly hold weight, yet Sandler contends that fostering virtuous dispositions holds equal gravity for responsible conduct, aligning strikingly with discussions surrounding ESG practices. This perspective shines a spotlight on the pivotal role of philosophy in influencing a sustainable and compassionate approach to business, thereby resonating with the latent dynamics of societal progress. As we reflect on these dimensions, it becomes evident that this perspective warrants its rightful recognition in environmental ethics, firmly intertwined with the essence of ESG—an ethos that extends beyond compliance to encompass a holistic transformation in attitudes. A transition beyond the confines of unchecked greed emerges as an imperative step on this journey towards a conscientious and harmonious coexistence.

The relentless pursuit of growth within capitalism, often touted as the epitome of efficiency, warrants scrutiny due to its implications. This pursuit, driven by profit maximization, has led to concerns such as resource depletion, environmental degradation, and income inequality. The financial crises of recent decades, from the Enron scandal to the 2008 global financial crisis, have unveiled the vulnerabilities of unbridled growth-driven capitalism. These events have cultivated an ethical zeitgeist, a collective response to the tumultuous aftermath of unchecked corporate power and financial recklessness. This evolving consciousness is reshaping paradigms, catalyzing the ascent of ESG as a countermeasure. As businesses and societies reevaluate their priorities in this backdrop, philosophy emerges as an essential guiding force, steering capitalism towards a more equitable and sustainable path, and ushering in an era where virtue and ethical considerations are foundational.

The underlying philosophy of ESG finds its roots in the realm of environmental philosophy, as illustrated by Sandler in *Character and Environment*. This pivotal work accentuates the importance of virtuous character in ethical conduct and decision-making. The future philosophy of ESG lies within the domain of virtue ethics, encompassing the purpose of life itself. To repeat, this pursuit necessitates ongoing reflection, aligned with the evolving notions of Eudaimonia, the ethical north star that both shapes and is shaped by the prevailing philosophy. In this dynamic interplay, philosophy remains an ongoing process intrinsically woven with its conclusions. This symbiotic relationship ensures its perpetual relevance to the business landscape, echoing through time. However, it is pertinent to acknowledge that the current ESG outlook rests on a foundation that may be deemed shallow, inviting a reevaluation and reinforcement of its philosophical bedrock to foster enduring ethical progress.

> *Good environmental character is not only valuable insofar as it leads to proper actions. It is also beneficial to those who possess it. Dispositions to appreciate, respect, wonder, and love nature enable people to find reward, satisfaction, and comfort from their relationship with nature.* [Sandler 2007, 2]

In our ongoing pursuit of progress, regular reevaluation becomes vital, particularly in light of evolving conceptions of Eudaimonia—a guiding principle. This interaction not only shapes our philosophical framework but is also reciprocally influenced by it, as exemplified by the "objects influencing each other" literature. Philosophy's essence lies in its perpetual evolution, an inherent part of its conclusions. This intrinsic quality ensures its lasting relevance in the business realm, infusing it with a dynamic vitality that extends beyond theoretical discourse.

Presently, the philosophical underpinnings of the ESG position might benefit from a stronger foundation. A more robust philosophical base aligns with a greater potential for the logical outcomes of ESG practices, rooted in their vision and core philosophy, to be realized. By bolstering the philosophical groundwork, we enhance the prospects of ESG progressing beyond a compliance-based and metrics-driven framework, towards an ethos of purpose-driven ethics. This fortification transforms a potential challenge into an opportunity for transformation, ushering in an era where ethics, business, and societal and environmental well-being converge seamlessly.

Philosophers: A Call to Action

Drawing from the insights of Dominic Barton and his gravitational forces, the pace of change in our landscape is truly breathtaking. As prominent public intellectual Yuval Noah Harari aptly puts it:

> *....artificial intelligence and biotechnology are giving humanity the power to reshape and re-engineer life. Very soon somebody will have to decide how to use this power—based on some implicit or explicit story about the meaning of life.*
>
> *Philosophers are very patient people, but engineers are far less patient, and investors are the least patient of all.* [Harari 2019]

In light of this, delving into Tagore's ideas, particularly from his work *Sadhana: The Realization of Life* holds promise as a foundation for guiding virtue ethics within the realm of business. While Tagore doesn't explicitly use the term "Eudaimonia," his profound reflections on the interplay between individual fulfillment and harmonious existence with the universe provide a rich tapestry upon which to build such a concept. His exploration of life's purpose, the pursuit of joy through self-realization, and the unity of self and cosmos offer potent points of reference for this development.

To summarize, our current context presents a unique stage for action. Within this theater, the philosophy of business finds its platform through virtue ethics, aligning seamlessly with Barton's emphasis on the interplay of "who you are vs. what you do." It's notable that Barton, even without explicitly naming or elaborating on it, has effectively popularized virtue ethics. Barton's stature as a business leader reinforces the significance of this approach, marked not by armchair philosophy, but by practical implementation.

The case for ESG remains firm and essential, yet it evolves with the spirit of our times. Likewise, our conception of ethics must continue to adapt and strengthen as the landscape shifts. We stand at the threshold of a new era in world philosophy, where the journey has just begun and there is indeed much more to explore and accomplish.

Conclusion

In the above I have attempted to argue for inclusion of virtue ethics, combining the wisdom of the East, where the Indian perspective constitutes an important ingredient, all in the business world of today. Being situated in the heart of the corporate world myself, I hope to see such inclusion unfold itself in a meaningful way with an immediate effect, perhaps starting with the shaping of the ESG dimension in the corporate sector.

I have approached this paper following the invitation of Barton to expose leaders and future leaders in the business world to philosophy, while suggesting a pathway for philosophers to become more relevant to the business world. I would like to conclude by reiterating the difference between philosophical reasoning and scientific reasoning, and its importance on questions of ethics as they relate to business or any other field: whereas we might profitably use the conclusions of science without being scientists ourselves, in philosophy we cannot use conclusions without arriving at them in our own way of exercising philosophical reasoning. We readily incorporate the outcomes of scientific research into our lives, such as those related to the medical field, without individually verifying each study. In contrast, our existential understanding doesn't come solely from external information; it emerges from the personal journey of philosophical exploration. Experiencing the impact of philosophy requires actively engaging in the philosophical process. This paper has been my endeavor in that regard, and I anticipate its potential value for future scholars in this field.

References

Alzola, M. (2017). "Character-Based Business Ethics". In N. E. Snow (Ed.), *Oxford Handbook of Virtue* (pp. 591–620).

Alzola, M., Hennig, A., & Romar, E. (2020). Thematic Symposium Editorial: Virtue Ethics Between East and West. *Journal of Business Ethics, 165*, 177–189. https://doi.org/10.1007/s10551-019-04317-2

Aristotle. (1941). *Nicomachean Ethics*. In R. McKeon (Ed.). *The Basic Works of Aristotle*. New York: Random House.

Beach, Kate. "Leadership in the 21st Century and Global Forces." Darden School of Business, University of Virginia, 9 September 2016. https://blogs.darden.virginia.edu/international/2016/09/09/leadership-in-the-21st-century-and-global-forces-dominic-barton/

Freeman, R. E. (2010). *Strategic Management: A Stakeholder Approach*. Cambridge University Press.

Guha, C. (2018). *Bridging East and West: Rabindranath Tagore and Romain Rolland Correspondence* (1919–1940). Oxford University Press.

Harari, Y. N. (2019). *21 Lessons for the 21st Century*. Vintage. Introduction (xiv).

Sandler, R. L. (2007). *Character and Environment: A Virtue-Oriented Approach to Environmental Ethics*. Columbia University Press.

Smith, A. (2002). *The Theory of Moral Sentiments*. K. Haakonssen (Ed.), Cambridge University Press.

Sorensen, Chris. "Honorary degree recipient Dominic Barton encourages U of T grads to adopt a global outlook." University of Toronto, 12 June 2018, https://www.utoronto.ca/news/honorary-degree-recipient-dominic-barton-encourages-u-t-grads-adopt-global-outlook.

Tagore, R. (1932). *Sadhana: The Realisation of Life*. Macmillan.

UNESCO. Director-General, 2017- (Azoulay, A.). (2022). Message from Ms Audrey Azoulay, Director-General of UNESCO, on the occasion of World Philosophy Day, 17 November 2022. https://unesdoc.unesco.org/ark:/48223/pf0000383675_eng

Vandekerckhove, W. (2014). *Virtue Ethics and Management*. In S. van Hooft (Ed.), The Handbook of Virtue Ethics (pp. 341–351). Acumen Publishing.

Williams, B. (2011). *Ethics and the Limits of Philosophy*. Routledge.

CHAPTER 9

Reflections on Teaching Virtue Ethics in a Business Curriculum

Dennis Wittmer

So, you want to become a business person of the future. Well, what will that future look like, and what will be required of you to be successful? What attributes are needed to succeed in business? By the way, what does success mean to you? Indeed, how will business success be measured in this new future? These are some of the questions that I love to discuss with my students in courses that I am so fortunate to teach to bachelors, masters, and doctoral students in business.

This essay will attempt to synthesize some of my previous writing on the subject of virtue ethics, practical wisdom as a key virtue in business, and strategies for teaching and educating business students. This chapter has provided me with an opportunity to review a continuing theme in my thinking, writing, and teaching—the relevance of ageless concepts and traditions of philosophy in the world of business today.

The concept I will primarily use to organize my thoughts reaches back to ancient Greece and Aristotelean virtue ethics, as well as India and its

D. Wittmer (✉)
Daniels College of Business, University of Denver, Denver, CO, USA
e-mail: dwittmer@du.edu

S. S. Chakravarti et al. (ed.), *Traditional Indian Virtue Ethics for Today*, Palgrave Studies in Comparative East-West Philosophy,
https://doi.org/10.1007/978-3-031-47972-4_9

own tradition of virtue ethics. Previously I offered a playful exploration of the virtues and nature of a "good businessperson," honoring a dear mentor and friend, titled *Agoricus: A Platonic Exploration of the "Good" Businessperson* (Wittmer 2012). That mentor guided me into the joys of ancient Greek philosophy, and particularly Plato and Aristotle. The principal question in that essay was, "What constitutes the essence of a 'good' businessperson?" In that search I explored various virtues of a good businessperson. I have also described an approach for teaching virtue ethics in a business curriculum in *The Virtue of "Virtue Ethics" in Business and Business Education* (Wittmer and O'Brien 2014). The article provides a theoretical framework for the importance of virtue ethics in a business curriculum, as well as describing an ethics module used for undergraduate, graduate, and executive training programs in business.

Additionally, I have published a couple of pieces focused on a particular virtue I see at the heart of business education, practical wisdom. In *Developing practical wisdom in ethical decision making: A flight simulator program for 21st century business students* (Wittmer 2013) I argued for a focus on developing practical wisdom in business education and offered methods and approaches to develop that virtue in a formal education setting. In *Educating future business leaders to be practically wise: Designing an MBA curriculum to strengthen good decision making* (Wittmer and Fukami 2016) a colleague and I also used an Aristotelian framework to suggest how one might approach developing practical wisdom as a central virtue for MBA students.

I review these publications in order to help readers understand that my own journey of connecting virtue ethics, business management, and leadership has evolved in a teaching career of over thirty years. I have been joined in these curriculum reform by creative and kind colleagues, as evidenced by my co-authors above and most recently as it applies to positioning a course on AI and business, including the ethics of AI (Allen et al., 2022). A constant during this time has been a commitment to teaching business students the importance of virtue ethics in their future business lives and careers, but also in their personal relationships and community responsibilities. This chapter is based on the assumption that future business leaders will be well served by reflecting on the intersection of the challenges of a rapidly changing world and an ancient and enduring philosophy of ethics. Some might think it rather strange, if not anachronistic, to merge these worlds, but from my perspective it brings together quite naturally these worlds of business and philosophy. Some of the ideas from these previous publications will be adapted for the synthesis in this chapter.

The presocratic philosopher, Heraclitus, said, "You cannot step in the same river twice," since the water is constantly changing. And yet, of course, we do call it the same river by its location and position in space and time, allowing us to reasonably say it is the same river. So, his statement is true in one way and not in another. That distinction itself is very Aristotelian as a method for improved understanding of the world and our human experience of it. Some of the virtues required for leading organizations would seem to be constant in that they are time tested, successful adaptations for humans in communities (the same river), while the specific practices (and perhaps specific virtues) are changing in this era of modern business. Either way, facilitating discussions and reflections on attributes (virtues) of success in life and business should be a critical part of a business education.

The following sections are organized around different topics and questions from my approach for incorporating virtue ethics in the curriculum of business education. I follow more general and theoretical discussions with particular strategies I have used in classes from undergraduate to executive education programs.

One qualification should be added before explaining my particular approach to teaching virtue ethics to business students. While my discussion in this chapter is focused on virtue ethics, I do not mean to suggest that I teach virtue ethics to the exclusion other normative theories and frameworks for ethical decision-making. To the contrary, I do spend some time first framing the social function of morality and ethics in our human experience. Here I use contemporary experiential exercises employing prisoner dilemma scenarios, and I then connect that to philosophers such as Thomas Hobbes and social contract theory, as well as more contemporary thinking such as Garrett Hardin's Tragedy of the Commons. I frame essential elements of ethical or moral decisions and dilemmas. That is followed by using the classical normative theories of utilitarian (Bentham, Mill) and deontological (Kant) thinking as providing different decision rules for arriving at morally justifiable courses of action. I then position Aristotle and virtue ethics as an alternative to those ethical theories. I do also introduce students to the descriptive and behavioral side of ethics, utilizing social science theories and empirical research that bears on ethics and ethical decisions (e.g., Joshua Greene and the "trolley problem," moral psychology more broadly, as well as other social psychology research such as the Milgram Experiments). These preliminary topics provide business students with a broad understanding of ethics and morality, followed by about half the class being applications to specific issues and topics related to business ethics (e.g., employee privacy in the workplace, whistleblowing, sexual harassment, AI and its implication, and other topics). Thus virtue ethics is one part of a course that is wide-ranging as it applies to business ethics and ethical leadership.

The Nature and Purpose of Business

It seems that I am regularly drawn back to basic questions in my contributions to business education, including the theory and practice of business. One of those questions relates to the fundamental nature or purpose of business. A starting point might be that business is simply organizing resources (e.g., land, labor, and capital) to produce and deliver products and services to meet the needs of customers. In a capitalist economy, this involves allowing freedom, innovation, and the forces of competition to measure success in the production of those goods and services. Yet, there has been an ongoing debate related to what is now framed as shareholder versus stakeholder capitalism. Milton Friedman (1970) and his followers advocated the primacy of maximizing financial returns for the shareholders and investors of business enterprises. While that view held sway for 30–40 years, the business community more recently adopted a much broader perspective, reflected in a philosophy of stakeholder capitalism. According to this view, business and its leaders have an obligation and are best served when working and leading to optimize value for all stakeholders (employees, customers, suppliers, communities, the environment, and not last or least investors/shareholders). Indeed, in 2019 the Business Roundtable (an organization of the CEO's of major companies in the U.S.) revised its "Statement on the Purpose of a Corporation" to reflect stakeholder capitalism (see https://opportunity.businessroundtable.org/ourcommitment/). As the statement reads, "While each of our individual companies serves its own corporate purpose, we share a fundamental commitment to all of our stakeholders."

We will leave the theoretical debate about shareholder and stakeholder capitalism aside for purposes of this chapter. Instead we will focus on pedagogical approaches for engaging students in that debate, having students develop their own conception of the purpose of business. Adopting stakeholder capitalism as our theoretical lens, the role and purpose of business is to create value and happiness for everyone affected by a business. Stakeholder capitalism in this view is an enterprise to produce the good (and improved) life for all in the community.

A Teaching Strategy 1: *In terms of engaging students on the question of the fundamental purpose of business as an enterprise and major element of the larger social system, my colleagues and I use videos, readings, and a critical thinking assignment. We use video examples of the Mango House, a business started by a physician in Denver to address the health needs of immigrants. We use the REBBL, a beverage company dedicated to addressing human trafficking in Peru and helping indigenous people to expand local economies related to Brazil nuts and other agricultural products. We show them a video of Subaru in Indiana and the company success in eliminating solid waste in this major production plant. Students then read Milton Friedman's New York Times classic article on the purpose of business, as well as the Business Roundtable's 2019 restatement of the purpose of business. Students are assigned to write a rather brief critical thinking paper, assessing these points of view and finishing with an articulation of their own conception of the purpose of business. We view this assignment as very important for business students, as they complete their business education and enter the world of practice.*

The Good Life (Happiness, Reason, and Virtue)

The purpose of business is well aligned with another fundamental question for students, harkening back to debates in ancient philosophy. What is the purpose of a human life? Said differently, what constitutes a good and fulfilling life? With great humility (a virtue, I presume) I offer my brief exposition of Aristotle's vision (theoria) of happiness and the good life. In his works on ethics and politics Aristotle was fundamentally trying to understand the nature of a good and happy human life and the nature of a good political community, including its business components. Aristotle's methodology seemed to be that of dissecting human life around him in Greece and the ancient world. He begins his inquiry in the *Nichomachean Ethics* with the simple and disarming observation, "Every art and every inquiry, and similarly every action and pursuit, is thought to aim at some good; and for this reason the good has rightly been declared to be that at which all things aim." (NE 1094a1). Humans pursue many goods, of course, and a good human life will include having such goods such as health, wealth, friends, good looks, and good fortunate. But Aristotle is after something more, namely the highest good (summum bonum) or most encompassing aim of humans.

He is a functionalist by nature, assuming that the best way to understand a thing or a being is to examine its purpose, function, work, its unique features, or in his word, its distinctive virtue (arete). He is a teleologist, believing that insights and understanding can be achieved by examining the ends and purposes (telos) of things and beings. Like his predecessors and teachers, Socrates and Plato, he probes with analogies and examples. His examples include flute players, lyre players, carpenters, and tanners. His biological orientation leads him to think in terms of the function of eyes, feet, and hands to get at the deeper function of a human being. He dismisses nutrition and growth (mere survival) as the final or highest good for humans, since those are necessities for all living organisms, not distinguishing of the special virtue humans possess. Similarly, as it relates to business, profits are the blood of the business. Profits are necessary for a business to survive, but profits are not the purpose or fundamental virtue of a business. Eventually, Aristotle identifies reason as the distinct virtue or attribute of humans, a fact he thinks is intuitively clear.

The main function of business and its leaders, as discussed above, embraces the goal of producing good or value for all stakeholders. An extreme, but not isolated example in business today is the apparel company, Patagonia. The company mission is, "We're in the business to save our home planet." The mission is heroic and inspiring, and difficult to achieve.

To better understand goods that humans value, Aristotle distinguishes goods that are valued for their extrinsic worth (e.g., wealth), since these extrinsic goods are means to some other end (see Fig. 9.1). Such extrinsic goods are distinguished from other goods that have intrinsic worth (e.g.,

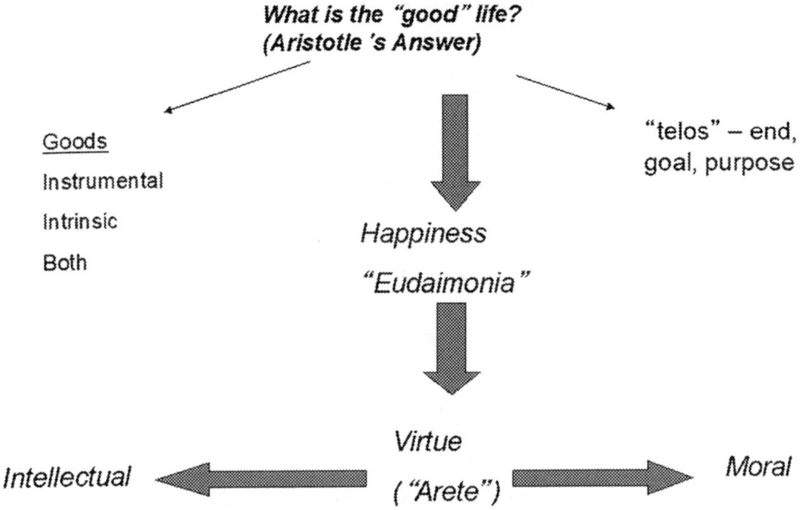

Fig. 9.1 Graphic representation of Aristotle's Theory of Virtue

health or friendship), since they are valued for their own sake, not merely as a means to some other good. In applying this distinction to professions and the world of work, the final end (intrinsic good) of the practice of medicine is health, while for architecture it is the creation of a building (house). Aristotle posits that we all would say that the final or highest good for humans is happiness (eudaimonia) or flourishing (eu zen).

> Now such a thing happiness, above all else, is held to be; for this we choose always for self and never for the sake of something else, but honor, pleasure, reason, and every virtue we choose indeed for themselves (for if nothing resulted from them we should still choose each of them), but we choose them also for the sake of happiness, judging that by means of them we shall be happy. (NE, Bk I, Ch 7)

We can now connect the distinctive function or virtue of humans (reason) with the ultimate end or good for humans (happiness). Like the heroic journey of Patagonia as a business, humans can be thought of as on a heroic journey that can be both inspiring and yet difficult to achieve.

> …if this is the case, and we state the function of man to be a certain kind of life, and this to be an activity or actions of the soul implying a rational principle, and the function of a good man to be the good and noble performance of these, and if any action is well performed when it is performed in accordance with the appropriate excellence: if this is the case, human good turns out to be activity of soul in accordance with virtue, and if there are more than one virtue, in accordance with the best and most complete. (NE, Bk I, Ch 7)

So, for Aristotle the happy or flourishing human life is a life of reason in all its dimensions. It might be in the sphere of theoretical inquiry, resulting in scientific knowledge (episteme) with its end (telos) being truth and understanding. Reason can be applied to the art of and making things with its end as production (poiesis, techne). Reason is also required in the study and practice of practical arts such as politics and ethics (praxis), with the end (telos) being behavior and action in the interaction of members of a community (polis). **As Aristotle succinctly puts it: "…happiness is an activity of soul in accordance with perfect virtue (arete)"** (NE, Bk I, Ch 13).

As related to business, one might extend Aristotelian analysis to the happy or flourishing business person or business leader. Virtuous and happy business people use their reason to create happiness (value, good) for all stakeholders affected by their decisions. **The truly happy CEO, then, is one who uses the various skills and talents required to accomplish the purpose of business, namely, creating value and happiness for all stakeholders**.

Happiness is not so much a state of mind but an activity for Aristotle. It is the excellent practice, virtuous activity itself, that constitutes happiness. From an Aristotelian perspective the happy knife, if it had a soul (psyche) would be the sharp knife engaged in the practice of cutting, the happy eye would be a healthy eye engaged in the practice of seeing, or to use a modern business example, the happy financial planner would be the well trained and knowledgeable Certified Financial Planner (CFP) engaged in the activity of designing an excellent retirement portfolio for a client. Happiness is in the doing, a human engaged in the activity related to a particular function and doing so in an excellent or virtuous way. By analogy, the happy CEO is again that leader who excels or is virtuous in producing value for all stakeholders.

A Teaching Strategy 2: *One approach we have used to engage students in reflecting on the nature of a fulfilling, good, and happy life relates to combining an Aristotelean conception with a contemporary theory from psychology and business. We employ Richard Boyatzis' (*2006*) Intentional Change Theory (ICT), along with Aristotle's theory, to help students better understand their conception of a good and fulfilling life and career in business or elsewhere. We have used this approach with younger students (typically 23–28 years) in a graduate MS-Management program. The Boyatzis model uses a model of intentional personal change that moves students through five discoveries, beginning with a clarification of their ideal self, that is the kind of person they wish to be in their future careers and life. For about three weeks students work through a series of exercises they do individually and then discuss with rotating partners in the class. The exercises include identifying their most important and core values. Another exercise, "catch your dreams," asks students to explore their personal aspirations and dreams. Students are then asked to create a personal vision statement, modeled on vision and values states of organizations and businesses. This leads to another exercise focused on imagining and exploring their dream jobs. Continuing this process, the next exercise focuses on having students reflect on and clarify thinking about money and success, using "what is money" and "what is success" as organizing prompts. The final exercise focuses on identify the possible "right jobs" that might integrate and align the results of all of these various exercises. The culmination of this process is a short reflective essay that calls for students to write a personal vision statement. "For this assignment, you will provide a description of your ideal self, as*

> *assessed through the exercises, readings,' discussion, and lectures in class." Students are then exposed to Aristotle's approach by thinking about a good and fulfilling life, focusing on happiness as virtuous activity, utilizing the unique and individual passions and talents that each student brings to a career in business and a community.*

It is relevant and important to consider the specific moral virtues required to achieve happiness, fulfillment, and the life of a good business-person, a natural transition to showing the relevance of Aristotle's theory of virtue ethics.

Virtue Ethics

Aristotle applies these ideas about virtue, reason, and happiness to the domain of ethics and morality, the sphere of our actions and interactions with other citizens in the community. He wants to make it clear that his goal is not just theoretical but very practical in trying to elucidate how citizens should act toward one another. Indeed, moral or ethical virtue can only be practiced in a community (polis). The very nature of moral virtue is a social thing; it is inherently about how we behave with and toward each other. This might seem obvious, and yet it is worth emphasizing, it seems, by way of contrast with private meditation and private strategies to achieve peace, unity, understanding, insight and nirvana. Aristotle's *Nicomachean Ethics* is an exploration of moral virtue and a discussion about how we might **become** good, ethical, or moral.

> Since, then, the present inquiry does not aim at theoretical knowledge like the others (for we are inquiring not in order to know what virtue is, but in order to become good, since otherwise our inquiry would have been of no use), we must examine the nature of actions, namely how we ought to do them;... (NE, Bk II, Ch 2)

While Aristotle's writings are descriptive in the sense of capturing what he observes and records about moral behavior, his writings are also highly normative or prescriptive. He does provide a descriptive account of what moral virtue is, how we acquire moral virtue, a list of moral virtues practiced, and other dimensions of morality and ethics, including a distinction between intellectual and moral virtue (See Fig. 9.1).

> Virtue, then, being of two kinds, intellectual and moral, intellectual virtue in the main owes both its birth and its growth to teaching (for which reason it requires experience and time), while moral virtue comes about as a result of habit, whence also its name (ethike) is one that is formed by a slight variation from the word ethos (habit). (NE, Bk II, Ch 1)

> Virtue, then, is a state of character concerned with choice, lying in a mean, i.e. the mean relative to us, this being determined by a rational principle, and by that principle by which the man of practical wisdom would determine it. Now it is a mean between two vices, that which depends on excess and that which depends on defect... (NE, Bk II, Ch 6)

For Aristotle, of course, we acquire and perfect virtues (or vices) through practice and habit. We go the gym or recreation center to re-create or strengthen our physical muscles (strength, agility, flexibility), and accordingly we engage with other humans to daily re-create or practice (strengthening or weakening) our moral muscles, as it were. Accordingly, we become honest by consistently practicing the practice of truth telling, or we become generous by appropriately demonstrating our generous spirit.

> ...but the virtues we get by first exercising them, as also happens in the case of the arts as well. For the things we have to learn before we can do them, we learn by doing them, e.g. men become builders by building and lyre-players by playing the lyre; so too we become just by doing just acts, temperate by doing temperate acts, brave by doing brave acts. (Aristotle 1941, p. 952)

The Virtues of Good (and Ethical) Business Leaders

What are the virtues that matter in life and business, and particularly those deemed moral and ethical? Nearly 30 years ago, Robert Solomon (1993) used a virtue ethics perspective for business managers and leaders. The book, *Ethics and Excellence: Cooperation and Integrity in Business*, provides an account of how to approach business and corporate life by using an Aristotelian and virtue ethics perspective. Solomon's book discusses what he believes are the basic business virtues (**honesty, fairness, trust, toughness**), as well as virtues of what he refers to as the corporate self (**friendliness, honor, loyalty, and shame**). Of these, Solomon (1993) says, "**Honesty** is the first virtue of business life" (p. 210).

Focusing on leadership, Kouzes and Posner (1993) identify four virtues or qualities as central for "credible" leaders: ***honesty, competence, forward-looking, and inspiring***. Their list reflects a mixture of moral and intellectual virtues.

James O'Toole (2005), a decade later, explicitly used an Aristotelian framework in detailing important virtues for a happy life. His focus was the moral dimension of leadership. "Hence, in addition to effectiveness, leadership has a moral dimension: the capacity to discern and provide **justice**" (p. 199).

James Autry (2001), also focused on leadership, adopting a virtue ethics perspective in his book, *The Servant Leader*. He advocated for "five ways of being" for effective leadership, and these ways of being are essentially five critical virtues of effective leaders: ***Be Authentic, Be Vulnerable, Be Accepting, Be Present, and Be Useful.***

Teams are pervasive in business and organizations more broadly. When it comes to being a *virtuous team member* in an organization or business, LaFasto and Larson (2001) suggest that the following characteristics form the basis for being an excellent or virtuous team member: **experienced, productive problem solver, open, supportive, personal initiative and positive style**. All of these virtues appear to be nonmoral excellences, but other moral virtues seem to be required of both followers and leaders, e.g., **honesty and truthfulness**.

Looking more broadly, Peterson and Seligman (2004) found six broad categories or families of related virtues in their empirically grounded work: **wisdom, courage, humanity, justice, temperance, and transcendence**. Wisdom, for example, as a family includes attributes such as curiosity, love of learning, judgment, ingenuity, emotional intelligence, and perspective.

The research cited above is by means comprehensive. It does reveal the importance of attributes or characteristics of leaders and managers in business, whether they are called "virtues" or not. To refer to these qualities as characteristics is consonant with an Aristotelian approach. Aristotle would say that virtues (or vices) are dispositions to behave in certain ways and reveal the very ***character*** of the person or leader, i.e., one's ***characteristics***.

Aristotle offers his own set of virtues. These are not intended to be exhaustive, and my representation (See Table 9.1) is intended to show the structure of his framework, with virtues or vices emanating from various emotions or feelings, calling for some kind of action or behavioral response.

Table 9.1 Aristotelian virtues and vices

Feeling/Emotion	*Virtue*	*Vice (Deficiency)*	*Vice (Excess)*
Fear/Confidence	Courage	Coward	Reckless
Pleasure/Pain	Self-Control	"Insensitive"	Self-indulgent
Giving/Taking Money (Small)	Generosity	Stinginess	Extravagance
Giving/Taking Money (Large)	Magnificence	Niggardliness	Gaudiness Vulgarity
Honor/Dishonor (Great)	High-Mindedness	Small-Mindedness	Vanity
Honor/Dishonor (Small)	No Name	Unambitious	Ambitious
Anger	Gentleness	Apathetic	Short-tempered
Speech/Action (truth)	Truthfulness	Self-deprecation	Boastfulness
Speech/Action (pleasantness in amusement)	Wittiness	Boorish	Buffoon
Speech/Action (pleasantness in daily life)	Friendliness	Grouchy Quarrelsome	Obsequious Flatterer
Shame	Modesty	Shameless	Terror-Stricken
Pain/pleasure (Fortunes of Neighbors)	Righteous Indignation	Spite	Envy

Teaching Strategy 3: *In order to engage students into the search of virtues, I engage them in an online discussion, wherein they provide responses to the question, "What do you think are the most important qualities or attributes of a good person, good manager, and good leader. In class and in small groups students share their responses and report out, and I record the results on a whiteboard with columns for good person, good manager, and good leader. Students are also asked to do an online exercise in which they identify the top seven virtues of a good leader from a list of 20 attributes used by Kouzes and Posner (see Fig. 9.2 and Table 9.2). The class profile is compared to national samples from Kouzes and Posner. Students are asked to read the case of "Joe*

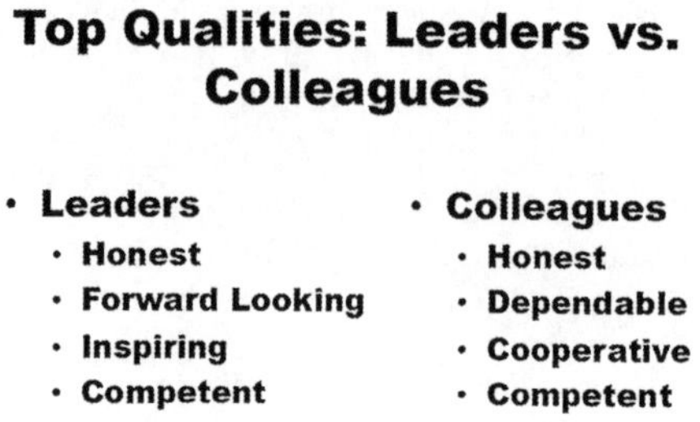
Top Qualities: Leaders vs. Colleagues
• Leaders
• Honest
• Forward Looking
• Inspiring
• Competent
• Colleagues
• Honest
• Dependable
• Cooperative
• Competent

Fig. 9.2 Most important characteristics—leaders and colleagues. (Kouzes and Posner)

Table 9.2 Leadership characteristics survey

Leadership Characteristics Survey
(Check the seven most important characteristics of a leader)
____ *Ambitious*
____ *Broad-minded*
____ *Caring*
____ *Competent*
____ *Cooperative*
____ *Courageous*
____ *Dependable*
____ *Determined*
____ *Fair-minded*
____ *Forward Looking*
____ *Honest*
____ *Imaginative*
____ *Independent*
____ *Inspiring*
____ *Intelligent*
____ *Loyal*
____ *Mature*
____ *Self-controlled*
____ *Straightforward*
____ *Supportive*

Source: Kouzes, J. M. and B. Z. *Posner, Credibility: How Leaders Gain and Lose It* (1993)

Sullivan," which is the story of a local Denver businessperson, who restamps the alcohol content of 350 cases of beer in order to satisfy the order of a coveted customer. In small groups students dissect the qualities of the main character, identifying both virtues and vices of the businessperson. The decision of restamping the beer is discussed in this context. At the end of the class discussion, an additional part to the case is revealed in which Joe Sullivan commits suicide after the aftermath of being caught and losing his liquor license in Colorado. The case is impactful for students in terms of the complexity of human character and the tragic consequences of poor decision making and a frailty of character.

Practical Wisdom

A virtue of particular importance in business is practical wisdom (phronesis). Practical wisdom is, of course, an excellence or attribute that is important in many spheres of life. We have emphasized it especially with MBA students, who are preparing to assume various leadership positions in organizations. These students will be called upon to make many judgments that call for consideration of many factors, applying general principles and values to specific, particular, and unique situations and people. Determining a good or right course of action requires a level of wisdom, good sense, or good judgment. In short, these future leaders will be called upon to be practically wise business leaders and managers.

Kip Tindell, founder and CEO of the Container Store, faced a very difficult decision during the economic downturn of 2008. He prided himself on not having laid off associates, since employees were the heart and soul of his retail model, paying them perhaps double the average salary of other retail businesses. Yet, the loss of revenues were significant during the financial crisis, and so he was forced to consider layoffs as an option. In his book, "Uncontainable," Tindell (2014) relates the story of the dilemma he faced while on his property in Colorado. He decided that he would include his stakeholders in the decision, since he embraced the philosophy of Conscious Capitalism, a philosophy of business that emphasizes stakeholder integration and shared decision making. In the end, he found a way that rejected trade-offs and embraced creative win-win-win solutions. He navigated a set of shared cost cutting strategies that stakeholders supported, resulting in not having to resort to significant layoffs. Southwest Airlines, likewise rejected a course of action followed by other airlines with respect to charging fees for baggage. Even though it meant forgoing significant revenues from charging for bags, the company's leadership considered its fundamental vision to "democratize the skies." Leadership considered a move to charge for bags as contrary to the mission itself. Instead, they saw the potential of a differentiating strategy, which worked to gain competitive advantage in the industry and satisfy all stakeholder, including flight attendants, who would not have to help passengers with so many carry-on bags. These cases exemplify principled, as well as practically wise, leadership.

Practical wisdom can be demonstrated at all levels of the organization. A custodian, Luke, cleaned the hospital room of a very ill young man, whose father had been consistently at his son's bedside, but happened to be absent during this day's cleaning. Since he did not see the custodian clean the room, he proceeded to berate the custodian, demanding that Luke clean the room immediately. After some brief consideration, Luke simply cleaned the room again. An interview with Luke later revealed that Luke had an understandable initial reaction of being defensive and a bit angry. He could have toldthe father that he cleaned the room and reported the incident to his supervisor. He could have held out for what was fair and just. He could have protected his honor. Moreover, he could have asserted his right to be treated fairly and with dignity. Or he could have brought in a supervisor immediately to handle the conflict. However, when he thought about the stress the father was experiencing and the fact that the father was convinced the room had not been cleaned, Luke decided to simply clean the room again. Luke said, "But I wasn't angry with him. I guess I could understand."

Schwartz and Sharpe (2010) cite this example in their book, "Practical Wisdom: The Right Way to Do the Right Thing." They say, "It [practical wisdom] depends on our ability to perceive the situation, to have the appropriate feelings or desires about it, to deliberate about what is appropriate in the circumstances, and to act" (p. 5).

Practical wisdom, as defined by Aristotle, is basically knowing what to do in specific situations. At the heart of it, practical wisdom is the capacity and skill to grasp the particular context and relevant features of situations, the capacity to deliberate, and the ability to decide and act. Practical wisdom (phronesis) "is a true and reasoned state of capacity to act with regard to the things that are good or bad for man" (Aristotle 1941, p. 1026). For Aristotle, practical wisdom is not theoretical wisdom or knowledge. Theoretical wisdom and knowledge (sophia and episteme) involve understanding the nature and relationships of things. As Aristotle says, "Scientific knowledge is judgement about things that are universal and necessary..." (Aristotle 1941, p. 1027). Practical wisdom, on the other hand, "is identified especially with that form of it which is concerned with a man himself—with the individual..." (Aristotle 1941, p. 1029).

Specific practices involved in the acquisition and practice of practical wisdom would seem to include:

- Reflection on the *telos* or fundamental purpose, vision, or mission of the particular business;
- Simulation or cases as a vehicle for strengthening skills and competencies;
- Debriefing as a critical component in learning;
- Group decision making and team management as a mechanism for getting better decision making;
- Focus on the particulars of a situation, rather than only abstract ideas and rules disconnected from real word problems;
- Development of empathy and social context by considering numerous stakeholders;
- Practice in balancing principles and particulars, balancing the competing interests of stakeholders and balancing the various skills and talents of member of a team.

A Teaching Strategy 4: *In order to have students practice their moral muscles and ethical decision making skills, I use a method I call "pilot and crew simulations." This approach is adopted by an account of improving pilot decisions in simulated situations, as described in Johnathan Lehrer's book, "How We Decide." Lehrer frames the benefit well, when he says, "But the best decision-makers don't despair. Instead, they become students of error, determined to learn from what went wrong" (Lehrer 2009, p. 249). Accordingly, I use brief scenarios or case studies, some written by previous business students. A template (see Table 9.3) for analyzing the scenario is completed by students prior to class, and small groups are formed. One student volunteers to be the pilot, explaining the pilot's assessment of the situation and decision. Then the crew (other students in*

Table 9.3 Case analysis template

Please fill in this template with your responses and post it as a Word document on the Assignments page of Canvas.		
	Your responses	*Debrief feedback when piloting*
What would you do in this situation? What is your first reaction to the situation? What does your "fast brain" think should be done?		
Case Analysis		
Who are the key decision makers and players in the case?		
What alternative courses of action are available?		
What significant harm and good may result from each of these choices? Identify harm and good relative to each alternative.		
What relevant ethical norms, standards, or principles deserve consideration?		
Normative Analysis: What decision making concepts and frameworks apply best?		
(Duties/Rights, Virtues/Vices, Consequences) What is the right course of action? Justify/Explain.		
Recommendations		
What course of action do you recommend for the key individuals involved?		

the group) provide feedback and their own assessments. The pilot takes notes and turns in the feedback on the template. A debriefing follows, in which there is discussion related to how the feedback confirmed or enhanced the pilot's assessment and recommendation. One of the objectives of this class exercise is to demonstrate the value of having others involved in ethical decision making. Another objective is to practice moral decision making in order to strengthen moral decision making. Athletes exhibit their skills in games,, and in preparation for competition, athletes practice and practice and practice in order to perform better in real athletic contests. Likewise, my contention, which should not be all that controversial, is that practicing ethical and moral decision making will make business stu-

dents better at moral and ethical decision making. In a word, the use of ethical and moral simulations may ***stimulate moral imagination and strengthen practical wisdom****.*

Concluding Thoughts

Virtue ethics is ancient as well as timely for our contemporary world, including the world of business and commerce. In my own 32-year career, business ethics has advanced, with ebbs and flows, in terms of being embedded into the curricula of undergraduate and graduate business programs. To the extent that students are exposed to normative decision-making frameworks, the traditional frameworks of utilitarian and Kantian theories, as well as Aristotelian virtue ethics, would be found in business ethics syllabi. Moreover, in terms of academic researchers in business, virtue ethics can be found when researching concepts such as ethical leadership (Neubert et al. 2009), ethical identity (Weaver 2006), or ethical culture (Kaptein 2008). Yet, of course, the likelihood that virtue ethics is taught to business students does not have the same probability compared to learning about return on investment (ROI). I have been fortunate in my own career to have a business college that values and allows me to teach business ethics, including educating students about the virtue of virtue ethics.

I have had the privilege and joy of teaching business students at all levels, I have found that Aristotelian virtue ethics is one of the most resonant and practical frameworks for engaging students to reflect on ethics. Without systematically collecting data from students, my anecdotal experience with students has been very positive in terms of their receptivity to virtue ethics, and business ethics more generally. However, my course is an elective for both management and legal studies. Students are exposed to virtue ethics in their freshman year as part of the Foundations of Business Law course.

Aristotle has been referred to as a common-sense philosopher, and my experience is that business students embrace the sensible and practical value of virtue ethics as a theoretically sound and practically valuable framework. It helps students organize their thinking with respect to the nature and essence of business, their responsibilities as future leaders, and clarification of the qualities and attributes they wish to exhibit. Moreover, the case study I wrote and use has such a dramatic and tragic ending that students better understand the critical importance of having a solid character and set of ingrained virtues. In short, students welcome the opportunity to define the virtuous person they wish to be, and I am fortunate to work with them in the time that is mine to be.

References

Allen, D. B., Fukami, C. V., & Wittmer, D. P. (2022). A course on the future of work: Building the scaffold while standing on it. *Journal of Management Education*, *46*(1), 178–209.

Aristotle (1941). Nicomachean ethics. In R. McKeon (Ed.). *The basic works of Aristotle*. New York: Random House.

Autry, J. (2001), *The Servant Leader: How to Build a Creative Team, Great Morale, and Improve Bottom-Line Performance*, Roseville, CA: Prima Publishing.

Boyatzis, R. E. (2006). An overview of intentional change from a complexity perspective. *Journal of management development*.

Fukami, C. V., Allen, D. B., & Wittmer, D. P. (2022). Teaching Management in the Fourth Industrial Revolution. In *The Future of Management Education* (pp. 153–171). Routledge.

Friedman, M. (1970). A Friedman doctrine: The social responsibility of business is to increase its profits. *The New York Times Magazine*, *13*(1970), 32–33.

Kaptein, M. (2008). Developing and testing a measure for the ethical culture of organizations: The corporate ethical virtues model. *Journal of Organizational Behavior: The International Journal of Industrial, Occupational and Organizational Psychology and Behavior*, 29(7), 923–947.

Kouzes, J. M. and B. Z. Posner (1993), *Credibility: How Leaders Gain and Lose It, Why People Demand It*, San Francisco, CA: Jossey-Bass.

LaFasto, F. and C. Larson (2001), *When Teams Work Best*, Thousand Oaks, CA: Sage.

Lehrer, J. (2009), *How We Decide*, New York, NY: Mariner Books, Houghton Mifflin Harcourt.

Neubert, M. J., Carlson, D. S., Kacmar, K. M., Roberts, J. A., & Chonko, L. B. (2009). The virtuous influence of ethical leadership behavior: Evidence from the field. *Journal of Business Ethics*, 90(2), 157–170.

O'Toole, J. (2005), *Creating the Good Life: Applying Aristotle's Wisdom to Find Meaning and Happiness*, New York, NY: Rodale Press.

Peterson, C. and M. E. P. Seligman (2004), *Character Strengths and Virtues: A Handbook and Classification*, Washington, D.C.: American Psychological Association and Oxford University Press.

Schwartz, B. & Sharpe, K. (2010). *Practical wisdom: The right way to do the right thing*. New York: Riverhead Books.

Solomon, R. C. (1993), *Ethics and Excellence: Cooperation and Integrity in Business*, New York, NY: Oxford University Press.

Tindell, K. (2014). *Uncontainable: How passion, commitment, and conscious capitalism built a business where everyone thrives.* Hachette UK.

Weaver, G. R. (2006). Virtue in organizations: Moral identity as a foundation for moral agency. *Organization studies*, 27(3), 341–368.

Wittmer, D. (2012). Agoricus: A Platonic Exploration of the "Good" Businessperson. *Journal of Business Ethics Education*, *9*, 309–324.

Wittmer, D. W., & Fukami, C. V. (2016). Educating future business leaders to be practically wise: Designing an MBA curriculum to strengthen good decision-making. In *Wisdom Learning* (pp. 245–263). Gower.

Wittmer, D., & O'Brien, K. (2014). The virtue of "virtue ethics" in business and business education. *Journal of Business Ethics Education*, *11*, 261–278.

Wittmer, D. (2013). Developing practical wisdom in ethical decision making: A flight simulator program for 21st century business students. *Journal of Business Ethics Education*, *10*, 169–183.

CHAPTER 10

Kautilya's Ethics-based Economics vs Modern Economics

Balbir Singh Sihag

Introduction

India's Golden Age: Vedic sages developed *dharma*, the ethical infrastructure to live in peace and harmony. Charaka believed that life expectancy depended on human efforts and not on the whims of gods. He redacted Āgniveś's *Saṃhitā*, which is now known as Charaka's *Saṃhitā* during the 8th century BCE. It is a manual on how to live longer, healthier, and happier. Suśhruta, forerunner in surgical procedures, wrote his own Samhita. Yājñavalkya, the first world philosopher and a prolific writer composed the following texts: Bṛhadaranyaka Upaniṣad, Yājñavalkya Smṛti Yājñavalkya Śākha, Pratijnā Sutra, Śaṭapatha Brāhmana, Yoga-Yājñavalkya. Vishnugupta Chanakya (son of Chanaka) Kautilya (4th Century BCE/1992) wrote *The Arthaśāstra* for engineering shared prosperity built on ethical foundation (all quotes except one are from this reference). Creation of

B. S. Sihag (✉)
University of Massachusetts Lowell,
Lowell, MA, USA
e-mail: Balbir_Sihag@uml.edu

S. S. Chakravarti et al. (ed.), *Traditional Indian Virtue Ethics for Today*, Palgrave Studies in Comparative East-West Philosophy,
https://doi.org/10.1007/978-3-031-47972-4_10

knowledge was taking place in every sphere of human activity for its own sake and more importantly to realize the cherished dream: life full of joy and riches.

• Many helpful suggestions by Lisa Widdison are deeply appreciated

According to ancient seers in India, the virtues of truthfulness and non-violence create a cohesive, anxiety free, and trusting society. That is, socio-political trust flourishes only in an ethical environment. No society can be sustained in the absence of ethics. They devoted a considerable amount of their intellectual energy to building an ethical infrastructure. They identified the system creating secular virtues, such as truthfulness and compassion. They also identified the system destroying vices, such as anger, greed, and lust. They understood that system-creating virtues promoted trust in each other and feelings of generosity whereas system-destroying vices were the root cause of suspecting each other and promoted grabbing tendencies. The significance of this point demands attention in Section I.

Vishnugupta Chanakya (son of Chanaka) Kautilya was known as an Āchārya (professor). He was the kingmaker and more importantly maker of his age. He lived a very simple and virtuous life. He was a man of letters, creative, secular, wise, and humble. He was an action-oriented visionary. He envisioned an ethical, prosperous, secure, and secular nation. He wrote *The Arthashastra* to realize his vision. It has 150 chapters distributed among 15 books. Books 1, 2 and 8 deal primarily with economic policies and economic administration, Books 3 and 4 discuss crime and punishment and administration of justice, Books 6, 7, 9, 11 and 12 primarily deal with foreign policies and Books 10 and 13 deal with issues related to war. Interestingly, "The Method of Science," is placed at the end rather than in the beginning of *The Arthaśāstra*.

Modern economics may not be a dismal science, but it is an amoral science. Every consumer, investor, producer, bureaucrat, or a politician is assumed to be a utility maximizer, serving his/her own interest. These interests are conceptualized in terms of contracts. Solely relying on rights-based contracts has crowded-out conscience-based commitments. Both modern economics and Kautilyan economics use economic concepts. However, economic decisions are guided by ethics in Kautilyan economics whereas self-interest is the guiding force in modern economics. It is argued that Kautilya's *Arthaśāstra* may be correctly designated as *Dharmanomics*: economics built on an ethical foundation projecting economics and economic policy in a more meaningful and socially desirable perspective. Trust creates what may be called Kautilyan ethical surplus: the difference between the level of Gross Domestic Product (GDP) if people were guided by ethics and the level of GDP if people were guided by self-interest. Ethical surplus might be a $1trillion every year. Relevance of Kautilya's insights to (A) engineering highest possible and equitable economic growth, (B) reduction in unproductive and unethical activities, and (C) mitigation of systemic risk is provided in Section II.

Current educational systems concentrate primarily on acquisition of knowledge and information. On the other hand, Kautilya put heavy emphasis on comprehensive education. He understood the necessity of each subject for ensuring that every child grew up as a foresighted, far-sighted, logical, consistent, steady, and coherent Jñānayogi by learning Ānvikshiki (philosophy), ethical Karmayogi by studying and following Vedas and Dharmaśāstras and proficient in understanding worldly affairs by studying economics and political science. Kautilya wholeheartedly embraced the message in *The Gita* related to the spiritual wellbeing. His objective was to complement spiritual wellbeing with material wellbeing for making life fuller and richer of every citizen. Section III presents Kautilya's educational curriculum. Section IV contains a few final observations.

I. Kautilya's Predecessors on Building an Ethical Infrastructure

This World is Upheld by Dharma. (Atharva Veda 12-1-17)

Vedas (books of ethics and knowledge) emphasized charity, truth, honesty, love, harmony, non-violence, and self-discipline. According to the Vedic seers, ethical virtues are very different from other excellences, only these virtues hold the society together. They built up the assumption that trust flourished only in an ethical society. They developed these secular virtues to build a trusting, cohesive, and caring society. Trust serves as a bridge between individuals. It may be noted that physical infrastructure deals with building bridges to connect different physical places, human infrastructure is related to building every individual's full potential, but both would be provided at suboptimal levels without first building an ethical infrastructure. These virtues went beyond the intrinsic value—not just self-improvement for its own sake but also to uplift others without expecting anything in return: "render good to all," "extend helping hand to all." A few quotes (English translations of the quotes of Vedas are from Talreja (1982)) that indicate the intrinsic value of these Vedic virtues (Table 10.1).

Table 10.1 List of dharmic (ethical) duties/virtues

Non-violence	*Truth and Benevolence:*	*Malice against no one*
Rishi (sage) Godha: "O enlightened men, We neither harm any one Nor impose ourselves on others, We act in accordance with Vedic doctrines and ideals, We co-exist and Co-operate in life With Akins as well as aliens To render good to all." Rig Veda (10-134-7)	"They follow eternal law Preach and practice truth Extend helping hand to all Act as unique guide and guardian Bounteous, benevolent, broad-minded And savior from sins." Rig Veda (5-67-4)	"I bless you to be free from malice To live with concord and unanimity Love one another as cow loves its new-born calf." Atharva Veda (3-30-1) "May we not hate anyone." Atharva Veda (12-1-24)
Charity Rishi (Sage) Angiras: "He who hoards provisions in vainAnd does not feed his elders and companions,Is inhuman, unkind and stingy,Verily he brings his own destruction.He who eats aloneIs a great sinner." Rig Veda (10-117-6).	Truth "The earth is sustained through truth." Atharva Veda (14-1-1)"He who performs selfless actionAccompanied by auspicious wordsFull of truth, joy and sweetnessIn the atmosphere of mutual co-operationReaches the goal." Yajur Veda (3-47)	Intrinsic value of Virtuous character Be pure and piousO worshipers Rig Veda (10-18-2)
Heavenly Rule of Ethics	Heavenly Rule of Ethics	Knowledge for its own sake

(*continued*)

Table 10.1 (continued)

Non-violence	*Truth and Benevolence:*	*Malice against no one*
"He who sees all beingsIn his own selfAnd finds the reflectionOf his own selfIn all beingsNever looks down upon anybody." Yajur Veda (40-6)	"Hence, (keeping these in mind), by self-control and by making dharma (right conduct) your main focus, treat others as you treat yourself." [Mahābhārata Shānti-Parva 167:9]	"Wide apart are these two, ignorance and what is known as wisdom, leading in opposite directions. I believe Nachiketas to be one who longs for wisdom, since many tempting objects have not turned thee aside." Katha Upanishad (II-4)

Heavenly Rule of Ethics: Vedic seers advanced the "Heavenly Rule" of ethics: treat others as you treat yourself. That is, live and help others live with dignity and self-respect. This Rule first appeared in Yajur Veda, which was composed around 3600 BCE. "He who sees all beings in his own self and finds the reflection of his own self in all beings never looks down upon anybody (Yajur Veda (40-6)." Everyone yearns for self-respect, dignity, and flourishing for himself. According to the expression "finds his own reflection in all beings" implies "do unto others what you would do unto yourself." There is no reciprocity involved in this expression. Such an individual is good to others without expecting any good in return from them. That is, it is an expectation from himself to be virtuous. It is also obvious that justice would prevail in such a society since no one would want to be unjust to oneself. If everyone follows this advice, there would be heaven on earth. This may be called the Heavenly Rule of Ethics. This rule is made more explicit in the *Mahabharata* (3100 BCE): "treat others as you treat yourself (Mahābhārata Shānti-Parva 167:9)."

Golden Rule of Ethics: "Do unto others what you would have them do unto you." Be kind and generous to others if you want generosity and kindness from them. There is an implicit expectation and clearly, reciprocity is implied by the Golden Rule.

Silver Rule of Ethics: "Do not do unto others what you do not wish to be done unto you" is called a Silver Rule. Often the Silver Rule is much more effective in conveying a strong message/warning. Ma*habharata* (5:1517): "This is the sum of duty: do not do to others what would cause pain if done to you." Kautilya (p. 138) remarks, "One who inflicts physical injury is likely to suffer the same fate from others (8.3.36)." Similarly, Gandhi made an insightful remark, "An eye for an eye will leave the whole world blind."

Platinum Rule of Ethics: "Do unto others as they would want to be done unto them." That is, treat others the way they want to be treated and not the way you want to be treated. It means one must know the likings and aversions of other individuals. Kautilya applied the Platinum Rule very effectively. Kautilya (4th Century BCE/2000, p. 116) suggested, "The miser should be won over by means of wealth, the proud man by offering respect, the fool by flattery, and the learned one by truthfulness." In business or in negotiating a treaty/contract, it is important to know the mental make-up of the other party.

All these metallic rules of ethics are used to promote good behavior and discourage bad behavior. These rules are necessary but not sufficient unless accompanied by ethical anchoring. These rules do serve some purpose but are only second best to the first best Heavenly Rule. Kautilya offers a comprehensive educational curriculum which includes ethical anchoring, development of self-discipline, and acquisition of wisdom, knowledge, and information (see below in Section III).

II. Kautilya's Conceptual Framework on Provision of *Yogakshema (Peaceful Enjoyment of Prosperity)*

> In the happiness of his subjects lies his happiness, in their welfare his welfare. He shall not consider as good only that which pleases him but treat as beneficial to him whatever pleases his subjects (1.19). (Kautilya, p. 149)

Kautilya on Foundational Role of Ethics: Kautilya promoted the foundational role of ethics. He repeatedly emphasized the importance of ethics. He (p. 106) wrote, "[The observance of] one's own dharma leads to heaven and eternal bliss. When dharma is transgressed, the resulting chaos leads to the extermination of this world." Kautilya advised the ruler to pursue actions that promoted *dharma*, *artha*, and *kāma*. He (p. 639) wrote, "Wealth is like a tree; its roots are dharma, and the fruit is pleasure. Achieving that kind of wealth which further promotes dharma, produces more wealth, and gives more pleasure is the achievement of all gains (sarvarthasiddhi) (9.7.81)." He (pp. 107–108) asserted, "For the world, when maintained in accordance with the Vedas, will ever prosper and not perish. Therefore, the king shall never allow the people to swerve from their dharma."

On the other hand, Adam Smith believed beneficence was merely ornamental. He ([1790] 1982, II. ii. 3. 3–4) wrote, "Beneficence, therefore, is less essential to the existence of society than justice. Society may subsist, though not in the most comfortable state, without beneficence; but the prevalence of injustice must utterly destroy it." He added, "It is the ornament which embellishes, not the foundation which supports the building, and which it was, therefore, sufficient to recommend, but by no means necessary to impose."

According to Kautilya, virtues, such as beneficence were not just ornamental but foundational. He argued that ethics paved the road to riches, was essential to the administration of justice, and to reduction in socially unproductive activities, and systemic risk. These are discussed in turn.

(A) Kautilya on Engineering highest possible and Equitable Economic Growth: Kautilya believed that poverty was death while living. His *Arthaśāstra* is a manual on how to engineer shared prosperity. He invariably offered a complete and comprehensive solution to a problem. He identified the factors which promoted shared prosperity and the factors that hindered it. He suggested maintenance of law and order to reduce risk and good governance, such as provision of infrastructure, and formulation and implementation of sound economic policies to raise the rate of return on investment in the private sector. He argued that *dharmic* (ethical) conduct paved the way to shared prosperity. According to Kautilya, a society based on contracts alone is less productive and more anxiety prone than the one based on conscience and compassion. If the social environment is predominantly ethical, there is less of a need to take defensive measures to protect against opportunism. The following Table captures his comprehensive approach to bringing prosperity and national security (Table 10.2).

Importance of Maintaining Law and Order: Kautilya (p. 108) observed, "By maintaining order, the king can preserve what he already has, acquire new possessions, augment his wealth, and power, and share the benefits of improvement with those worthy of such gifts. The progress of this world depends on the maintenance of order and the [proper functioning of] government (1.4)." Maintenance of law and order was also emphasized by Adam Smith (1776/1976, Bk. V, Ch. III, p. 445).

Table 10.2 Kautilya's manual on engineering shared prosperity

Metaphor	*Description*	*Policies to achieve Yogakshema*
Edifice = Yogakshema	Peaceful	(a) Elimination of threat of foreign aggression by developing comprehensive national security policies. *Self-Protection Measures against Foreign Aggression*: (i) building of forts, (ii) building a large army and armor, (iii) setting up an intelligence gathering and analysis unit and (iv) diplomatic initiatives.(b) Crime free society through (i) Ethical anchoring and (ii) formulation of clear, consistent, codified, and fair laws and their effective implementation.
	Enjoyment of shared Prosperity	Maintenance of law and orderProvision of infrastructurePro- growth economic policies
Pillar = Justice	Built-in Justice in the Ethical Infrastructure	See (Section I above)
	Law-based justice for those who commit crimes	Kautilya (p. 377): "It is the power of punishment alone, when exercised impartially in proportion to the guilt, and irrespective of whether the person punished is the King's son or an enemy, that protects this world and the next. (3.1)."
Foundation = Dharma (ethics)	Non-violence, truthfulness, freedom from malice, compassion, tolerance	Vedas, philosophy Ethical Anchoring (Section III)

Low Taxes with full Compliance: He was against putting any excessive tax burden on the people. For example, he (p. 181) suggested to the king, "He shall protect agriculture from being harassed by [onerous] fines, taxes and demands of labor (2.1.37)." Similarly, he did not want the tax collectors to be overzealous. He (p. 284) wrote, "He who produces double the [anticipated] revenue eats up the janapada [the countryside and its people, by leaving inadequate resources for survival and future production] (2.9)."

Administration of Justice: Kautilya (p. 377) wrote, "A king who observes his duty of protecting his people justly and according to law will go to heaven, whereas one who does not protect them or inflicts unjust punishment will not. It is the power of punishment alone, when exercised impartially in proportion to the guilt, and irrespective of whether the person punished is the King's son or an enemy, that protects this world and the next. (3.1)." Kautilya (p. 108) elaborated on this theme, "Whoever imposes just and deserved punishment is respected and honored. A well-considered and just punishment makes the people devoted to *dharma*, *artha* and *kāma* [righteousness, wealth and enjoyment]. Unjust punishment, whether awarded in greed, anger or ignorance, excites the fury of even [those who have renounced all worldly attachments like] forest recluses and ascetics, not to speak of householders. When, [conversely,] no punishment is awarded through misplaced leniency and no law prevails, then there is only the law of fish [i.e., the law of the jungle] (1.4)." That is, might is right.

Kautilya believed justice was the key to freedom, peace, and prosperity. According to him, there was no rule of law without justice and there was no justice without ethical and self-disciplined judges. He suggested to appoint a person as a judge only if he was incorruptible, self-disciplined and an expert in law so that he would not award an unjust verdict due to "greed, anger or ignorance."

Adam Smith did not write a single word on Justice: Adam Smith believed that justice was very important but did not define it or explain how to deliver it. He ([1790] 1982, II. ii. 4) wrote, "Justice, on the contrary, is the main pillar that upholds the whole edifice. If it is removed, the great, the immense fabric of human society,..., must in a moment crumble into atoms." If a pillar is to provide support, it must be strong, structurally sound, and aesthetically pleasing to enhance the magnificence and integrity of the edifice. More importantly, according to Kautilya, unless the pillar (justice) rests on the ethical foundation, it would remain wobbly.

On Physical Infrastructure: Kautilya (p. 553) suggested, "A king makes progress by building forts, irrigation works or trade routes, creating new settlements, elephant forests or productive forests, or opening new mines (7.1)."

On Good Governance: Kautilya suggested, (a) "remove all obstructions to economic activity" and (b) Provision of incentives: He (p. 231) recommended (1) *Tax Holidays*: "Anyone who brings new land under cultivation shall be granted exemption from payment of agricultural taxes for a period of two years. Similarly, “for building or improving irrigation facilities’ exemption from water rates shall be granted (3.9).” (2) *Concessionary Loans* (p. 179): “[On new settlements] the cultivators shall be granted grains, cattle, and money which they can repay at their convenience (2.1).” (3) *Duty Free Imports* (p. 238): “Any items that, at his discretion, the Chief Controller of Customs, may consider to be highly beneficial to the country (such as rare seeds)” (2.21) are to be exempt from import duties.

Kautilya’s Most Important Insight: Economic growth depends on maintenance of law and order and good governance, but both depend on the ethics of the ruler. He (p. 142) wrote, “The three sciences [philosophy, the three Vedas and economics] are dependent on the science of government. [For, without a just administration, no pursuit of learning or avocation would be possible.] [Government by] Rule of Law, which alone can guarantee security of life and welfare of the people, is, in turn, dependent on the self-discipline of the king (1.5.02).” He argued that only an ethical, intelligent, wise, and disciplined king, that is, only a ***Rajarishi (Jñanayogi and Karmayogi)*** could provide *Yogakshema*.

On Human Infrastructure: Kautilya insisted on protecting the weak and defenseless in the society. (1) He (p. 128) suggested, “Whenever danger threatens, the king shall protect all those afflicted like a father [protects his children] (4.3).”

(2) He (p. 180) recommended, “He shall, however, treat leniently, like a father [would treat his son], those whose exemptions have ceased to be effective (2.1).”

(3) He (p. 182) suggested, “King shall maintain, at state expense, children, the old, the destitute, those suffering from adversity, childless women, and the children of the destitute women (2.1).”

(4) He (p. 385) stated, “The judges themselves shall take charge of the affairs of gods, Brahmins, ascetics, women, minors, old people, the sick and those that are helpless [e.g., orphans], [even] when they do not approach the court. No suit of theirs shall be dismissed for want of jurisdiction, passage of time or adverse possession (3.2).”

Kautilya on Scope of Economics: Kautilya’s economics consists of two components: economic knowledge and its use for policy-making guided by ethical concerns. Modern economics is guided only by self-interest. Kautilya argued that ethics was the deep determinant. Both rule of law and governance are essential but not sufficient since they depend on the ethics of the legislators and enforcers (Table 10.3).

Table 10.3 Kautilya and Smith on the scope of economics

Kautilya	*Adam Smith*
Scope of The Arthaśastra: Kautilya (p. 100) writes, "By following [the principles set out in] this treatise one can not only create and preserve ***dharma*** [spiritual good], ***artha*** [material well-being] and ***kama*** [aesthetic pleasures] but also destroy [their opposites, i.e.,] unrighteousness, material loss and hatred. It is a guide not only for the acquisition of this world but also the next (15.1)."	**Scope of The Wealth of Nations**: Adam Smith (1776/1976, Book IV, p. 449) writes, "Political economy, considered as a branch of the science of a statesman or legislator, proposes two distinct objects: first, to provide a plentiful revenue or subsistence for the people, or more properly to enable them to provide such a revenue or subsistence for themselves; secondly, to supply the state or commonwealth with a revenue sufficient for the public services. It proposes to enrich both the people and the sovereign."

It is worth noting that Kautilya emphasizes preservation and promotion of *Dharma* (spiritual wellbeing) by putting it ahead of *Artha* (material wellbeing) in *The Arthaśastra*. There is no mention of spiritual wellbeing in *The Wealth of Nations* or in the modern economics.

(B) Reduction in Harmful Activities: Kautilya believed that ethical anchoring and self-discipline would reduce unproductive and harmful activities. Kautilya's insight may be captured by Table 10.4 below.

If people are greedy, that uncontrolled desire affects everything: charitable activities decline and socially harmful activities, such as monopolization, lobbying, and financial manipulations etc. increase. Over time activities which promote public interest shrink. He firmly believed that rape, murder, discrimination, bullying, oppression, exploitation, subjugation, sextual harassment, injustice, corruption, tax evasion, and cooking the books could never be prevented by laws and regulations alone. Laws could not prevent Ivan Boesky, Charles Keating, Michael Milken, Jack Grubman, Kenneth Lay, Bernard Ebers, and countless others from resorting to fraudulent practices. Laws deal with symptoms of egregious conduct and not with the underlying character disorder. Clearly, laws alone cannot prevent someone from breaking them.

Incidentally, Adam Smith (1776/1976, Bk. I, Ch. II, p. 18) took the easy way out and focused primarily on Case (1) in which there is no conflict between the private interest and the public interest. That is, Adam

Table 10.4 Kautilya and modern economics on public and private interests

	Public interest	*Against public interest*
Private Interest	Most of the activities: agriculture, cattle-rearing, and trade, manufacturing, provision of infrastructure etc. Case (1) (no conflict, ideal)	Discouragement to do harmful activities, such as Monopolization, lobbying, financial manipulation, regulatory arbitrage (such as shadow banking), shirking (writing personal emails in office time) etc. Case (3) (conflicts of interest)
Against Private Interest	Encouragement to do beneficial activities, such as charitable contributions, performing good deeds, risking one's life to defend the mother land (Emphasis on moral duty and Incentives) Case (2) (conflicts of interest)	Destructive actions (rape, murder, discrimination, bullying, oppression, exploitation, subjugation, sextual harassment, injustice, corruption, cooking the books, insider trading, backdating options) motivated by greed, anger, lust, jealousy, hate, arrogance, and addiction etc. Case (4) (worst case) **To be prevented**

Source: Sihag (2019, p. 11)

Smith did not deal with the relevant but challenging issues. On the other hand, Kautilya dealt with all the four cases. In fact, Kautilya's predecessors were also concerned, at least, about cases (3) and (4). Ancient sages identified the system-building virtues, such as non-violence, compassion, truthfulness, malice against none, tolerance, and cleanliness for creating a healthy, harmonious, and peaceful society. Non-violence meant not to harm anyone physically, financially, or emotionally implying case (3) would not arise in such an ethical society. Logically speaking, case (4) should not happen since it is against both private and public interests. However, according to Kautilya, it arises because an angry or greedy person loses his logical ability to process information and harms himself and others.

Kautilya on Building Ethical Infrastructure and Shared Prosperity: Ethical infrastructure not only is critical to preserving democracy but also it complements the physical and human infrastructures in enhancing competitive advantage and reducing gun violence. Ancient sages realized that genuine trust was an ethics-intensive concept since non-violence, truthfulness, honesty, and benevolence were the foundation for trust. Kautilya accepted that insight wholeheartedly. There is a confusion between confidence and trust. Confidence is a statistical concept whereas trust is an ethical concept. That is, trust as an ethic-intensive concept and can be sustained only in an ethical environment and in such an environment, the trustor does not doubt either the competence or the intentions of the trustee. Since one knows that the trustee would not promise something s/he was not capable of delivering it. In other words, the possible vulnerability of the trustor arises only in an unethical or a legalistic environment.

On the Critical Role of Trust in a Knowledge-based Economy: Trust may be an intangible asset/good but has the most tangible role in creating and sustaining the social, economic, cultural, and political structures. It is the brick and mortar to the building of inter-personal relationships. In an industrial economy, trust (a) reduces transaction costs by reducing opportunism, enhances a feeling of wellness by reducing anxiety and (b) also might increase GDP by reducing the demand for lawyers and turning them into engineers.

Trust is one of the most valuable assets in a knowledge-based economy. Both the creation and sharing of ideas depends on trust. The distinguishing characteristic of a knowledge-based economy is a frequent sharing of tacit (embodied) knowledge and exchange of information among the knowledge workers. As soon as a person codifies one's tacit knowledge everyone has access to it. Knowing this fact, a person will share tacit knowledge only if s/he is sure of not getting fired. That is, creating ethical-based trust is the key to realizing all the potential gains from creating and sharing of knowledge.

On the Link between Ethics-deficit and Budget-deficit: At present taxpayers do not trust the government that it would spend all the tax revenue on most productive projects and government in turn does not trust the taxpayers that they would pay their fair shares. As a result, (1) there is a lot of tax evasion and (2) waste of tax revenue on less productive projects because of kickbacks and political reasons. Elimination of ethical deficit would significantly reduce the budget deficit by (1) increasing tax revenue due to increased compliance and (2) by raising income resulting from judicious spending on infrastructure. As a result, there would be less of a need to resort to deficit financing. That would lower inflation and interest rate and increase investment in the private sector. Investment in infrastructure would increase and that would raise productivity in the private sector.

On the Link between Trust-deficit and Trade-deficit: Businesses do not trust the fairness of the system and resort to all kinds of maneuvers. Restoration of trust would have a positive impact on trade-deficit by reducing under invoicing and over invoicing of international transactions and more importantly by making the economy very competitive.

Trust-deficit and Productivity: Employers might believe that the workers were shirking, and workers might believe that they are not getting their fair share. Trust-deficit results in lower productivity.

Ethical Surplus= GDP (If people were ethical) – GDP (when they are guided by self-interest). This ethical surplus in India could be in hundreds of billions and at least a $trillion for the world.

A Sample List of the Sources of Kautilya's Ethical Surplus:

1. There is no need for supervisors because employees do not steal or shirk work.
2. There is no need for Corporate Board of Directors because there are no agency costs, since ethical managers do not need any supervision, that is, they take care of the stakeholders as expected.
3. Doctors do not do any unnecessary procedures or unnecessarily prescribe opioids.
4. Bank managers do not take excessive risks with depositors' money.
5. Stock- brokers take care of the investors' interest.
6. No need to write lengthy contracts.
7. Drug companies do not push harmful medicines.
8. Public servants formulate and implement good laws and sound policies.

(C) Poor Understanding of Economic System: Adam Smith (1795, p. 66) wrote, "Systems in many respects resemble machines. A machine is a little system, created to perform, as well as to connect together, in reality, those different movements and effects which the artist has occasion for. A system is an imaginary machine invented to connect together in the fancy those different movements and effects which are already in reality performed."

For over two hundred years an economic system has been compared to a machine. Such comparison is inappropriate since parts of a machine do not negotiate with each other the terms and conditions of engagement and similarly, no part of a machine ever displays moral hazard or strategic behavior but people, who are the primary constituents of an economic system, do.

On the other hand, Kautilya believed that a kingdom or a system consisted of people (policy-makers and others) and things. Such characterization of a system allows a more meaningful analysis of systemic risk. He (p. 116) suggested to the king: "In the interests of the prosperity of the country, a king should be diligent in foreseeing the possibility of calamities, try to avert them before they arise, overcome those which happen, remove all obstructions to economic activity and prevent loss of revenue to the state (8.4)."

In sum, Kautilya's contribution is superior to that of Adam Smith in every meaningful comparison. (a) Kautilya innovated more economic concepts, (b) identified not only the sources of economic growth but unlike Adam Smith, provided a manual on engineering shared prosperity, (c) considered ethics as foundational whereas Adam Smith considered ethics as ornamental, (d) understood sharing of knowledge was power whereas Adam Smith did not and (e) the *Arthaśāstra* is more rigorous than *Wealth of Nations* (see Sihag (2014) for details). Economists will be much more satisfied with their profession if they move towards Kautilyan economics and away from Smith's economics.

III. Kautilya on Acquisition of Wisdom and Ethical Anchoring

James Halteman and Edd Noell (2012) explore Adam Smith's ideas on ethics. They (p. 76) remark, "The social passions are generosity, compassion, and esteem. They are inherently good and bring forth virtuous behavior, but they are also scarce and not prevalent enough in everyday life to serve as the foundation of a successful social order." Clearly, Smith did not have a positive view of people and did not suggest any ethical education to make them ethical. His approach essentially was legalistic and very similar to that of Han Feitzu (280–233 BCE) another thinker from ancient China.

How to make sure that every child grows-up to be a *Rajarishi*? Kautilya suggested that a child needed to be taught ethics. In a democratic system every child is a prince or princess and could become a President/Prime Minster. Kautilya (pp. 155–156) wrote, "There can be no greater crime or sin," says Kautilya, "than making wicked impressions on an innocent mind. Just as a clean object is stained with whatever is smeared on it, so a prince, with a fresh mind, understands as the truth whatever is taught to him. Therefore, a prince should be taught what is dharma and artha, not what is unrighteous and materially harmful (1.17)." He (p. 169) added,

Table 10.5 Kautilya on the link between character and behavior

Ethical (Ruler, President)	*Unethical (Ruler, President)*
Kautilya (p. 145): "A *rajarishi* [a king, wise like a sage] is one who: has self-control, having conquered the [inimical temptations] of the senses, cultivates the intellect by association with elders, is ever active in promoting the security and welfare of the people, endears himself to his people by enriching them and doing good to them and avoids daydreaming, capriciousness, falsehood, and extravagance (1.7)."He (p. 149): "In the happiness of his subjects lies his happiness; in their welfare his welfare. He shall not consider as good only that which pleases him but treat as beneficial to him whatever pleases his subjects (1.19)."He (p. 121); "The wealth of the state shall be one acquired lawfully either by inheritance or by the king's efforts (6.10)." He (p. 231) added, "Water works such as reservoirs, embankments and tanks can be privately owned, and the owner shall be free to sell or mortgage them (3.9)."He (p. 149): "Hence the king shall be ever active in the management of the economy. The root of wealth is economic activity and lack of it brings material distress. In the absence of fruitful economic activity, both current prosperity and future growth are in danger of destruction. A king can achieve the desired objectives and abundance of riches by undertaking productive economic activity (1.19)."	Kautilya (p. 133): "A decadent king, on the other hand, oppresses the people by demanding gifts, seizing what he wants and grabbing for himself and his favourites the produce of the country [i.e., the king and his coterie consume more than their due share thus considerably impoverishing the treasury and the people.] (8.4)."He (p. 159): "Ignores the good [people] and favours the wicked, causes harm by new unrighteous practices; neglects the observation of the proper and righteous practices; does what ought not to be done and fails to what ought to be done; fails to give what ought to be given and exacts what he cannot rightly take; 'indulges in wasteful expenditure and destroys profitable undertakings';does not punish those who ought to be punished but punishes those who do not deserve to be; arrests those who should not be arrested but fails to arrest who should be seized; 'fails to protect the people from thieves and robs them himself'; 'does not recompense service done to him'; 'does not carry out his part of what had been agreed upon' 'by his indolence and negligence destroys the welfare of his people' (7.5)."

"An only son, if he is wicked, shall not [under any circumstances] be installed on the throne (1.17)." He listed the behavior of an ethical and unethical ruler as follows (Table 10.5):

Kautilya (p. 144) provided a list of some of the mightiest kings, such as Ravana and Duryodhana destroyed by any one of the vices, such as lust, anger, greed, conceit, arrogance, and foolhardiness. Kautilya (p. 144) concluded, "All these, and many others, lacking self-control and falling prey to the six enemies [lust, anger, greed, conceit, arrogance, and foolhardiness] perished with their kinsmen and kingdoms. On the other hand, kings like Jamadagnya and Ambarisha, who had conquered their senses, long enjoyed their kingship on earth (1.6)."

Kautilya explains why people fall prey to these vices. He (p. 137) writes, "Vices are due to ignorance and indiscipline; an unlearned man does not perceive the injurious consequences of his vices (8.3)." He (p. 144) stated, "The sole aim of all branches of knowledge is to inculcate restraint over the senses (1.6.3). Self-control, which is the basis of knowledge and discipline, is acquired by giving up lust, anger, greed, conceit, arrogance, and foolhardiness. Living in accordance with the *shastras* means avoiding over-indulgence in all pleasures of [the senses, i.e.,] hearing, touch, sight, taste, and smell (1.6.1, 2)."

Interestingly, Kautilya put study of philosophy ahead of Dharmashastras. He wrote, "One should study philosophy because it helps one to distinguish between dharma and adharma [evil] in the study of the Vedas, between material gain and loss in the study of economics and between good and bad policies in the study of politics. [Above all,] it teaches one the distinction between good and bad use of force. When the other sciences are studied by the light of philosophy, people are benefited because their minds are kept steady in adversity and prosperity, and they are made proficient in thought, speech, and action (1.2.11)." According to Kautilya (pp. 105–106), "Philosophy is the lamp that illuminates all sciences; it provides the techniques for all action; and it is the pillar, which supports dharma (1.2.12)." (Table 10.6).

According to Kautilya, prosperity depends on education which consists of development of intellect, acquisition of wisdom, ethical anchoring, and acquisition of knowledge and information. Technically, second chapter in *The Arthaśāstra* is the first chapter since chapter one is just the list of contents. The very first chapter in the *Arthaśāstra* is on acquisition of wisdom. The second chapter is on ethical anchoring. The third chapter is on acquisition of knowledge (economics, political science). The current educational system in India has not changed since 1858. Consequently, it puts emphasis only on knowledge (skills) and information (but not on our cultural history). It lacks acquisition of wisdom and ethics.

Table 10.6 Summary of roles of information, knowledge, wisdom, and ethics

	Description	*Objective*	*By studying:*
Wisdom	Sound judgement, Foresight, far-sight, and insight	Making one proactive, pragmatic, visionary, steady in adversity and prosperity, developing intellect and ability to think	Ānvikshiki: It is more than Tarkavidya, Atmavidya, Nitisara
Ethics	Non-violence, compassion, truthfulness, tolerance, malice against none	Making society cohesive, trusting, co-operating, caring, people-centric, fair-minded	Dharmashastras
Knowledge	Skills, tools to solve problems	Making one competent to be a leader, entrepreneur, scientist	Science, Technology, Engineering and Mathematics (STEM) and Humanities, Arts and Social Sciences (HAAS)
Information	Historical information on Economic and non-economic variables	Making one proud of rich cultural heritage and a source of ideas	History of creative achievements in arts and sciences starting from Vedic times and Indus Valley Civilization

IV. Concluding Observations

Since the times of Plato and Aristotle, justice in western countries has been rudderless. There has been no realization that in the absence of trust created through ethical grounding, justice would remain arbitrary. It is a derived virtue from foundational virtues. It, at best, has worked only for a privileged segment of the population. Often color and the economic or social status of a person have played undue influences in the administration of justice.

Modern economists adopt a "calculative" approach to trust, that is, treat trust as a risk and suggest taking necessary protective measures. For example, Williamson (1985, p. 47), who received Nobel prize in economics, characterizes the potential behavior of firms as: "calculated efforts to mislead, disguise, obfuscate, or otherwise confuse" and "seeking self-interest, but they do so with guile". In the prevailing opportunistic and legalistic environment, it would be naïve or even foolish to trust anyone since that would be too risky. As a result, trust- deficit has created a "culture of suspicion."

On the other hand, Kautilya believed that ethics was essential to the administration of justice and building of trust. He wholeheartedly accepted and promoted ethical virtues. He believed that rule of law and good governance were essential to economic growth. He argued that administration of justice, which was essential to maintenance of law and order, and good governance, such as formulation and implementation of efficient and equitable economic policies depended on the ethical conduct and self-discipline of the rulers. He strongly recommended ethical anchoring and development of self-discipline over destructive vices.

Kautilya believed that a nation needed physical infrastructure, human infrastructure, and most importantly an ethical infrastructure for making every citizen's life richer and fuller. It is obvious that building the Ethical infrastructure is a prerequisite to building the human infrastructure. Ethical anchoring works like a vaccine against moral decay. It is easy to repair and replace degraded physical infrastructure, but very hard to repair the degraded ethical infrastructure.

References

Halteman, James and Edd S. Noell, *Reckoning with Markets: Moral Reflection in Economics*, Oxford University Press, 2012

Kautilya, V. (4th Century BC). *The Arthashastra*, Edited, Rearranged, Translated and Introduced by L. N. Rangarajan. Penguin Books. 1992. New Delhi, New York.

———. (4th Century BCE/2000). *Maxims of Chanakya*, Translated by V. K. Subramanian. New Delhi: Shakti Malik, Abhinav Publications.

Sihag, Balbir S. (2014), *Kautilya: The True Founder of Economics*, Vitasta Publications, New Delhi.

———. (2019), *Kautilya on Moral Hazard, Poverty and Systemic Risk*, Vitasta Publications, New Delhi.

Smith, A. (1790/1982). *The Theory of Moral Sentiments* Edited by D.D. Raphael and A.L. Macfie: Liberty Fund, Indianapolis.

———. (1795), "The History of Astronomy" in Smith, Adam, Essays on Philosophical Subjects, ed. W.P.D. Wightman, Indianapols: Liberty Fund, pp 31–105.

———. (1776/1976). *An Inquiry into the Nature and Causes of the Wealth of Nations*, Edited and with an Introduction, Notes, Marginal Summary, and Index by E. Cannan. The University of Chicago Press, Chicago.

Talreja, Kanayalal (1982), *Philosophy of Vedas*, Talreja Publication, Bombay, India.

Williamson, O. E. (1985), *The Economic Institutions of Capitalism: Firms, Markets, Rational Contracting*. London: Collier Macmillan.

PART IV

Indian Virtue Ethics for Theory Building Today

CHAPTER 11

Why Virtue Ethics Comes Closest to Indian Moral Praxis

Amita Chatterjee

It is well accepted today that ethics as a separate discipline has never been a part of Indian tradition. To be precise, in no ancient tradition, disciplinary divides were clearly demarcated. However, in India, in particular, remarked Matilal, professional philosophers did not systematically discuss the moral questions ever, though they made important contributions in logic, epistemology and metaphysics. The ancient source books of moral philosophy, *The Dharmaśāstra*-s, contain treatises on classification of virtues and vices, individual and social duties but 'morality was never discussed as such in these texts' (Matilal 2002). Moreover, no attempt was made in these texts 'for providing any theoretical foundation whatsoever' (Mohanty 2000). Consequently, we find that contemporary interpreters have attempted to understand common Indian moral concerns by imposing categories from the dominant western moral theories like consequentialism, deontology and virtue ethics. Even the same text of the Gita has been given a deontological reading by Amartya Sen (2000), liberal utilitarian interpretation by Sitansu S. Chakravarti (2006) and a hybrid of

A. Chatterjee (✉)
Jadavpur University, Kolkata, India

S. S. Chakravarti et al. (ed.), *Traditional Indian Virtue Ethics for Today*, Palgrave Studies in Comparative East-West Philosophy,
https://doi.org/10.1007/978-3-031-47972-4_11

Duty and Virtue Ethics by Bina Gupta (2006). Of course, there are scholars who think 'Dharma-Ethics is the representative of an ethical ideology and ethical practices making it a unique model by itself' (Sanyal 2016). The presuppositions, the methodology as well as the basic concepts of Indian ethics are so disparate from those of the western meta-ethical theories that, they think, it is prudent not to impose any alien framework of interpretation on it. Notwithstanding such tension in the context of interpreting Indian concept of morality, I would like to offer arguments in favour of the thesis that dharma-centric Indian morality is a kind of virtue ethics, somewhat similar to but also different from the Aristotelian and McIntyre's version of virtue ethics.

It has been unanimously admitted that the concept of '*dharma*', centring which the Indian notions of morality has been developed is not well defined at all. This multi-layered concept has many connotations. In the Mahabhārata, it has been mentioned specifically, that *'dharma'* has been understood in different sourcebooks differently; the essence of *dharma* lies hidden in a cave and hence we should conduct our lives by following the moral exemplars or one's conscience. That is why P. V. Kane (1930–1962) begins his *History of Dharmashāstra* with the comment *'Dharma* is one of those Sanskrit words that defy all attempts at an exact rendering in English or any other tongue'. Etymologically, the word means that which sustains (the world). But the word has been used to mean *ṛta* (the cosmic order), *satya* (truth), *yajṇa* (rituals/ sacrifices/ performance of desireless actions), *brahma* (the ultimate reality/ the ultimate conscious principle), duties (relative duties—related to one's caste and one's station in life or universal duties), positive and negative injunctions (*vidhi-s and niṣedha-s)* enjoined by the scriptures—heard or remembered (*Śruti*-s and *Smṛti*-s). To quote from Matilal (2002, 37), 'In various contexts, the word *dharma* may mean: law, justice, custom, morality, ethics, religion, duty, nature, or virtue'. A few pages later (p. 50), he asserts, 'By the term *dharma* ..., I understand nothing short of moral virtue, or rather, a theory of moral behaviour, as it is found implicit in India's traditional wisdom'.

From this assertion of Matilal, we cannot jump to the conclusion that *dharma-ethics* was synonymous with virtue ethics, not only because *'dharma'* has been used in different senses but also because even when *dharma* has been defined as excellence of any object, it has not been used to stand for moral excellence only. We, therefore, need to construct the case for virtue ethics rather carefully. Keeping that in mind, let me digress a bit and offer a rough account of the characteristic features of virtue ethics. Virtue ethics has been developed as an agent-oriented personal ethics as opposed to action or duty oriented theories. Deontological or consequentialist theories also talk about virtues. But in those theories, virtue plays a second fiddle to action or duties while in virtue ethics virtues occupy the most fundamental place. The development of virtue ethics has run through three different courses: (a) eudaimonistic, i.e., human-flourishing-based theories, (b) agent-based theories and (c) ethics of care (Slote 1997). According to Aristotle (1906), virtue is all about character. A virtuous man knows how to behave 'at the right times, about the right things, towards the right people, for the right end, and the right way'. It is the essence of human nature to strive to be virtuous, to attain human excellence/flourishing/well-being. A virtuous person is supposed to follow the golden mean, avoiding two extremes. For example, courage is a virtue, between the two extremes of cowardice and recklessness. Aristotle didn't mean to say that the virtue is the fixed mid-point between two extremes. The golden mean varies from situation to situation. A virtuous person attains the skill of assessing a situation through experience by honing his strength and working on his weakness. This is how a virtuous person exhibits the joint excellence of reason and character and eventually this skill becomes a way of living, quite habitual. A life well lived is a life of accomplishment and fulfilment leading to happiness (eudaimon). That is why, 'Virtue ethics', opines Michael Slote, 'is more interested in the virtuous character of virtuous individuals than in the actions of such individuals. Virtue ethics should be grounded in aretaic concepts of goodness and excellence rather than in deontic notions like "ought", "right", "wrong" or "obligatory"' (Slote (1992), *From Morality to Virtue*). Therefore, the key question that any virtue ethical theory aims to address is, 'what kind of person should I be?' (Crisp (1996), Crisp and Slote (1997)) That is, according to this theory, the main aim of an individual moral agent is to live the good life by being a specific kind of person. McIntyre also maintains that a virtue is a positive trait that makes its possessor a good human being; it is a habit of mind in harmony with reason and the order of nature. 'It grounds the question what kind of life should I lead? and immediately translates into several other questions: "what kind of character should I construct?" "What kinds of virtues should I develop?" "What sorts of vice should I avoid or eradicate?" It is important that each agent strives to achieve that aim as an individual, with only secondary regard to the community.' (Floridi 2013, 164). Thus McIntyre's conception of virtue consists of three stages, (1) the concept of a practice, (2) the narrative order of a single human life, and (3) a moral education. (McIntyre 1984)

Perrett and Pettigrove (2015) suggested three ways of understanding virtue ethics. In the strictest sense, virtue ethics stands for a set of abstract thesis about how certain concepts are best fitted together in the moral realm where the concept of virtue is theoretically the most dominant (Watson 1990), i.e., the concepts like goodness, rightness, obligation, etc., will be defined in terms of virtue. Zagzebski's theory (2004) has been cited by Perrett and Pettigrove as an instance of such an ethics, the like of which, they think, is not available in Indian philosophical systems. The second way of understanding virtue ethics is to assign a fundamental role to virtues in explaining the normativity of the elements of a given ethical framework (Perrett 2005; Pettigrove 2014). This brand of virtue ethics is weaker than the first one because here all moral concepts need not be defined in terms of virtues. Virtue ethics in the widest sense 'consists primarily in the advocacy of virtue' (Crisp 1996) and cultivating them.

The widest description of virtue ethics instantly reminds us of the Rāmāyana, the oldest epic of India. The Ramayana narrative starts thus. Debarşi Nārada approached the sage Vālmīki and asked:

> 'In all the world, I pray thee,
> Who is virtuous, heroic, true?
> Firm in his vows, of grateful mind,
> To every creature good and kind?
> Bounteous and holy, just and wise
> Alone most fair to all men's eyes?
> Devoid of envy, firm and sage,
> Whose tranquil soul ne'er yields to rage? …
> Who is the best of princes, he
> Who loves his peoples' good to see?
> The store of bliss, the living mine
> Where brightest joys and virtues shine?'
>
> The sage Vālmīki replied,
>
> 'Hermit where
> Are graces form so high and rare?
> Yet, listen and my tongue shall tell
> In whom alone these virtues dwell.
> From old 'Ikshvaku' line he came

known to the world by Rama's name.'

[*Rāmāyana of Vālmīki*, tr. Ralph. T. H. Griffith (1871)]

Rāma, the king of Ayodhyā, the eldest son of King Daśaratha, has been deified by the people of India, because he was the embodiment of all noble virtues, though we don't know whether he was a historical figure at all. Many versions of this epic are extant in different parts of South-east Asia. It is believed that the original epic was composed by the sage Vālmīki, most probably after 600 BCE. For thousands of years Indians are attempting to emulate Rāma as the ideal son and the ideal king, his queen Sitā as the ideal wife and his brother Laxmaṇa as the ideal younger brother. A land where all men are happy, where Justice and Morality prevail, is named '*Rāma-rājya*', i.e., the kingdom of Rāma, even today. The Rāmāyana narrative therefore makes a perfect proto-type of virtue ethics in the widest sense, in accordance with the characteristic features of virtue morality mentioned above.

Virtue ethicists differ among themselves regarding the issue how to define a virtue, what are to be counted as virtues and whether it is possible to identify a virtue, which remains so in all circumstances. In the Mahābhārata as well as in the Gītā we find mention of the following list and also some guidelines for identifying virtues. 'Serenity, self-control, penance, purity, patience and uprightness, wisdom, judgment and piety are natural born dispositions of a brāhmin. Heroism, vigour, firmness, skill, not fleeing in a battle, charity and leadership are the natural born disposition of a warrior. Agriculture, animal-farming and trade and commerce are natural virtues of the business community and serving the other three classes is the natural duty of (the lowest social) class called *śūdra*' (*The Gītā*, 18: 42–4). Even a cursory glance at this list of natural duties makes it obvious that actually what has been enjoined is the practice of certain virtues by a morally aspiring agent whose place in society has been determined by the scriptures and the *Dharma-śāstra*-s. The above list is of duties related to one's class and station in life. The priority of virtues become all the more evident if we consider the list of universal duties provided by Manu—patience (*dhṛti*), forgiveness (*kṣamā*), restraint (*dama*), non-stealing (*cauryābhāva*), purity (*śauca*), repression of sense-organs (*indriya-nigraha*), wisdom (*dhī*), scholarship (*vidyā*), truthfulness (*satya*), absence of anger (*akrodha*). All these are dispositions or character-traits of individual agents in accordance with which they are supposed to act appropriately in a given situation. The list of virtues varied in different sourcebooks of Indian morality, but in all it has been maintained that the practice of these virtues will lead to the prosperity both in this world (*abhyudaya*) and in the world beyond and finally to liberation (*mokṣa/ niḥśreyasa*). This shows that in the Indian tradition too virtues point to a *telos* as in the Aristotelian Virtue Ethics. In fact, life in ancient India was guided by four ends of human life (*puruṣārtha*-s), viz., *artha* (wealth), *kāma* (sensuous pleasure) *dharma* (moral excellence) and *mokṣa* (freedom from the cycle of life and death). In liberation one realizes one's true nature. The Upaniṣad-s succinctly say that in liberation one not only knows the ultimate reality but becomes identical with the ultimate reality or Brahman which is of the nature of *sat* (existence), *cit* (consciousness) *and ānanda* (bliss). Thus it is transparent that in the Indian tradition, emphasis had always been on 'being something' than on 'doing something', though Indian philosophers did not always agree on the nature of the final end.

The second variety of virtue ethics, where virtues are taken to explain the normative character of the Indian ethical framework, may be traced to the Yoga philosophy, maintain Perrett and Pettigrove. Bilimoria (2014) too upholds that the *Yoga-Śramaṇa* tradition is the common fount of Indian virtue theories propounded in both orthodox and heterodox systems including Buddhism and Jainism. Five virtues, which have been identified as seminal in *Yoga-Sūtra-Bhāṣya* are: *Ahimsā* (non-violence), *Satya* (truthfulness), *Asteya* (non-stealing), *Brahmacarya* (celibacy in thought, word and deed), *Aparigraha* (non-covetousness). Of these five, non-violence is considered the principal virtue, the rest are subsidiary to it in the sense that the rest of the virtues merely unfold the essence of non-violence.

> Abstinence from injury (*ahimsā*) means the abstinence from malice towards all living creatures in every way and at all times. And the other abstentions (*yama*) and observations (*niyama*) are rooted in it. In so far as their aim is the perfection of it, they are taught in order to teach it. (*Yogabhāṣya*:178, tr. Woods 1927)

That is, if non-violence is inculcated, then all other virtues would be taken care of, since other virtues mentioned above are also meant to prevent some kind of violence/exploitation. A self-disciplined, non-selfish person can be truly non-violent because often violence is unleashed on the pretext of self-defence and protecting self-interest. Non-violence thus constitutes the core of Indian virtue ethics. Non-violence does not only signify non-killing or non-injury. It is an inner feeling of mind and heart. It means 'the largest love and greatest charity' (Gandhi 1983). It is a dynamic living force, a noble disposition, an instrument in the struggle for freedom and justice. The Buddhists and the Jaina-s preached and practiced these five moral virtues in the form of five precepts. Each precept enjoins a particular form of self-control, which promotes a noble virtue and avoids the correlative anti-virtue. The first precept exhorts to control violence and anger, the second cowardice and malevolence which generally leads to untruthfulness, the third craving for material possession, the fourth the lust for flesh, and the fifth greed including the desire for unwholesome excitement. The practice of these five precepts promotes the virtues of compassion, truthfulness, generosity, contentment, non-attachment and clarity of thought respectively. Practicing these virtues constitutes a necessary step to attaining liberation, the highest end or the *summum bonum* of human life.

Vātsyāyana in the *Nyāya-bhaṣya* proposed a thorough classification of virtues and vices, later endorsed also by Jayanta Bhaṭṭa in the Nyāya-manjarī, mainly under three heads: (a) the virtues of the body (*śarīra*), (b) the virtues of speech (*vāk*) and (c) the virtues of the mind (*manas*). The virtues of the body comprise of charity (*dāna*), succouring the distressed (*paritrāna*), social service (*paricaraṇṇa*) whereas the corresponding vices are theft (*caurya*), cruelty (*hiṃsā*) and forbidden sexual indulgence (*pratiṣiddha maithuna*); the virtues of speech consist of veracity (*satya*), beneficial speech (*hita-vacana)*, gentle speech (*priya-vacana*) and self-study of scriptures (*svādhyāya*) while the correlative vices are mendacity (*mithyā*), asperity (paruṣa), calumny (*sūcanā*) and gossip (*asambandha*); the virtues of mind include benevolence/kindness (*dayā*), detachment (*aspṛhā*) and reverence (*śraddhā*), the opposite anti-virtues being malevolence (*paradroha*), coveting what belongs to another (*paradravya-abhīpsā*) and irreverence/ lack of faith in the scriptures (*nāstikya*). S. K. Maitra (1963, 209) observed in this context that the opposition between social service and forbidden sexuality is not at all obvious. He conjectured that just as social service consists in doing good to society, so forbidden sexuality rends the social fabric by loosening the bond and weakening the stock. These enlisted virtues and vices are all temperamental traits some of which need not be manifested through specific overt acts, e.g., the virtue of kindness may remain non-manifest merely as a disposition but the virtue of social service becomes meaningless if never practiced. Another remarkable feature of these listed virtues is that these constitute the fabric of situational morality, not to be indulged in all circumstances. One may have to refrain from the practice of a noble virtue like truth-telling in circumstances where 'truth is falsehood and falsehood is truth', e.g., where life of a person is at risk (the Mahābhārata, *anuśāsana parva,* chapter 109). It is assumed that 'the ultimate purpose of speech was the good (*hita*) of the mankind and therefore if a rigid adherence to truth was likely to do more harm than good, the evil should be avoided by a lie, if necessary' (Maitra 1963, 210). It appears that this list presents a good mix of self-regarding and other-regarding virtues. These virtues are not innate but have to be cultivated through effort, practice and good intention, if one aims to attain absolute freedom from suffering and autonomy of the Self.

In Vedānta philosophy too, a path of self-transformation leading to liberation through attainment of self-knowledge presupposes the practice of certain virtues and avoidance of certain vices. The four virtues that are said to be pre-requisites of self-knowledge are: (a) *nityānityavastu-viveka* (ability to discriminate between eternal and non-eternal objects), (b) *ihāmutrārtha-phala-bhoga-virāga* (detachment from the enjoyment of fruits of one's actions here or in the other world), (c) *śamadamādi-sādhana-sampad* (cultivation of the virtues of peace of mind resulting from toleration, forbearance and endurance, self-control leading to a life of temperance and moderation), and (d) *mumukṣatva* (aspiration for liberation). One who successfully pursues such virtues sees the Self or Brahman, by becoming calm, subdued, satisfied, patient and collected. Indian virtue ethics thus prescribes a route from our existing state to the state where we ought to be. This reminds one of McIntyre's identification of 'the general form of the moral scheme' which involves highlighting a 'contrast between man-as-he happens to be and man-as-he-could-be-if–he-realized-his-essential-nature [and where] ethics is the science which is to enable man to understand how they make the transition from the former state to the latter' (McIntyre 1984, 52).

Following Slote (2001, 5), Perrett characterizes the yoga approach to virtue ethics as an agent-based approach as opposed to an agent-focused approach. An agent-based approach makes the evaluation of all admirable, virtuous or right actions dependent on the qualities of the agent who performed them. In an agent-focused approach, on the other hand, the evaluation of the excellent, the admirable or the virtuous is in some sense independent of the evaluation of the agent and her qualities. In Indian ethical scenario since act-evaluation depends on agent-evaluation, Perrett thinks, it fulfils the condition of an agent-based ethics.

Though the account of Indian ethics usually remains confined to moral philosophy as propounded in six orthodox and three heterodox systems of Indian philosophy, we shall be able to trace the rudiments of virtue morality even in the tenets of Islam (Appyagil 2014) and Sikhism, two other major religions practiced by sections of Indian people. In Islam too, virtue ethics is looked upon as a pursuit of the perfection of character or self-perfection. The Quran and Hadith endorse many virtues or good character traits, e.g., kindness to people and animals, charity, forgiveness, honesty, patience, justice, respecting parents and elders, keeping promises, controlling one's anger, etc. Miskawayh (932–1030 CE) identified wisdom, courage, chastity and justice as the four cardinal virtues prescribed in Islam, the opposite of which, viz., ignorance, cowardice, gluttony and lust, and injustice and tyranny were branded as vices. Following the Aristotelian tradition, Islamic ethicists of the medieval period analysed three faculties of the soul: intellectual, irascible and appetitive. The virtue in the intellectual faculty is said to be wisdom (*hikma*), comprising of the knowledge of the nature or dispositions of things, and who possesses such knowledge is called the wise man (*hakim*). The virtue in the irascible faculty is courage with its sub-virtues, viz., magnanimity, patience and compassion. The virtue in the appetitive faculty is temperance and its sub-varieties are moderation, tranquillity and contentment. Justice is a virtue of the soul, which arises from the three faculties acting in harmony with one another. The sub-virtues of Justice are: true love and friendship, consensus and union that help the management of livelihood. In fact, justice ranks as the noblest of virtues next to belief in God and the truth of the Prophet in Islam. It is also considered the strongest justification of man's stewardship of earth. The Quranic injunction of fairness is equally applicable globally to all people irrespective of caste, creed and colour.

Like all other religions, Sikhism also emphasizes the congruence between spiritual development and everyday moral conduct. According to Guru Nanak, 'Truth is the highest virtue but higher still is the truthful living'. The five virtues extolled in Sikhism are *sat* (truth), *dayā* (compassion), *santokh* (contentment), *nimratā* (humility) and *pyaar* (love).

An objection may be anticipated at this point. We have mentioned in the beginning that virtue ethics have been developed as agent-oriented ethics as opposed to duty-oriented ethics. But there has been a long tradition in both the Mīmāṃsā schools (the Bhāṭṭa and the Prābhākara) to define virtues and anti-virtues in terms of scriptural injunctions and prohibitions—compulsory and optional. Not only that, in Indian philosophical literature we come across imperatives (both positive and negative) for action corresponding to most virtues listed above. How could we then claim that Indian ethics is a kind of virtue ethics? In response it may be said that in virtue ethics too there is involvement of action. McIntyre did state clearly that just as one who wants to become a good violinist need to practice regularly following the instructions of his trainer, or one who wants to be a master of chess need to follow rules of the game meticulously, similarly, we maintain that one who wants to attain heaven or absolute freedom from suffering must habituate oneself to become generous, courageous, wise, truthful, compassionate and so on, following scriptural injunctions and prohibitions. The difference lies in focusing on concepts of virtue and vice rather than on concept of obligation. Thus being truthful is not exhausted by fulfilling promises when occasion arises but is to be viewed as a state of character that ought to be cultivated. Following scriptural injunctions one may gain external goods like money, power, fame, happiness in heaven, but the emphasis has been on achieving goods internal to the practices. To quote from Bina Gupta (2006), 'The concept of a practice in virtue ethics is concerned with the good of the whole of human life … They also help us in overcoming harmful temptations, and in doing so contribute to our self-knowledge and steer us in the relevant kind of quest for the good'. So the Mīmāŋsā emphasis on the concept of duty and discussions on springs of action do not go against the spirit of Virtue Ethics. By supporting this stance, I hope to show that the concept of morality that we learn from the Gītā is undoubtedly a brand of virtue ethics.

Many modern interpreters of the Gītā think that its underlying ethics is deontological because in the opening chapter of the text, Arjuna, the great warrior and who is taken to represent the view of common man, standing in the middle of the battle-field, told his friend and charioteer Lord Krishna, the God Incarnate, that he was grief-laden and horror-struck realizing that he would have to participate in the act of killing, shedding the blood of his own kinsmen and near and dear ones. His mind was groping in darkness and could not see where his duties lied. In response, Lord Krishna explained to him wherein lied his duty both from an absolute and from a relative standpoint. Krishna re-iterated that Arjuna should not give up fighting because in the absolute sense all talk of killing and being killed is meaningless. Atman alone is real and body is an appearance and 'Atman cannot be slain or be the slayer. Atman is unborn, undying, never ceasing, never beginning,; it is death-less, birth-less and unchanging forever; it is not wounded by weapons, not burned by fire, not dried by the wind, not wetted by water'. So Arjuna would not kill anyone; it only seems that he would kill; so he should never mourn for anyone. Relatively speaking, fighting is the caste-duty of a warrior so he ought not hesitate to fight. For, to a warrior there is nothing nobler than to fight in a righteous war. If, on the other hand, Arjuna refused to fight for a just cause, he would be violating his duty as one belonging to the warrior caste and he would be branded as a sinner and disgraced. Not only that, his spiritual growth would be impeded, since duties of an individual had been prescribed according to his capacities, his natural propensities, the stage of spiritual advancement he is in and his current situation. One was not allowed to assume one's duties arbitrarily because that would inevitably result in mental confusion. Hence Krishna advised, 'Prefer to die doing your own duty. The duty of another would lead you to great spiritual danger'. He further said, 'If, in your vanity, you say, "I will not fight", your resolve is vain. Your nature will drive you to the act'. Arjuna, therefore, should perform his duty, take up his bow and arrows and participate in the just war. But his duty, he must perform for the sake of duty alone, and never desire for the fruits of his action. This being the central teaching of the Gītā, why should one not consider its underlying ethics as de-ontological?

The briefest possible answer to this question is: performance of one's duties for the sake of duty is not the highest end of life. One's sense of duty, performance of all actions are geared to only one goal and that is to know the Indwelling Soul, and go beyond the wheel of rebirth and death. One can reach this goal only by being a particular kind of person and possessing certain virtues. In fact, in the Gītā, Lord Krishna in his discourse mentioned a large number of virtues. Gupta (2006) has given a list of 32 virtues which we come across in different chapters of the *Gītā*, viz., fearlessness, sincerity, non-violence, amity, modesty, non-hatred, non-anger, freedom from greed, humility, absence of fault finding, uprightness, simplicity, abstinence, self-control, charity, forgiveness, patience, compassion, friendship, gentleness, equanimity, peace, truthfulness, purity, heroism, determination, reverence, penance, vigour, endurance, detachment, humility and restraint. Vices are hypocrisy, arrogance, vanity, anger, harshness which have been finally reduced to three primary ones, viz., desire (*kāma*), anger (krodha) and greed (*lobha*) which lead to three-fold gates of hell. Apparently, some of these virtues need to be cultivated for self-improvement and some are directed towards the benefit of others or society as a whole. In the ultimate analysis, one can find that cultivation of all these virtues contribute to harmonious living in this world and final release from the empirical world of life and death. That is achievable through self-knowledge, which is nothing but unitive knowledge of the Godhead leading to eternal life and beatitude.

The duty of an individual, according to the Gītā is determined by one's nature or *svabhāva*, which is constituted of three *guṇa*-s -- *sattva*, *rajas* and *tamas*. These three guṇas combine in different proportions depending on the past actions of an individual and bind him to the world. Of *sattva,* knowledge is born; of *rajas* the greed; *tamas* brings forth bewilderment, delusion and darkness. It is further stated, 'abiding in *sattva* man goes to higher realms; remaining in *rajas*, he remains in this world; sunk in *tamas*, his lowest nature, he sinks to the underworld. Though *sattva* can show the Atman by its pure light, it still binds the individual through search for happiness and longing for knowledge'. So one should attempt to go beyond the realm of these three *guṇa*-s even transcend *sattva* by practising virtues, performing one's duties with non-attachment to go beyond birth and death, pain and decay and become immortal.

Another interesting feature that becomes transparent from the said discourse is, amidst all these virtues *samatvam* (equanimity) or a balanced attitude has been identified as the master-virtue or the key-virtue. We have seen that in other prominent lists of virtues available in different sourcebooks of the Hindu morality and philosophical systems, *ahimsā* or non-violence has been given the highest place. But true to the narrative of the Mahābhārata, Lord Krishna upheld that taking up arms against enemy (*himsā*) is not only justified but also is a duty of a warrior for the right cause, when all other means of peaceful intervention fail. Hence though *ahimsā* and its correlates like amity, non-hatred, non-anger, charity, compassion, gentleness, etc. have been enumerated as virtues repeatedly, the Gītā does not preach unconditional non-violence as the highest virtue. However, even when one indulges in violence of some form by way of performing his/her duty, one must perform with the right attitude and in the right spirit of disinterest, being established in the intellect (*buddhi-yukta*), i.e., renouncing both good and evil, treating alike pleasure and pain, gain and loss, success and defeat. Krishna praised this evenness of character (*samatvam*), equanimity in thought and action without being affected by the changing emotions all through the Gītā. In the fifth chapter Krishna further elaborates on this virtue of evenness when he said, 'A wise man sees with an equal eye a priest, a cow, an elephant, a dog or an outcaste. One who masters evenness can overcome all obstacles in this world. The Infinite Indwelling Spirit is without any flaws and is the same in all human beings and one who attains evenness is established in the Infinite Spirit'.

Samatvam is the basis of all three yogas—*Jnāna,bhakti and karma*- the ways knowledge, devotion and selfless action to liberation. It is a virtue of the mind and also the golden mean between the extremes of asceticism and self-discipline. We re-iterate that this virtue of evenness of mind or *samatvam* plays the same role in the moral system of the Bhagavad-Gītā as the virtue of non-violence or Ahimsa plays in other systems of philosophy. 'A person who cultivates *samatvam* also masters other virtues, such as endurance, courage and wisdom', (Gupta 2006). Hence Virtue Ethics of the Gītā also falls in the second category according to the classification given by Perrett and Pettigrove. This virtue of *samatvam* has percolated to the people of India though the ages, help them ignore seemingly intolerable contradictions. In the language of C.G. Jung (1964) 'The Indian does not fish out infinitesimal details from the universe. His ambition is to have a vision of the whole'. Some have objected that since the Indian mind strives to go beyond good and evil, it lacks a clear-cut criterion to distinguish between good and evil, right and wrong. As a result, moral excellence falls by the wayside when one is at the thresh-hold of attaining the summum bonum of human life, i.e., self-realization or 'realization of the divinity already existing in man'. But this is a misconceived idea because no one can attain the highest end of human life without going through the strict moral discipline. Hence moral excellence has never been ignored in practice and theory even at the highest level of meditation. Even to go beyond good and evil, one must possess the discriminatory knowledge between moral and immoral and follow the moral path as long as one is in this empirical world. A wise person's behaviour is morally impeccable. He behaves morally without prompting; moral virtues become a part of his nature. So, in sum, it may be said that the unique feature of Indian morality reveals the fact that what all moral philosophers and common men, scientists and activists of India are continually trying to find an answer to is the eternal query: 'What am I?' This is also the quest of Virtue Ethics as a constituent of perennial philosophy.

References

Appyagil, R. (2014). "Virtue in Islam" in *The Handbook of Virtue Ethics,* ed. Stan van Hooft, Acumen, U.S.A. pp. 318-326.

Aristotle (1906) *Nichomachean Ethics*, Tr. J.E.C. Welldon, Mcmillan, New York.

Bilimoria, Purushottama (2014) "Ethics and Virtue in Classical Indian Thinking", *The Handbook of Virtue Ethics,* Stan van Hooft (ed.) Acumen, Durham. pp. 294–305.

Chakravarti, Sitansu S. (2006). *Ethics in the Mahabharata: A Philosophical Inquiry for Today*, Munshiram Manoharlal Publishers Pvt. Ltd., New Delhi.

Crisp, R. (1996). "Modern Moral Philosophy and the Virtues" in R. Crissp (ed,) *How Should one Live? Essays on the Virtues,* Oxford University Press, Oxford.

Crisp, Roger and Michael Slote, eds. (1997), *Virtue Ethics,* Oxford University Press, New York.

Floridi L. (2013). *The Ethics of information*, Oxford University Press, Oxford.

Gandhi, M. K. (1983). *Gandhi: An Autobiography*, Beacon Press, Boston, MA.

Gupta, Bina (2006). "Bhagavad-Gītā as Duty and Virtue Ethics: Some Reflections", *Journal of Religious Ethics,* Wiley, pp. 373–95.

Jung C.G. (1964). "What India can Teach Us?" Originally published in English in *Asia*, New York, 1939, included in *Civilization in Transition*, *The Collected Works of C.G. Jung,* vol.10, tr. R.F.C. Hull, Princeton University Press, Princeton.

Kane P.V. (1930–1962). *History of Dharmashastra* in 10 volumes, Bhandarkar Oriental Research Institute, Pune.

Maitra S. K. (1963). *The Ethics of the Hindus,* 3rd edition, University of Calcutta, Calcutta.

Matilal, B.K. (2002). "Dharma and Rationality", *Ethics and Epics: The Collected Essays of Bimal Krishna Matilal,* vol.2, ed. Jonardon Ganeri, Oxford University Press, New Delhi.

McIntyre, Alasdyre (1984). *After Virtue,* University of Notre Dame Presss, Notredame, Ind.

Mohanty, J.N. (2000). *Classical Indian Philossophy*, Rowman & Littlefield, Maryland, USA.

Perrett, R. (2005). "Hindu Ethics?" in W. Schweiker (ed.) *The Blackwell Companion to Religious Ethics,* Blackwell: Oxford.

Pettigrove, G. (2014). "Virtue Ethics, Virtue Theory and Moral Theology" in Stan van Hooft (ed.) *The Handbook of Virtue Ethics,* Acumen, Durham.

Perrett, Roy W. & Pettigrove, Glen (2015). "Hindu Virtue Ethics", *The Routledge Companion to Virtue Ethics*, eds. M. Slote & L. Besser-Jones, New York.

Sanyal, Indrani (2016). *Through The Lens of Dharma-Ethics*, Jadavpur Studies in Philosophy, Suryodaya Books, New Delhi.

Sen, Amartya (2000). 'Consequential Evolution and Practical Reason', *The Journal of Philosophy*, Vol. XCVII, No. 9., New York, USA.

Slote, M. (1992). *From Morality to Virtue*, Oxford University Press, USA.

———. (1997). *Three Methods of Ethics* eds M. Baron, P. Pettit and M. Slote, Blackwell: Oxford.

———. (2001). *Morals from Motives*, Oxford University Press, Oxford, MA.

Valmiki, *The Ramayana of Valmiki*, tr. into English by Griffith Ralph T.H. (1871), Trubner and Co., London.

Watson, G. (1990)."On the Primacy of Character in O. Flanagan and A. Rorty (eds), *Identity, Character and Morality: Essays in Moral Psychology*. M.I.T. Press, Cambridge, MA.

Woods, J. (1927). *The Yoga System of Patanjali, 2nd edition*, Harvard University Press, Cambridge, MA, USA.

Zagzebski, L. (2004). *Divine Motivation Theory*, Cambridge University Press, Cambridge, U.K.

CHAPTER 12

Environmental Virtue Ethics: A Traditional Indian Perspective on Hursthouse's Quest

Sitansu S. Chakravarti

Earlier versions of the paper were delivered at New College, University of Toronto (in sessions arranged by June Larkin, Vice Principal), and at the department of Philosophy, Jadavpur University, Kolkata, India. I am especially thankful to Rosalind, Hursthouse for the many comments on the earlier versions sent to her; words of encouragement received from her are gratefully acknowledged. I am indebted to Sarnath Basu for philosophical help relating to the Gita, Bhagavad Gītā, and Sri Aurobindo's interpretations on the Gita, Bhagavad Gītā. I am thankful to my son Ananda for giving me the opportunity to discuss the contents of the paper, and the editing comments received from him over time. I thank Amita Chatterjee for having a look at the paper in the midst of all her preoccupations.

S. S. Chakravarti (✉)
New College, University of Toronto, Toronto, ON, Canada

S. S. Chakravarti et al. (ed.), *Traditional Indian Virtue Ethics for Today*, Palgrave Studies in Comparative East-West Philosophy,
https://doi.org/10.1007/978-3-031-47972-4_12

Introduction

In her thorough exploratory article 'Environmental Virtue Ethics',[1] Rosalind Hursthouse chalks out a blueprint for viable future work in the area promising true allegiance to the spirit of ethics. She looks for an accepted virtue, or virtues, which, 'given a new interpretation', (p. 155) are expected to act as foundation for the extended task at hand of building this fairly new branch of ethics alongside the traditional human centred kind in existence where human interactions are the subject of study. Concurrently, she keeps her eyes open for any new virtues, outside of the ones traditionally in use in virtue ethics, which might be found suitable exclusively for the purpose of building environmental ethics in case the existing ones fail in the task. She considers the relevance of 'the old virtues of prudence, practical wisdom, compassion and proper humility' (158) in this venture, while alerting us to the analytical consequences that the corresponding 'old vices of greed, self-indulgence, short-sightedness, cruelty, pride, vanity, dishonesty, and arrogance' lead on to. She, however, hastens to point out that the aforesaid virtues may not count as decisive toward building an environmental virtue ethics we want, free of the charge of being human centric (158–9). As for the possible new virtues, Hursthouse proposes two for consideration. The first one she indicates is connected to the healthy emotion, *wonder*, while she cannot come up with a name in the abstract noun form for it. She has an apprehension, though, that the virtue may not be adequate for environmental ethics as the emotion of wonder is not exclusively directed to nature, thus possibly potent with seeds of human centricity. The second one in her list is 'respect for nature', or rather 'being rightly oriented to nature', as she prefers to call it. Attractive as the new virtues are, they need to be clearly chalked out in concrete, non-question-begging terms, on top of being not human centric. Certainly, no philosophical grounding can be secured, to our satisfaction, in the area of environmental virtue ethics, she cautions, so long as a virtue that is expected to provide the basis for the right explanation is missing. Such a failure in the quest for the right kind of virtue or virtues indeed falls in line with failures in attempts at doing environmental ethics outside of the area of virtue ethics in so far as such attempts simply end up in issuance of 'some fairly obvious prohibitions against wanton, gratuitous, selfish, materialistic, and short-sighted consumption, harm,

[1] Hursthouse 2007, pp. 155–71.

destruction and despoliation' (167). Success in the area, it appears, might have practical relevance as well, on top of the theoretical, for in providing the reasons for right actions, vis-à-vis the wrong ones, the ground is laid for inculcating a virtue that motivates the agent toward initiating appropriate actions on her journey to flourishing or living well.

A Virtue from the Indic Tradition

In this essay I propose to posit a non-conventional virtue for consideration along the line Hursthouse has drawn for us in her paper. This, to my mind, will not only lay the foundation for environmental ethics from the virtue ethical perspective, but also for ethics as such, in conformity with the expectation Hursthouse expresses at the beginning of her article:

> …it may well be that if we could find a way of releasing many human beings from the grip of [the] familiar vices, the change in our current ways of going on would be so extraordinarily radical that it would indeed adequately set the scene for all the changes the environmentalists dream of. After all, no one suggests that we need a new ethic to deal with the human-centred moral problems of poverty, war, and, quite generally, 'man's inhumanity to man'. We suppose if (and what a big 'if') we could somehow induce many more of ourselves to be truly compassionate, benevolent, unselfish, honest, unmaterialistic, long-sighted, just, patient—virtuous, in familiar ways, in short—the way human beings live would be radically different, and the entirely human-centred moral problems that our own vices create would become things of the past. And if these hitherto intractable human-centred ones, why not the environmental ones as well? (157)

Thus we would not be in need of separate virtues to account for the different areas of ethics, while one single virtue covers all areas. The advantage in the virtue ethical treatment of environmental ethics, we hope to see, lies in providing the needed philosophical explanations, thus paving the ground for instilling the relevant virtue in individuals in society, starting from childhood, not through imposition, but internalization instead, ensuring thereby that the society is rightly tuned ethically, in contrast to the prevailing situation today. The virtue I am going to propose here is not Aristotelian; in fact, it comes from a tradition outside the western, though not culture-specific per se on that count, as the Aristotelian virtues are not specific to the ancient Greek culture. The virtue is ***harmony within***. We will see how the virtue provides the needed foundation in the human centric area of ethics relating to justice and care in society, while at the same time helps us build environmental ethics on its basis.

Harmony and Ethics

The expression 'harmony' has two senses: (1) The first refers to a harmonious state that obtains on its own out there, or is brought about on the basis of actions undertaken. The harmony one finds present in nature is of the former kind. Human intervention toward mass exploitation of nature eats into it and ecological imbalance results. Those who believe in Gandhian socialism think that the societal harmony it aims at is to be brought about by human involvement the right way. (2) The other sense pertains to an attitude, to wit, a disposition (courage is a mental disposition), typically a character state, which again one can work on toward its furtherance, as one can on courage. Gandhian socialism is dependent on building this harmonious state within, on the basis of which one would be motivated toward proper actions leading to the goal of building a harmonious society. *Harmony within* is a disposition that inspires to build harmony around, resulting in doing good to others as well as contributing to ecological harmony. Here harmony is not just balance or equilibrium; like harmony in music, it is creative in its aesthetic mode present in the ethical dimension, and is pleasing overall,—certainly not binding or depriving, either to oneself or to the other. Thus, harmony is not simply self-control that Aristotle talks about as a measure against self-indulgence or intemperance, but adds a meaning to the onward flow of life. Harmony in this second sense is a virtue.

The virtue *harmony within* is a character state that equips, and prompts, the possessor of the virtue to furtherance of harmony within and without, a process accompanied by a sustaining, unconditional joy manifest even in the midst of failures and the many challenges on the way,—an intrinsic value, which an individual intends to share with others. The more one approximates the limiting concept of perfect harmony within, the more is one away from greed and possessiveness, along with the other vices, viz., self-indulgence, short-sightedness, cruelty, pride, vanity, dishonesty, and arrogance, as enumerated by Hursthouse, absence of which is a necessary, and perhaps sufficient condition indeed for maintenance and furtherance of the inner, as well as the outer harmony.

We humans do cause harm to ecology short of the inner harmony. A society that promotes cultivation of this virtue paves the way to ending human exploitation associated with the vices mentioned, severally or in combination. Retributive measures embedded in the legal system by themselves have been seen to have failed to lead to the goal expected. This is demonstrated in recent history by the Wall Street crisis taking place on the heels of the Enron scandal while no effective, real solution is in sight relating to greed-management in spite of the legal checks and balances put in place to correct the wrongs.[2] It might be relevant in this connection to bring to mind the spate of bullying lately at schools in North America leading often to deaths, of mindless mass-killings opening random fire at public places, in astoundingly quick succession of repeats of similar events, and the abundance of other forms of violence in society, including the sexual, in spite of the legal deterrence in operation. The legal system, on its own, simply fails to ensure that people are happy, contented and in peace, so that the irresistible inclination to indulge in violent overtures, arising out of a deep-rooted discontent and unhappiness do not get to a widespread, if not epidemic proportion in society, as many observe, has happened today. A pandemic opioid crisis, rooted in societal boredom leading to depression, alongside other maladies mentioned above, highlights the need for ethico-spiritual solutions when traditional measures fail. Here comes the need to cultivate the virtue *harmony within* following the spirit of virtue ethics. To sum up the ideas above, I gratefully borrow the words Hursthouse used as she summarized my position in her email correspondence on a very early version of this paper:

> Harmony has a threefold aspect: (a) the *harmony within*, which is the virtue leading to the wellbeing of the agent herself; (b) the harmony amongst human beings—in one's own society and the whole social world—that the virtue is meant to, and helps promote; and (c) the harmony of the individual and every society with the natural world, which we delight in and promote on the basis of the virtue.

The primary source of satisfaction in life for the one, who has imbibed the virtue *harmony within* to an extent, lies within, in the virtue itself, and not in extraction of satisfaction from sources outside oneself. The virtue stands for an intrinsic value in life providing satisfaction in joy in the phenomenological state of contentedness around harmony, in contrast with

[2] Cf, 'Ethical Message of the Mahabharata in the Wake of the Global Financial Crisis' in Part III of this anthology.

harping on conditional enjoyment randomly derived from enjoyment of the senses leading on its way to a state of depression in the individual and the society. With the virtue *harmony within*, or *inner harmony* in place, accommodating a meaning of life that is inclusive, the animate as well as the inanimate entities around are not looked upon as means only to the individual's, or at best to humanity's, goals set apart in isolation. With the virtue in place, in other words, people may not be ready to look for substituting the satisfaction they find in it with that originating outside. There is, however, a continuous flow between the inner and the outer, so that no watertight dichotomy holds between the two.

Enjoyment of the state of harmony in the peace of contentedness is a prominent ingredient of the wellbeing of the individual while no incongruity holds with the wellbeing of others around, as we spell out the logic of *harmony within* with *intentionality* built into it. It is not only the case that the wellbeing of the individual leads on to the wellbeing of others, and vice versa, but others' wellbeing is a part and parcel of the individual's, as harmony manifests itself only in an inclusive atmosphere where others have not been left out. We will deal with this in some detail later in the following section. A feeling of wellbeing, as relating to having been considerably established in *harmony within*, is not a mirror image of the feeling associated with the wellbeing in having a good health in so far as the latter is individual centric, while the former accommodates all in its domain following the logic of inclusiveness imbedded in *harmony within*. If the people in charge of the society make room for *harmony within* at the macro level of social planning, they would be preparing for the virtue to take shape at the individual level, making room for the individuals to grow into happy, mature and truly autonomous beings, shunning slavery to the goal of sense satisfaction exploited by today's business world to its own narrow and self-defeating ends. As individuals in society get the opportunity and encouragement for developing *harmony within*, the foundation is set for a strong platform for social harmony. The first requisite for the administrators, and academics in a society, is to be aware of the importance and significance of the virtue *harmony within* in the life of an individual as well as the society she is a part of.

Inner harmony for a person means harmony achieved at the cognitive, affective and conative levels. Her cognitive world is harmoniously arranged as she keeps her mind open to new horizons; she has affective harmony within that manifests itself in the expression of dignity in relating to animate and inanimate objects, and forbids eccentricities as inner peace and joy prevail, even in the midst of challenging circumstances. The actions she performs hold together in a harmonious way, too, without being incongruous, haphazard, or the least absurd and exclusive,[3] while she is involved in helping ameliorate disharmony around,[4] according to capacity and inclination. There is a concurrent harmony holding here across the board combining all the three levels, so that if harmony is found missing anywhere around (cognitive level), the situation affects the person (affective level), triggering her thought process (cognitive level), which may lead to a suitable action befitting the situation (conative level).[5] Although she attempts to ensure that harmony is maintained within and without, she does not lose her cool if the actions planned fail to lead to the desired consequences; neither is she off her balance in a fit of ecstasy if they do lead her on.[6] The meaning of life based on *harmony within*, which is 'intentional' in character, prompts one to look for harmony all the way, and help maintain, and build it if found missing by any chance, not just because it 'is the best policy'(160), but for some deeper existential reason. It is but natural that one established to an extent in inner harmony is sensitive to the harmony, or lack of it, within or around. Harmony for such a person spills over beyond the possessor of the virtue, crossing the narrow bound of the limited self, which ceases to posit a limit to the operation of harmony crossing the narrow limits of the possessor. Such a person is as much observant of things out there as she is self-critical. Thus, a person embedded in the virtue *harmony within* not only does not feel prone to building satisfaction upon exploitation of fellow beings, with cruelty meted out while vanity reigns supreme, as dishonesty and short-sightedness, resting on self-indulgence, find expression in arrogance; she looks forward to doing good to others, including non-humans, and taking care of the inanimate world with a feeling of affection and respect.[7] She relates to the environment around with a feeling of humility and honour arising out of an affectionate bond. It is possible to translate the ways of

[3] A person in a state of harmony is not hateful of the vicious people, or even of vice itself, in as much as she transcends the level of vice, in a harmonious way, and sees, with equanimity, its presence in society.

[4] Gita, 5/25, 12/4 'sarva-bhuta-hite ratah. (Engaged in doing good to all beings).

[5] Cf, 'All these apparently disparate elements can form a unity in human nature; that is, they can be recognized as a way a human being, given human psychology, could be'. (Hursthouse 2007, p. 160).

[6] The Gita, 2/56, 57.

[7] The Gita, 5/25, 12/4 (See Footnote 5 for more details.)

harmony for the sake of children, for educational purposes, fulfilling an important requirement condition pointed out by Hursthouse for a viable environmental virtue ethics (160–1). Here are a few lines from Tagore that leave an overall impression of the state of *harmony within* as taking shape in society:

> Where the mind is without fear and the head is held high;
> Where knowledge is free;
> Where the world has not been broken up into fragments
> by narrow domestic walls;
> Where words come out from the depth of truth;
> Where tireless striving stretches its arms towards perfection;
> Where the clear stream of reason has not lost its way
> into the dreary desert sand of dead habit;
> Where the mind is led forward by thee
> into ever-widening thought and action—
> Into that heaven of freedom, my Father, let my country awake.
> —Tagore, *Gitanjali (Song Offerings)*

The concept of wellness centring around *harmony within* is not human centric, for it connects wellness of all around—humans, animate beings as well as inanimate objects via the *intentionality* pertaining to the virtue *harmony within*.

More on *Harmony Within*: A Philosophical Look Into the Gita

The above considerations bring into focus what the states of being unmaterialistic, unselfish, honest, compassionate, benevolent, long-sighted, just and patient (157) that Hursthouse eloquently praises, analytically amount to for us in terms of their grounding in the anchor virtue *harmony within*. The vices that Hursthouse mentions in her list, viz., greed, self-indulgence, short-sightedness, cruelty, pride, vanity, dishonesty and arrogance are negated by the virtue *harmony within*. Other virtues like sympathy, or empathy, on which virtue ethics has been built traditionally, follow from the anchor virtue, while *harmony within* has the advantage of covering even a broader ethical area as it accommodates the environmental dimension within its fold,—a feature we have touched upon already. Building *harmony within* is a process of existential becoming which I feel tempted to view as a secular spiritual involvement in palpable contrast with the religious. In the philosophical engagement of ours we find a meeting ground for all, in harmony, on the basis of an analytical understanding of the human nature.

The above brings to light the unity of virtues, as the diverse virtues are shown to follow from the anchor virtue *harmony within*, a job neither Plato nor Aristotle succeeded in completing. This feature of distinction pertaining to the anchor virtue was brought to my attention by Hursthouse in one of her email correspondences with me on a very early version of this paper. I feel tempted to quote briefly what she said, with a view to sharing the philosophical points she makes, in her own words:

> [An] aspect of the paper ... I ... found particularly interesting was the way in which the virtue of harmony provides a very un-Aristotelian account of the *unity* of the virtues. Of course Plato talks of virtue as bringing the human psyche into harmony, but it's nothing more than the thin notion of the (dubious) tripartite division of the psyche being harmonious. And Aristotle has a hint of it, but one might say, his i[s] even thinner because it's just getting the desiderative and the rational parts into harmony. But yours displays all the traditional virtues as *subsumed* under harmony, and thereby gives one a significant, content-rich, concept ... The virtues are what we need to live well, and we live—are actively engaged with— not just in social groups, and not even just in the global village, but, as we are just beginning to realise—in the natural world. ... If we had been thinking in terms of harmony, we wouldn't have had to realise that—it would have been luminously obvious long before we started to destroy it.

Before proceeding any further, I would like to go to the Hindu scripture The Bhagavad Gita which is saturated with philosophical wisdom pertaining to psycho-philosophical issues, arising out of a dialectical engagement between the teacher and the student, for some light on the virtue *harmony within* toward sharing possible philosophical knowledge of relevance from there. In the Gita, starting in the Second Chapter, the words 'sama', adjective and its abstract noun form 'samatva' are introduced in course of streamlining the optimum mental attitude of the performer of an action. Sri Aurobindo is prone to translate 'sama' as 'equal', while 'samatva' becomes 'equality'. In the 48th verse, the noun 'samatva', in its significant use in the book, is indicated as defining the concept Yoga. Buddhi Yoga, or *Yoga of the Intelligent Will*, in the excellent translation by Sri Aurobindo, relates to Yoga in the context of performance of actions, i.e., in the broadly ethical context, and has been defined as the technique of right action (*skill in works*, says Sri Aurobindo) (2.50). In the 48th verse this technique is posited as informed by 'samatva', i.e., by 'equality', if we proceed on with Sri Aurobindo's suggested translation of 'sama' as 'equal'. All this results in the advice of Sri Krishna to Arjuna in the verse 38 that the latter takes 'happiness and suffering, gain and loss, as well as victory and defeat as 'equal'' 'and proceeds on with the fight'. Certainly, there is an extended sense in which the opposites of happiness and suffering, gain and loss, victory and defeat can be taken as equal, meaning equanimity advocated for one's right frame of mind setting grounds for actions to perform (vide 2.38). However, taken literally, the translation does cause uneasiness, in so far as the translated verses can be produced as justification for sadistic overtures, for happiness and suffering are advised to be taken as equal, with the suggested translation, in the verse 38, preparing the ground for the definition of 'samatva' in 2.48. Also, the translation apparently fails to furnish a proper motivation for work, setting a goal an action is supposed to help us reach. If, in other words, victory and defeat amount to be the same, or are equal, what would Arjuna be motivated to fight for, and how is the fight to be conducted, geared to which end in view? Doesn't the fight, like all actions, encompass a plan toward a goal to reach? Sri Krishna certainly advises Arjuna to fight, and have a balanced state of mind where defeat does not spell a shattering state of mental disaster, nor does victory usher in an exuberance of overwhelming joy to celebrate with a champagne bath. He advises Arjuna to fight for victory, even as victory and defeat are suggested to be considered as hanging in a balance in sloka 38. In the verses 5.25 and 12.4 Sri Krishna suggests that the yogis who are involved in the task of doing benefits to all beings, are on the road to reaching the highest existential goal in life, of being situated in a feeling of contentment in the peace of joy unconditional (2.64, 65; 6.27, 28). Here he does not posit the opposites of causing benefits as well as harms as equal. In fact, there is only one goal suggested here for their actions to reach, viz., causing benefits to all beings—humans or otherwise. Following the same spirit, in 2.38 the advice to the disciple may be taken as for reaching happiness, making gains, and obtaining victory, shunning the dichotomy in the opposites, in a spirit of harmony within, where the opposites do not pose a mental turbulence.

Gandhi has accepted 'samatvam' as 'even-mindedness'. Radhakrishnan has followed the same route in his own translation of the Gita. I take the liberty of translating 'samatvam' as 'harmony within', the virtue which is expected to set the tone, and substance of our actions. Certainly, the necessary and sufficient condition of even-mindedness is harmony within. Imbibed in the virtue *harmony within*, one is properly equipped to perform an action. It provides the spirit of its performance in a positive mood, that incorporates a moment of detachment contributing to the performance of an act in all seriousness and determination. It is the virtue *harmony within* that leads one to the performance of the right action needed, with its feature of *intentionality* built into it. Harmony within leads on to actions relating to harmony without, as we mentioned before. It is worth mentioning that the concept *intentionality* has been in operation in Non-Dualistic Vedanta epistemology for centuries as the philosophers in the tradition analyse perception in terms of consciousness reaching out on to the object out there.

In the Gita the word 'sama' has occurred at many other places where 'equal' cannot be claimed as the intended meaning. For example, when Sri Krishna advises the disciple to sit in a meditative posture where the trunk of the body, the head and the neck are held straight (6.13), we may perhaps say, held in harmony, but not certainly as equal.

Since actions tend to spring naturally from the virtue toward amelioration of disharmony around, if human beings are adversely affected either by natural causes or as a result of injustice, it is but normal that the situation generates sympathy, or empathy, in the agent motivated enough by the virtue. We must note that sympathy, or even empathy by itself may not be enough in a situation for the appropriate moral acts to follow, for it has to be backed by proper knowledge and understanding of the situation, and the required expertise relating to it, on which a right act can stand. Otherwise, even harm can result when unguarded sympathy or empathy are at play. *Harmony within* here comes to our rescue in so far as humility as well as prudence and practical reason are built into it, which hold the agent from ending up in doing harm instead. True, the agent can still be open to mistakes and miscalculations regarding choice of actions, while imbedded in the virtue, as a physician might be, in spite of her training, experience, authenticity, perseverance and thoroughness, i.e., in spite of her possessing the virtues and qualifications needed in a situation. However, the actions of a person have a mooring in spontaneity, while based on the virtue *harmony*, and are not primarily motivated by the consequential considerations of what benefits they bring in their wake, even as the consequential dimension for any voluntary action undertaken needs to be considered as constituting an important aspect of the morality of a situation. The drowning man certainly must be helped to life promptly, according to the capacity of the onlooker.

We need to take a break here to ponder briefly on the role of sympathy, or empathy, operating in isolation, on their own, on our actions. Popular singers of today, while pursuing their way of instilling joy in the suffering souls—out of empathy, we can assume—with enchanting songs as listeners dance in ecstasy to the fast, pounding beats, often end up transmitting their way of life in drug and sex addiction in the process to the masses captivated by the songs. This happens as in empathy the agent treats the other as an extension of oneself and finds no objection in transmitting to the other what he values most in his own life even as the values he bases himself on are found unsustainable by society, vouchsafed by the statistics of a high suicide rate in the lives of these performers. They often are found dead with excess drug levels present in their blood. Nobody doubts the great intentions involved on the part of these entertainers. However, the question as to what effect the intentions may leave on the fans along with transmission of the values on which they mount their empathy demands a minute look. Certainly, sympathy, or empathy need to operate under the concept wellbeing in order for them to reach desired ends. Unhinged sympathy or empathy, having a free flow of their own, may end up in causing disaster instead. This simply points out that empathy not grounded on a sustaining value, like *harmony within* may simply lead us astray, following the logic of empathy. Assuming that the two stalwarts of modern-day activism, Freud and Marx, devised their ways for betterment of the world out of empathy for the suffering masses, they strictly skipped the route of character building for us in the process they bequeathed to the world. Freud shunned the traditional values with a view to giving the libido its precedence for the sake of his theory, in the name of science, and opposed the pleadings of Romain Rolland in support of building the 'oceanic feeling' in us.[8] Freud denied empirical evidence in favour of the yogic absorption in a phenomenological state of joyous trance that Rolland referred to with his coinage of the expression 'oceanic feeling' as the culmination of human life. Romain Rolland was a master craftsman of aesthetic creation that brought great joy to the readers of his literary work unmatched by the conditional joys extracted from sensuous satisfaction. He was touched by

[8] More on Rolland and Freud in the Introduction of this book. Cf, Parsons, (Appendix to book, 'The Letters of Sigmund Freud and Romain Rolland' especially the letters from Rolland dated Dec. 5, 1927, July 7, 1929, July 24, 1929, May 3, 1931), pp. 173–8.

the ideas of Indic spirituality spelt out by Swami Vivekananda in the West, and Ramakrishna Paramahamsa in India, the guru of the Swami, and saw the relevance of building the inner spiritual joy of saturation in the oceanic feeling in everyday life, to whatever extent possible. Freud's insistence on reducing all human values to the value of the libidinal force led him to dump all civilizational values in favour of exclusive protection of the libidinal value, as he blames the civilizational values to generate and strengthen with deontological commandments of the superego Freud finds unwelcome for the good of the society. We need to notice that Rolland's steadfast commitment to the 'oceanic feeling' totally lacks in any deontological backing as its support. In fact, nobody urges, wielding a stick in hand: 'Do get induced to the oceanic feeling', which certainly would be self-defeating for the cause. Since we are approaching the issue from a Virtue Ethical perspective, we stick to the virtue/virtues that strengthen the feeling. It is *harmony within* that we find worth cultivating in the context, without a deontological mooring in the least. It helps keeping in mind that Freud fails to provide a special place to the aesthetic value apart from, if not preferable to, the libidinal urge in the case of humans, at some level. True, the libido has its demands that must be properly heeded to. However, that does not necessitate reduction of all our values to the libidinal. To repeat, Rolland's position does not rest on a deontological underpinning, and Freud does not need to reserve an exclusive dominance of the libido on the humans. His theory, applied toward the wellness of humans, has taken little time to the creation of Hugh Hefner, Harvey Weinstein and the ilk in line to follow, a breed of culture creators we are witnessing the first time in human history. This can be seen as an outcome of Freud's bounty to humanity following from his empathy. It is significant to note that the Gita dwells at some length on imbibing the virtue *harmony within*, or *even-mindedness*, earlier on in Chap. 2, the discussion leading on to the concept of steady wisdom at the end of the chapter, before finally mentioning empathy in Chap. 6 (6.29). We do not touch on Marx's theory here in any detail; we only keep in view the spates of disquiet culminating into incidence of ongoing rampant violence that the practice of his theory has unleashed in the history of humankind throughout societies, causing immense suffering to people at large.

The non-consequential dimension in the virtue ethics developed in this paper centres around the virtue *harmony within*, which ensures the authenticity, spontaneity and at the same time effectiveness of actions undertaken, keeping the needed focus on the recipient of the action, a follow-up indeed of the intrinsic value, bereft of which welfare activities, meticulously planned and drafted, laudable as they are, simply may fail to deliver. Trappings of bureaucracy, adventitious greed or self-seeking interests, often found invariably present in the process, may eat into the success of the ventures undertaken. The consequential dimension of an act in the virtue ethics developed here relates to the thrust for all, oneself included, along with the animate as well as the inanimate objects outside of humanity's fold. Consequential consideration is built here into the logic of the virtue *harmony within*, as indicated before. Without a grounding in the virtue, a 'right action' arrived at solely on grounds of consequential calculations, indeed a scientific decision procedure, may not lead us far. The virtue has its intrinsic value, which motivates one to proper actions, although there is always room for human mistakes, to which mechanical decision procedures are hardly any antidotes by themselves. Such procedures, on top of their own share of mistakes, are severed from the heart of the human action situation, away from a mooring in the virtue. Without the proper mental set-up in place anchored to the virtue, they fail to lead us on. The logic of morality centres around a psychological setting grounded in the virtue *harmony within*. Consequential consideration, to repeat, an important aspect as it is of the morality of an act, derives its sustainability and efficacy from the intrinsic nature of the virtue.

Many a modern day secular philanthropic organization geared to people's wellbeing is in the hands of a founder anchored to the virtue, while a considerable number of employees share the situation with the employer, to the success of the organization's mission.

When the moral propriety of an action is considered, questions are quite legitimate regarding its efficacy toward the end. This is the consequential aspect of the morality of an action where the action's fit is taken into account. The other aspect of morality involved in the performance of an action relates to *the way* of its performance, signifying the *moral tone*.[9] It is not enough that a proper action must be performed, but the performance must be associated with all dignity, earnestness and the needed dedication centred around the virtue *harmony within*. The two aspects, however, do not hang loose, for the right kind of moral tone contributes to the choice of the action as well as its success in so far as the associated moral tone helps in its proper performance, while at the same time leading to the agent's own flourishing. Apart from consequential considerations,

[9] Cf. Chakravarti 2006.

however, the moral tone has its own intrinsic value which we have pointed out before. The virtue *harmony within*, we may say, is teleological in the eudemonic way in that its importance lies in leading us to our own flourishing, as well as of the whole of humanity, in harmony with the world around. In the role of a virtue, *harmony within* is a means to reaching the end of life which is joy in a state of self-contentment and peace, as harmony within has taken its shape in us while we keep working on harmony around, intensifying its presence further within ourselves. Here flourishing of the individual coalesces with flourishing around as a logical follow up of *harmony within*, to emphasize a point made already. In the Indian system, *harmony within* is a virtue, the anchor virtue, for that matter, we may repeat once again, relating to the actions we humans perform for all, ourselves included, while it is there as holding the eudemonic end for all. In the Gita we find:

> The even-minded one sees oneself in every being while feeling the presence of all beings in oneself, as she connects herself to (the practice of) yoga. (6.29)

Imbibing *harmony within* induces one to such a state, so the right mood takes shape for transcendence of the limited self, confined within itself, toward performance of actions directed to others. The passage from self to others gets clearly indicated here. The non-dualism present in Vedanta, and not less significantly in the Tantras, facilitates the process of transcendence. Here I confine my attention to the phenomenological aspect of the situation involved in the epistemic context away from the metaphysical analysis existent in the tradition relating to it.

East-West Confluence: Naturalism and *Harmony Within*

The claim that a virtue is naturalistic in so far as it leads to naturalistic ends, prompts Sandler to posit three ‘promising candidates’[10] for such ends ‘appropriate to us [human beings] in virtue of our rationality’,[11] while he tries to salvage Hursthouse’s failed attempts to find any specific end at the level of rationality per se. ‘Our rationality’, Sandler says, ‘gives rise to additional eudaimonistic ends, beyond those appropriate to us as

[10] Sandler, p. 23.
[11] Hursthouse 1999, p. 218.

living, sentient, social animals'. The possible three ends Sandler proposes for consideration are: meaningfulness, knowledge and autonomy. Taking the first candidate, viz., meaningfulness by itself, he continues: 'Thus, there is at least one end appropriate to us as rational animals, above and beyond those appropriate to us as living, sentient, social animals'.[12] My position, however, is that although reason does have its important role to play for a human being in an existentially meaningful situation, it may perhaps not be the most important element in shaping a meaningful life that rather needs a proper buildup of the virtue *harmony within* as the guiding force. That it is rational for us to have the virtue for human flourishing,—and reason, to repeat, has its part to play here,—does not mean that the process of being settled in the virtue, as well as being led by it, is primarily a rational process. What is involved here is existential becoming which has a strong non-rational underpinning. That it is rational for human beings to follow the pursuit of art if they have an aptitude as well as inclination for it, means simply that pursuit of art is a human form of life, while it is an acceptable way to pursue and express the meaning of life. It does not follow thereby that the pursuit itself is indulging in a primarily rational process even as it does not fall totally outside of the application of reason. That a specific state X is seen to follow Y 'rationally' in a chemistry experiment, does not mean that the physical act of following is a rational act itself out there mirroring the rational process of logical implication of one step in an argument from a previous one, nor are X and Y to be considered rational entities. To find that an animal, characteristically for the species it belongs to, is equipped with a reasonable mechanism for defending itself in the face of attacks, does not mean that the animal involves itself in a rational attempt while trying to defend itself. The recent spurt in occurrences of mindless violence in North America that we referred to before does not simply show that the agents cease to have an overall strong hold on the rational faculty, but, more importantly, that the non-rational asset of character, viz., integrity, as expected to be shaped by the virtue *harmony within*, is at the root of the problem in being significantly absent, and the basis for the smooth functioning of reason is missing. While Hursthouse fails to come up with a 'fifth end'[13] in relation to the human species attaining rationality in the evolutionary process, on top of the ends she enumerates pertaining simply to the aspects of living, sentient, social

[12] Sandler, p. 23.
[13] Hursthouse 1999, p. 218.

animals they are, realization of human values relating to harmony, in and through the process of existential becoming, may be posited as such an end. Here, as we have seen, reason has its important but limited role to play. The value here is secularly spiritual, and does not presuppose supernatural commitments Hursthouse would like to avoid.[14] What many see as a modern-day malaise being frequently exhibited in today's society can be taken care of if we pay the needed attention to this value, and imbibe the associated virtue individually as well as socially. Treating nature with dignity and reason follows.

Harmony within posits a meaning to life, while it does accommodate knowledge, as the latter is a necessary condition for the proper shaping of the virtue in an individual. Also, autonomy, circumscribed by the true freedom for us, from the life we live as captivated by our sensual moorings, is embedded in the meaning of life that *harmony within* fosters. Thus, the three ends Sandler proposes go concurrently together.

Conclusion

The above hopefully brings a new perspective to virtue ethics, with a non-Aristotelian basis for it, while providing a ground for benefitting from the truths in the other theories, viz., consequentialism, deontology and contractarianism. A contract can be meaningfully reached at, and is effective, with people having attained some level of *harmony within*. Categorical imperatives may make effective operational sense only on the basis of this virtue, and not reason alone. Consequential considerations also are held in their proper ethical setting in the context of the virtue. Philip Pettit's recourse to a distinction between *honouring* and *promoting* a value may not explain the difference pertaining to virtue ethics and consequentialism, the former allegedly adhering to honouring a value, e.g., peace, while the latter to promoting it even when honouring may need to be compromised. Gandhi indeed seems to posit a counterexample here, for in his campaign against colonial rule (not certainly against the ruler), he *promotes* his value *in* honouring it, and never compromising with the honouring. The following reflections, in personal communication, from Hursthouse are pertinent at this point:

[14] Ibid., p. 218.

> [T]here is no such thing as an impractical ethics, and no such phenomenon as someone's honouring a value if they never lift a finger to promote it; [s]ometimes—very often indeed—the only right way to honour a value is to promote it (in some sense) and that that is so gives no credence whatsoever to consequentialism. I think too that there are often occasions or cases in which the only way to promote a value, long term, is to honour it and that this is what, I think Westerners see Gandhi as having done.[15]

What we have said before, lays a foundation for Environmental ethics in the spirit of virtue ethics in so far as *harmony within* equips us to deal with nature, along with human beings, with dignity, which is the opposite of rampant exploitation, exposing the colonial, demonic mind at work. The mindset can be built satisfactorily with the foundation laid on *harmony within*, bereft of which legal actions simply fall severely off the desired goals to reach. What I have tried to argue for is that without the mindset there, actions can hardly follow, in the right spirit. More importantly, it is the mindset that is at the very root. Such is the stand of virtue ethics, as I understand it. To repeat, if the opioid addict does not have an inkling of what human nature is, no medications can come to his rescue. Or, in other words, the drug addiction pandemic needs to be faced as a moral issue. Before we end, my position on *harmony within* and the self is that the virtue has an innateness about it, in so far as it attempts to manifest itself in the surface of consciousness, paving the way for flourishing, while the individual has the existential choice to accept it as the proper ingredient for one's own nature. Here certainly reason has its role to play.

References

The Bhagavadgita, with Sanskrit Text, and English translation by S Radhakrishnan, Blackie & Son (India), Bombay, 1977.

Chakravarti, Sitansu S. *Ethics in the Mahabharata: A Philosophical Inquiry for Today*, Munshiram Manoharlal, New Delhi, 2006.

———. 'Tagore-Wittgenstein Interface: The Poet's Activism and Virtue Ethics,' *Tagore, Einstein and the Nature of Reality: Literary and Philosophical Reflections*, ed. Partha Ghose, Routledge, Oxford, 2019.

Freud, Sigmund. *Civilization and its Discontents*, W.W. Norton, New York, 1961.

Hursthouse, Rosalind. *On Virtue Ethics*, Oxford University Press, New York, 1999.

[15] from email correspondence.

———. 'Environmental Virtue Ethics,' *Working Virtue*, eds. Rebecca Walker, Philip J Ivanhoe, Oxford University Press, New York, 2007.

Parsons, William B. *The Enigma of Oceanic Feeling: Revisioning the Psychoanalytic Theory of Mysticism*, With an *Appendix* 'The Letters of Sigmund Freud and Romain Rolland,' Oxford University Press, New York, 1999.

Rolland, Romain. *The Life of Ramakrishna*, Translated from the original French by E.F. Malcolm-Smith, Advaita Ashrama, Calcutta, 1984.

———. *The Life of Vivekananda: And the Universal Gospel*, Translated from the original French by E.F. Malcolm-Smith, Advaita Ashrama, Calcutta, 1984.

Sandler, Ronald L. *Character and Environment*, Columbia University Press, New York, 2007.

Sen, Amartya. 'Consequential Evaluation and Practical Reason, '*The Journal of Philosophy*, vol. XCVII. No. 9, September 2000.

Slote, Michael A. *The Ethics of Care and Empathy*, Routledge, London, 2007.

Tagore, Rabindranath. *Gitanjali (Song Offerings)*. Macmillan, London, 1953.

CHAPTER 13

Emotion Concepts for Virtue Theory: From Aesthetic to Epistemic and Moral

Lisa Widdison

The Self is a dancer (actor)—
—the soul being the stage.
Śiva Sūtram III. 9–10

What connection can there be between the villain's heart, hard as the wild date,
and songs of poets, tender as blooming jasmine?
Be not amazed, but note the marvel that is told of the moon,

L. Widdison (✉)
St. Mary's University, San Antonio, TX, USA
e-mail: lisa888@hawaii.edu

S. S. Chakravarti et al. (ed.), *Traditional Indian Virtue Ethics for Today*, Palgrave Studies in Comparative East-West Philosophy,
https://doi.org/10.1007/978-3-031-47972-4_13

that with its nectared light, it brings a stone to tears.
Vidyākara's Treasury of Poems[1]

Of whom stays unmoved, all desires enter
—as waters enter the ocean, filled from all sides—
being not a lover of desires, tranquility is reached.
Bhagavad Gītā II.70[2]

Introduction

This chapter is an inquiry into the relation between virtue, emotions and aesthetic appreciation. Emotions are critically important in motivating a virtue. Yet, the right kinds of character traits for virtue are mostly understood descriptively, as dispositions. In virtue theory we expect to have a more nuanced account of emotions, though. (If a charitable action is performed grudgingly, then we say it is not virtuous.) Aesthetic sentiments suggest that a desire to share, and that all such actions *we ought to desire* and ways *we ought to feel* are liberating. As such, sublime-emotions guide us to having the right attitude for virtuous character traits in ways that other emotions cannot. This is my central claim, which is supported by a tradition, the *rasa-bhāva* theory from Sanskrit literature that holds across multiple philosophies, sciences, medicine and aesthetics. *Rasa*, is a term that arises in Vedic mantras as 'essence' or water. '*Rasa*' in aesthetic theory is traced to the sage Bharatamuni (200 CE). The meaning as an 'elixir' is continuous with the life-science, Āyurveda, Yoga psychology, Bhakti devotional faith, Śaiva theology, philosophical schools of metaphysics, and especially poetics. Although we expect any complete theory of emotions to explain what emotion responses in art and religion have in common with emotion concepts in ethics, there are few to none aside from the theory of *rasa*. The *rasa-bhāva* account of emotion expression and conditioning is explanatorily powerful. Bharata's theory can do what has not

[1] Vidyākara, and Daniel Henry Holmes. Ingalls, trans., Kosambi and Gokhale, eds. (1957). *Subhāṣitaratnakoṣa: Sanskrit Poetry, from Vidyākara's Treasurȳ.* Cambridge Harvard Oriental Series.

In the original Sanskrit page 226: khlānāṃ kharjūrakṣitaruhakaṭhoraṃ kva ca manaḥ / kva conmīlanmallīkusumasukumārāḥ kavigiraḥ / itīmaṃ vyāmohaṃ parihara vicitrāḥ śṛṇu kathā / yathāyaṃ pīyūṣadyutirupalakhaṇḍaṃ dravayati //. Translated in Sanskrit Poetry from Vidyākara's Treasury, by Daniel H. Ingalls (1965) 1278/page 253.

[2] Quoted from the *Gītā* II:70.

been done before in virtue theory, which is to demarcate freely willed emotions from those that go against moral responsibility. We observe this shift, from stone-cold dispositions, to free and reflective feeling, in a confluence of aesthetic ideas flowing from the transcendental philosophies of Abhinavagupta, and Immanuel Kant, who noted that a moving poem may bring reason and emotion to our conceptual limits. The aesthetic descriptions of *taste*, *sublime*, and *rasa* can assist our account of epistemic and moral virtue, as the link to creating dispositions (*sthayībhāvas*), with distilled emotion (*rasa*), in the cultivated transcendence of normally biased and unreflective emotions (*bhāvas*).

Classical Sanskrit aesthetic theory of emotions, as traced to Second Century Bharatamuni, anchors traditional instruction on all aspects of theatre, dance, music, costume and style in the thirty-six chapters of a *Treatise on Drama*, the *Nāṭyaśāstra* (NS). The text has overlap with Sāṃkhya-Yoga philosophy and the Āyurvedic compendium of Caraka (Second Century). Most importantly, two full chapters of NS are devoted to the ontology, production, and class distinctions of "aesthetic emotion," or *rasa*, and a realistic logic of ordinary emotion (*bhāva*). '*Rasa*' is naturally associated with essences. Abhinavagupta and Bharatamuni (1992) The meaning in the kitchen is *taste*. In scriptures, *rasa* is associated with the divinity of conscious enjoyment, and in alchemy, an elixir or pure-substance, water, or juice. The ideas of '*rasa*' seamlessly transition from the Vedas, to medicine, cooking, literature, the moods of love and play between Krishna and his charming devotees, and contemporary cinema. Used as a formal concept of charm in poetics, there was a critical point that *rasa* developed into an aesthetic idea entailing that the suggestion of an apt emotional contrast is essential in all kinds of art.[3] With a widespread consensus in practice that the aim of art is to suggest *rasa*, the tradition flourished. Dancers trained to evoke *rasa* worship Śiva, though some classical Śaiva philosophers were philosophically interested in the ontology of aesthetic production for the sake of liberation. The theory of emotion in art, music, theater and poetry converged with a theism of human agency in the Kashmiri, Abhinavagupta's non-dualistic tradition of Śaiva Philosophy. *Rasa*, as a phenomenon, was applied in analyses of all kinds of literature, including Buddhist plays, and Prakrit erotic poetry, with key theorists, such as Kṣemendra (Eleventh Century) taking a discursive turn

[3] See Lawrence McCrea on the theistic teleological progression of poetic theory into the established aesthetic theory of aesthetic emotion in 11th CE Kashmir. McCrea (2009)

into the practice of expressing taste-constructions. Ideals of *sublime courage*, *pathos* and other emotions, recur in aestheticized forms as cultivars of *rasa*. In any case, the tradition is living, and has been explicitly referenced in cross-cultural aesthetics, contemporary poetry, theater and cinema. Perennially, *rasa* recurs in the emotional consciousness of communities, invites questioning, and promotes agentive responses on the part of critical knowers, which impact ethical practices and character.

An initial question is how such a transcendental emotion is possible. A second difficulty is that it has been overlooked by the West. Sri Sitansu Sekhar has observed that: "The world of creative literature is very rich in India from ancient times. Drama occupies a special place there. In Sanskrit a play is known as 'the *Drishsya-kavya*,' i.e., a poetic creation that is to be 'viewed' (by the audience')." The temple and dance tradition also belongs together. The aesthetic dimension of the audience has been analyzed in the tradition in terms of a cognitive-emotional shift seen in the act of devotion. A connection between knowing and feeling in an audience is continuous from the expressive tradition to the lived tradition. Thus, Sri Sitansu Sekhar notes that "the aesthetic dimension present in the Hindu tradition relating to the concept of divinity [appears] strikingly absent in the monotheistic tradition … Divinity after all is a divine play in the aesthetic domain, rather than a metaphysical supposition." He therefore posed the following questions: "Is *rasa* pertaining to the aesthetic dimension is everything there? Does *rasa* lead to *bhāva*? How do the two relate? Is delving in *rasa* a necessary condition for the latter? In other words, what is the relation between *rasa* and *bhāva*, both belonging to the emotive dimension?" I am very grateful for these questions, and wish to respond. According to Bharata, no meaning proceeds [in art] without *rasa* (NS VI. 31). Taken as meaning about possibility, or what *we can do in life*, not just *what happens*, there is no meaning of an ordinary emotion (*bhāva*) beyond a description of causes and conditions, unless there is this reflection on the affective essences of humanity. *Rasa*s are also emotions, but they are not dispositions. Rather, *rasa*s are open-ended occurrences in which we relish the choice to feel one way or another. A *rasa* produces awareness that we ought to feel a certain way, given a presentation such as the *Drishsya-kavya*, and it changes dispositions reflectively through the power of feeling a spontaneous emotion.

Sri Sitansu Sekhar has further seen the import of this inquiry by commenting that *rasa* leads to the conative dimension, there is little doubt. "In the case of the Indian sub-continent, two wars were fought inspired by the rasas emanating from the songs of Tagore: (1) in India against the British colonial rule, and (2) in Bangladesh against the rule of Pakistan. We didn't find a parallel uprising inspired by Shakespeare's writings, or by Wordsworth's anywhere." The *bhāva* realm does in fact lead us a bit further, but only on the condition that an openness to questioning, reflecting, and relishing has its occasion, and for this we need *rasa* ushering us into the spiritual, where after all the conative is securely embedded. In what follows, I introduce the aesthetic dimension which is not segregated from the conative or the spiritual dimension of sādhana in the long tradition of Hinduism. Against the fast and simplistic negative assessment of the passions in Indian philosophies, we can speak of a place, with Gītā and all, in a very interesting presentation of spirituality in the aesthetic mode, pace Bhagavan Dās (1953) who illustrated a scientific moral psychology continuous with aesthetic and medicinal terminology.

Drawing together some key points here, a ground of emotive agency relevant to character virtues may be examined from the perspective of Sanskrit aesthetics. The aims of an ongoing discourse in global virtue ethics in the philosophical vision of Sri Sitansu Sekhar have been to first develop an ethical structure using the analytical tools of philosophy, and virtue ethics, and "to contribute to the Virtue Ethics of today with age-old visions from the classical Indian perspective, converging in the virtue of *samatva*, harmony within which leads to the other requisite ethical virtues such as courage, benevolence, sympathy or empathy." In part, we saw that classical literature used as a starting point, the Bhagavad Gītā in particular, does not fit into a single Western ethical paradigm such as Deontology. This is confirmed by examining the work of the tantric polymath Abhinavagupta (nineth–eleventh centuries CE) who was the most prolific commentator in the Pratyābhijñā school, and author of the *Tantrāloka*. The proper relation between reason, emotion, and action, are central to a conception of virtue for Aristotle, who used *character* as a starting point for ethics education. As we know, the ethical sense of 'character' employed as *ethos* is to be distinguished from the theatrical sense of 'character' in a play—comedy, tragedy, etc., on the grounds that we are primarily discussing moral agency. Only in the Pratyābhijñā school of Indian Philosophy do we see that the two senses of 'character' are fused in moral-agency. Far from being a trivial view, this transcendental argument holds that all beings are one consciousness expressed in our different characters. Just as an actor in a play has a part, the agent of moral judgment has a part to play of Śiva consciousness—the divine player within—to be recognized as all of us, everywhere, all the time. The implication is not that agency is to be taken less seriously, though. In fact, the Pratyābhijñā school emphasizes the complete freedom of the agent, and the reality of aesthetic experiences to emotionally awaken us to the power we have as an enactor. Thus, in reflective moments when we watch a play, read a poem, or reflect on art, we may become absorbed into the characters so much that we recognize glimpses of our real self in another, the veil falls away so to speak.

In the ethics of the Bhagavad Gītā, the theory of karma implies that there are causal connections between thought, action and character. Sanskrit classical literature includes considerations on the ethical aims of life, including musings on the proper means to categorical values of: pleasure, material wealth, personal responsibility and spiritual liberation. Abhinavagupta claims that Gītā II.70/72 critically answers an earlier question of Arjuna's, posed in Gītā II.56: "What are the signs of a man whose intellect is steady, who is absorbed in the Self, O Kesava? How does the man of steady intellect speak, how does he sit, how does he walk?"[4] These are the ethical questions, of course. According to Abhinavagupta, the reason for this questioning is in order to reach *samādhi*. The wider narrative will bring a range of emotions to the mind of the connoisseur who understands the purpose of the characters involved, even if the final end of liberation is not yet felt. The audience has its own desires which are reflecting in the background as possibilities in the play events of characters and the context we imagine them to navigate. Epic literature is affectively moving because the characters are cognitively moving. A final settling of the process, culminates in the exemplar's renunciation, and the *rasa* of *śānta*, or peace in the audience. In Abhinavagupta's commentary on the Gītā, he remarks about the above verse pertaining to desire:

> A yogin is not purposefully seeking to engage in worldly activities just to fulfil his desires. However, he remains engaged in the activities of this world because this is the nature of the sense organs. Sense organs that run through him (but are not part of his real nature) do not create waves of anger in him. In the same way, the movement of the river does not disturb the ocean. [*numbering shifting to II.72 in Abhinavagupta's edition*][5]

[4] ibid., (2004, 70).

[5] Boris Marjanovic trans. Abhinavagupta, *Gitartha Samgraha,* (2004, 78).

This verse matters to Abhinavagupta as a teacher, and author of the *Tantrāloka*. If Abhinavagupta is consistent, we can understand our bodies as an ethical starting point. To act in practice presupposes a thinker redirects, *not* retreats from sense experience, the body or desire. As he sees consciousness to be the logical basis for bodies, *rasa* aesthetics is all the more relevant as embodied knowing. The path of Arjuna in the Mahābhārata is an ethical journey we are to recognize through narrated conditions. The embodied mind is the initial way we experience self-awareness in consciousness. Just as divergent streams of water flow in to the ocean, so do different emotions flow as desires through the body. Ordinary persons struggle more to be rid of desire, or to satisfy desire, than to be unmoved by desire.

Intellectual virtues are fitting to bring into this discourse contingent on a theory that does not exclude the epistemic and aesthetic dimensions of emotion. In part, a Western oversight of theoretical unity of consciousness with emotion in Indian philosophies persists, which is something that Sanskrit aesthetic criticism challenges. Views on emotions are well discussed in Sanskrit texts but some misconceptions remain about the basis of emotions, as modifications of thoughts and desires in ethical matters well beyond poetic theory. The fallout is apparent, as spiritual implications of the non-dualist Pratyābhijñā school having drawn on traditional ethical sources was overlooked. In many cases, classical theories make a continuous connection between feeling, thought and action that Abhinavagupta synthesizes into a single theory of embodied consciousness. Abhinavagupta offers a realistic analysis of aesthetic rapture as well as yogic joy. New for Western philosophy is a categorical view of aestheticized emotion as part of the reality of the world. In a meta-philosophical critique of virtue theory, the concept of *rasa* provides a path to re-conceptualize the unity of consciousness with emotion.

In classical Sanskrit philosophy, poetry, drama and medicine, an emotional transformation is implicit in any cognitive activity. From the kitchen to the theater, *rasa* pertains to a subtle essence. This dual sense of taste, kitchen-wise, and theater-wise, carries the normative weight of what it is proper to empathetically feel, in line with but beyond the 18th CE German Enlightenment. In Advaita Vedānta we know 'joy' as a dimension of Pure Consciousness (*puruṣa*). In Yoga philosophy, the nature of matter (*prakṛti*) is theorized to be insentient, but is itself taken as three-fold strands (*guna*) of affective constitutions (which surpasses the western distinction between active and passive affects). Furthermore, 'reason and emotion' are ontologically unified in classical Sanskrit literature more often than not. Emotion-concepts and a moral psychology may be overlooked on account of being omnipresent. Though we look to the Bhagavad Gītā as philosophical literature in many ways, as an inquiry on freedom and action (*karma*), or as a moral psychology (employing the phenomenology of *guna*s: delight, *sattva*; dynamicity, *rajas*; and dullness, *tamas*) or a guide to morality (*dharma*), readings which bridge ethics with moral beauty and the sublime also result in deeper responses to questions of agency. Aesthetic ideas of Kant's sublime track the unfathomable magnitude of Nature, but that includes tragic art, and moral beauty Lyotard (1991); Abhinavagupta's soul-stage is the Nature within. One sublime consciousness in the dance of Śiva. We are to recognize divine-identity from within, the villain also has a heart to make the old world affectively new.

Only a few emotions are sublime according to Kant, as emotion rarely involves the use of reason. The idea "sublime" captures awe and reverence, and an interesting reversal of desire. Tragic theater makes one go from imaginatively resisting a presentation that is too much to handle, to relishing the magnitude of extraordinary circumstances. Reflective judgment plays with conceptual possibilities. A spectrum of emotion states is essential to imagination and understanding in the Śaiva interpretation of aesthetic experience, because consciousness is itself affective—we affectively think what we ought to do. Following the theory of suggested emotion's lead, Abhinavagupta's *Abhinavabhāratī* (Tenth Century NS commentary), peace (*śānta*) emerges as the ultimate *rasa*. Rather than act on desire, the agent takes in and transforms desire, as one identifies *rasa* in a character that reveals one's own playful *imagination*. In theorizing emotion for the sake of answering universal questions about virtue, we believe that the *rasa* experience enhances the moral imagination and understanding from an impartial perspective. Moral action may follow by accepting anger and sorrow and transforming it into a dissolution of emotions into peace, or *śānta*. *Rasa* as a theory was applied in analyses of all kinds of literature, including Buddhist plays, and Prakrit erotic poetry, theorists taking a discursive turn into the practice and ethics of expressing taste. Ideals of sublime courage, empathy and other emotions recurs in aestheticized forms realistically as cultivars of *rasa*. Thus, *rasa* theory tracks a social aesthetic of agentive responses in the course of actions that have an impact on character. This integral technical term for reflective or aesthetic emotions we now see as *rasa*, has forms of which *śānta* is but one of many aesthetic ideas, like the erotic, comedy, or tragedy denoting an atmosphere such as peaceful, sexy, funny or sad. The aesthetic ideas differ from ordinary ideas though, because unlike ethical ideas and concepts the emotions are reflective. This distinction marks the transition of an emotion concept from epistemic to moral via the aesthetic. Reflecting on concepts that are given to us a priori as *Śiva consciousness* is a convergence point with the Kantian subjective powers of imagination and understanding reaching out towards a synthesis of recognition. The Śaiva grants a subject has freedom of knowing, remembering and distinguishing through the imagination.

Aestheticized Emotion

Rasa, we noted is cross-modally used to mean *taste*. The core meaning of aesthetic taste is rooted in its direct perception of a feeling. Aesthetic enjoyment is 'savoring' or immersion, in a manner of cooking an emotion. The "Rasa Sutra" of the *Nāṭyaśāstra* dictates that where determinations of fleeting emotive expressions conjoin with possible experiences in a contextualized dramatic setting, "aestheticized emotion," i.e., *rasa*, arises (NS VI.32: *tatra vibhāvānubhava vavyābhichari samyogād rasaḥ niṣpattiḥ*). Cautiously, the aphorism omits reference to ordinary feelings like personal sadness, instead picking out only the conjunction of necessary conditions: determinants, consequents, and transient states, as the sufficient condition for producing aesthetic savor. '*Rasa*' is the aesthetic enjoyment of: *śṛṅgāra* (the erotic), *karuṇa* (pathos), *adbhuta* (wonder), *bībhatsa* (disgust), *bhyānaka* (terror), *raudra* (anger), *vīra* (the heroic), and *hāsya* (comedy). In the paradigm any emotion, culturally specific or universal, may be aestheticized. Like an atmosphere, anyone can feel *rasa*. Even dark emotions can be beautifully transformed, and telling. Mixed *rasa*s like: disgust-fear, fear-wonder, wonder-heroism, are very contextual but epistemically normative, and about sensing the way desire, thought and action hang together in real relations, than matters of fact. *Rasa* is no less real though, the relations are not merely a character's feelings, nor only the emotion of an artist, musician, or poet causally responsible for a presentation. Rather, *rasa* awareness is theorized like *sensus communis* by Kant, who attributes the status of "universal" to aesthetic reflective judgment.[6] A *judgment of taste* is a universal call to interpretive communities who are a priori sentient. Universal communicability in self-consciousness recognizes the sameness of faculties of consciousness.

[6] Pluhar trans. 2010, 87,238§.

A confusion about *rasa* sometimes arises from the assumption that aesthetic emotions are unreal because they are associated with the fictional matters of literature. The critical insight on this issue is that while aesthetic constructions can be based on fact or fiction, in the process of aestheticization the reality of affective consciousness is suddenly accessible. Emotions are of the nature of consciousness in feelings for life, whether it be in home, work, worship, or art. Emotions can be cashed out as judgments across traditions, but this does not mean that judgments about fictions are ontologically inferior to determinations and personal emotions. The *evaluative* nature of emotion-judgments is common to moral judgments and to liking art.[7] Thus, affective phenomena are theorized by Abhinavagupta in terms of an inner stage: 'the conjunction' (*saṃyoga*) of the "Rasa Sūtra" occurs in the embodied imagination of the spectator. In a time-stopping performance, a certain fittingness of feeling, the right sentiment for a station on the life-stage, is aptly generalized as a sufficient condition for *rasa*.[8] Bharata describes the causal efficacy of a *rasa experience*, pervading the body-mind-stage of the spectator in aesthetic harmony like fire consumes dry wood, as a "discourse of the heart."[9] In turn, Abhinavagupta describes the function of a setting and props (*vibhāvādi*) in producing transcendental aesthetic enjoyment as different from that of ordinary conditioned experiences. Rather than viewing theater as a narrative of settled events in space and time, aesthetic constructions must be seen as extemporaneous real counterparts of emotion-occurrence, if not more real in their indeterminate and contemplative overflow of meaning. At odds with their ideas of *rasa* is a view where the mind is disembodied.

The way Bharata theorizes personal and communal emotions, the distinction between ordinary and aesthetic emotions is only possible insofar as dramatized, poetic emotions run on the same channels of feeling as ordinary embodied emotions in a spectator. The duration, quality and effects of aestheticized emotions are different, though. The cause of ordinary emotion is a judgment determining good or badness as such, and so dictating desire. In aesthetic experience, emotions are not just qualities of

[7] Boruah remarks, the paradox of emotion in fiction disappears by taking existential and evaluative beliefs as separate (1988, 125).

[8] (NS 7.7) *tatrāṣṭau bāvāḥ sthāyinaḥ / trayastriṃśadvyabhicāriṇaḥ / aṣṭau sātvikā iti bhedāḥ / evamete kāvyarasabhivyaktihetava ekonapañcāśadbhāvāḥ pratyavagantavyāḥ / ebhyaśca sāmānyaguṇayogena rasā niṣpadyante //*.

[9] *bhavati cātra ślokaḥ— yo'rtho hṛdayasaṃvādi tasya bhāvo rasodbhavaḥ / śarīraṃ vyāpyate tena śuṣkaṃ kāṣṭhabhivāgninā* (NS 7.7).

the characters in drama, spectator emotions are also a feature of the audience's embodied response minus unreflective desires.[10] According to K.C. Bhattacharya in "The Concept of Rasa" (1930):

> The feeling of ugliness is itself a contemplative feeling but the artistic spirit may retire to a deeper level and rejoicingly contemplate the ugly in an attitude of superior detachment. It rejoices either in having eluded its touch and in being able to watch it from a secure distance or in the sense of power to blow it away and turn it into thought—I mean the explosive power of laughter, these being the two directions of the feeling of the ludicrous. The other aesthetic attitude in which ugliness can be negotiated is what I have characterised as the patient faith of courageous love. The faith that the ugly can be transmuted into beauty is familiar enough in the artistic sphere. It is in fact what makes aesthetic education possible. (Battacharya 2011, 206)

When we read literature or watch a play, etc. we usually want a break, or a change in the direction of thought and feelings to a different or more valuable experience of reality. Contexts and images with *characters* serve the negative function of removing obstacles for the mind to touch upon new possibilities of moving an agent. Creating a contextual break is key to bringing about the *rasa* experience as we become absorbed into all of the characters who are presented to us as in the context. Boring things in life can become interesting in art. Unknown possibilities in one's own experience can become familiar in poetry. The familiar can become new and strange again. To evoke conceptually thick emotions is essentially to call attention to the faculty of reason to produce ideas that go unquestioned in their ordinary historical context. Bernard Williams thought that the study of the history of philosophy is important because it allows us to notice previously unnoticed and unquestioned assumptions in our thought (Williams, 2001). Sentient modes of thought are historically left out of the questioning. Here, it is precisely because certain alien feelings seem so familiar to us that it can lead us re-think our contemporary "common sense" conceptions. Abhinavagupta describes the function of theatrical context in producing aesthetic enjoyment as parallel to, though different from, ordinary factors in experience. The sentient nature of consciousness itself is ahistorical.

[10] Aristotle, *Poetics,* IX.

Often, an emotion is pictured as cognitive if it involves a belief or determination about objects or persons as causes of pleasure and pain. As such, Kant pictures veridical judgments of beauty to be non-cognitive but also non-emotional. In Yoga philosophy, the mind is viewed as entirely embodied, irrespective of consciousness. Mind (*manas*), is a synthesizing inner-sense-organ of sentience or the "heart." Subverting the traditional Sāṃkhya-Yoga view, Abhinavagupta theorized consciousness as continuous with the body as well. Consciousness is then ultimately the sentient nature of reality. Emotional sentiments in aesthetics, or *rasa*-s (*rasāḥ*) are set apart from as refinements of consciousness. Yet, conditioned, build-up dispositional and occurrent states (*bhāvāḥ*) are experiential only on account of *rasa*. As such, refined responses do not necessarily depend on beliefs about how things are, but on imaginative conditions of the body in reflection. The transcendental nature of art has continuity with the transcendental philosophy of Kashmir Śaiva that is to move us beyond ordinary ways of thinking. Therein, the inner, imaginative world depends on this ability to expand feeling that comes alive by drinking in a performance. Bringing judgments of beauty back to the body as such crosses into the realm of the sublime. The quintessential term of art for *rasa* enjoyment, *camatkāra*, is supposed to be the yogic-experience of "unobstructed consciousness." The significance of such a moment is that it invites thought-play, and the choice to relish consciousness' freedom.

Kant claims that judgments of beauty reflectively serve as a symbol of morality, illuminating the imagination and our power to act freely. Although Kant linked judgments of preference to merely personal emotions, he argued that the reflective branch of aesthetic pleasure is free from sensual preferences. He also gave us two ways to conceptualize emotion in judgment. First, the logic of personal emotion is such that it involves desire. Where there is a personal desire, there will always be some pain involved in cycles of hope and failing. Emotional distillation of the dynamic is seen in the universal communicability of aesthetic experience, which is marked by being unattached, and disjoined from desire or aversion. In aesthetic experience there are "judgments of emotion" (e.g., this is comic, or erotic), but we ought not to experience the sentiments as personal emotions, nor should we see characters as objects of our desire. With distanced desire, patient observation increases. As Paul Guyer points out in response to Noë (2017) on the cognitive value of art appreciation: "Edward Bullough in his 1907 Cambridge lectures on aesthetics, argued that precisely by distancing ourselves from our own personal emotions, art allows us to experience a fuller range of human emotions than any one of us could otherwise experience in his or her quotidian life, or would even want to." (Guyer 2017). Aesthetic distance theorists all maintain that there is a steady stream of emotional consciousness, and judgments of taste are both free and qualitatively normative. Hanfling (2000) articulates distance in five ways as such, including cutting out the practical side of observing feelings. Arguably, the aesthetic idea of rasa that Abhinavagupta anticipated transcends psychic distancing as a mere placeholder of attention, to achieve an agentive spiritual focus. To be at a loss for emotional response is as equally problematic as having a merely practical reaction to art, and humanity. Though Kant is precise that moral judgments are determinate, not reflective, the relationship between virtue and reflective judgment holds on the basis of self-recognition in the judgment rather than recognition in the concept. The power to judge reveals the freedom of the subject. In Śaiva philosophy (quoted above) the "subject" sees the actor in the self. To recognize the subject of experience as free is also to affectively move thought and action. Synthesizing the philosophies, we can picture *rasa*-s as distanced forms of aesthetic judgment qua being reflective about *how one ought to feel* in taking up actions. Far from being indifferent to moral action, one is more attuned to the basis of morality in compassion as one feels awe in communal emotions. Far from being an outdated view, this aesthetic humanism is confirmed by in-depth studies on awe. In *Awe: The Transformative Power of Everyday Wonder*, Dacher Keltner advises that we seek out awe, *in moral beauty*, or wherever possible and to follow that mystery. Keltner (2023) Wonder brings us together; we harmonize physiologically when watching performances, and we feel an agentive unity beyond individual identities. Abhinavagupta emphasized the constant wonderment inherent to the nature of reflective awareness that like an a priori basis for the *rasa* experience is also the basis for an ever-new rediscovery of the Self. The same awe ordinary people glimpse in transformative moments, is sustained unfading novelty that a yogin feels because of being spiritually liberated in unity with the divine. *Camatkāra* is an occurrent novelty for the ordinary connoisseur, but enlightened persons would understand it ontologically, as a priori.[11] Aesthetic, or reflective wonder nourishes the intellectual virtue of 'wisdom' for ordinary persons, because of the flashes of recognition it affords the imagination in trying to stretch across the unity of consciousness. A

[11] Gnoli, (1956, 60).

yogin would have constant, insight into the unity of consciousness, but also compassion on the basis of directly perceiving the mutual vulnerability of limited beings. In accord with his teacher, Utpaladeva, who reasoned that every moment of consciousness has the wonder self-recognition, Abhinavagupta claims to be teaching out of compassion.

The next link in the emotion concept chain is from epistemic to moral, an ongoing task. *Rasa*, evaluative like an emotion, and reflective like thought, is free like a judgment of taste. The fallout is that there is a refinement of emotion in terms of clarity (Skt. *sattva*), disinterestedness in terms of universality, and impartiality in terms of personal distance. If emotion can be distanced, then it fits with the character trait of impartiality, and may be resistant to personal bias. To achieve such an emotion, desire enters the mind but does not move arbitrarily. In fact, Othello does teach us of jealousy's trappings and dangerous delusion. Madame Bovary conveys the lesson that delusion leads to self-destruction. Though these lessons happen to be apt, the link to virtue is somewhat arbitrary. Less arbitrary, and bringing in a matter of choice, proper disinterestedness is moderated against the extremes of over distancing and under distancing in encountering aesthetic objects. Edward Bullough, taking the logic of aesthetic emotion at face value in the Western tradition, clearly saw that picturing aesthetic emotion as "psychic distance" does not imply personal and subjective perspectives are lost. Likewise, in all forms of distance there is some aspect of the spatial-temporal distancing Abhinavagupta speaks of in describing *rasa* as personally moving, extraordinary, timeless and other worldly.[12] As Kant linked *beauty as a symbol of morality* to a reflective judgment, our hybrid view is that distanced sentiments are kinds of *judgments of taste*.[13] The epistemological advantage is that aesthetic audiences have a 'not-merely-personal stance' in comparison with the 'merely-personal-perspective' of everyday life. It is by way of lingering in possibility that emotions are integral to epistemic and practical virtue. Judging apt-sentiments asserts taste, which expresses an epistemic practice of an agent more than as factual knowledge. The agent has morally relevant imaginative-play route. The shift is favorable to virtue theory that places emphasis on the character of the knower in practice. Generalized emotions have a place in the mutual harmony within and between communities, epistemic communities included. The process of aesthetic judgment

[12] Abh. VI, See Gnoli (1956, 26).
[13] CJ §59, 229.

internally links an individual to a community in terms of attunement to compassionate values. Anyhow, aesthetic reflection invites the question of what a sentiment is at all, beyond causes. The occasion to reflect is just as much a way of breaking with a community feeling as a conscientious resonance in a critical judgment. An aesthetic response is a choice (agentively) of how to feel, over and above externally being caused to feel.

Emotion and Judgment

At first, there may not seem to be a need for considering this aesthetic idea that amounts to *reflection*, in virtue theory. Virtue ethics seeks to regulate or train emotion-dispositions within ordinary, mundane life. Emotions, extreme or mild, are also seen as a perennial source of bias. From Plato, we have been warned to pay attention to the way artistic emotional appeals are used to manipulate us, particularly with the seemingly innocuous poets who could as well be mad in their reveling.[14] Praising emotion as a reliable aid to virtue is equally problematic, since the occurrence of any emotion qua kind of judgment, need not track what is true. Emotional judgment can go against reason, towards delusion. What then to make of the firm unity of consciousness with emotion? Might the relevant aesthetic emotions actually lead to changes in our motivational and emotional dispositions resulting in moral and epistemic vice (rather than virtue) under certain conditions? Perhaps because emotion-sentiments in the arts reveal the flood-like force of communal sentiments, emotion is also an instrumental resource of vice. We accept that weaponized emotions in the public sphere have rightly earned a dangerous reputation. On this problem (a foil we could call the fallacy of appealing to art-emotion), it seems that both Immanuel Kant, and the stoic, Seneca, both of whom were generally distrustful of such emotions, offer direction as aesthetes. I wish to elucidate how Aristotelian, Stoic and Kantian insights may leave us at the threshold of *rasa* theory, a precise vocabulary of aesthetic generalization where the aesthete is emotionally moved to care and yet unmoved to act in anger. Both Kant and Abhinavagupta evade discoursing on the misuses of art for the unaesthetic end of manipulating ideas and political control. Seneca used the theater precisely to question the misuse of power. From there we

[14] Plato (1997), in the *Ion* reveals the poets to be more of a conduit of divine transmission than divinely inspired visionaries, in part because Ion has no idea what it is his poetry actually means himself.

can make a case in in favor of *reflective emotions* that are critical for cultivating aesthetic, epistemic and moral virtues. The refinement of emotion for a successful virtue is manifested in terms of a motivational function, as we shall see further on.

In the sense that there is an ethics of how to know the world, epistemology has a normative dimension. The master virtue for harmony, *wisdom* requires a conscientious agent. Epistemic dispositions to inquire and cultivate character traits that lead to intellectual virtue are motivated. Zagzebski (2001) In Aristotelian terms, emotions function as motivational components in a virtuously constituted character insofar as they cohere with good judgement, temperance, and balanced dispositions. Balancing virtues requires the wisdom of a skillful practice (*phronesis*). Some Stoics did distinguish between mere embodied affects, and [Aristotelian] emotions as (cognitive) judgments that motivate virtue or vice. Conversely, many stoics linked emotion's role in moral dispositions to total error. In line with virtue ethicists, virtue epistemologists also construe emotions as embodied judgements which express moral and epistemic value. In asking what an emotion in aesthetic experience consists in, we need to know if and how it functions in relation to beliefs, and whether or not the beliefs are evaluative.[15]

Aristotle discusses two kinds of virtue in the *Nicomachean Ethics* Book II: virtues of thought and virtues of character. Aristotle (1984) "Virtue, is a state that is willed which consists in a mean relative to an individual, defined by reference to reason, just as prudent person would define it. (1107a). Of course, practical virtue is supposed to be habitual, and not just in terms of acting, but also in terms of feeling. A virtuous state is not a mere feeling either, because feelings do not determine goodness or

[15] Beginning with a cognitive theory of emotions defended by the Stoic philosopher, Seneca, affective response or feeling in aesthetic experience is not necessarily considered to be an emotion, mainly because it is not construed as an evaluative judgment to which the agent assents. In a stoic cognitivism of 'emotions,' 'first movements,' or embodied affective responses, abide on a non-cognitive lower level. "Real" emotions are taken as higher order cognitive evaluations reaching assent to judgment. This is not the case for Posidonius, for whom the irrational nature of affect is attuned in aesthetic experience precisely because both poetics and affect function through harmonization of a distinct part of the soul. On Seneca's picture, what one names aestheticized-emotions are merely a first-order responses, which abide below the threshold of cognitive evaluation, and are thereby insufficient to constitute the paradigmatic minimally two-tiered structure of real 'emotions.' Seneca's own argument rests on the non-propositional nature of wordless music, and the lack of a determinate object on which to base a judgment of it. See Richard Sorabji, *Emotion and Peace of Mind*.

badness. Insofar as emotion functions as a motivational component in a virtuously constituted character, virtue is no *mere* disposition; it must be exercised. As such, even practical virtue is dependent on some intellectual virtue to determine its propriety. The trickiness of developing virtue means that being a good judge requires as broad as possible of an education (1095a). At the same time, education should be specialized, like medical treatment (1180b7–9). One must learn how to habituate emotions by a practice of moderation and pleasure in the right objects—a difficult task not lost on karma theorists. Education for aesthetic appreciation generates character traits such as carefulness, creativity and imagination. Enactments of emotion, if not positive in moral value, ought to tend toward positive understanding. Imaginative causes and effects, remove the obstacles of pragmatic, egotistical, and even intellectual concern as a matter of play.[16] Accordingly, Bijoy Boruah claims: "Distilled of egocentric first-personal salience and entertained in contemplative imagination, aesthetic emotions are a transmutation of ordinary emotions into what might be called essence-illuminating emotions. Whether it is the depiction of sorrow, love, jealousy, hatred, guilt, fear, repentance, or agony, the contemplative appreciation of affective response to such an artistic depiction is an emotional experience that illuminates what it is like to be in any such emotional state." Boruah (2016, 141) For this reason, a different questioning arises from the object, that of imaginable possibility, inviting a contemplative wonder. However, as Abhinavagupta confirms, we appreciate *rasa* more as a source of enjoyment than any sort of lesson. The "transformative power" of the aesthetic emotions is still necessarily positive in regulating inquiry in a truth-oriented way, for the realization of virtue or feeling out what is good for its own sake. *Virtue* and *rasa,* are intrinsic goods of a higher order perspective on truth and reality. The difference in paths to either virtue or vice is the form of desire-channeling disinterestedness (*Gītā* II.70) that flows at the heart of aesthetic inquiry. In Aristotle's poetics, aesthetic appreciation has a cathartic effect of channeling and balancing emotions, though the sketchy insights are limited to cognitive states linked to belief and the mere possibility of consequences of actions.

In the Stoic view, aesthetic emotions could only help us if they promote 'tranquility' and sublimate passion. The emotion-cognitivist and neo-Stoic, Martha Nussbaum notes an intentional object in any given emotion

[16] The process of imaginative role-play is a (*āvaraṇa-bhaṅga*) breaking of obscurity, see Chakrabarti (2009, 197).

with moral valence for an agent who is making a kind of judgment. Isolating epistemological emotions, which Nussbaum terms "upheavals" shows that emotions are not always irrational forces contrary to practical reason. As Nussbaum puts it, they also have a rational pull which expresses value judgments in a kind of shorthand about their intentional object. Nussbaum (2008) Thus, there is a stoic counter-position to *apatheia*. The right fit of key emotions can be useful for knowing the world by orienting the knower through key practices truth seeking. She improves upon Chrysippus strong position that all emotions are cognitions which are based on erroneous judgments.[17] A rival position from Posidonius is that emotions are not entirely reducible to judgments. Nussbaum interprets Posidonius' position as non-cognitive.[18] From the Stoics we get two insights. One is that we can picture at least some emotions to be evaluative. The other is that the mark of freedom (from viciousness) is emotional liberation from erroneous judgments, and someone who judges well has an ultra-balanced emotional disposition.

Seneca, who improved on the Platonic view by bringing in the Stoic model of emotions as judgments, did not view aesthetic experiences to manifest cognitive emotions. He wrote intense dramas as he attempted Nero's emotional training. Seneca is the first in the Greco-Roman tradition to make a fine-tuned distinction between ordinary emotions and quasi-emotions in the arts. In his moral-psychological theory of anger, he analyzed the shifting place of rationality in assenting to a cognitive judgment. The precursor to an emotion is an automated, non-voluntary embodied response Seneca calls a first movement (e.g., reflex or mirrored response). An emotion is an appraisal of sorts that follows up on it. He calls the judgment stage a full-fledged emotion.[19] Anger is an emotion that moves a step beyond merely cognitive emotions—it overturns reason and carries one away. However, if one can slow the process and recognize the causal sequence of rapture, then one can halt assent to its terms. Logical

[17] The Stoics linked emotion's place in moral dispositions to naturally follow from emotion's role in epistemic dispositions. Stoics naturally advocate disciplining emotional dispositions for an agent's benefit. Sorabji, 7.

[18] Nussbaum (1993) follows Galen on this: "Posidonius 'completely departed' (*telos apechorisen*), both from Chrysippus' view that they are identical with judgments and from Zeno's view that they supervene on and are necessarily produced by judgments: Nor he does not regard the passions either as judgments or as supervening upon judgments, but as coming about through the thumoeidetic and epithumetic power" (*Passions and Perceptions,* 110).

[19] Seneca, *De Ira, Book II.*

intervention in the process thwarts error. Seneca saw all real emotions as having this two-tiered structure, but in the third stage of some particularly vicious ones, such as anger, the agent lets go of, and loses one's self, not an activity that generally occurs at the theater. It is the opposite extreme of abandoning one's selfish ego. The cognitive distinction between ordinary and aesthetic instances of irrationality indicates that a distinction between 'fear as a state of suffering' and 'fear as contemplation' is possible. The structure of judgment is reversed, which is demonstrated by the non-cognitive feelings qua impulses in the enjoyment of music. Aesthetic experiences never get past the first stage, because aesthetic rapture supposedly lacks a judgment with a desired object. Being that there is no real object to fear in a horror novel, fear in response to its imagery is no more irrational than the initial flinch, sneezing or shivering. Thus, like Seneca, the cognitivist can reject "aesthetic emotions" are real emotions at all, by claiming first movements are responsible.[20] Aesthetic rapture remains unexplained on that count, though. Seneca's own distinctions should lead one to wonder what he saw the purpose of drama to be, especially since he was himself a dramatist, and was engaged in emotionally laden satire.[21] As revealed in Nussbaum's analysis Seneca uses distance to expose the viciousness of his enemy, and it is about an insight into character:

> Seneca's portrayal of [Claudius'] opportunistic murders and thoroughly vindictive character is correct. The chilling incident in which [Claudius] first has his wife Messalina executed and then asks why she has not come to the dinner table is just one example of his warped personality, and Seneca gets it right ... Our sources portray Claudius as paranoid and ruthless—able to find threats everywhere, and determined always to extirpate their imagined source without a fair hearing. ... On balance, then, Seneca is right about the

[20] It is worth differentiating the view of Posidonius from Chrysiuppus and Zeno on this point, the latter of whom Seneca follows. For Chrysiuppus, all emotions are faulty judgments and should be eradicated. If emotions are construed as irrational then they make us epistemically vulnerable. For the sake of explaining why the Stoics take up poetry as a practice, given the call for attacking it beginning with the rationalist, Plato, Martha Nussbaum has the positions mapped out: "The paradox of Stoic poetry," according to Nussbaum, is about the consensus of Hellenistic philosophers: "that poetry makes its impact on the soul above all by altering its passions" but ironically, many influential Stoics were themselves marvels of poetic erudition. (*Passions and Perceptions,* 98).

[21] Seneca 2010. "The Pumpkinification of Claudius the God" (*Apocolocyntosis*). See: *Seneca: Anger, Mercy, Revenge*. Martha Nussbaum, trans.

> man's character, though—perhaps for reasons of genre—he underrates [Claudius'] intellectual capacity and political skill.[22]

The way Seneca hotly ridicules actions of anger is countered in his cooler judgment of a man's character—which is a particular kind of skill—reaching the stoic ideal of total emotional distance. To be "aestheticized" is for an emotion to take on generality and distance. Like Plato, the Stoics did not deny that erroneous emotional judgments, irrational emotions, and quasi-emotions have the power to move us. A practice of affective damage control is needed to realign one's self in virtue with the cosmic order, though. Sorabji (2000)[23] In turn, Stoics seem to choose their poets very carefully. If anything, theistic stoicism invites us to make, and further clarify the distinction between distanced aesthetic emotions and reactive ordinary emotions. Even for Plato, what it truly means to love the beautiful (love of truth) is at the heart of his critique against the indulgent vanity of poets. In the moment of aesthetic appreciation in a Platonic sense could not be fast and easy, there would certainly be an absence of rushing, and presence of reflection, and transcendence. Plato's most significant aesthetic lesson for approaching wisdom was really that we ought to have patience for the process of loving and reaching truth. Like the process of learning classics, attitude is essential. Conversely, if overtaken and drowning in the trappings of personal desires then are agitated, in a hurry and fail to achieve a reflective mode of enjoyment. Emerging from *the conjunction* is novel *interested-disinterestedness* or a pathos by choice. At the very least, in the impersonal subjectivity of *reflection*, the process of sympathy unfolds contemplatively, if only for a while. The fragility of such moments, while feeling timeless, renders the *rasa experience* fleeting, marking *rasa* as distinct from stable dispositions and occurrent states. We have a kind of 'judgment' about emotions as they are encountered in aesthetic experience, but it is crystalized in a universal rather than particular judgment. On this much Aristotle agreed in the *Poetics*—aestheticized pathos, as an affect caused by poetry, teaches universal knowledge, while history teaches particulars. The result of aesthetic engagement is not a universal standard of beauty, nor merely beauty as a symbol of morality

[22] Ibid., p. 202.

[23] Seneca, in particular prescribes a program of discipline in his counsel to extirpate all practices leading to anger.

but rather is a self-critical test of impartiality, sensitivity, thoughtfulness and character.

Imagination

As final lead, Kant critically remarked that to ask how "aesthetic judgments are possible a priori" we must deal with a lesser question, namely, how we become conscious, in a judgment of taste, of a reciprocal subjective *harmony* between the cognitive powers: is it aesthetically, through mere inner sense and sensation? or is it intellectually, through consciousness of the intentional activity by which we bring these powers into play?[24] The pleasure cannot be merely intellectual because "the quickening of the two powers" (of the imagination and understanding) bypasses concepts. The pleasure is not felt in ordinary sensation either because inward directed aesthetic judgements bypass the concept of an object of sensation.[25] The 'liking' in all judgments of the sublime, which is similar to 'liking' in taste, is connected to the power of exhibition (the imagination) being in harmony with the power of reaching concepts (the understanding). Then, while the experiencer finds herself at a loss to fully size up some incomprehensible thing, concepts take root in determining 'Nature' to be *terrifying*.[26] 'Affect,' which relates to sublimity, remains if the feeling may be what is referred to as *noble*. In the "Exposition" Kant reveals that in aesthetically sublime experience:

> Only a cast of mind of that sort is called noble—[though] the term has since come to be applied to things as well, such as a building, a garment, a literary style, a person's bearing, and so on—namely, if it arouses not so much *amazement* (an affect [that occurs] when we present novelty that exceeds our expectation) as *admiration* (an amazement that does not cease once the novelty is gone), which happens when ideas in their exhibition harmonize, unintentionally and without art, without our aesthetic liking. Every affect of the VIGOROUS KIND (i.e., which makes us conscious that we have forces to overcome any resistance, is *aesthetically sublime* (CJ 273, Pluhar, 133)

[24] Ibid., 219, pp. 63.

[25] CJ 187 Pluhar, 26 [This cryptic phrasing might be one reason to suppose that aesthetic pleasure precedes the process of judging, but logically, as we shall see this thought should be avoided.]

[26] 209 Kant, CJ 268, Pluhar, pp. 127210 Kant, OBS 47–8.

An ordinary wonder occurs when novelty exceeds our expectation. But *admiration* [*Bewunderung*] is a form of aesthetic wonder which persists beyond the novelty of a presentation, based on the aesthetic phenomena. Subsequently, affects are distinguishable by either *vigorous* or *languid* kinds. Kant himself mockingly expresses wonder at the uniqueness of this superior emotion: Admiration is sublime aesthetically, because it imparts a momentum whose effects are mightier and more permanent than those of an impulse produced by sense. The agent who experiences a harmony between the imagination and understanding with the feeling of an emotion, has a telling state about the fittingness of emotion for the circumstance. In this way, aesthetic rapture reinforces the capacity to judge a range of emotions with personal distance. Reflective judging ties together the different modes of judging taste, sublime, and the *rasa* experience with (evaluative and descriptively rich) thick emotions. Aesthetic enjoyment is an intrinsic good or end in itself, but towards being a good knower, conscious harmony between the imagination and understanding also bring about self-reflexivity, and self-trust.

The imagination has some functions which are objective, and others of which are more playful in Kant's *lawful freedom of imagination*. Though more can be said on epistemic value of play, at this point we have to address a possible objection: the foil of cognitive contact with reality is also an active conductor of that contact—*the imagination*. For something to be purely imaginary is 'to lack a grip on reality.' A virtuous transformation ought to make one prone to understanding reality better, but the thought process involved in aesthetic experience is not tethered to how things really are, and this gives rise to skepticism about imaginative embellishments. In response, Aristotle held a view of art-experience which served as a precursor to the imagination's role in achieving intellectual virtue. One can argue he has a notion of *poetic truth*, as modal truth in the *Poetics*. Unlike ordinary circumstances, theater gets at probable 'impossibilities,' in which case drama produces a logical judgment, of *possibility*. Possibilities are also imaginatively produced in theater when one generalizes a character's plight to be understood as a 'real possibility of one's own.' Furthermore, Aristotle claims: "For it is the nature of a riddle to attach impossibilities to real things," which implies the creative act is not distinct from acts of negative understanding. An interesting thing about coming up against such imaginative resistance in inquiry is that it sends the understanding towards some other certainty. Virtue epistemologist, Linda Zagzebski notes: "The *technai* of art, music, and literature can produce a state that has epistemic value ... Understanding works of art and literature is probably one step removed from understanding basic features of reality, since the arts are in part an attempt to understand reality."[27] However, few epistemologists would agree. A general Stoic insight capable of deflating imaginatively constructed emotions is the ill effect of a pathological disposition to fantasize. The value of art cannot be that it produces knowledge. Rather, we expect enjoyment. If sensitivity or a technical skill is enhanced, we arguably will find it in the understanding, but as a non-propositional ability to grasp relations between the self, and subjects of experience.

In his Critique of Judgment, Kant provides a theory of reflective judgment, as such.[28] The ability is an aesthetic capacity that Kant may have seen as a "hidden art of the soul" which is a condition for having propositional knowledge, not itself conceptual and determined.

The productive imagination, a means of emergent knowledge, follows rules of truth-oriented-ness in its disinterestedness from personal desires. By aptly judging in a *rasa experience*, "judgments of 'taste" non-cognitive, open-ended, but intellectually sublime. Kant claims that genius is (1) an art, not a science, (2) presupposes a purpose and hence, understanding, (3) expresses an aesthetic idea, and (4) is not rule based, but is lawfully in harmony with the imagination and understanding, presupposing attunement of the powers in an "unstudied, unintentional subjective purposiveness" brought about only by nature[29] (CJ 186/318). This necessitates the faculties of imagination and understanding are "at play" without reaching a cognitive, or fixed judgment. Grounded in a disinterested stance, a 'moment of universality' in a supposed *judgment of taste* places assurance on the correctness in judgment, irrespective of others' failure to assent to it, because of an internal harmony between the *imagination and understanding* that does not the least concern the power of desire. Thus, objective and private feelings can be contrasted with subjective, but universally valid feelings. The former is the occurrence of objectivity in cognitive or

[27] Zagzebski, Linda. *Virtues of the Mind*. 2002, 243.

[28] Kant's theory of reflective judging is integral to this account, but up to this point we could just as well consider David Hume's *of the Standard of Taste*. The key feature of Kant's theory here, is that the judgment of taste must be theoretically communicable. The aesthetic experience is one in which we can imagine others would likely feel the same way in similar circumstances, even if embodied responses, such as trembling or crying differ between members of the audience. The judgment of taste is communicable in a way that is unlike lower-order affective responses.

[29] CJ Pluhar, 186/318.

logical judgments while the latter is a subjectivity of "reflective judgement." This point is key to theorizing ideas of aesthetic emotion so we may distinguish merely personal, from 'disinterested,' as in de-personalized, feelings. Yet, aesthetic judgments are not disinterested in the sense that salient interests are dulled. An emotional investment expands, only what is at stake is changed. The kinds of judgments an artist makes have continuity with judgments a connoisseur makes in *rasa* theory, even if they disagree on the sentiment. A special form of genius, or *pratibhā*, is the ability to grasp relations where an idea or a play on words and meaning come spontaneously to the knower.

Aesthetic Character

The inter-personal metaphysical problem of the relation between unity and multiplicity is a problem of how the mind makes contact with the manifold of experiences in bodies. The agent of aesthetic enjoyment is an active observer, who takes in the array of feelings, but does not desire their objects. A form of joy qua imaginative freedom in attaining harmony within, will lead to building and maintaining harmony throughout, signifying the overflow of meaning of in existence. Aesthetic appreciation in fact plays a significant role in altering ingrained emotional dispositions, and character virtues where personal interests are reconsidered. As an occasion to become better, we all have a special interest in cultivating some forms of artistic appreciation. Abhinavagupta clearly indicates that the point of producing the *emotional context* (i.e., making an aesthetic cause with theater, dance and song) is to remove personal obstacles for the mind to rest in the self—in a refined experience. Thus, the pleasure of aesthetic experience is metaphorically referred to as "repose in the heart," or *viṣrānti*. Emotions, for better or worse, move an agent to act or refrain from acting. Aestheticized emotions lead to repose, because an agent is moved Chakrabarti (2005). The actual physical characteristics of the body and an embodied mind (*manas*), make *rasa* movements relatable to motivating personal emotions[30] The judgment of aesthetic emotion is sublime—elevated, and discriminating or endowed *with taste*. If imagination and creativity are intellectual virtues, and we believe they are, then aestheticized emotions create avenues of contemplation and understanding by touching on certain emotional dispositions. The moment involves a

[30] Sen *Aesthetic Enjoyment*, XXI.

motivational shift towards a newfound freedom from desire for things, or ego. *Śāntarasa* is freely achieved "when one leaves all ways of desire untouched, *śānta* alone remains" (*Gītā* 22.71/73). "Śanta" here is *śāntarasa*, the sentiment of quietism or tranquillity that Abhinavagupta names as a ninth basic emotion to be suggested in a drama. Traditionally repetition of '*śāntiḥ*' three times at the end of a mantra manifests an aim of freedom from the three kinds of afflictions (*tāpatrayas*), including those which are out of our control (*ādidaivika*) from forces of nature, those immediate relations to which we ought to aptly respond (*ādhyātmika*), and inner discord of the mind and emotions (*ādibhautika*). A connoisseur, or *rasika*, has knowing a taste of freedom from such afflictions, an inward flow of *śāntarasa*, which in an aesthetic judgment is felt as a playful break from vanity, remorse, heartbreak, or a hostile world.

Arguably, even in Immanuel Kant's theory of taste, a reflective harmony Kant describes as "lawfulness"[31] (in the form of the *free play of imagination and understanding*), may move an agent towards intentionally exercising intellectual and moral virtue with the threefold aspect that Sri Sitansu Sekhar has suggested: "(a) the harmony within, which is the virtue; (b) the harmony amongst human beings—in one's own society and the whole social world—that the virtue is meant to, and helps promote; and (c) the harmony of the individual and every society with the natural world," (Chakravarti 2019, 153). It matters that it is a world in which we delight in and promote on the basis of the virtue. The new grounds for virtue are the earth itself, the dancer and the questioner. It is no wonder then that in a Śaivāgama commentary on Tantric scripture called the *Parā Trīśikā Vivarṇa*, Abhinavagupta explains the state of *samatā* for the embodied questioner, Devī, is oneness with the supreme consciousness. He says: "That very *khecari* is perceived separately (from the Divine) in the form of desire, anger, etc. However, the *samatā* or sameness of *khecari* means the perception of her full divine nature everywhere [all sound, sight, taste, smell, touch] because of her being of the perfect nature of Bhairava ..." who is pure consciousness.[32] Of note is that "*samatā*" here means oneness with the unconditioned and undetermined consciousness as an ethical agent. We unenlightened are not able to perceive the moral agency in the other. The ideal vision is not a state that is first habituated and then exercised as a virtue, it is liberation. Thus, in this context, *samatā*

[31] Pluhar, 2010, 91 §241.

[32] Abhinavagupta (2014), Jaideva Singh trans, 2014, 39.

is not an Aristotelian virtue such as equanimity. In aesthetic rapture is not moderate in feeling, either. *Samatā* in the aesthetic context is a regulative ideal of relational consciousness. The Kantian aesthetic pleasure rests on a surplus of self-consciousness rather than preference for individual preferences that Eva Schaper (2009) speaks of as impure judgments of [hedonic] value. It is not possible to instantly transition from selfishness to the self in all except through play reversing an order in feeling. So here we have to practice love, and the virtue is rare and sublime. This view is not only a Śaiva view of the reality of phenomenal consciousness as a product of agency, but in that reading, *rasa* is explicitly connected to freely willed emotions, and thus grants a new route to theorize emotions as purposive for ethical action.

The reality of aesthetic generalization is demonstrated by way of a practice of spontaneous feeling responsible for virtues of imagination and creativity. As in Wittgenstein's *Tractatus*, one has to go beyond the world to look for this value. The point is to return to the ordinary world, with aesthetic sensibility. As, *Tractatus* 6.41 holds: "The meaning of the world must lie outside the world …"[33] we can respond that in *Śrī Tantrāloka*, Abhinavagupta identifies the only possible meaning outside the world as grace. The moved agent acts with a free desire:

> Nothing remains as to do for him (the aspirant) in last doings except the compassion towards people like an axe frees a person from all bondages of sufferings.
>
> This world does effort by assuming 'this is my duty'. But it never does any work for others. But he, who is full of Bhairavibhāva (feeling and existence of power) after destroying all the worldly impurities, does his duties only for the sake of the happiness of people. (Tantrāloka II.38–39, Abhinavagupta (2008), 55-6).[34]
>
> [*Thus … Abhinavgupta later reflects*]:
>
> Some beings are enlightened only for their own liberation, but others for the sake of redeeming the whole world—just as a firefly shines only for itself, jewels shine for others, the stars shine for more, the moon shines for still more, and the sun bestows light on the whole universe. (Tantraloka XIII. 159)

[33] Wittgenstein & Kolak 1998, 48.

[34] Chatterjee. Trans. Śrī Tantrāloka 2008, 55–56.

As the spade turns here for emotion concepts, those emotions that are reflecting on the world and overflowing with meaning, are the essence, or *rasa*, of pure consciousness that connects inner and outer awareness through the body. Reflective awareness is significant for the shift in perspective an agent has in relation to others—one that dissolves. *Distilled emotions, distanced emotions, or a possible dissolution of one's own selfish ego and problems, into the feeling of the world* is part of the mystery of existence. "The feeling of the world as a bounded whole is the mystical feeling."[35] Taking into account Sri Sitansu Sekhar's critical insight: "However, once one has reached the mystic state having gone beyond, looking back at the world is never the same again. With the mystic transformation having taken shape in the subject, the facts (i.e., how things stand) have got a touch of value on them." (Chakravarti 2019, 151) The result is that the ordinary world *becomes* touched, infused, or colored with value. Pratyābhijñā philosophy has this path of rediscovery of the divine Self through harmony with every being. *Rasa* was waiting for us as a solution because we sought truth. We find more than we were looking for, though. The value of sentience overflows into life, as a reflective knowing, which harmonizes with the character of *sameness* as unity in multiplicity. A world infused with value is sought by the Pratyābhijñā philosopher as conducive to liberation even if *rasa* is a rare experience of attunement and of harmonizing with others. Unlike liberation, though, aesthetic experience is fleeting. Where *rasa* is fleeting, so is *samatā*. One must cultivate the insight in here and now relations only by practices. With grace, one acts with insight and compassion. If one has self-recognition then one also has *samatā* and *rasa*. If this reading of *samatā* is new to this confluence of ideas, we again echo the point: "harmony is not simply self-control that Aristotle talks about as a measure against self-indulgence or intemperance, but adds a meaning to the onward flow of life." (Chakravarti 2019, 153) Aristotle saw that virtue requires instantiations, but our virtue of *harmony within* is something special. The *inner condition of harmony* can transcend spatial-temporal limitations. The fact that emotional *samatā* is an aesthetic concept is crucial. Just as beauty transforms a symbol of morality beyond any rational end and as it is not a fixed outcome of a strictly rational process, reason is very much involved as a guiding principle. Aesthetic pleasure allows one to linger on the negative emotion (e.g., Othello's envy) without feeling the hatred of Othello. The aestheticizing agent is

[35] Ibid., 49.

observant, and not passively so. The aesthetic judgement is a truth about sublime *character*, and the self-refinement of the *knower* is a moving target in a virtue.

The pivot of an emotion for virtue is the a priori of *rasa* in consciousness as transcendental emotion. Affectively, our problematic emotions require that a "solution of the riddle of life in space and time lies *outside* space and time" as conditions of possibility we all have access to—awe, love, grief, anger, mirth, disgust, fear, courage, and the wonderfully *samatā* tranquil peace of rest in *wanting-not*. We have desires, and desire-based emotions, owing to exercising reflective possibilities of *rasa*. Just as space and time are conditions for the possibility of experience, reflective wonder, pathos and harmony are affective conditions of consciousness. Consciousness is playing but lawful.[36] It is not just a truth about the way things hang together, as it were, though there is a certain fittingness to the parts of a poetic image which can only be grasped by getting at the whole. As a Sanskrit critic, Kṣemendra, elucidated with the concept of propriety (*aucitya*), in order to manifest *rasa*, we feel apt judgments of valued qualities. The character of *rasa-judgment*, is realized like an aesthetic atmosphere because the artwork, poem, etc., captures a way desire goes in life.[37] Just as a priori concepts were a condition for making a judgment of taste, a priori sentience as Śiva consciousness is idealist basis of divine aptness of a *rasa*, or in Kantian terms, a playing imagination and understanding. The logic of *rasa* is such that though consciousness is inherently free, ethical choices determine us as moral players. All possibilities are to be savored in the imagination and understanding. *Rasa* is most real, or the essential delight in the transformations of consciousness which drinks in the logic of desire, and lets it rest.

Aesthetic emotion begins as art made for the pleasure of contemplation, if anything. Yet, for our purposes, and even Aristotle's, an emotion concept for virtue should be just that, *a contemplative feeling, fit to judge self-refinement and responsive action truthfully*. The aesthetic sentiment is not a movement with a worldly goal or objective, though. It is a reflective flutter. Precisely because there is an inner harmony to *rasa*, the connoisseur feels negative emotions with equanimity, or without the subversive desires that make ordinary emotions painful and blind. In the above ethos

[36] Kant, Pluhar trans. 2010, 91.

[37] Kṣemdra (1964), *Aucityavicārcarcā* 118, *Aucitya* is literally a concept of propriety, fitness, and appropriateness, but could be translated as aptness.

of the poet Vidyākara, the normative appeal is to an epistemic virtue, that of sensitivity. A poet has the sensitivity to *inquire with the heart*, which hyperbolically stands in contrast to a *rasa* elevated heart of stone.

On the level of aesthetic judgment for sentient beings, *rasa* is relishing of our communal inquiry that reflectively tracks the unity in multiplicity of consciousness. The theory supports the sentient nature of consciousness in virtue. Aesthetic emotions are not virtues, though. Aesthetic emotion initiates a self-conscious reflective transition away from conditioned dispositional emotions towards affective freedom. Whereas our ordinary emotions draw out our conflicting desires, *rasa* experiences draw fragmented beings together. Connoisseurs share open-ended discourses. The harmony that exists within the communities of *rasa* appreciation carries with it a sensitivity to contexts rather than merely to individual concerns. In relational terms, the *rasika* audience aspires to a friendly discourse of the heart with the minds of all others, or life itself. In epistemic terms, the enjoyer (*sahṛdaya*) is reflective. By attuning one's self to meaningful conditions, *rasa*'s interpersonal harmony is ground for apt responses to suffering. The unconstrained ability to be disinterested, yet to discriminately infuse worldly interests with pathos, is a meaningful harmony internal to the knower. In agentive terms, the audience (*samājika*) is free to find agreement or not in a *rasa* without loss. *Samatā* is an extraordinary and resonant epistemic virtue towards which a practice of aesthetic immersion is regulative. Though our individual aesthetic paths only sustain the inquiry, the moral questioning stays open and ongoing. Without any loss of artistic sources revealing how the personal transformation of desire is possible, emotion concepts for virtue theory from epistemic to moral transcends utility with aesthetic considerations.

References

Abhinavagupta. 2014. Singh, J., Joo, L., & Bäumer, B. *Parā-Trīśikā-vivaraṇa: The secret of tantric mysticism*. Motilal Banarsidass Publishers.

Abhinavagupta. 2004. Marjanovic, Boris. Trans. *Gītārthasaṁgraha*. Varanasi: Indica Books.

Abhinavagupta. 2008. Chatterjee, Gautam. Trans. *Śrī Tantrālokaḥ*. Indian Mind, Varanasi.

Abhinavagupta and Bharatamuni. 1992. *The Nāṭyaśāstra of Bharata, with the Abhinavabhāratī of Abhinavagupta*, Vol. 1, 4th ed. Ed. K. Krishnamoorthy. Baroda: Oriental Institute.

Aristotle. 1984. *The Complete Works of Aristotle: The Revised Oxford Translation.* Vol. 2. Jonathan Barnes, trans. Princeton University Press: 2316–40.

Bhattacharyya, K. C. 2011. "The Concept of Rasa (1930)." *Indian Philosophy in English from Renaissance to Independence.* edited by Nalini Bhushan and Jay L. Garfield. Oxford University Press.

Boruah, Bijoy. 2016. Arindam Chakrabarti, ed. "The impersonal Subjectivity of Aesthetic Emotion" in *Bloomsbury research handbook of Indian aesthetics and the philosophy of art.* London: Bloomsbury Academic.

Chakrabarti, Arindam. 2009. "Play, Pleasure, Pain: Ownerless Emotions in Rasa-Aesthetics." *In History of Science, Philosophy, and Culture in Indian Civilization. Vol. XV Part III.* ed. D.P. Chattopadhyaya and Amiya Dev (New Delhi: Center for Study in Civilizations). pp. 189–202.

Chakrabarti, Arindam. 2005."Heart of Repose, The Repose of the Heart: A Phenomenological Analysis of the Concept of Viśrānti" in *Samarasya: Studies in Indian Arts, Philosophy, and Interreligious Dialogue: in Honour of Bettina Bäumer.* Edited by Sadananda Das and Ernst Fürlinger. New Delhi: D.K. Printworld.

Chakravarti, Sitansu Sekhar. 2019. "Tagore-Wittgenstein Interface: The poet's activism and virtue ethics." Tagore, Einstein and the Nature of Reality: Literary and Philosophical Reflections. Partha Ghose (ed.) London: Routledge.

Dās, Bhagavan. 1953. *The science of emotions.* Madras, India: Theosophical Pub. House.

Gnoli, Raniero. 1956. *The aesthetic experience according to Abhinavagupta.* Roma: Is. M.E.O.

Guyer, Paul. "Alva Noë, Strange Tools: Art and Human Nature" Philosophy and Phenomenological Research Vol. XCIV No. 1, January 2017.

Hanfling, Oswald. "Five Kinds of Distance" *British Journal of Aesthetics*, Vol. 40, No. 1, January 2000 p 89–102

Kant, Immanuel. 2010. Werner S. Pluhar. trans. *Critique of Judgment.* Indianapolis: Hackett.

Keltner, Dacher. 2023 *Awe: The Transformative Power of Everyday Wonder.* Penguin.

Kṣemendra. 1964. Ācārya Śri Brajmohan Jhā. Ed. *Aucityavicārcarcā.* Vidyabhawan Sanskrit Granthamala, Chowkhamba.

Lyotard, Jean François. 1991. Lessons on the Analytic of the sublime Kant's Critique of judgment, sections §23–29. Translated by Elizaberh Ronenberg. Meridian.

McCrea, L. J. (2009). *The teleology of poetics in medieval Kashmir.* Published by the Dept. of Sanskrit and Indian Studies, Harvard University.

Noë, Alva "Strange Tools: Art and Human Nature: A Precis" *Philosophy and Phenomenological Research.* Vol. XCIV No. 1, January 2017.

Nussbaum, Martha C. 2008. *Upheavals of thought: the intelligence of emotions.* Indianapolis, Hackett

Nussbaum, Martha C. 1993. "Poetry and the Passions: two Stoic views" in *Passions and Perceptions: studies in Hellenistic philosophy of mind.* Edited by Jacques Brunschwig, and Martha C. Nussbaum. Cambridge University Press.

Plato. 1997 John M. Cooper Ed., Paul Woodruff trans. "Ion" in *Complete Works.* Cambridge; Hackett.

Seneca, Lucius Annaeus. 2010. Nussbaum, Martha. Trans. "The Pumpkinification of Claudius the God". *and* "On Anger" trans. Kaster. *In Anger, Mercy, Revenge.* Chicago University Press.

Schaper, Eva. Pleasure, preference and value: studies in philosophical aesthetics. Cambridge: Cambridge Univ. Pr., 2009.

Sorabji, Richard. 2000. *Emotion and Peace of Mind: From Stoic Agitation To Christian Temptation The Gifford Lectures.* Oxford University Press

Vidyākara, and Daniel Henry Holmes. Ingalls, trans., Kosambi and Gokhale, eds. (1957). *Subhāṣitaratnakoṣa: Sanskrit Poetry, from Vidyākara's Treasury.* Cambridge Harvard Oriental Series.

Williams, Bernard. Spring 2001 "Philosophy as a Humanistic Discipline" *The Three penny Review.*

Wittgenstein, L., & Kolak, D. (1998). *Wittgenstein's tractatus.* Mayfield Publishing Company.

Zagzebski, Linda Trinkaus. 2002. *Virtues of the mind: an inquiry into the nature of virtue and the ethical foundations of knowledge.* Cambridge University Press.

Zagzebski, Linda Trinkaus. 2001. "Rediscovering Understanding" in Knowledge, Truth and Duty, edited by Matthias Steup. Oxford University Press.

CHAPTER 14

Science, Spirituality and Virtue Ethics

V. Kumar Murty

Introduction

The goal of this article is to discuss science, and specifically its practice and expression, in relation to virtue ethics, and the living of a spiritual life.

Apart from popular literature, questions of ethics and spirituality are not normally associated with science in the sense that we expect science to provide any answers or insights. Rather, these questions arise in philosophy, and perhaps also in religion, and are for the most part discussed by practitioners of these disciplines. Our point of view is that there is a person behind the science, and it is this person who also asks about ethics and spirituality in a way that is complementary and not contradictory to the science.

People debate whether cloning or genetic modification is ethical or whether artificial intelligence can ever reflect human values. These are not only questions asked by observers, but by scientists themselves who are perhaps looking for a normative framework that will help them to pursue,

V. K. Murty (✉)
University of Toronto, Toronto, ON, Canada
e-mail: murty@math.utoronto.ca

S. S. Chakravarti et al. (ed.), *Traditional Indian Virtue Ethics for Today*, Palgrave Studies in Comparative East-West Philosophy,
https://doi.org/10.1007/978-3-031-47972-4_14

or to support, a given direction of scientific research in a way that is consistent with their humanity.

In moral philosophy, the virtue ethics point of view places emphasis on the development of character. This is in contrast to utilitarianism which emphasizes the consequences of action and deontology which emphasizes duty. In virtue ethics, the focus of attention is on the moral agent developing strength of character.

The Western perspective locates the concepts of virtue ethics almost exclusively in the work of Aristotle. Thus, the Aristotelian point of view has dominated this aspect of Western moral philosophy. However, the writings of contemporary philosophers, especially Michael Slote, make clear that a virtue-ethical perspective is to be found in many non-Western philosophical traditions. Slote writes 'What strikes me as most salient about virtue ethics in this increasingly internationalized world we live in is how widespread and practically pervasive virtue ethics and virtue-ethical thinking are in the world's ethical thinking'. (Slote 2013) With the backdrop of Slote's point of view, we shall examine the virtue-ethical component of our topic from the perspective of Vedanta, especially as elucidated in the works of Vivekananda.

As we said, virtue ethics places emphasis on the development of character. According to Aristotle, a strong moral character leads to flourishing, or success, of the individual. In practice, it is to be observed that what constitutes flourishing or success will differ from individual to individual. From the perspective of Vedanta, a strong character makes possible a *transformation* and growth that leads to more effective action. But beyond that, it leads to awareness of oneself and one's identity, and manifestation of one's perfection. Moreover, this perfection is actually perfection of the whole, consisting in an awareness of the interconnectedness of everything. Vivekananda asserts 'God, though everywhere, can be known to us in and through human character' (Vivekananda, What we believe in, 1978, 356).

The relationship between strength of character, transformation and growth of the individual, and manifestation of one's perfection connect virtue ethics to Vivekananda's concept of education: 'Education is the manifestation of the perfection already in man' (Vivekananda, What we believe in, 1978, 358).

Speaking to the virtue-ethical foundation of education, Vivekananda asserts 'We want that education by which character is formed, strength of mind is increased, the intellect is expanded, and by which one can stand on one's own feet' (Vivekananda, Conversation with Surendra Nath Sen, 1979a, 342).

Moreover, he stated 'Education is not the amount of information that is put into your brain and runs riot there, undigested, all your life. We must have life-building, man-making, character-making assimilation of ideas. If you have assimilated five ideas and made them your life and character, you have more education than any man who has got by heart a whole library' (Vivekananda, The future of India, 1979b, 302).

In stressing growth of the individual, Vedanta asserts that spirituality is not a belief or a proclamation, but a transformation and a becoming. Thus, Vivekananda said that the Upanishads that describe the philosophy of Vedanta do not speak of salvation, but of freedom and that this freedom is already within us. (Vivekananda, Vedanta and Indian life, 1979c, 238–239).

Moreover, even transformation is not the final word: one has to *live and act* in the light of that transformation. This state is referred to in Vedanta as *jivanmukta* which roughly translates to 'free while living'. It is a way of living and moving and interacting that takes into account the apparent multiplicity of the empirical world without forgetting the unity at the spiritual dimension.

Returning from these Himalayan peaks to the activity that the scientist engages in, it has to be acknowledged that the great advances of science in describing our world and predicting events have given science an almost religious following. In almost all fields of human activity, there is an effort to formulate ideas in a scientific frame of reference. Spinoza's work on Ethics is an attempt to develop a mathematical approach to ethics, or at least a mathematically styled presentation, and his work is actually delineated in terms of Lemmas and Propositions. Even art has been affected by the scientific tendency as can be seen in schools like Picasso's cubism.

There is a feeling that ideas derive greater credibility when they have a scientific sanction. While some of these efforts succeed more than others, the very attempt shows the power wielded by science in affecting human behaviour. We find people eager to justify behaviour in terms of being 'scientific' and deriding behaviour that cannot be so described. You will find marketing literature using words like 'scientist-approved' and 'laboratory-tested' to give whatever they are advocating more credibility. All of this is to show that science has a hold on the minds of people and that they attach greater credibility to statements that are connected to science in some way.

At the same time, many thinkers will agree that there are limitations to what science can achieve and it is unrealistic to look to science for authority in dealing with phenomena that lie outside the scope of science. Foremost amongst thinkers who express this view are practising scientists themselves. The limits of science are quite keenly felt by practitioners of science, but perhaps are not well understood by those who follow science in a popular way.

A better understanding of what science is, and what guides its practice and its form of expression, can help us see its potential and its limitation. We especially want to cast a spotlight on the *person* who is doing science as that will bring out the ethical and spiritual dimensions of her activity. While our focus is on science, we must remember that 'the moral agent in her role as scientist should not be thought of as separate from the moral agent as a person' (Chen 2015). Any concept of the development of character must include integrity or wholeness of the individual.

What Is Science?

Etymologically, the word 'science' comes from the Latin root 'scindere' which means to divide or dissect. The idea is that the scientific approach to knowledge is to dissect a complex phenomenon into simpler constituent parts. By understanding these parts, one gets an idea of the more complex phenomenon. Whether one is studying the cosmos or human anatomy or the structure of the living cell, the approach of science tends to be to decompose the complex phenomenon in front of us into simpler constituent pieces and to attempt to gain an understanding of those pieces.

There is a further effort to find the *ultimate* building blocks of which even these constituent pieces are composed. And this is a theme in science including in mathematics. It is reminiscent of the Upanishadic query 'what is that by knowing which all else becomes known?' Though the query in the Upanishads may be targeting a broader conception of knowledge than what science is accustomed to, the idea is the same, namely to understand the fundamental building blocks or some knowledge from which all other knowledge can be reconstructed.

Strictly speaking, knowing the building blocks is not the end of the story. One has to supplement the knowledge of the parts with how they work together. How are the constituent pieces put together to assemble the more complex phenomenon? We know that the human genome is made up of just four nucleotides. However, sequencing the human genome was a major achievement. In what order are these four basic building blocks assembled to create the human genome? And even knowing the sequence is just the beginning, as it is not yet known what alteration or alterations of the sequence has what effect. And until that is known, the genome sequence is not a useful tool. Going even further, one knows that it is not just the sequence, but the geometric arrangement (folding) that also has tremendous significance for example, in gene transcription.

I mentioned the etymology of the word 'science'. I might point out here that the word 'religion' also comes from a Latin root 'religio' which means 'that which holds together'. Incidentally, the Sanskrit word 'dharma' also means the same thing. From this point of view, to understand complex phenomena, we need both science and religion where I am interpreting these words strictly in terms of their etymological origin. We need to understand the constituent parts of a complex phenomenon, but we also have to understand how those parts fit together and interact with each other. It is only with this combined approach that we might get a meaningful or comprehensive understanding of complex phenomena. And it is only with this combined approach that we can turn knowledge into action, and with this come the ethical issues.

R. Fouchier and Y. Kawaoka, virology researchers from the Netherlands and the United States (respectively), showed in 2011 how to genetically modify an avian influenza virus H5N1 so that it became an airborne virus that could spread between ferrets. They felt that such 'gain of function' research was important for understanding the public health implications of such mutations, including the production of effective vaccines should there arise a mutation to which humans were susceptible. The research was only possible because both the sequencing of the virus and the way in which the genome could be engineered to modify its transmissibility, were understood.

Fouchier and Kawaoka's research understandably sparked much concern in the scientific community, especially as they wanted to publish their research. Their work was eventually published, but only after the development of a policy framework around such research. In 2013, they published a subsequent paper (Fouchier and Kawaoka 2013) in *Nature* in which they proposed experimenting with another strain of avian influenza virus H7N9 to change its properties, including transmissibility, and other fundamental properties.

Notice that these discussions took place just 8 years before the COVID-19 pandemic and there are still debates about whether COVID was a human engineered virus that 'escaped' the laboratory. Certainly, gain-of-function research counts as one of the most significant ethical issues that science has had to deal with in the recent past. However, we note that this ethical question is not one that could be discussed, debated and settled by scientists alone as they do not have the expertise needed to consider all the issues and implications that are involved. It is interesting to note that already in 1989, funding agencies, including the National Institutes of Health, had asked scientists to broaden their expertise by taking a course or other training on 'the responsible conduct of research whose curricula includes topics on science's social contexts and consequences' (Chen 2015, 89).

As science progresses, it is clear that these kinds of ethical issues are going to appear with increasing frequency and complexity. We are currently facing one now in the debate about artificial intelligence. There are a large number of leaders in the AI community who feel that it is necessary to slow the pace of research, or even to halt it. Such calls, whether they be practical or not, are a clear manifestation of the ethical responsibility that scientists have and are becoming aware of. For the most part, halting of research is probably impractical as it would attempt to put back into a bottle a genie who has already been released. A more practical approach for the virtue ethicist might be to educate users and regulate uses of the technology.

At the end of the day, it is our understanding that has to be awakened. For when that happens, we regulate ourselves. This point is made emphatically in one of the oldest hymns of the Ṛg Veda, namely the famous Gayatri mantra. This hymn, recited daily by millions of people around the world, is a prayer for understanding. Moreover, the use of the word *naḥ* (our) in this mantra emphasizes that it is a prayer not only for *my* understanding, but for *our* understanding.

Returning to science wanting to know not only the constituent parts but also how they are put together to form the whole, we find a similar statement can be made about a comprehensive Upanishadic assertion such as *sarvam khalvidam Brahma*. A rough translation of this is 'everything here is the manifestation of an underlying spiritual reality; would you not agree?' This statement, to which many accord the status of a *mahāvākya* (great statement) asserts a fundamental unity and invites discussion. But the task of understanding how that unity manifests in practice is still before us. This last point is what I described earlier as the state of the *jivanmukta*.

In this context, it might be worthwhile also mentioning the *Isha Upanishad* and especially its first verse. Unlike the above statement, the *Isha Upanishad* speaks to both aspects: the interconnectedness and how one might navigate it in practice. The first verse states a principle of a fundamental unity: *ishā vāsyam idam sarvam yat kiñca jagatyā m jagat* (the spiritual reality permeates or resides in everything). In the light of that, how should one behave? *Tena tyaktena bhuñjīthā mā gṛdhaḥ kasya svid dhanam* (by that awareness, enjoy, but do not covet the wealth of others).

The Practice of Science

Let us return now to science and its practice. The practice of science (other than mathematics) is contingent on several principles. One is the empirical principle. The empirical principle is the idea that there is order in the universe. What has happened repeatedly in the past will happen again. The sun rises in the east and has done so over millennia of observation and so we expect that tomorrow, all other factors remaining constant, the sun will rise in the east. If I drop an object while standing on the earth, it will fall down. This has been observed countless many times and so barring any reason to think that something has changed, we expect that if I drop the object again, it will fall down just as before. This principle is not unique to science. It is also used in philosophy and is what is called *vyā pti* in logic.

Note that the empirical principle helps us to describe a phenomenon and perhaps even elevate it to a principle or law. Thus, it helps us to elucidate 'what', but has no answer to the question of 'why'. But our commitment to the empirical principle is such that we will accept the 'what' even when it defies our intuition and we have no answer to 'why'.

An example of this is the way in which the concept of gravity as a force met with a great deal of scepticism but was nevertheless accepted on empirical grounds. Force as it had been understood till then involved an object acting on another object and gravity did not seem to fit that paradigm. One could not say that the earth was acting on an object to pull it down. And there was no good explanation of why such an attraction even existed. However, the formulation of gravity as a force whose strength could be mathematically modelled and tested on empirical grounds led to its acceptance.

It is interesting that when Newton was asked the question of why there is gravity, he simply refused to speculate. On the other hand, Einstein's answer was a metaphor, namely that space may be thought of as an elastic fabric and planets may be seen as billiard balls of different sizes placed on that fabric. They cause an indentation. Now if two billiard balls are placed nearby, the smaller one will fall towards the larger one. A smaller ball given momentum in a normal direction to the larger ball and at a right distance will even orbit the larger one. This is not an answer to the question of why there is gravity. Rather it is a metaphor which gives us a way of conceptualizing it.

This is typical of the scientific approach: we understand through models or metaphors. I don't know how well this is known outside of science. Science develops a model to understand a phenomenon, and then studies the model and uses it to make predictions which then have to be validated. The model is not the phenomenon, any more than space is actually an elastic fabric. But it captures certain essential features of the phenomenon that can be studied through the model.

Where does the model come from? It comes from arguing by analogy and by invoking one's imagination. These abilities represent a maturing of the more well-known tools of comparison and hypothesis. These tools are important in making any serious discovery and it is necessary to understand them.

In the context of the instruments of knowledge (the *pramāṇas*) that are enumerated in Indian epistemology, we find perception, inference, verbal testimony, comparison, hypothesis and non-perception. However, as knowledge becomes deeper, these undergo a metamorphosis in which we seek 'knowledge beyond knowledge' as it were. This leads to a category of knowledge which goes beyond Russell's 'knowledge by acquaintance' to a level that we term 'knowledge by identity' (*tat tvam asi* as the Upanishad states). Accessing this level of knowledge, which is experience, is what we might say is the spiritual dimension, as opposed to knowledge which is a function of mind. It is not to say that there is an opposition between the two, but rather a completion and fulfilment. In the process of reaching that stage, the very tools of knowledge, the *pramāṇas*, undergo a metamorphosis. Thus, perception becomes *viveka* (discernment), inference becomes intuition, verbal testimony becomes supersensuous knowledge, comparison becomes metaphor, hypothesis becomes imagination, and non-perception becomes nondualism. (Murty 2018), Chapter 6.

To return to the empirical principle, we note that it is also used in mathematics in order to form an idea or a guess of what might be true. We look at examples and special cases and it is a very subjective matter to know when you have found a pattern or when you are just looking at an anomaly. But any practising mathematician will agree that looking at things empirically is a good place to start in trying to get to the truth. The difference in mathematics is that it is only a place to start and that whatever heuristics we may have must then be vindicated by logic. This is something that beginning students of mathematics find very difficult to understand. The concept of proof in mathematics is very exacting.

Thus, in all cases, science believes that the universe has a certain orderliness. Note that we do not have an objective proof that the universe is orderly. We assert it only by appealing to the empirical principle which we *believe* to be true. Scientists may bristle at this description, but at heart, science is predicated on an unproven article of faith, that the universe is orderly and that that orderliness can be discovered and expressed. To be clear, the definition of faith is to accept something as true that is not the outcome of reason. And our acceptance of the empirical principle does seem to fit that description.

In addition to this belief in the empirical principle, there is a further belief, namely that order can be discovered and described. This also is faith, because before we solve a problem, we have no argument through reason to prove that we can solve it. And yet we proceed with full energy to try and solve it. If one says that one has solved similar problems in the past and that is what gives one confidence in being able to solve the problem at hand, I would point out that one is again appealing to the empirical principle which itself is an article of faith. Thus, we believe there is order and we believe that we can discover and describe it. Moreover, when we look for a scientific explanation, we need to invoke imagination and think metaphorically.

Let us now consider the process of discovery. The popular literature depicts the scientist as pursuing a forensic process of experimentation, observation and reasoning. However, any practising scientist will tell you that no substantial discovery is made in this way. We have already seen that it involves metaphors and imagination. To access that level of thought requires a purity and power of concentration that are not available without ethical discipline. The word that is used in Indian philosophy is *tapas* which literally means 'to heat'. Metaphorically, we may say that we have to 'warm to a subject', or we may say that we need to 'cook the ingredients over a fire' to produce the culinary delight.

Vivekananda writes 'It has also been found, on careful inquiry in the sphere of material knowledge, that those higher truths which have now and then been discovered by great scientific men have flashed like sudden floods of light in their mental atmosphere, which they had only to catch and formulate. But such truths never appear in the mind of an uncultured and wild savage. All these go to prove that hard *tapasya*, or practice of austerities in the shape of devout contemplation and constant study of a subject is at the root of all illumination in its respective spheres. What we call extraordinary, superconscious inspiration is only the result of a higher development of ordinary consciousness, gained by long and continued effort. The difference between the ordinary and the extraordinary is merely one of degree in manifestation. Conscious efforts lead the way to superconscious illumination' (Vivekananda, Knowledge: its source and acquirement, 1980).

The Expression of Science

Next, we discuss the way in which science expresses its thought. The language in which it is described is mathematics. Amongst all languages used by humans, mathematics has the distinctive feature of being unambiguous. A statement which is ambiguous, even if clothed in mathematical symbols, will not be considered to be a mathematical statement. We find sometimes social scientists or humanists trying to describe a principle by expressing it as an equation. However suggestive and useful as a metaphor, such an 'equation' is not considered to be a mathematical statement unless it is unambiguous. As mathematics is the language of science, such an 'equation' cannot be considered a scientific statement either.

The flip side of this unambiguous nature of mathematical statements is that this attribute has been obtained at a price. There is an uncertainty principle in language in which precision and breadth compete with each other. The only way to achieve precision in language is by restricting the breadth of ideas that can be expressed in that language. A concept such as 'happy' is ambiguous and so cannot be described mathematically. At the other extreme are languages such as most spoken languages in which one can express a great wealth of ideas, such as being happy. But we do at the price of sacrificing precision. I do not know how to define 'happy'. We can describe certain attributes that one might see in a person who is happy. But what 'happy' itself means as an abstraction cannot be described unambiguously. It is a miracle that in and through that ambiguity, we actually communicate meaning.

Ambiguity is not a defect or 'bug' of spoken languages, but a feature. It is because languages such as English or Hindi are so ambiguous that we are able to give expression to so many ideas. It is because of the ambiguity that we have poetry and literature, in which the multiple meanings of words are considered praiseworthy. So, we note that science, by adopting the language of mathematics, has restricted the range of ideas that it is able to express and therefore discuss.

Another principle for the expression of science is the primacy of reason. The tool that the scientist uses to express how diverse observations have been woven together into a coherent and consistent explanation is reason. Given the importance attached to reason, we have to understand both its power and its limits. This is as important to the scientist as to the philosopher. Reason establishes a relationship between facts or observations. Note that it has no power to obtain those facts or observations. Reason only begins after we have, by some means or other, obtained facts and observations. Reason is then finding cohesion according to certain rules of logic.

To make matters worse, the rules of logic are themselves not the outcome of reason. A basic principle like the law of the excluded middle - if statement A is true, then the negation of A is false – is not the outcome of reason. The power of reason to discover connections cannot be underestimated and the success of science can be attributed to this power. However, we also have to understand what reason is not capable of. It cannot get the facts to which reason is applied. Those have to be obtained in some other way.

To get those facts, we say that we have some objective method of observation. These form the input into the process of reasoning. The problem with this is that observation is never objective. This is something that philosophy teaches us. At least in some cases, the act of observation actually changes what is being observed. We certainly know this in human behaviour, but it is also true in the behaviour of matter.

But it is not only philosophy that warns us about the subjective nature of perception. There is also physiological evidence. The eye functions through the use of a large number of sensors called rods and cones. These sensors assemble a coarse image in the brain. But our vision is not coarse. We see straight edges and exact shapes. This is possible only because the brain 'straightens out' the coarse picture. It is like a computer-enhanced picture that we see from satellites. On what basis does the brain 'straighten out' the coarse image? Whatever basis it is, it is not based on perception. It seems to be based on what we expect to see perhaps from past experience. There is a saying amongst surgeons that after you open the patient, you will only see what you expect to see. The subjective nature of perception is a physiological fact.

This is, of course, a problem for science as it casts objectivity in a difficult light. The only way this is addressed is by collecting observations repeatedly and independently, and by inviting others to repeat the experiment. Now we appeal to the uncorrelated quality of the different observations to minimize the impact of subjectivity.

It is a miracle that with these huge limitations, science is as successful as it has been in describing our world. We may therefore ask whether these methods could be applied in other spheres of human activity, especially in the field of spiritual truth. If the great teachers of religion spoke from the point of view of actual experience, and we have some record of what they said, then can we—on empirical grounds—extract spiritual truth from it.

Note that I am speaking of an empirical approach to spiritual truth and not an experiential one. If these teachers spoke at different times in different places and if we have no evidence that they were influenced by one another, then even with the coarseness of the record of their teachings, might we extract those statements that are common and view them as spiritual principles established on empirical grounds? That is a challenge that most of us do not dare to take. But if we dare, and I think it is only academics that could dare, then we have a new approach to spiritual truth.

Summarizing, science uses the empirical principle and the power of reason to arrive at truth. To the extent that we are trying to describe an objective reality, these tools are quite powerful. But the question we now want to ask is whether they are of any use in discussing questions of ethics and of spirituality. These are not questions about the objective universe but are deeply intertwined with our subjective identity. We are asking questions about ourselves, or of others.

If we imagine society as an objective reality and models of social organization as being subject to empirical orderliness, we might try to apply the methods of science to discuss ethics and values. This is, for example, the approach taken by Mill in his utilitarianism or by Rawls in his concepts of social justice. Mill says that an action is right or moral if it maximizes the 'happiness' function amongst the members of society. The difficulty with this is that 'happiness' itself is not well-defined. Rawls says that an action is moral if it is something that we would all agree with if we were objective. The problem with this is that there is no objective way of determining whether one is being objective. Another problem with both of these approaches is that in a given instance, we do not have the means to determine whether the conditions of morality or 'rightness' are satisfied.

In the virtue approach, action has to be consistent with virtue. Unlike the deontological and the consequentialist approaches, virtue ethics is not primarily rational, but it is more holistic taking into account the entire experience, not only of the individual, but also of one's surroundings and environment. Sri Sitansu Sekhar Chakravarti explains 'According to the virtue ethicist, however, morality is not primarily an area of rationality, in so far as what counts here are virtues, not pertaining only to doing good to others, but to the overall shining forth of the human existence, in balance and conformity with the animate as well as inanimate environment' (Chakravarti 2009, 99).

What Can Science Teach Us About Ethics and Human Values?

We have said that science, as a discipline, cannot analyse subjective concepts such as ethics and human values. However, the practice of science can teach us something about this. The reason is that in the doing of science, there are certain social norms that the community has accepted. The first is commitment to truth. Even if the data points to an explanation that we do not like, we cannot escape the conclusion and we cannot falsify the data. If corrupted data is knowingly used in a scientific discussion, the community is quite harsh in condemning both the work and the individuals involved. Thus, the practice of science teaches us about commitment to truth. Moreover, a model that intrinsically promotes inequality will meet with resistance from the community. In other words, if in the name of science, propositions are advanced that conflict with concepts of human values or ethics, such propositions will be challenged.

Another principle that one learns through the practice of science is how it can unite people. While nationality, ethnicity and other attributes can serve to divide people, the scientific community is a global one. A theorem proved in Chennai is the same as a theorem proved in Toronto (provided neither made a mistake). Science can overcome political or other divisions amongst people. One learns to look at the science and not the personality.

Both of these – a commitment to truth and working as a global community – are virtues that are not uncommon to practitioners of science. If they could absorb those virtues into their entire life (and not just their scientific life) then it would have served the purpose of virtue ethics.

But what about concepts of right and wrong? The problem can be illustrated in the story of the aftermath of the Manhattan project. After an atomic device was successfully tested in the desert and the means of delivery were made available, the question was how to use this new weapon in the war then underway. Science did not provide an equation that significantly factored in the loss of life and human suffering this would create amongst people who had essentially nothing to do with the war effort other than to be born at the wrong place at the wrong time.

Nevertheless, there were some in the scientific community who felt that the atomic bomb had to be used to prevent the further loss of life that conventional warfare would entail. On the other hand, there were many scientists who were horrified at the prospect of its actual use, as the awful destructive potential had already been demonstrated. In taking these positions, scientists were reaching beyond science and towards their humanity. This moral conversation had its consequences, not in terms of giving an objective answer to the dilemma – for there isn't one – but in developing the inner soul-searching about the value of life and the need to proactively search for peace.

It was this conversation that led the Massachusetts Institute of Technology (MIT) to appoint the Lewis Committee in January 1947 to 'reexamine the principles of education that had served as a guide to academic policy at MIT for almost ninety years, and to determine whether they were applicable to the conditions of a new era emerging from social upheaval and the disasters of war' (MIT Libraries 1995).

The main recommendation of the Lewis Committee Report issued in 1949 was the creation of a School of Humanities and Social Science on an equal footing with the science and engineering schools of the Institute. Around the same time, James Killian, President of MIT during 1948 to 1959, asked for a plan to construct a non-denominational chapel on the MIT campus. One might regard both the issue and the corrective actions taken as belonging to a virtue ethics perspective of inviting each individual to ask what kind of person one wants to be and to examine how their actions and pursuits can help them to become that kind of person.

Unity as a Foundation for Ethics

I want to suggest that there is one common basis from which to understand both the spiritual quest as well as the pursuit of science. In science, we are trying to find harmony. Scientific discovery, even mathematical discovery, is about uncovering a relationship between two things that were not known to be related or connected. Of course, the scientific context requires us to express that relationship mathematically. But the attempt to discover unity in the diverse phenomena of the objective universe can be thought of as a fundamental goal of science.

Indian spiritual works go even further and suggest that the answers to the questions of ethics and values are also to be found in the search for unity. A case in point is the final hymn of the Ṛg Veda. This is the hymn on unity which says 'Let us walk together. Let us speak in harmony. Let our minds apprehend alike. Common be the end of our assembly. United be our thoughts. United be our hearts. Perfect be our unity'. So, the answer to the question of science giving us any insight into ethics or human values is that both the pursuit of science and the search for ethics are about discovering a fundamental and unalterable unity and to act in the light of that unity.

While science is forced to stop at the objective universe, the unity that Vedanta proposes goes to the heart of the subjective question of who we are. The question of identity has been raised in both the West and the East but the answers have been different. While the West identified the individual with the mind, the Vedantic perspective is that we are consciousness and that consciousness can exist independent of mind. Moreover, consciousness is indivisible and thus the perceived multiplicity of conscious beings is only apparent. In reality, there is a unity at the level of consciousness. And with that assertion in hand, ethics is derived as character and behaviour that is consistent with that fundamental unity and interconnectedness.

I want to close by describing another aspect of identity that is important to both science and spirituality, and that is love. Love is the destruction of distinction and so it is the tool to operationalize the principle of unity, whether it is in terms of ethical behaviour, or in terms of scientific discovery or in terms of spiritual experience.

Let me start with scientific discovery. If the picture we have of scientific discovery is a forensic application of observation and reason, it is completely off the mark. Scientific discovery is almost never made like that and if a discovery is really made that way, it tends to be superficial. The story of Archimedes and his *eureka* moment are well-known. What made him run down the street in that way? Discovery is almost always accompanied with an aesthetic experience, the *rasa* and for a time, discoverer and discovery are united in that.

Vedanta says that the answer to the question of our identity is *chidānanda* or in English, consciousness and love. This is the nature of *sat* or Being. Moreover, consciousness and love cannot be separated. As far as I know, this idea is not present in the Western discussion of consciousness, not even in contemporary philosophy of mind such as in the work of Chalmers and others. Consciousness is seen by them as an instrument of knowledge. What is needed now is to insert this idea of the inseparability of consciousness and love into contemporary discussion.

Returning to two verses that I quoted earlier on, I want to draw attention to the use of the word *khalu* in *sarvam khalvidam brahma*. One can feel the joy of the rishi through the use of this word. Similarly, the verse of the Isha Upanishad mentioned earlier uses the word *bhuñjīthā* which means to enjoy. All to suggest that both the search for, and the experience and the operationalization of, the unity of existence is rooted in love and joy. And this seems to apply even if we narrow the field of unity to something like scientific inquiry.

By failing to recognize the importance of love as fundamental to our humanity, we run the risk of an identity crisis. The most important philosophical question of our time is 'what does it mean to be human?' It was mentioned earlier that CEOs are taking philosophy courses. I would say that everyone will need to be taking philosophy courses to get an answer to this question. And while the Indian tradition has profound insights to offer, we have much to gain by exploring a world philosophy and this requires a synthesis.

The actual challenge in front of young philosophers is to produce a grander synthesis than has yet been attempted, by harmonizing the different traditions. Moreover, such a comparative study and synthesis, while of interest from a purely academic point of view, is also going to be needed in our changing world, where new existential challenges are waiting for us. The revolution in artificial intelligence is going to bring front and centre the problem of defining our humanity. This will be needed not only to define the rights of the new species that we are creating, but also to explain to ourselves why we need to live. Society will turn to its philosophers to help them deal with this impending existential crisis.

In the process of defining who we are, of answering yet again the ancient ontological question of what it means to be human, we will also have to deal with the question of what we mean by truth. We are already in the midst of a crisis of belief in which the sources of information that we have become accustomed to relying on are being vilified and tainted as offering 'fake news'. We used to say that 'seeing is believing' and *pratyakṣa* was the first of the six *pramāṇa*. But we have now such sophisticated Photoshop and video editing technology that we can make anyone apparently say and do anything. The tools which were meant to connect us and to empower ordinary groups of people, and which played a crucial role in significant social and political movements such as the Arab spring, have now been revealed to also have the power to mislead and confuse.

Humanity has barely learnt to grapple with the old problems of peace, justice, and sustainable development when it is already being confronted with new forces that threaten to undo whatever progress has been made. But the one consolation we have is this, namely that we have been here before in a different form. When atomic power was first discovered and weaponized, it took a concerted and united global effort to ensure that it would be put under control and that its use would be for peaceful purposes. We need perhaps a similar global effort now to face the new challenges that technology is presenting us with. But at the back of such a global effort has to be a new philosophical understanding of the fundamental problems of truth and the identity of the human being. And that understanding is probably best obtained by forming a new grand synthesis of the philosophical wisdom of all of the world's traditions. That is the task and the challenge in front of us and I wish that all of us would focus our energies in this direction.

References

Chakravarti, S. S. (2009). Ethical message of the Mahabharata in the wake of the global financial crisis. *Journal of Human Values, 15*(2), 97–105.

Chen, J.-Y. (2015). Virtue and the scientist: using virtue ethics to examine science's ethical and moral challenges. *Science and Engineering Ethics, 21*, 75–94.

Fouchier, R. A., & Kawaoka, Y. (2013). Gain-of-function experiments on H7N9. *Nature, 500*, 150–151.

MIT Libraries. (1995, November). *Committee on Educational Survey.* Retrieved from MIT History: https://libraries.mit.edu/mithistory/institute/committees/committee-on-educational-survey/

Murty, V. K. (2018). *Knowledge, Identity and Behaviour.* Toronto: Manuscript.
Slote, M. (2013, March). On virtue ethics. *Frontiers of Philosophy in China, 8*(1), pp. 22–30.
Vivekananda, S. (1978). What we believe in. In S. Vivekananda, *The Complete Works of Swami Vivekananda* (Vol. 4, pp. 356–360). Mayavati, India: Advaita Ashrama.
Vivekananda, S. (1979a). Conversation with Surendra Nath Sen. In S. Vivekananda, *The Complete Works of Swami Vivekananda* (Vol. 5, pp. 339–343). Mayavati, India: Advaita Ashrama.
Vivekananda, S. (1979b). The future of India. In S. Vivekananda, *The Complete Works of Swami Vivekananda* (Vol. 3, pp. 285–304). Mayavati, India: Advaita Ashrama.
Vivekananda, S. (1979c). Vedanta and Indian life. In S. Vivekananda, *The Complete Works of Swami Vivekananda* (Vol. 3, pp. 228–247). Mayavati, India: Advaita Ashrama.
Vivekananda, S. (1980). Knowledge: its source and acquirement. In S. Vivekananda, *The Complete Works of Swami Vivekananda* (Vol. 4, p. 362). Mayavati, India: Advaita Ashrama.

CHAPTER 15

The Challenge to being Virtuous: A Lesson from the Mahābhārata

Nirmalya Narayan Chakraborty

Introduction

The Mahābhārata is an epic tale of war and peace, tolerance and ignonimity, truth and lies, vengeance and forgiveness. It is a store house of moral dilemmas, where characters face complex situations and confront difficult alternatives, alternatives that are not only exclusive, but are also opposed to each other. In our present discussion of virtue, I will focus on the morality of deception.[1] A moral player, Yudhiṣṭhira's deception leads

An earlier version of the paper was published in *Studies in Humanities and Social Science*, XXVI, No.1 2019.

[1] In this paper I address the issues raised by Jonardon Ganeri in Chap. 3 of his book *The Concealed Art of the Soul: Theories of Self and Practices of Truth in Indian Ethics and Epistemology*, Oxford University Press, Oxford, 2007. The chapter is entitled 'A Cloak of Clever Words: The Deconstruction of Deceit in the Mahābhārata.

N. N. Chakraborty (✉)
Rabindra Bharati University, Kolkata, India

S. S. Chakravarti et al. (ed.), *Traditional Indian Virtue Ethics for Today*, Palgrave Studies in Comparative East-West Philosophy,
https://doi.org/10.1007/978-3-031-47972-4_15

Droṇa to lay down his weapons in a pivotal conflict. As we shall see, Kṛṣṇa, Bhīma and Arjuna have different assessments of Yudhiṣṭhira's deceit. An account of all these will help us navigate the moral maze leading to Yudhiṣṭhira's act of deception. Droṇa's relinquishing of an imminent victory in an epic battle is an important turning point in the war, and his exit is the direct effect of Yudhiṣṭhira's deceit. Is it right for Yudhiṣṭhira, who is an embodiment of truth, to lie to his teacher Droṇa? Even more strange and condemnable, Yudhiṣṭhira attempts to make his false statement appear like the truth; he seems to deceive himself about his own fall from virtue.

The Moral Maze of Deception: Differing Perspectives of Agents

The Mahābhārata Book VII, 'Droṇaparva', is especially relevant to the geography of moral dilemmas. Duryodhana, apprehensive of losing the battle, comes up with a devastating plan. He advises Droṇa to capture Yudhiṣṭhira and then to tell the latter to request the Pāṇḍavas to surrender. The Pāṇḍavas cannot deny a request from Yudhiṣṭhira, for Yudhiṣṭhira is well known for his unquestionable commitment to truth. The success of the plan depends on Droṇa's ability to capture Yudhiṣṭhira alive and then coercing Yudhiṣṭhira as directed by Duryodhana. Twice Arjuna tries in vain to capture Droṇa. Arjuna faces Droṇa at one point and requests him to stay back to have a conversation, but Droṇa flees. Instead, he returns as if from successful espionage and begins to corner the Pāṇḍava army. The Pāṇḍavas are left scared and Arjuna, alone, who has the sole ability to defeat Droṇa, still refuses to fight his former teacher. At this juncture Kṛṣṇa makes a cunning suggestion:

> He cannot be defeated by force in battle. Leaving aside dharma, O Pāṇḍavas! follow a method fit for victory, so that Droṇa might not kill everyone in the battle. I think he will not fight, if (his son) Aśvatthāman were killed. Let some man say that he has been slain in the battle of Mahābhārata.[2]

It is interesting to note how different the reactions are to this controversial suggestion of Kṛṣṇa. Arjuna disagrees with its aptness for obtaining

[2] *Mahābhārata*, 7/164/67–69. For all the references to *Mahābhārata*, I have relied on *Mahābhāratam*, Haridas Siddhantavagisa (ed. & Trans.), Visvavani Prakashani, Kolkata, 1387(beng.).

a just victory. Yudhiṣṭhira hesitates, but falteringly condones the option. Bhīma enthusiastically endorses it, thus Bhīma kills an elephant belonging to the Pāṇḍava side whose name happens to be Aśvatthāman and then informs Yudhiṣṭhira that *Aśvatthāman has been killed*. Vyāsa informs the reader that bearing in mind that it is an elephant, Bhima speaks falsely in saying "Aśvatthāman has been killed". Not aware of the equivocation, after listening to the news, Droṇa goes on rampage slaying a large number of Pāṇḍava soldiers. At this point in the story, a number of sages enter the scene to convince Droṇa not to perform this heinous act, for this is both unjust and unbecoming of his status as a brahmin. Droṇa then starts questioning himself and wonders whether if what Bhīma says is true or not. Here Droṇa turns to Yudhiṣṭhira to ascertain the truth of Bhīma's statement, for Droṇa believes that Yudhiṣṭhira is the one person who would never tell a lie. Kṛṣṇa is well aware of Droṇa's trust on Yudhiṣṭhira. Kṛṣṇa advises the following:

If Droṇa fights in anger for even half a day, I believe, your army will be destroyed. In order to protect our side from Droṇa, it is better to speak a falsehood (*anṛta*) than the truth (*satya*). A falsehood uttered for the sake of a life is not touched by error.[3] Bhīma informs Yudhiṣṭhira of the killing of the Pāṇḍava elephant called Aśvatthāman and Yudhiṣṭhira thereby succumbs to Kṛṣṇa's 'devious divinity', to use B.K. Matilal's expression, and this is what follows:

Sinking in fear and addicted to victory, Yudhiṣṭhira equivocating spoke out 'Lord, He is slain, the elephant'.[4]

Yudhiṣṭhira's announcement has the desired result. Droṇa collapses in sadness and lays down his weapons. Yudhiṣṭhira's fall from virtue is undeniable. In a brilliant metaphor, Vyāsa tells us that by making this statement, Yudhiṣṭhira's chariot which used to ride a few inches high above the ground, now touches the ground. The battle still took an ugly turn for the Pāṇḍavas. Aśvatthāman tries to avenge his father's retreat from the battle, saving narrowly from a last intervention by Arjuna. The whole ordeal puts Arjuna in an agonizing situation of which he thinks he would be free only by embracing death: *See what a mess is created by Kṛṣṇa's advice! Or, may be, this mess facilitates the unfolding of events that are destined to happen. All of the agents have elbow room, a little space to exercise their freedom. But then the whole episode moves towards a final end, a result that is predestined.*

[3] Mahābhārata, 7/164/98–99.

[4] Mahābhārata, 7/164/106.

Kṛṣṇa ensures that the final goal is reached and intervenes only when human actions deviate from the determinate path towards the final destination.

It is quite illuminating to see how the episode leading to Droṇa's death is assessed from different viewpoints. As the story goes, after finding Droṇa defenceless, Dhṛṣṭadyumma, a disciple of Bhīma, not only kills Droṇa, he severs Droṇa's head and parades it much to the dislike of Arjuna. When the Kaurava army panics after Drona's death, which Aśvathāman is not aware of, he enquires as to the reason for the Kaurava army's retreat, and thereby comes to know of Droṇa's killing. Aśvatthāman accepts that the act of killing in a war is not wrong, but feels that to parade the head of *his father* who is trustworthy and rightfully engaged in a battle cannot be defended as right.[5] Aśvatthāman also condemns the act of deceit performed by Yudhiṣṭhira as the ultimate cause of the injustice. Aśvatthāman so argues that Yudhiṣṭhira has failed in his unique duty of trustworthiness. In believing Yudhiṣṭhira, Droṇa put himself in Yudhiṣṭhira's care as it were and Yudhiṣṭhira betrayed the trust of Droṇa.

Arjuna's assessment is noteworthy. He is in clear disagreement with Yudhiṣṭhira.[6] According to Arjuna, this act of deceit is performed by a person who clearly knows what is right and what is wrong. Yudhiṣṭhira's statement is a falsehood that wears a mask of truth. *This, to a teacher!* For Arjuna, it is clearly an act of treachery performed while driven by the vice of greed, longing to regain the kingdom. For Aśvatthāman what is objectionable is the deceit itself, not the killing. For Arjuna, on the other hand, the locus of moral injustice is the act of killing itself. It is not only Yudhiṣṭhira's fall from an otherwise unflinching allegiance to truth, rather it is his involvement in the conspiracy leading to the death of Droṇa that is condemnable. Bhīma thinks otherwise. He argues that Droṇa's behaviour is unbecoming of his *varṇa* viz. *brāhmaṇa*. In engaging himself in a war, he behaved more like a *kṣatriya*. The Pāṇḍavas, on the other hand, are just doing the actual duty of their *varṇa*, viz., *kṣatriya*.[7] Moreover, Yudhiṣṭhira has not actually told a lie, he merely fights one illusion with another. These three stances speak of three different moral voices. Breaking of trust is the worst thing that one can do, to Aśvatthāman. Arjuna also emphasizes this breach of trust between a student and a teacher as illicit. Yudhiṣṭhira is normally a moral exemplar, but he falters in exercising his

[5] Mahābhārata, 7/166/ 19–27.
[6] Mahābhārata, 7/167/33–41.
[7] Mahābhārata, 7/168/14–16.

characteristic virtue. He does not straightforwardly follow Kṛṣṇa by making a simple false statement, nor does he side with Arjuna in unequivocal condemnation of deceit.

Yudhiṣṭhira, ready to lay down his own life, feels remorse after the death of Droṇa, but not without giving a list of Droṇa's wrong acts, bearing the consequences. When Kṛṣṇa advises the Pāṇḍavas to lay down their arms for time being to shield themselves from a deadly weapon, the *nārāyaṇa*, Aśvatthāman takes that opportunity to further the attack on the Pāṇḍava brothers. Kṛṣṇa, Arjuna and Bhīma are all seriously injured. Arjuna attacks Aśvatthāman with all his might in return. Aśvatthāman then becomes perplexed and exits the battle with a significant statement: "all this is false".[8] The power of weaponry, and knowledge of rightness of action, are all false and enigmatic. Morality appears ever elusive. The war finally ends after five days of destruction. Yet as Vyāsa continues telling the story, and relating the text to the post-apocalyptic present, Aśvatthāman begins to understand its significance and he grows respect for Kṛṣṇa. Vyāsa's message is that the battle and related events are illusory images of the cosmos, that hint towards moral imprecision in real life. Through weaving many substories, about a battle that has already taken place Vyāsa underscores the point. In the end it seems that both parties in the battle are not fighting against each other, rather they are fighting against a common enemy. The real enemy is illusion in multiple manifestations, including delusion. The way to rid oneself of illusion is to reflect on the self, and rest in *śānta rasa* (aesthetic peacefulness).

It is quite well-known that in many scriptures, from Upaniṣads into Dharmaśāstras, the act of truth-telling is exhorted. Nonetheless, in some instances lying is regarded as morally permissible. Manu makes the suggestion that one ought not speak [openly] of a coveted truth: "*mā bruyāt satyamapriyaṁ*".[9] When the alternative to telling an unpleasant truth is telling a pleasant lie, one's duty is perhaps not to say anything that might impel an undesirable course of action. Yudhiṣṭhira finds himself in a situation where if he tells the truth, the result would be the unrighteous defeat of the Pāṇḍavas (the defeat of truth). On the other hand, if he tells the lie, it would achieve victory for the Pāṇḍavas. Yudhiṣṭhira cannot wholeheartedly accept either course of action. He does not tell a straightforward lie, but rather a lie that masquerades as truth. It is a twisted truth. A problem

[8] Mahābhārata, 7/172/42.

[9] *Manusaṃhitā*, 4/138, see also *Vaśiṣṭha Smṛti* 16/36 and *Gautama Smṛti* 23/29.

here for evaluating moral action is that it is notoriously difficult to make a moral distinction between a straightforward lie and a deception carried out through twisting the truth. One could argue that it is morally opaque to tell a straightforward lie, for at least the speaker owns up to her responsibility of telling lie. In the case of twisted truth, the speaker implies an act of telling the truth, when really the presentation of truth is rigged or fudged. Perhaps Kṛṣṇa's suggestion to tell a lie is a move toward clarity. Kṛṣṇa thinks that straightforward lying is morally defensible in some circumstances.

In many places in the Bhīṣmaparva,[10] Bhīṣma advises Yudhiṣṭhira not to follow a moral rule blindly, instead one should apply one's intelligence (*buddhi*). One such example occurs in the story of a brāhmin, Viśvāmitra, who chooses to eat dog-meat rather than starve to death, even though it is in violation of Viśvāmitra's *varṇa dharma*. "The *kṣatriyas* should learn such moral rules from alternate sources, and not follow any rule blindly." To this Yudhiṣṭhira raises the possibility of moral anarchy viz. any act that could be morally rationalized by anybody. Yudhiṣṭhira questions Bhīṣma whether there is any moral rule that must be followed without an exception. Bhīṣma's rather enigmatic reply is that one should always follow the learned and pious *brāhmins* which is a difficult advice to hear for Yudhiṣṭhira, because Yudhiṣṭhira's statement led to the death of such a pious *brāhmin*, Droṇa. Moreover, Bhīṣma's reply is not conclusive, for there are pious *brāhmins* whose advice do not always cohere with each other. Yudhiṣṭhira's rule–following moral reasoning does not gain support from Bhīṣma. Dharmaśāstra, however, aids Bhīṣma in providing exceptions to rules, especially to the rule 'always tell the truth'. Elsewhere,[11] Bhīṣma tells us that it is morally right to remain silent or speak falsely if the questioner aims to appropriate another's wealth, or if the questioner wants to imprison the speaker, or if the questioner will lose trust in the speaker. Bhīṣma's point seems to be that if only one has the legitimate entitlement to hear a truth, then a truth should be told, and not otherwise. All of this depends on the individual case.

The difficult situation that Yudhisthira has to face is not uncommon in moral life. Often we are torn apart by conflicting intuitions, and there is no easy way out. The question arises: Is there *any* moral code that we could follow in order to 'be virtuous'? What is the way to *dharma*? The

[10] Mahābhārata, 12/ 139/94.
[11] Mahābhārata, 12/110/1.

Mahābhārata seems to tell us that there is no fast-track to *dharma*. The maze of moral reasoning is baffling. Many of the characters articulate an oft repeated claim: where there is *dharma*, there is victory (*yato dharmastato jayah*[12]). In the technical sense of the term 'significance' (*tā tparya*),[13] the import of the Mahābhārata is this very statement. Thus it is clear that the main message of the Mahābhārata pertains to the establishment of the path of *dharma*.

According to Nīlakaṇtha, a key commentator on the philosophical meaning of Mahābhārata, the following verse sums up the moral message of the Mahābhārata as a text:[14]

> *duryodhana manyumoyo mah ādrumah, skandhah karṇah śakunistasya śā khā ah /*
> *duhśā sane puṣpaphale samṛddheh, mū laṃ rā jā dhṛtarā ṣtroamanīṣī //*

The real meaning of this verse is this: one must rid oneself of attachment as this attachment is like a tree whose main stem is anger and greed, etc., which manifest violence, and has stealing as its branches. Attachment is caused by ignorance, and so ignorance is to be eradicated. Furthermore, ignorance may be destroyed by performing Vedic rituals while showing respect to the Vedas and *brā hmins*. Then alone *dharma* ripens as the fruit. The moral fruit comes in the form of a direct perception of 'the real'. Moral fruition is the result of a tree nourished by truth etc., on which its stem is made, while *dhyā na*, *dhā raṇā*, etc., maintain its branches. In this context, *dharma* is synonymous with liberation. But in other places, *dharma* is regarded as one of the four *puruṣā rtha*s, the final *puruṣā rtha* being *mukti*. *Dharma* ought to bring happiness both in this world and in the world after. Since people are naturally inclined to be happy, people should follow *dharma*. As the ultimate result that people desire, *dharma* is the way to happiness.

According to Nīlakaṇtha, in the 'Sabhāparva' and the 'Vanaparva' of the Mahābhārata, *dharma* is defended where truthfulness, patience,

[12] Mahābhārata, 5.39.9, 5, 148, 16.

[13] There are six recognized ways of determining the significance of a text. For details see *Bharatiya darsansastrer samanvaya*, Jogendranath Tarkatirtha, Calcutta, University of Calcutta, 1958.

[14] Mahabharate caturvarga, Sukhamay Bhattacharya, Calcutta, Sanskrit College, 1972, p. 2.

taking care of teachers and friends are prescribed.[15] There are two etymological explanations of the term '*dharma*'. If the verb root *ṛ* is added with the prefix *dhana* and with the suffix *mak*, then the etymological meaning of '*dharma*' stands for that out of which both mundane and supramundane wealth comes. On this meaning, *dharma* is the source of all worldly pleasure and pleasure in the after-world. Another etymological analysis of the term '*dharma*' arises when the term is formed by adding the suffix *man* to the root verb *dhṛñ* (that which holds), thus meaning that which holds together, especially in societal context. The former meaning denotes the individual aspect of *dharma* where personal wellbeing is the focus. The latter etymological analysis is directed to the collective human welfare. So a complete understanding of *dharma* requires an explanation of the role of *dharma* in both individual and social spheres. And this dual aspect of *dharma* is encapsulated in an old saying: *ātmano mokṣārthaṃ jagaddhitāya ca*, employing both meanings towards individual emancipation, and the collective welfare. Where the word '*dharma*' has been used in the Mahābhārata, it can mean either of these two aspects. The other two values (*puruṣārthas*) viz. *artha* and *kāma* are to be guided by *dharma*. If *artha* stands for principles of statecraft[16] and *kāma* stands for principles of pleasure-seeking by an individual, then the supervisory role of *dharma* clearly indicates individual and social aspects of the principles of *dharma*. *Dharma* can be understood in terms of morally permissible behaviour (*anindya ācaraṇa*). This morally not-condemnable behaviour not only denotes external behaviour, it also includes mental dispositions. Thus all *dharma* is directed at both the individual and society. Even though the performance of rituals prescribed by it, *dharma* requires some effort and toil on behalf of the individual that results in giving up immediate individual comfort and selfish desires. The prescribed rituals are further directed to individual mental purification, and sometimes even directed at social welfare, or benefits to be gained in the after-life.

[15] Ibid., p. 3.

[16] For this, lease see *Pracin Bharater Dandaniti*, Jogendranath Tarkatirtha, Calcutta, Pracyavani Mandir, 1356 (beng.), introduction.

Two Aspects of *Dharma*

Scepticism about moral reasoning arises when these two aspects of *dharma* viz. the individual excellence and the social demand seem to clash with each other. This kind of question around the dharmic moral grounding grew into a practical problem for Yudhiṣthira and so he approached Bhīṣma for a response. Bhīṣma emphasizes the social mooring of *dharma* in the case where such conflicts arise—the prescriptions of *dharma* are meant for the social cohesion (*lokayā trā rtham eva iha dharmasya niyamah kṛtah*).[17] Individual aspects of *dharma* have to be occasionally violated for the sake of social wellbeing. Where *dharma* is said to lead to liberation, the idea of liberation need not be understood in terms of a final state only to be achieved either within life, or in a post-mortal state. After performing the rituals prescribed by one's *dharma* where the mental realm is purified, one is not likely to be controlled by fleeting whims and desires. This self-control constitutes individual excellence. The more one performs this actively, the more one transcends the immediate circumstance. This is an individual's agentive visa granting entry into the realm of an ethical standpoint. Once a society of individuals have attained excellence in this sense, this grounding would automatically lead to an ethical society. *Dharma* in its individual aspects lends itself to social wellbeing for a community.

While speaking about the sources of knowledge of *dharma*, the Vedas are given top priority in the Mahābhārata. Vedic prescriptions are to be treated as *dharma* and the Vedic prohibitions are to be regarded as contrary to *dharma*. The Smṛti Śāstras are also important sources of knowledge of *dharma*. In many places in Mahābhārata, Vyāsa defends his position by referring to the Manu Smṛti. The author of the Mahābhārata even refers to another epic, the Rāmāyaṇa, while defending his conclusion. The Rāmāyaṇa is also considered a source of knowledge in *dharma*. Other than textual sources, behaviour of cultured people (*śiṣṭā cā ra*) is another source of knowledge in *dharma*. The behaviour of cultured people is supported by the founding scriptures and honest people in general. The veridicality of *dharma* prescriptions are derivative from the Vedas and the Smṛti Śāstras, implying that if the behaviour of the cultured people is not in tune with the Vedic or Smṛti prescriptions, it cannot be regarded as *dharmic*.

[17] *Mahābhārata*, 12/258.4–6.

This is indeed a messy situation. While responding to the questions of Yakṣa, Yudhiṣthira recognizes that there is a labyrinth surrounding *dharma*:

> *tarkopratiṣthah śrutayo bibhinnā naika ṛṣiryasya mataṃ pramānaṃ I*
> *dharmasya tattvaṃ nihitaṃ guhāyāṃ mahājano yena gatah sa panthāh II.*[18]

Reasoning is unable to determine *dharma*, for it is always possible to come up with a counter reason. Even the Vedas are amenable to differing interpretations. The moral disquietude that Yudhiṣthira suffers from leads him to proclaim that only the path followed by the great people (exemplars) ought to be pursued. Although moral reasoning disregarding the Vedas and the Smṛtis has been discouraged, in case there appears any conflict between the Vedas or between the Smṛti, the only thing that one could fall back on is the behaviour of the cultured people. In many places in the Mahābhārata there are similar exhortations to follow the path of the cultured people.

Yudhiṣthira, himself being the embodiment of *dharma* in theory, is perhaps at a critical stage of being torn between following the principles of *dharma*, and the dictates of practical reasoning. The author of the Mahābhārata portrays this angst in its full intensity in Yudhiṣthira's character. Again and again Yudhiṣthira asks Bhīṣma: "People are confounded with the nature of *dharma*. What is *dharma*? Where does it stay?".[19] Bhīṣma's answer is worth noting: "Right behaviour, the Vedas and Smṛtis are what constitute *dharma*."[20] Learned people also regard *artha* as *dharma*. The commentator thus interprets '*artha*' as meaning doing good to others. Bhīṣma himself holds that whatever one desires for himself, one should desire for others:

> *yad yadātmani ceccheta tat parasyāpi cintayet /*[21]

It is in this context that one finds talk about family duties (*kuladharma*), a larger manifestation of which is *varṇa dharma*, that finds its allusion in a big way as *svadharma* in the Bhagavad Gītā. Following the paths of forefathers constitutes an important part of *dharma* in general.

Noting the social aspect of *dharma*, Bhīṣma implores us to be aware of the *dharma* in specific places:

[18] Mahābhārata, 3, 312, 117.
[19] Mahābhārata, 12, 258, 1.
[20] Mahābhārata, 12, 258, 22.
[21] Ibid.

deś ajā tikulā nā ñca dharmajñosmi janā rdana[22]

Local *dharma* is very much conventionally recognized. In its universality, this dimension of *dharma* includes physically performing rituals, linguistic performances like truth-telling etc., and entertaining good thoughts in the mind. These three aspects of *dharma*, viz, the physical behaviour, the linguistic performance and the mental disposition, contribute both to individual excellences and to social upliftment. In many places in the Mahābhārata, one comes across dialogues where people from the so-called lower strata or professions are engaged in explaining the nature of *dharma* to the so-called learned people.[23]

It is true that in many places the Mahābhārata emphasizes the importance of thinking good for all and non-violence to all as *dharma*. This raises the issue of performing sacrifices where animals are supposed to be killed. In the *Mokṣaparva* of the Mahābhārata one finds a debate between gods and the sages regarding the validity of sacrificing animals in the *yajñas*. The gods advocated animal sacrifice, while the sages expressed opposition. This brings up an issue regarding the permissibility of violence in a religiously oriented society. In one dialogue between a brāhmin and a hunter, we find the hunter arguing that in every sphere of our livelihood, we end up killing animals of different kinds. The hunter concludes: "There is no one who is non-violent."[24] At the same time, the hunter holds that killing animals for the sake of protecting one's life and livelihood does not contradict *dharma*. So the hunter's activity is not contrary to *dharma*. Similarly killing animals in *yajñas* performed for the sake of departed forefathers, etc., is not contrary to *dharma*, because it is sanctified by reciting Vedic mantras. Even killing and consuming the meat of hunted animals is not contrary to *dharma*, for it is the *vaṇna dharma* of the *kṣatriyas* to perform hunting.

In spite of declaring again and again that truth-telling is the greatest sacrament, if truth telling amounts to the destruction of a life, then not to tell the truth becomes one's *dharma*. If one does good to cows, *brā hmins*, women, poor, sick, etc., by not telling the truth, then lying becomes the *dharma*. Lying could be justified for self-protection.

[22] Mahābhārata, 12, 54, 20.
[23] Mahābhārata, (jajali samvada), 12, 261, 5–9.
[24] Mahābhārata, 3, 207.

Moral Particularism in the Mahābhārata

This discussion about exceptions to moral rules suggests a kind of moral particularism. Bhīṣma is perhaps the champion of this view. Yudhiṣṭhira is still ambivalent, but nevertheless feels the urge to entertain a particularist conception of morality and so takes recourse to telling a 'twisted-truth'. Kṛṣṇa, in his own way, feels attracted to this view of morality. Particularists think that there is no essential connection between making moral judgements and appealing to moral principles.[25] One does not need a set of moral principles in order to be a moral agent. This view should not be viewed as an attack on morality itself, just as Yudhiṣṭhira apprehended. If Bhīṣma's suggestion is taken seriously, then delinking morality from moral rules is a way of defending moral practice, and not a fall into relativism. This is, in a way, counter-commonsensical, for we normally look down upon people who do not have any moral principles. Moreover, it is widely held that without moral principles it is impossible to distinguish right from wrong and it is the sole task of ethics to discover a set of moral principles in the light of which one can account for the morality of right and wrong.

There are three questions with reference to which we tend to appeal to principles and they are: (1) Who is a moral person? (2) How can one to make moral decision? *and* (3) How is it possible for an act to be morally right, or wrong?[26]A moral person [or an ethical agent] is supposed to be a person with the knowledge of moral principles. [An agent] can make a moral decision by applying a moral principle to the particular case in hand. Finally, an act can be regarded right or wrong only if the act can be subsumed under a moral rule.

Particularism denies all this. There are two possible courses of action that a particularist can follow and retain agency: (1) To show that no moral rule is flexible enough that can cover a specific moral situation and consequently they cannot do the job that we want them to do. Each instance of moral life is unique and so complex that no single moral rule can be expected to subsume all the specific moral instances of the same kind. Sameness, in terms of moral judgment is too difficult to maintain in our moral lives when circumstances are constantly changing between individuals, and for any one individual. Bhīṣma's advice to Yudhiṣṭhira retains this spirit. Bhīṣma's brand of particularism exhorts us not to depend on

[25] Jonathan Dancy, *Ethics without Principles*, Oxford: Clarendon Press, 2004, p. 1.
[26] Ibid.

rules blindly, for a context requires unique treatment for which we need to apply our individual intelligence. Secondly, one can argue against the idea that morality rests on supply of principles. Here, one needs to show that morality can get along even better without imposition of principles. In order to prove this point, one has to give an account of how moral reasoning works. This would require a meta-level study in the sense that this is not directly concerned with the moral rightness or wrongness of an action. But then the idea is that a description of moral reasoning will help us see that we can have moral thought and judgement and we can distinguish moral right and wrong without any appeal to moral principles. Moral judgement can go very well from the ground up without talking about top down moral principles.

One way of constructing the relation of morality to moral principles can be called the "subsumptive option".[27] On this view, when we engage in moral reasoning, we approach new cases with a set of moral principles and try to find out which of these moral principles subsume the present case. The thought is that either it is impossible for the case to fall under more than one principle, or if more than one principle is applicable, then all given principles must recommend the same course of action. There are several problems with this account. This makes the notion of genuine moral conflict impossible. In a moral conflict we think that there are conflicting reasons in a given case for or against a particular course of action. Subsumptive options rule out such a possibility, for according to this view when one principle is applicable to a particular case, it is decisive and all the available reasons must be coherent with that principle. Yudhiṣṭhira's indecisiveness shows the inadequacy of the subsumption option. Secondly, this account fails to make room for moral regret. However, we do have experiences where there are compelling reasons to do otherwise. On the subsumptive option the principle is determinate and so it is wrong to do otherwise. Thus, there is no reason to feel bad for not doing otherwise. Of course, the logical, meta-ethical question about the justification of the right set of principles looms large in the background. Obviously the justification of principles cannot be extracted from the moral judgements concerning particular cases on the pain of circularity.

Rejection of the subsumptive option does not automatically lead to particularism. One could stop midway by taking recourse to 'prima facie duties'. Therein, the idea is that each action has some features of which

[27] Ibid., p. 3.

some are favourable, while others are not in its favour. Critically, for each feature there is then a principle of prima facie duty that should specify whether that feature counts in favour, or against the act. Notice, different features of an act call for different prima facie duties, and they are different from the subsumptive option. There is hardly any way of weighing conflicting prima facie duties, except by an appeal to our intuitive judgement. This is surely an improvement on any subsumptive option. But the idea of prima facie duty still bears a vestige of the subsumptive option by claiming that if a feature justifies the decision to favour an action, then that feature lends favourable decision to all cases wherever it appears. This is precisely what takes one from the recognition of the presence of the feature to a knowledge of a general principle, to the notion of prima facie duty. Particularists go further by claiming that what is relevant in one case is not necessarily relevant in another case. For them, possibility of moral reasoning and judgement does not rest on the applicability of moral principles. They also hold the feature that whatever constitutes a reason in one case might not necessarily be a reason in another case. And this is where particularism differs from the idea of a prima facie duty.

While analysing Yudhiṣthira's act of deception, it could be argued that in judging the moral worth of an action, one should note the particular features that might support a positive evaluation of an action, but in a different context could just as well be treated as defending a negative evaluation of the same action. The fact that Mr. X would be present in the meeting could be a good reason for me to attend a meeting, and at the same time the absence of Mr. X in another context could be a good reason for me to attend. It depends on the contextual factors involved. Of course, one must note that here 'reason' is used in a normative sense and not in the sense of an explanatory cause. In the statement 'The long lockdown is the reason behind slowdown in economy' 'reason' is used to determine the cause of the economic slowdown. In the present context, however, 'reason' is used to refer to a norm that could be said to fix the evaluation of an action. Reason in the sense of explanatory cause involves temporal order. The event of lockdown precedes the economic slowdown. Reason in the sense of explanatory norm is atemporal. This normative reason is located in the space of norm, a space that moral reasoning creates, a space that scaffolds the structure of morality. This scaffolding is flexible enough to admit, or discard, individual norms and associated ideas. This alternating amenability explains why one feature contributes to a positive evaluation of an action while the same feature negates the positive evaluation of the same action in another context.

Admittedly this idea of 'reason' as the explanatory norm requires unpacking. Explanatory norms do not come individually. There might be one face of the explanatory norm, but it might have many limbs all of which try to make the face appear prominent. If promise keeping, for example, is the face of the explanatory norm, then the added proposition that a promise was not taken under compulsion, or that the person who made the promise is able to perform the promised act etc., are auxiliary explanatory norms.

Viewed in this way, Bhīṣma can be understood to offer an explanation of 'reason' as explanatory norm. Bhīṣma draws our attention to the flexible nature of the normative scaffolding. If the space of norms is to be taken seriously, then Bhīṣma's appeal not to look for moral principles each time we make a moral judgement is worth listening to. Bhīṣma could very well argue that the feature serving as a reason for Yudhiṣthira to perform the act of deception may be a reason for not performing the act of deception in a different context. This, of course, is not a license to moral anarchy. This only hints at rejecting the idea that moral thoughts and judgements depend on the availability of a set of moral principles.

The variety of particularism being explored here could be contrasted with a generalism that claims that the very possibility of entertaining moral thought depends on a supply of suitable moral principles. This claim of generalism could be reformulated: No one would be capable of having moral judgements without there being suitable moral principles. This again could be restructured: No one could be able to entertain moral judgements unless she knows a relevant moral principle. While the emphasis in the former is on the ontological status of moral principles, the latter is more concerned with the epistemology of these principles. Since we are talking about the evaluation of the action where the agentive aspect is of crucial importance, the latter epistemological formulation of generalism is relevant for our purpose. Notice that this epistemological generalism talks about the possibility of moral judgement and not about the possibility of true moral judgement. It also does not offer any suggestion that moral thought is impossible unless some moral propositions are true. This is a tricky area. It is indeed a matter of great debate whether moral propositions are truth-apt or not. Nevertheless, it is expected that knowledge of moral principles would have some bearing on the relevant moral judgement and the onus is on a defender of particularism to specify the nature of this bearing. In order to stop particularism from falling into the hands of moral anarchist, one must claim that particularism does not deny that there are true moral principles. It only redefines the relation between moral judgement and moral principle. Particularists claim that possibility of having moral judgement does require the truth of moral principles. Bhisma's call for freeing us from the clutches of moral principles echoes this particularist claim.

Echoing Wittgenstein's idea of mathematical propositions[28] one could think of moral principles as rules of a game and the particular moral judgements are moves in a game, following the rules of the game. Then individual moral judgements cease to be truth-apt, simply because they are not factual in nature. The moral principles are not descriptive of states of affairs in the world. If the world of morality precludes truth-centric discourse, does it signal the end of ethics? I am inclined to reply 'no'. And this is where the idea of virtuous life becomes relevant. I shall come to this point little later.

Normally deductive reasoning is monotonic in the sense that whenever an inference is logically valid, it remains so, no matter if another [contradictory] premise is added. The addition of a premise to a valid inference cannot make it more or less valid. But in non-monotonic reasoning, adding a premise can reverse a cogent inference. Think of the following example:[29]

1. If one causes someone pain, one is doing something normally wrong $(p \rightarrow q)$.
2. If p and the pain is a legalised form of punishment for a recognized offence, then one is not doing something morally wrong $(p \& r) \rightarrow -q$.
3. If p and r and the punishee is unfairly convicted, then one is doing something wrong $(p \& r) \& s) \rightarrow q)$.

Notice how in this case addition of a premise reverses the whole inference. This is an example of moral reasoning that is non-monotonic in nature. This shows that a feature which lends support in one case, does not lend

[28] A detail explanation of Wittgenstein's views on this can be found in Crispin Wright's *Wittgenstein on the Foundations of Mathematics*, Duckworth, London, 1980.

[29] Jonathan Dancy, *Ethics without Principles*, p. 8.

support in another case. Looked at this way, particularism does justice to the non-monotonic nature of moral reasoning.

I would like to propose, we interpret Bhīṣma as giving us a non-monotonic model of moral reasoning. For him, lying may be wrong in one case, but not wrong in another case. So the addition of a premise reverses a moral inference. And my hunch is that Kṛṣṇa and Yudhiṣṭhira are a step closer to particularism, though Yudhiṣṭhira's attitude is rather cautious and hesitant. Arjuna, of course, is not happy with particularism and still wants to be rely on the subsumptive option. And so he is not happy with Yudhiṣṭhira's deceit leading to Droṇa's killing.

If ethics is concerned with responding to the question 'How should one live?', then one way of looking at the question is through the prism of a virtuous person. Bhīṣma's prescription to follow the path of the *mahājanas* seems to point towards virtuosity. This immediately raises the question: In what way does a person possess a virtue? If telling the truth is a virtue, then a person's action of truth-telling cannot be the result of a blind habit, or instinct. Therefore, that the situation requires a certain sort of behaviour (for example, telling the truth) is the reason for him behaving in that particular way.[30] The truthful person has a kind of sensitivity to a kind of requirement that a relevant situation imposes on the agent. Understood this way, the knowledge that is formed from contextual sensitivity is a necessary condition of possessing the virtue. Possession of the characteristic could be said to explain the actions that manifest the sensitivity, and in this way sensitivity itself results in action that is considered virtuous. It is in this sense virtue produces only right conduct. This, in fact, makes room for the possibility that an agent may envision what a virtuous person would do in a given circumstance, yet fails to be virtuous because sensitivity is blinded/blocked by a desire to do the contrary. Recall Duryodhana's confession: "*jānāmi dharmaṃ, na ca me pravṛtti*".

Morality as Rule-Following: Wittgenstein via Kripke's Prism

Getting back to the example of truth-telling as a virtue, one could reformulate this principle in the form of a practical syllogism: the major premise might consist of the universal knowledge that truth-telling is a virtue. The

[30] John McDowell, 'Virtue and Reason', in his Mind, Value and Reality, Cambridge, Mass. Harvard University Press, 1998, p. 52.

relevant particular situation might be the content of the minor premise. And the judgement expressing what should be done in the particular case turns out to be the conclusion. The major premise formulating the universal principle is perhaps the most important ingredient in this syllogism and precisely here a profound problem lurks behind. The idea of rationality resting on consistently following a rule has been under attack by Wittgenstein, as interpreted by Kripke.

Wittgenstein formulates a paradox in this context, as follows: No course of action could be determined by a rule, because every course of action can be made to accord with the rule. For Kripke, this paradox is actually a new form of philosophical scepticism. Kripke presents this scepticism with the help of an example from mathematics.[31] Like all the English speakers, I use 'plus' and '+' to refer to the function of addition. By referring to external symbolic representation and by mental exercise I grasp the rule of addition. Kripke draws our attention to the notion of grasp. Although I have performed addition to a very large number of cases, the rule can be applied and I can perform addition in countless number of cases that I have never previously performed. So in learning a mathematical function I grasp a rule in the sense that my past intention regarding the meaning of addition determines uniquely the answer for indefinitely many cases in future. Suppose that I have never performed the addition 86+75. But I have performed many additions in the past. In fact these finite number of additions that I have performed in the past imply that such an example exists, example exceeding previously performed computations. Thus, I perform the addition and get the result '161'. I am confident that this is the correct answer in the mathematical computational sense and also in the sense that I have used the symbol '+' the way I have used it in past.

This is precisely where scepticism enters in. The sceptic questions my being certain about the performance of addition. She might argue that on the basis of the way I used the term 'plus' in past, I intended the answer of the present addition to be 10! Of course the gut reaction to the sceptic's suggestion is that she should go back to school and refresh her arithmetical knowledge. But the sceptic drives the point home that how can I be so sure that I have used the symbol '+' in the present case exactly the way I have used it before. Even if I claim to apply the same function as before, I perform a separate computation in this new instance and I got

[31] Saul Kripke, *Wittgenstein on Rules and Private Language*, Cambridge, Mass., Harvard University Press, 1982, p. 7.

the result '161'. What function was it that I performed in the past? The numbers that I have dealt with in the past are smaller than 75. The sceptic continues, perhaps in the past I have used the 'plus' to denote a function that may be called 'klus' that may be symbolized as +O. One could define this function as x +O y = 10 if x, y < 75. Here the function of klus has been substituted by plus and in earlier instances I have performed klus where the numbers were less than 75. One cannot rule out this possibility, according to the sceptic. Maybe this is what I meant by 'plus' in the past. I am misinterpreting my previous use of 'plus'. Maybe I have always meant klus, and used the operation accordingly. The sceptic's question might sound bizarre, but it is not logically impossible. In order to silence the sceptic, one has to cite some fact of the matter, a fact about my past usage to show that by 'plus' I meant addition and nothing else. What is the guarantee in asserting that I have not misinterpreted my past usage? And on the basis of my understanding of my past usage I perform the present computation. The main thrust of the sceptic is this: When I compute '86+75', I do not do it the way I like. Nor is it a random calculation. I follow directions that I followed in my previous usages of '+' and this precisely determines the result of my present computation where I say, the result is 161. But what are those directions that I followed in my past usages? This direction certainly does not include that I should say 161 as the result of the present computation. This is a new instance of computation. This direction cannot suggest 'do the same thing as you did before', for in the past the rule that I followed could be a rule for plus and klus as well. This could go on forever backward to trace the history of my past usage.

The sceptic's question could be divided into two sub-questions: (1) Whether there is any fact of the matter that could show that in my past usages I did mean plus and not klus. (2) What is the reason for my being confident that the result of the present computation is 161 and not 10? Needless to say, these two sub-questions are related. I am confident of my present computation because the answer agrees with what I meant by this function in my past usages. It is not the question about my ability to compute, nor is it about the power of my memory. If I meant 'plus' in my earlier usages of the same function, then certainly I am justified in claiming that the result of the present computation is 161 and not 10. The sceptic could be answered only if we can come up with some fact about my mental state that captures my meaning plus, and not klus, in my earlier usages. Also, it must be shown that any such fact about my mental state will be able to apply itself to any putative case of a relevantly similar kind. Only this would account for my being confident about the result of my present computation.

Wittgenstein's sceptic argues that the idea of following a rule in principle always overdetermines the formulation of a universal principle. There is no fact of the matter on the basis of which one could justify his following a rule consistently. And this is surely a great threat to rationality. Bhīṣma's reluctance to follow a universal moral principle could be substantiated by the Wittgensteinian sceptic. If rationality requires consistency in the application of universal principles, then the very idea of being guided by a universal principle is susceptible to doubt and this is the conclusion that both Bhīṣma and Wittgenstein's sceptic are sympathetic to. Neither does the sceptic nor does Bhīṣma reject that we follow a rule. What they seem to question is the conception and ground of following a rule that we normally tend to believe in. Out of our fear that we will lose objectivity in mathematics or in morals, we take refuge in the idea of following a rule. This is nothing but a "consoling myth".[32]

All these reconstructions of Bhīṣma's allegiance to non-monotonic reasoning and his scepticism about universal rule-following imply that a philosophical account of moral reasoning cannot be given from some external standpoint, outside *lokavyavahāra* or form of life. Bhīṣma draws our attention to the contingencies of our existence, to the vagaries of our moral life. So instead of focussing on the specific moral moments of our life, it would be profitable to look at the life as a whole and then participate in moral life in the background of this canvass. This is where the idea of a virtuous life becomes important. How should we live a fulfilled life is more important than what should we do (morally speaking) on a particular occasion.

[32] Ibid., p. 61.

CHAPTER 16

Epilogue: Incorporating Ideas from the Mahabharata

Review article of: *Ethics in the Mahabharata: A Philosophical Inquiry for Today*, Sitansu S. Chakravarti

Amita Chatterjee

The great epic, The Mahabharata, is the richest document available on the society, polity and value systems of ancient India. It also serves as a watershed between the Vedic (śrauta) and the post-Vedic (smārta) life-world. Rightly looked upon as the Panchama Veda, the Mahabharata also helps us

Paper originally appeared:
Amita Chatterjee, Book Reviews. *Journal of Human Values*, 13:2 (2007), pp. 179–184. DOI: https://doi.org/10.1177/097168580701300208. Sage Publications. Copyright Holder: Management Centre for Human Values, Indian Institute of Management, Calcutta.

A. Chatterjee (✉)
Jadavpur University, Kolkata, India

S. S. Chakravarti et al. (ed.), *Traditional Indian Virtue Ethics for Today*, Palgrave Studies in Comparative East-West Philosophy,
https://doi.org/10.1007/978-3-031-47972-4_16

understand the continuity between the Vedic and the Upanisadic thoughts. Though the tradition as reflected in the epic was very much self-conscious about moral values, the epic has remained an unexplored gold mine of moral philosophical thinking. Volumes have been written on the Mahabharata from different perspectives, but not from the moral perspective and not by academic philosophers. The late Spalding Professor Bimal Krishna Matilal began pioneering work in the area. But his untimely death prevented him from giving us a systematic philosophical account of the moral philosophies in the epics. Chakravarti's work on the ethics of the Mahabharata has very effectively filled up the gap in the moral philosophical literature. In a sense, Chakravarti has gone beyond Matilal by providing a philosophical interpretation of the Mahabharata **as a whole** and the possible universal message of the epic, which is still relevant in the twenty first century.

The book has been dedicated to the late Professor Gopinath Bhattacharya and Mahamahopadhyaya Anantalal Thakur, two doyens who have shaped the minds of many contemporary philosophers of India. The former is famous for doing philosophy analytically and the latter for his discovery and reconstruction of many important manuscripts of Indian philosophy. No wonder, the book combines superb analysis with deep traditional scholarship. The author has taken pains to maintain an easy flow of the ideas and has refrained from giving it a formidable scholarly look by not using original Sanskrit technical terms with diacritical marks wherever avoidable. The book comes complete with a glossary for the readers who are not acquainted with the Mahabharata at all and a very useful bibliography.

Chakravarti began exploring moral ideas in the Mahabharata by pointing out that ethics of the epic is mainly duty-based. The ethical duties listed in the Mahabharata can be divided into three categories:

1. Universal duties (*sadharana dharma*-s);
2. Duties emanating from the concept of debt (*ṛṇa*); and
3. Duties relative to one's station of life (*varnasrama-dharama*).

Besides, the concept of *dharma* has been used in two different senses: one corresponding to the practices or act-*dharma*-s and the other defining the principles on which the practices are based, attitude-*dharma*-s. The author rightly emphasizes on the precept of the epic that performance of virtuous acts mechanically do not constitute morality but these are to be performed in the right spirit. Performance of virtuous acts may not be free from blemishes, but 'as attitudes, they have a serenity constitutive of them that eludes the defects.' An example may help understand the point. One may say to one's offender 'you are forgiven,' while the fire of revenge still smoulders in his heart. That is not a proper act of forgiveness. Only when one can imbibe the attitude of forgiveness, the moral quality of the act shines forth.

In the grand scheme of the epic, four virtues have been identified as the principles underlying all virtuous acts. These are: truth, forgiveness, sympathy to others and non-attachment to the objects of the senses. Of these, truth has been mentioned as the supreme principle of morality. But sometimes we find that truth has been given a lower rank than non-violence. Take, for instance, the narrative mentioned in the *Karnaparvan*. Arjuna once took a vow that he would kill the person who denounced the power of his favourite weapon, the Gandiva-bow, a gift from Agni, the fire-god. We find that Yudhisthira after getting a good beating in the hands of Karna was angry with Arjuna, doubted the capability of the latter to win the war and slighted the Gandiva-bow. Now Arjuna was really in a moral dilemma. He would have either to break his vow or kill his beloved elder brother. Faced with these two choices, Arjuna decided to take up the second course of action. Like Kant, Arjuna also thought that a promise is to be kept at all cost. Krishna, however, dissuaded Arjuna with the argument that insult to a respected elder is as good as killing him. Hence, if Arjuna insulted Yudhisthira, he would be able to keep his vow. At first, Arjuna was not convinced. So, Krishna told him the following story. There was a hermit named Kausika who took a vow of telling the truth, come what may. One day Kausika saw a traveller being pursued by a group of bandits. The bandits intended to rob the traveller and kill him. The traveller came to a crossroad where Kausika was sitting. The traveller took one of the paths and fled. Soon after came the bandits and asked Kausika which path the traveller had taken. Kausika told them the truth. The bandits caught the traveller and killed him. Kausika remained true to his vow but did not attain heaven because of this act of cruelty. Hence, concluded Krishna, one can break one's promise in order to save an innocent life.

That keeping one's vow is an instance of the universal moral duty of being truthful in speech and act has been accepted in the Mahabharata. In fact, it is rated very highly in the epic and when Yudhisthira told a lie to Dronacarya, the wheels of his chariot touched the ground and he had to visit hell once. But when promise keeping and truth telling are pitted against saving an innocent life, it appears that the ethos of the Mahabharata considered the latter as a stronger duty and enjoined its performance by foregoing the former. There are at least two problems here. First, truth loses to non-violence in the hierarchy of the moral principles. Second, Krishna has been accused of duplicity because of offering such advice to Arjuna. Not only once, but Krishna has been found to deviate from established principles of morality many times. Matilal took recourse to situational morality for handling the apparent anomalies. He wrote, 'under situational constraints, there might be stronger grounds for rejecting truth-telling as a duty and accepting the stronger duty of saving an innocent life. This encapsulates a very strong moral insight, although it is not Kantian.'[1] Chakravarti, however, has given a more thorough, in-depth and consistent analysis of the situation under discussion. He has tackled the first problem by showing the relationship between the four cardinal principles of morality and then by distinguishing between two conceptions of truth—truth that corresponds to facts and truth as existential transformation. The four cardinal principles are interconnected in the sense that 'each is a necessary and sufficient condition for the rest. Truth, for instance, manifests in forgiveness and forgiveness itself is truth.'[2] The relation between truth and forgiveness becomes clear from Chakravarti's citation of Narada's speech as mentioned in the third chapter of the epic. 'Non-violence is the greatest virtue, forgiveness the utmost strength, self-knowledge, the highest knowledge; nothing, however, surpasses the truth. Even though truth in words is by far preferable, that which is conducive to good, indeed, should be said. Truth, in my mind is that which brings about great benefits to all living beings.'[3] This liberal utilitarianism, says Chakravarti, is the cornerstone of the morality in the epic.

In the whole discussion of duty, Chakravarti has not said anything about the concept of rights. However, I think, the simple idea of right can be derived as the converse of obligation or duty in the context of the epic. For example, non-violence as a duty entails the right to life, non-stealing implies the right to property, the converse of benevolence is the right to lead a good life, truth entails the right to demand fulfilment of promise and the right to correct information, etc.

[1] 'Moral Dilemmas', *Moral Dilemmas in the Mahabharata*, Indian Institute of Advanced Study, Shimla, p. 10.

[2] Chakravarti, Sitansu S., *Ethics in the Mahabharata*, Munshiram Manoharlal, New Delhi, 2006, p. 11.

[3] Ibid., p. 15.

Chakravarti draws our attention to the point that truth has a loftier dimension than the mere practices of truth telling and promise keeping, which he calls *ṛta*. In the tradition, '*ṛta*' stands for the implicit idea of justice, the cosmic moral principle that gets manifested in all spheres of existence. Chakravarti links *ṛta* in the human context with the concept of *mokṣa*, the ultimate freedom. *Ṛta*, according to him, is truth as becoming, as existential transformation into what one really is in one's state of freedom. '*Ṛta* transcends the domain of facts insofar as it incorporates the existential moment. Freedom, being one's true nature, is neither a brute fact, nor an institutional one; it is only an existential truth, a matter of choice, a commitment.'[4] This existential conception of freedom, thinks Chakravarti, lies at the basis of the freedom of choice, being the norm that guides our choice in our worldly existence. When one's transformation is complete, one is free to perform moral acts in the right spirit, ensuring the well-being of all spontaneously. Truth in the highest sense thus merges with non-violence and forgiveness. This is how Chakravarti also explains Gandhi's identification of truth and non-violence.

Regarding Krishna's resolution of Arjuna's moral dilemma in an unconventional manner, Chakravarti introduces the idea of two different value systems prevalent in the epic. Bhisma was taken as the protagonist of the traditional value system where performance of certain duties as enjoined by the scripture was considered the objective of morality. This value system promoted individual moral excellence. Krishna, however, introduced a new value system the objective of which was welfare of all. This is based on spiritual foundation, where verbal truth does not always take the top ethical priority, though truth as *ṛta* does. 'The old system lacks in innovative input into positive acts towards addressing the debts, in all directions. The new value system emphasizes this aspect, and in a way makes it mandatory for people to work innovatively according to their capabilities towards the benefit of others. Sri Krishna works hard to ensure that a just and proper system takes root in the subcontinent, so that everybody can prosper.'[5] Seen in this light, all so-called Machiavellian suggestions of Krishna appear perfectly moral.

It is, however, extremely difficult to decipher the spirit of truth or *ṛta* and hence the eternal prayer of the Upanisadic sages, 'remove the cover and let us see the face of truth and morality.' It needs 'an imaginative poet'

[4] Ibid., p. 60.
[5] Ibid., p. 54.

with extra-ordinary moral sensitivity to reinterpret *ṛta* suitably for each age. This is the view of both Chakravarti and Matilal. But, why a poet? A quotation from P.B. Shelley's 'Prometheus Unbound' will aptly answer the question. 'To be a poet is to apprehend the truth and the beautiful, in a word, the good. The poets are the institutors of laws and civil society. Because the poets not only behold intensely the present as it is and discover those laws according to which present things ought to be ordered, but they hold the future in the present.' Grasping and implementing the highest truth in a particular context requires a paradigm shift in the moral thought, a poetic vision, which ordinary men lack.

Such emphasis on moral intuition and imaginative vision of a poet leads Chakravarti to give up reason-based morality. He seemed to be unwilling to place the ethics of the epic within the reason-based frame of morality right from the beginning as is evident from his quotation from Bernard Williams. He asserts in unequivocal term that *ṛta* transcends the realm of science and a poet's existential understanding of *ṛta* is the right understanding. Therefore, Chakravarti finds the greatest resonance of the existential spirituality of the Mahabharata in the writings of our poet extraordinaire, Rabindranath Tagore. Tagore rightly understood the spiritual message of the epic, which is detachment from sensual pleasures, and attainment of peace in a state of equilibrium away from the shackles of worldly attachment. Chakravarti embeds reason-based morality within a non-cognitive frame. He writes, 'The grounding of justice is after all in love… This core of love is not rationally induced in human beings to start with, its furtherance or curtailment is achieved existentially, and not on rational grounds, although reason might have a part to play there.'[6]

It has been admitted in the Mahabharata that an act, which is morally obligatory for one may not be binding on others. Besides, as morality centres on humanity, the change in time and scenario, changes the human perception of morality. Yet, Chakravarti admits 'a core ground of morality running through diverse moral systems.' He has developed his theory by extending Chomsky's linguistic theory[7] to the realm of morality. He writes, 'Morality has an inner core at the deep level, 'translating' itself at the surface level in the various systems of morality prevalent in societies. The deep level incorporates the basic moral principles—a priori, though

[6] Ibid., p. 105.

[7] Chomsky, Noam, *Aspects of the Theory of Syntax*, MIT Press, Cambridge, MA, 1965.

contingent—and helps shape the moral practices of individuals in diverse cultures in an existential setting.'

Chakravarti's interpretation of the *Gita* is really off the beaten track. The Gita has played a very significant role in almost all aspects of Indian life. It not only contains the crux of the teachings of the Mahabharata, but also is a text, which has the largest number of commentaries. Pandit Anantalal Thakur is, however, of the opinion that the best commentary on the Gita is the rest of the Mahabharata wherein all the couplets of the Gita are contained in spirit, if not verbatim. Being inspired by this theory, Chakravarti asserts a very startling thesis. The Gita has always received a deontological reading from almost all the modern commentators. Chakravarti goes against the tide and holds that the Gita too epitomizes the liberal utilitarian point of view. He says that Krishna is not advocating duty for duty's sake in the Kantian way. His advice to Arjuna comes from consequential considerations minus selfish motives. For Kant, goodness of an action consists in the goodwill determined by the motive of an action, apart from the benefits flowing from it as a consequence. According to the Gita, on the other hand, consequential considerations are important. The Gita upholds that actions undertaken for the benefit of others, taking all life into consideration, results in a balance in the animate as well as the inanimate world and is the part of the unfolding process of the existential truth. Chakravarti has argued very ably in support of this thesis. He has successfully explained two important concepts of the Gita, *svadharma* and *karmayoga* in consonance with his new interpretation of *ṛta* as authentic existential transformation leading to freedom and this enables him to place the consequentialist strand of the Gita above its deontological strand.

Before ending, I will like to mention one important point of disagreement between Chakravarti and Matilal. Bimal Krishna Matilal considers the disrobing of Draupadi in the royal court a women's rights issue, while Chakravarti wants to take it as a moral issue. Here I am more inclined to agree with Chakravarti than with Matilal. Matilal wrote that the question that Draupadi asked, viz., whether her husband staked her after having slaved himself, was more concerned with the rights or legality of her husband's action than with the morality of the situation. Nobody raised any objection to the fact that Draupadi was not being treated as an independent person but as a 'property' of her husbands, which could be staked in a gambling match. Matilal saw this point but concluded 'if Draupadi's questions were properly answered, it would have required a paradigm shift in India's social thought.' I find this conclusion baffling for two reasons.

Matilal considered Krishna's actions morally justified, even when these required a paradigm shift in the moral interpretation. Then why shouldn't Draupadi's question be taken as a moral question? Maybe, he would doubt that Draupadi possessed the right moral intuition, which Krishna had. His conclusion appears all the more curious because he stated that Draupadi was standing up for the rights and autonomy of the entire womanhood of that time. Then how could he maintain at the same time that this is not a moral issue at all? If the issue of granting autonomy to a person does not fall within the realm of morality, then what will constitute a moral question? He definitely admitted that Draupadi's question led to a dilemma, albeit a legal dilemma. He, therefore, did not include this incident as a case of moral dilemma. Why was he so reluctant to take it as a moral issue? Did he believe that the question of the right of the individual was not that important in a non-atomistic social structure? Yudhishtira did not gamble with Draupadi alone. He used his younger brothers too as stakes. Probably Matilal thought that the moot issue here is the right of an individual in ancient Indian society under which the question of woman's/wife's right can be brought as a special case. Chakravarti writes succinctly that there is need to go deep into the situation to see the issue here in a wider context. It goes to the credit of Chakravarti that he not only considers it a human rights issue but also deplores it as an immoral act. Violation of one's privacy is violation of a universal human right and is immoral irrespective of the fact whoever the violated person is. Having thus agreed with Chakravarti regarding the immorality of the act of disrobing Draupadi, I would still maintain that women's problems should not be reduced to human problems as such. Homogenizing problems of different marginalized groups perpetuates social inequality.

Chakravarti has raised many other issues and has woven them very sensitively to arrive at a moral theory without violating the spirit of the traditional reading of the epic. He has given detailed and meticulous arguments in favour of his theses making it almost impossible to raise internal criticisms. Somebody may disagree with his reading (which is neither too exalted nor too derogatory about our tradition but is a quite balanced one) but that is an entirely different matter. What is, however, the most remarkable is how easily he commutes between the Indian and western philosophy without being inauthentic to either of the traditions. The book has been prepared with loving care and dedication. The cover design is very pleasing and the book design is reader-friendly.

The Mahabharata is a mammoth book of wisdom. It is not possible to throw light on all relevant moral issues within the two covers of a slim book. Chakravarti's attempt is to be commended as an excellent beginning. In this strife-torn, loveless, mechanized world, his love and welfare-based moral theory, which he assures is perfectly practicable, lifts our spirit, raises our hopes. In places (e.g., his views on the caste system, on spirituality, on the Freudian concept of love, etc.) his comments and conclusions are provocative enough to generate a lot of debates. I hope his readers will appreciate his efforts by engaging in debates with him. That will surely contribute to the progress of moral philosophy.

Index[1]

[1] Note: Page numbers followed by 'n' refer to notes.

S. S. Chakravarti et al. (ed.), *Traditional Indian Virtue Ethics for Today*, Palgrave Studies in Comparative East-West Philosophy,
https://doi.org/10.1007/978-3-031-47972-4

B

C

D

Q

R

Printed in the United States
by Baker & Taylor Publisher Services